AF443044

Advances in Artificial Intelligence

Martin Charles Golumbic
Editor

Advances in Artificial Intelligence

Natural Language and Knowledge-based Systems

With 64 Figures

Springer-Verlag
New York Berlin Heidelberg
London Paris Tokyo Hong Kong

Martin Charles Golumbic
IBM T.J. Watson Research Center
Yorktown Heights, NY 10598

IBM Israel Scientific Center
Technion City
Haifa, Israel

Printed on acid-free paper.

Camera-ready text prepared by the authors.
Printed and bound by R.R. Donnelley & Sons, Harrisonburg, Virginia.
Printed in the United States of America.

9 8 7 6 5 4 3 2 1

ISBN 0-387-97355-9 Springer-Verlag New York Berlin Heidelberg
ISBN 3-540-97355-9 Springer-Verlag Berlin Heidelberg New York

If a man declares to you that he has found facts and confirmed them by experience — even though this man is considered most reliable and highly authoritative, be cautious ... Weigh his opinions and theories critically according to the requirements of pure reason.

Moses Maimonides (1135-1204)

Contents

Introduction

Research in artificial intelligence, natural language processing and knowledge-based systems has blossomed during the past decade. At national and international symposia as well as in research centers and universities all over the world, these subjects have been the focus of intense debate and study. This is equally true in Israel which has hosted several international forums on these topics. The articles in this book represent a selection of contributions presented at recent AI conferences held in Israel.

A theoretical model for a system that learns from its own experience in playing board games is presented in *Learning from Experience in Board Games* by Ze'ev Ben-Porat and Martin Golumbic. The model enables such a system to enhance and improve its playing capabilities through the use of a learning mechanism which extracts knowledge from actual playing experience. The learning process requires no external guidance or assistance. This model was implemented and tested on a variant of "Chinese Checkers." The paper shows the feasibility and validity of the proposed model and investigates the parameters that affect its performance traits. The experimental results give evidence of the validity of the model as a powerful learning mechanism. Original and general algorithms for knowledge extraction and pattern matching were designed and tested as part of the prototype computer system. Analysis of the performance characteristics of these algorithms indicates that they can handle large knowledge bases in an efficient manner. After an initial amount of knowledge has been acquired, further learning can take place with practically no effect on the response time of the system. Further research is necessary in order to realize the full potential of this model and its applicability to different domains.

In *PRODS: A Prototype Based Design Shell for Prototype Selection and Prototype Refinement*, Rivka Oxman presents a system for encoding and employing multiple prototypes in design. In knowledge-based systems, prototypes provide a basis for the generation of localized designs that are made specific through modification within a refinement process. They also enable the generalization of situations and constraints into prototypical contexts and problem contexts. The PRODS system provides a representation of two complementary types of knowledge which operate in a refinement process. Generative knowledge describes the design solution space by predefined refinement stages; interpretive knowledge enables selection and control. It is suggested that such systems can be made to interface with external CAD systems and to incorporate other kinds of design knowledge.

In the paper *What's in a Joke?* by Michal Ephratt, a preference algorithm is formulated for identifying and grasping the unexpected meaning, i.e., the punch line, of a linguistic joke. The usual task in computational linguistics is identifying and resolving ambiguity in favor of the most probable or likely meaning. By contrast here, a modification called "partial reverse preference" is applied to a variety of preference parsers, such as

Schubert's trade-off preference algorithm, turning them into electronic comedians. Watch out Bob Hope! This is demonstrated in the paper with several side-splitters.

Machinery for Hebrew Word Formation by Uzzi Ornan provides a new formal and arguably computer-implementable approach to morphological inflexion and derivation, while applying it to Hebrew. Since Hebrew text is generally written without vowels, written words display a higher degree of ambiguity presenting more of a challenge to computational linguistics than many other languages. Moreover, Hebrew grammar reflects concepts which allow interpretation of texts from ancient through medieval into modern times. The author's erudition as one of Israel's foremost Hebrew linguists leads us to view in a new light the processes of obtaining new roots, generating compound words, adopting foreign words, forming of "new" words by children, plus additional aspects of the morphological machinery.

In contrast to Hebrew, which has been in continuous use from Biblical times to the present, the Etruscan language of the pre-Roman civilization of northern Italy has been totally dead and buried for almost two millennia. In his paper *Theory Formation for Interpreting an Unknown Language*, Ephraim Nissan relates a methodology of research interpreting the surviving corpus of this ancient language. It is suggested that the problem of deciphering Etruscan is but one of many ways in which AI methodology could be applied to the deciphering of unknown languages.

Victor Raskin argues for a formal foundation of meaning representation in natural language artificial intelligence in the paper *Ontology, Sublanguage, and Semantic Networks in Natural Language Processing*. State of the art techniques neither in linguistic semantics nor in model-theoretic semantics provide solutions to the major problems of natural language processing semantics. An alternative is proposed that exploits the sublanguage orientation nature of NLPS and the ability to predefine the grain size of the required meaning analysis by combining the ontological and semantic network bases approaches.

Conceptual clustering has been introduced in machine learning research both as an extension to numerical clustering and as a method of learning by observation. The goal of conceptual clustering is not only to identify a cluster as a group of similar objects, as in classical numerical clustering, but also to determine its implicit conceptual structure. Incremental clustering techniques are especially desirable for applications in which context constantly evolves, but they are very sensitive to the ordering of the initial input. In *An Incremental Conceptual Clustering Algorithm that Reduces Input-Ordering Bias*, Yoëlle Maarek provides a hierarchical clustering method which allows for overlapping of clusters. This overlap requires ordering biases by periodically upgrading the whole hierarchy. The algorithm is presented both from the viewpoint of machine learning and of cluster analysis theory. A formal analysis of its computational complexity is given.

In the process of generating text, writers generally take into consideration the effect their words are likely to have on their listeners. In particular, they try to prevent possible comprehension problems which are likely to be triggered by the text. In her paper *Anticipating a Listener's Response in Text Planning*, Ingrid Zukerman presents a mechanism which emulates this behavior in the generation of discourse to convey an intended message. This mechanism anticipates the effect of a given message on a model of listener's beliefs, and proposes rhetorical devices to preclude possible adverse effects.

To understand and effectively use a sophisticated statistical, numerical, or other large software package requires many hours of training and guided practice with an expert. In *Towards an Intelligent Finite Element Training System*, Alex Bykat describes the construction of a knowledge-based consulting and training system for a finite element package. After presenting the overall design, the paper concentrates on the system's natural language communication.

Bayesian Inference in an Expert System without Assuming Independence by Alex Gammerman and A.R. Thatcher describes an application of Bayesian inference to the problem of estimating from past data, the probabilities that patients with certain symptoms have certain diseases. The study relates to 2000 patients at a hospital in Scotland who suffered acute abdominal pain. The methodology applies Bayes' Theorem without assuming independence of the symptoms and yet without an unmanageable increase in complexity. Moreover, using a limited database, it is shown how to select combinations of symptoms which allow the calculation of confidence bounds for the probabilities most relevant to the diagnosis of each disease.

Two papers address the problem of formulating practical semantics for constraint based systems: *A Partial Orders Semantics for Constraint Based Systems* by Steven Battle and *Partial Orders as a Basis for KBS Semantics* by Simon Morgan and John Gammack. Central to this problem is the issue of partial solutions which give rise to partially ordered structures of representational states. The partial order and the operations that may be performed upon it provide a general way of talking about constraint based systems without the need for specifics of any particular representational scheme.

In their paper *A Heuristic Search Approach to Planning and Scheduling Software Manufacturing Projects*, Ali Safavi and Stephen Smith discuss an incremental approach to scheduling which allows trade-offs between productions with different resource capacities and requirements. Since software project planning is seen more as a schedule revision problem than a schedule generation problem, an incremental strategy is advised. A formal treatment of revision operators is presented for application during the scheduling process, and the findings of an implementation of their model are reported.

Research into knowledge bases is an area still under evolution. Slowly, however, basic principles are emerging which seem to have the resilience to stand up to scientific rigor. In *From Data to Knowledge Bases*, Martin Golumbic and Dennis Grinberg reflect on and analyze the progress made so far and identify problems which can reasonably be attacked in the near term. Included as an appendix, is the edited transcript of a panel discussion on the subject, held at the *Third International Conference on Data and Knowledge Bases* (Jerusalem, June 1988).

Acknowledgements

First and foremost, I would like to thank the authors whose papers reflect so well the advances being made in artificial intelligence, natural language and knowledge-based systems. The first four papers were prepared for this volume as an outgrowth of talks presented in 1987 and 1988 at the *Israeli National Conference on Artificial Intelligence* held annually at the end of December. The remaining papers are based on the applications track of BISFAI-89, the *Bar-Ilan Symposium on the Foundations of Artificial Intelligence* (June 1989), sponsored by the Research Institute for the Mathematical Sciences at Bar-Ilan University with additional support from IBM Israel. (Several theoretical papers from that symposium will appear in a special issue of the *Annals of Mathematics and Artificial Intelligence*.)

I would like to take this opportunity to thank Ariel Frank, my co-chairman of BISFAI-89, for his suburb effort in handling all of the organizational, financial and logistic arrangements. Without his help and participation the symposium could never have been the success that it was. We express our appreciation to our colleague Uri Schild who was in charge of the social arrangements. Special thanks go to the invited hour speakers: Joseph Halpern (IBM Research) "Reasoning about Knowledge and Probability," Johann A. Makowsky (Technion) "The Architecture of Concepts," John McCarthy (Stanford University) "Formalized Common Sense Knowledge and Reasoning," Judea Pearl (U.C.L.A.) "Graphoids and the Representation of Dependencies," and Ronald Rivest (M.I.T.) "Recent Developments in Machine Learning Theory." Their enlightening lectures gave focus to the entire symposium.

I am especially grateful to my wife, Lynn Pollak Golumbic, who assisted with the editing during breaks from her environmental activities and who has constantly helped to provide an environment conducive to my professional activities. I would like to express my appreciation to Lynn Montz, formerly of Springer-Verlag, who was instrumental in initiating the appearance of this volume. Most of the effort spent editing this book was while I was a visitor at the IBM Thomas J. Watson Research Center, Yorktown Heights, New York, and I thank them for their support. Finally, I am indebted to the referees whose comments and suggestions improved many of the expositions.

MARTIN CHARLES GOLUMBIC

Contributors

Steven A. Battle
Transputer Centre
Bristol Polytechnic
Coldharbour Lane, Frenchay
Bristol BS16 1QY, England

Ze′ev Ben-Porat
Dept. of Math and Computer Science
Bar-Ilan University
Ramat Gan, Israel

Alex Bykat
Center for Computer Applications
University of Tennessee at Chattanooga
Chattanooga, TN 37402 U.S.A.
  email: bykat@utcvm.bitnet

Michal Ephratt
Department of Hebrew Language
Haifa University
Haifa, Israel
  email· rhlh702@haifauvm.bitnet

John G. Gammack
Bristol Business School
Coldharbour Lane, Frenchay
Bristol BS16 1QY, England

Alex Gammerman
Computer Science Department
Heriot-Watt University
79 Grassmarket
Edinburgh EH1 2HJ, Scotland
  email: alex@cs.hw.ac.uk

Martin Charles Golumbic
IBM Israel Scientific Center
Technion City
Haifa, Israel
  email: golumbic@israearn.bitnet

Dennis Grinberg
Dept. of Math and Computer Science
Bar-Ilan University
Ramat Gan, Israel

Yoëlle S. Maarek
IBM Thomas J.Watson Research Center
P.O.B. 704
Yorktown Heights, NY 10598 U.S.A.
  email: yoelle@ibm.com

Simon P. H. Morgan
Department of Computer Science
University of Exeter
Exeter, Devon EX4 4PT, U.K.
  email: smo@cs.exeter.ac.uk

Ephraim Nissan
Dept. of Math and Computer Science
Ben Gurion University of the Negev
Beer-Sheva 84105, Israel
  email: onomata@bengus.bitnet

Uzzi Ornan
Department of Computer Science
Technion - Israel Institute of Technology
Haifa, Israel
  email: ornan@techsel.bitnet

Rivka E. Oxman
Faculty of Architecture and Town Planning
Technion - Israel Institute of Technology
Haifa, Israel
email: arrro01@techunix.bitnet

Victor Raskin
Natural Language Processing Laboratory
Purdue University
West Lafayette, Indiana 47907 U.S.A.
email: raskin@ee.ecn.purdue.edu

Stephen F. Smith
School of Computer Science
Carnegie Mellon University
Pittsburgh, PA 15213 U.S.A.
email: sfs@isl1.ri.cmu.edu

Ali Safavi
School of Computer Science
Carnegie Mellon University
Pittsburgh, PA 15213 U.S.A.
email: ali.safavi@isl1.ri.cmu.edu

A. R. Thatcher
129 Thetford Road
New Malden
Surrey KT3 5DS, U.K.

Ingrid Zukerman
Department of Computer Science
Monash University
Clayton, Victoria 3168, Australia
email: ingrid@bruce.cs.monash.oz.au

Learning from Experience in Board Games

Ze′ev Ben-Porat

Department of Mathematics
and Computer Science
Bar-Ilan University
Ramat Gan, Israel

Martin Charles Golumbic*

IBM Israel Scientific Center
Technion City
Haifa, Israel

1. Introduction

A theoretical model for a system that learns from its experience has been conceived and developed. The model, titled "LEFEX" (LEarning From EXperience), operates in the domain of board games played on a rectangular board between two contestants who alternately move pieces on the board. The model is "game-independent" and may be applied to any game of the above type. All knowledge of specific game details is "hidden" from the learning portion of the system in three external routines: *INITPOS* gives initial positioning of pieces on the board, *MOVEGEN* generates all legal move in a given board position, *BASIC-SEF* performs an approximate evaluation of the worth of a given position (e.g., material balance). By replacing these routines the system may be applied to different games such as Chess, Checkers, GO, etc.

The model has been tested by the implementation of a prototype system which realizes major portions of the theoretical model. The model has evolved via a series of experiments with the prototype system for a variant of "Chinese Checkers," and was shown to be valid, i.e., effective learning was achieved by the model′s algorithms.

The system operates either in a *learning mode* or in a *playing mode*. Input to the learning mechanism is the score of a complete game. The game could have been played by any two players (e.g., system against itself, system against an external opponent or two external opponents playing each other). The system analyzes the game and looks for candidate learning instances. Those are sections of the game in which the system′s estimation of the position changes markedly within a small number of moves. The system identifies the source of its "prediction-failure" in the original position, and appends the extracted knowledge to a knowledge base.

---

* Revisions of this work were completed while the second author was a visitor at the IBM Thomas J. Watson Research Center, Yorktown Heights, NY.

The extracted knowledge is composed of a piece-pattern (a subset of the original board position including all pieces relevant to the observed "prediction failure") and the variation that was played from the original position of the learning instance. This knowledge base will be used in future games to prevent similar "prediction failures."

When playing a game, the LEFEX system employs a regular MINIMAX algorithm in order to select its next move from any given position. However, the basic (externally given) *static evaluation function* (SEF) is **modified** and **corrected** according to the knowledge that has been accumulated in the knowledge base by the learning mechanism. When the system identifies known patterns on the board, it uses the value associated with these patterns to correct the value calculated by the SEF. The variations associated with these patterns are treated as most probable continuations and direct the search in the game-tree.

A new method of automated "game-playing" has evolved as a by-product of the "LEFEX" model. This method consists of a search through a patterns' knowledge base which enhances and directs (or even replaces) the traditional search of the game-tree. When a known piece-pattern is recognized by the system, it directs its attention to the variation that was successfully played when that pattern appeared in previous games. For games in which the patterns on the board change slowly (e.g., chess, checkers) this pattern matching task can be carried out incrementally and efficiently.

Structure of the work

Section 2 presents the general LEFEX model, its related structures and its special algorithms. This is the heart of the paper and represents the main theoretical contribution. Section 3 describes the application of the LEFEX model to a variant of "Chinese checkers" and discusses the experimental results that have been observed with the prototype partial implementation of the model. It is here that the learning performance is analyzed, giving convincing evidence of the validity of the general LEFEX model. Section 4 compares the proposed model to several important "game-learning" AI systems, including the well-known classical work by Samuel [9, 18, 19] for Checkers and more recent research [11, 12, 16], Section 5 concludes with open issues and possible further research topics.

In [3], we provide the full version of the algorithms, annotated examples of learning instances, knowledge extraction, knowledge base structure and pattern matching. It also lists a representative sample of the 240 patterns of the knowledge base that have been accumulated by the system in one of its test runs, and compares the proposed model to several important "game-learning" AI systems, including the well-known classical work by Samuel [9, 18, 19] for Checkers and more recent research [4, 6, 11, 12, 16, 20].

In view of our experience with Chinese checkers, the LEFEX model appears to be a very powerful and promising method of learning. It is distinguished from similar existing learning systems due to its unique combination of features:

- **Fully Independent Learning:** The learning process is fully automatic. No external guidance is required and learning instances are identified by the system itself. The results discussed in section 3 of this paper have been produced by the system when it ran unattended for a number of days.

- **Wide Scope of Applicability:** As discussed above, the LEFEX model is game-independent and may be applied to a large number of board games. The system's algorithms are general and may be applicable to other domains.

- **Effective Learning:** The learning process has produced significant improvement in the playing strength of the system. Due to the nature of the game environment the improvement can be easily observed and accurately measured. There does not seem to be a theoretical limit to such an improvement that is inherent within the model (despite some practical limitations of the prototype implementation).

- **Efficient Learning/Playing Performance:** An exact quantitative analysis of the system's algorithms' performance was not carried out. However, both experimental results and qualitative analysis indicate that the performance of these algorithms is efficient and well behaved. As the size of the knowledge base increases, the response time of the system (both for learning and playing) converges to a relatively constant value. Thus, after an initial period of knowledge acquisition, further learning can be carried out with no degradation in the response time of the system.

- **Simplicity:** Conceptually, the LEFEX model is very simple and straightforward. The extracted knowledge is directly related to the actual experience of the system, and the extraction process is simple and direct. This strengthens the belief that this might be a general and effective method of learning from experience.

2. Schematic description of the proposed LEFEX model

Most game-playing systems select the move to be played in a given situation with the following type of mechanism:

(a) A forward search of the game-tree determines possible continuations (with various levels of exhaustion in the search).

(b) A static evaluation function (SEF) estimates the worth of the resulting positions.

(c) A MINIMAX algorithm (or some variation of this algorithm) is used to select the optimum continuation.

The basic assumption and source of motivation of the proposed model is that *the SEF is invariably faulty,* at least at some positions in the game. Had the SEF been correct for all game situations, there would have been no need for a search of the game tree that is deeper than 1-ply. A simple calculation of the SEF value for all positions that can be reached in 1 move (i.e., all legal moves for the side to move) would always point to the best possible move in any given position.

The main idea behind the "LEarning From EXperience" model is to identify those occurrences where the SEF fails to predict the future game development, to analyze and discover the reason for the failure and to use the discovered results to prevent similar future failures. The knowledge that is extracted from the analysis of SEF prediction failures is added to a knowledge base. This knowledge base is used to complement the SEF in evaluating future game situations.

The SEF itself is given to the system externally and does not change in the learning process. This given SEF defines the starting point for the learning process, and it should be noted that different levels of SEF will produce different learning behaviors.

The learning mechanism receives as input complete game traces. The input games may have been played by the system itself or by anyone else (i.e., the system can learn from existing Masters' games as well as from its own experience). The system replays the game moves and attempts to learn from them.[1]

2.1 WHEN and HOW to Learn: Identification and Analysis of Possible Learning Instances

The commonsense procedure for learning from experience in a game situation is to identify the move (or moves) that influenced the result of the game. Thus one might attempt to identify the losing move(s) of the losing side or the winning move(s) of the winning side. Once these moves have been identified, it is necessary to understand why they are bad (or good) -- so that it will be possible to generalize from the experience and to produce a general "rule" embodying the newly-learned game-knowledge. In the simplest case one can just record and remember the specific occurrence and avoid repeating the same mistake in the same situation.

---

[1]   It was originally intended that the system would identify candidate learning instances while actual playing was taking place. This idea was abandoned because it would have complicated the playing mechanism (and slow it down) without yielding any advantages. When learning from a complete game, the system concentrates on learning alone, and learning from an arbitrary given game has the additional advantage of letting the system learn from games that were played by others.

The problem of identifying the move(s) responsible for the result of the game (Credit Assignment Problem - see Rich [17, section 11.4]) is generally speaking very hard and in many cases not solvable (within reasonable time constraints). For example, *White* (computer) makes a bad move at the beginning of the game. The game continues for N (large) more good moves (no mistakes by either side) and then *White* loses. In this case identifying the "losing" move means making a full search of the game-tree to a depth of N, and had such a search been feasible to start with, the computer could probably have avoided the mistake by making that search during the game. Samuel's Checkers program [18, 19], for example, sidesteps this problem by identifying all of the moves (actually positions) that led to a victory as "good" and all moves that led to a loss as "bad."

In order to avoid the general Credit Assignment Problem, we propose a method where the learning is done by identifying local defects in the SEF in that area of the game where the system finally "realizes" it is in a bad state. It should be noted immediately that the error responsible for the bad state may lie far back in the game.

Learning instances for the LEFEX model are those sections of a game in which, within a small number of moves, the SEF values for the position changed markedly. The worth of the position at time (move) T_1 is defined as the value of the SEF for the board position at that time. The predicted value of the position at time T_2 when evaluated at time T_1, where T_2 is after T_1 (i.e., $T_2 > T_1$), depends on the value of $SEF(T_1)$ in the following manner:

$$
\begin{aligned}
SEF_{pred}(T_2) &\geq SEF(T_1) &\quad \text{if} \quad SEF(T_1) &\geq 0 \\
SEF_{pred}(T_2) &= 0 &\quad \text{if} \quad SEF(T_1) &= 0 \\
SEF_{pred}(T_2) &\leq SEF(T_1) &\quad \text{if} \quad SEF(T_1) &\leq 0
\end{aligned}
$$

i.e.,

- If *White* has the advantage, he is expected to keep it or (slowly) increase it.
- If the position is balanced, it is expected to stay so.
- If *Black* has the advantage, he is expected to keep it or (slowly) increase it.

Any large change in SEF values over a small section of the game may point to a failure in the SEF. This is true not only for the case where the advantage changes sides, $\text{SIGN}(SEF(T_1)) \neq \text{SIGN}(SEF(T_2))$, but also for cases where the advantage of one side increases or decreases rapidly (e.g., a variation that was played and increased *White's* existing advantage may, in a different position, move the advantage from *Black* to *White*).

When the expectations for $SEF(T_2)$, as calculated by $SEF(T_1)$ turn out to be wrong, there are three possible explanations:

- One of the sides made a bad move (one or more) between T_1 and T_2.
- The value of the static evaluation function at T_1 was incorrect.
- The position at T_2 is not stable (noise) and the SEF value there is incorrect.

In order to find out which of these possibilities is correct, the system performs its first algorithm, called A-1, to verify the validity of a candidate learning instance. This consists of an exhaustive search of the game-tree starting at the position of the game at time T_2 (POS(T_2)) to a predefined depth N (a learning parameter) and recalculation of the value of POS(T_2) based on that search. This is followed by an exhaustive search of the game-tree starting at the position of the game at time T_1 (POS(T_1)) to a predefined depth N (a learning parameter, $N \geq T_2 - T_1$). The result of this search will be to find the best variation (for both sides) starting at POS(T_1).

2.2 WHAT to Learn: Pattern extraction

Once a learning instance has been validated by the procedure in Algorithm A-1, the system attempts to extract from this instance useful information. The knowledge that we want will be in the form of a piece pattern (a subset of the original starting position of the learning instance) in which the original variation can still be played and leads to the same (or similar) change in the SEF value.

In order to maximize the expected benefits from the newly-learned pattern, it is desirable to discover the **minimal pattern** that fulfills the above conditions. (The original position itself certainly qualifies as a (non-minimal) such pattern, however, the chances for this exact position to reappear are not very great.) In any case we might hope that this new "pattern" can aid the SEF in many possible positions in the game-tree.

In order to find a pattern that involves a small enough number of pieces and squares, it may be necessary (and beneficial) to relax the condition that the change in the SEF values will be the same as the original change, and allow the system to select patterns in which the change is only partial (up to some percentage of the original.) Our next algorithm (A-2) extracts a minimal pattern from learning instance.

This consists of identifying the area of the board in which squares relevant to the pattern exist (all squares that are occupied by pieces or must be empty) and checking the scope of pattern over the board by trying to move the pattern area over the entire board (up, down, left, and right). This process will identify the true limits of the pattern (e.g., it may be that the pattern holds only at the edge of the board and not in the central region.)

Algorithm A-2 does not guarantee the minimal possible pattern, but in most practical cases this problem will not appear. If irrelevant pieces are added to the knowledge base together with the correct pattern, then it is most probable that at some time in the future this pattern will reappear without the irrelevant pieces and our knowledge management function can discover the irrelevant pieces and discard them. A bad pattern may also be "forgotten" by the system since it would appear rarely in future games, (because of the additional irrelevant pieces) while its correct counterpart will appear more often and have a greater chance of survival.

2.3 Knowledge Organization -- the Pattern Matching Tree

The patterns extracted by Algorithm A-2 are added to an accumulated knowledge base, to be used by the playing mechanism to improve its capabilities. Each pattern is given a unique identification number by the system, and all of the data that is relevant to the pattern is stored. In order to facilitate efficient pattern matching during the game, the patterns are also coded into a *pattern matching tree* that is built by the system. The pattern matching tree is a central construct of the model, and can be described as follows.

Each pattern corresponds to a path P that leads from the root to a certain node in the tree. Each node of the tree defines a test that should be carried out, and when the test defined by a node succeeds, one can proceed to its children, checking the tests that they define. When, for a given piece X on the board, all tests along the path P succceed, this pattern exists on the board and the piece X is the *anchor* of the pattern (i.e., it can move and initiate the variation that is associated with that pattern).

As patterns are discovered, they are added to the tree by our algorithm A-3. The trees constructed are quite compact and allow efficient pattern matching by our final algorithm A-4. One important reason for getting compact trees is that the system first learns simple patterns, and later learns more complex patterns (that are usually made up of simple patterns with some additional conditions). When a complex pattern is recognized which has a known simple pattern as a sub-pattern, the entire path defining the simple pattern will probably be used before any new nodes need to be defined for the more complex pattern.

The patterns with their associated variations are used by the playing mechanism of the system to augment and correct the basic SEF during the game. The system keeps track of all of the patterns that exist on the board for each of the pieces in any position (including hypothetical positions that are considered by the lookahead procedure). The patterns can be used by the system in two different ways:

Static usage: The patterns that exist in a given situation are evaluated and the result of this evaluation is added to the basic SEF value of the position.

Dynamic usage: The best patterns on the board are used as move selectors in the lookahead procedure.

In [3] we discuss the different aspects of these two types of knowledge usage in more detail. A general conclusion of that discussion is that *the static usage of the patterns is most useful for the defensive task* (recognizing potential dangers and destroying opponent's patterns) and less useful for the offensive task. The reason for this is that the system can give enemy patterns their full value, but it cannot do so for its own patterns.

Measurable improvement of playing capabilities has been achieved in the prototype implementation using the learned patterns only statically, but severe limitations were also detected. It is quite clear that these patterns should also be used dynamically in order to yield the maximum benefit.

3. A prototype application of the LEFEX model

In order to validate the proposed "LEFEX" model and to investigate its sensitivity to different parameters, a prototype system has been implemented which is described in this section. We present the experimental results that have been observed with the prototype, and provide an extensive analysis of the learning process. Finally, we investigate the performance characteristics of the pattern matching algorithm.

3.1 Selection of a model game and playing environment

A variant of Chinese Checkers has been selected as the prototype game. This is a game for two players which is played on an 8 × 8 board (like Chess and Checkers). The initial position has 9 white pieces in the upper left corner of the board and 9 black pieces in the opposite corner. The purpose of each player is to move its pieces to the squares in the opposite corner that are occupied in the initial position by the opponent's pieces. The winner is the first player that either (1) moves all his pieces to the target area, or (2) locks an opponent's piece (so that it cannot move) in any of the squares where the opponent's pieces are initially located. A move may be either:

- A vertical or horizontal shift of a piece to an adjacent empty square
  (from $\{x,y\}$ to $\{x+1,y\}$, $\{x-1,y\}$, $\{x,y+1\}$ or $\{x,y-1\}$,) or

- A series of one or more consecutive vertical or horizontal jumps
  of one piece over another piece (of either color).

This game was selected for the following reasons:

Simple game rules: The move generation function and the entire game-playing environment are relatively easy to set up, and thus facilitate testing the learning model.

Simple basic SEF: The cumulative distance of the pieces from the target squares provides a suitable basic SEF (i.e., it is approximately correct, it changes in a relatively slow and constant fashion and it is more accurate for deeper nodes in the game-tree, if players move in the correct direction.)

Complex game-tree: The average branching factor of this game is close to 30. This value should be compared to an average branching factor of 7.2 for Checkers, and indicates that this game is quite complex. The complexity of the game-tree results in many patterns that can be learned and profitably used by the system to improve the SEF.

Relatively stable game: The status of the position changes in a slow and smooth fashion, due to the fact that material does not appear, disappear, or change color. This minimizes the "noise" level of the game and provides suitable conditions for learning.

Simple measure for playing strength: The strength of a player relative to its opponent can be measured by the distance of the losing side from its final destination when the game is completed. This makes it possible to measure the relative strength of several players, without having to play a full tournament between all of them, by having all of them compete against one common opponent.

Three different types of "players" were set up in order to allow different applications and experiments with the system:

(1) a *human player,*

(2) a *constant (non-learning) "smart" player* that used a MINIMAX lookahead procedure with α-β PRUNING, and

(3) a *learning player* that uses the first m (parameter) patterns that exist in the knowledge base. This last type of a player performs only 1-ply lookahead and will henceforth be called LP[m].

A number of playing environments were set up to facilitate the experiments with the system:

(a) A *single game* between any 2 players.

(b) A *set of alternating playing and learning sessions* (with two learning players using all available knowledge).

(c) A *tournament of type "1"* : A group of learning players (LP[k*n], for a parametric n and $k = s$ to e by j) play against a common opponent.

(d)   A *tournament of type "2"* : A similar group of learning players (LP[$k*n$] playing against themselves. Each player scores p_1 (a parameter) percent of the full value of his own patterns plays against a player with the same level of knowledge who scores p_2 percent of the full value of his own patterns.

Note: Each player always scores 100% of the value for his opponent's patterns.

Because the tournaments included many games and took place over a large period of time (usually 24 consecutive hours) a checkpoint mechanism was incorporated to ensure storage of partial results in case of any unexpected interruption of the process.

3.2 Pattern discovery

Many learning sessions were carried out during the development of the prototype model. The results that will be described in this section were created by 12 applications of the following procedure:

(i) Play a game between two "learning-players," both using all available knowledge.

(ii) Try to learn from the game. Learn at most 20 new patterns from each game.

A total of 240 patterns were thus discovered. As expected, the system first discovers 1-ply variations. As its knowledge base expands, it is less often "surprised" by 1-ply variations and therefore starts to learn 3-ply and later 5-ply variations.

Learning a 1-ply variation can be viewed as relearning the move-generation rules of the game. However, only a small fraction of all legal moves was actually "relearned," and these are the moves that produce large changes in the SEF (i.e., probable moves with marked influence on the status of the position in which they occur).

3.3 Learning curves

In order to check the influence of the discovered patterns on the playing strength of the system, several tournaments of type "1" were set up. Each player LP[m] plays t (a parameter) games as *White* (the common opponent playing *Black*) and t more games as *Black* (opponent plays *White*). A randomizing move selection scheme is used in order to produce many different games (when two given players play each other a number of times).

The result of each game is determined by the distance (measured by the basic SEF) of the losing side from its goal. If the tested player wins, the result is simply that distance. If the tested player loses, the result is the negative of the distance. The result of a tournament between a tested player and the common opponent is defined as the average of the results of all of the $2t$ tournament games.

The graph in Figure 1 displays the results of a tournament "T-1" with $t = 4$ (i.e., 8 games for each player), common opponent = LP[64] , and tested players = LP[$k*16$] , $k = 0$ to 8. The bold points connected by the line going across the graph are the averaged results of the tournaments. The vertical line segments show the standard deviations for each of the tournaments. The asterisks denote maximal and minimal results of each tournament. The following observations should be noted:

- All players with less than 64 patterns lost to LP[64].
- All players with more than 64 patterns beat LP[64].
- The improvement of the players is clearly seen up to LP[96],
  but at that point it levels off and even deteriorates.
  LP[112] and LP[128] seem weaker than LP[80] and LP[96].

The conclusion from these results is that *the system is learning*. It changes its behavior by using the accumulated knowledge extracted from its past experience. However, some questions remain unclear in connection with tournament "T-1":

- Why does the improvement stop (and some deterioration can even be observed) after 96 patterns?
- Is the number of games (8 per player) large enough to provide statistical confidence in the results?
- What would happen when players with more knowledge participate, i.e., would the observed trend of deterioration continue?

In order to investigate these questions, the results of a second tournament "T-2," where the range of the players' knowledge was increased, is displayed in Figure 2. Similar results were achieved for similar or identical players (note results of LP[0], LP[48] and LP[96]), increasing the confidence in the averaged results. The trend of play-strength changes is similar to that observed for "T-1" -- fast improvement that levels out and then some deterioration (LP[168] even loses the tournament to LP[64]). These results confirm the initial observations from "T-1."

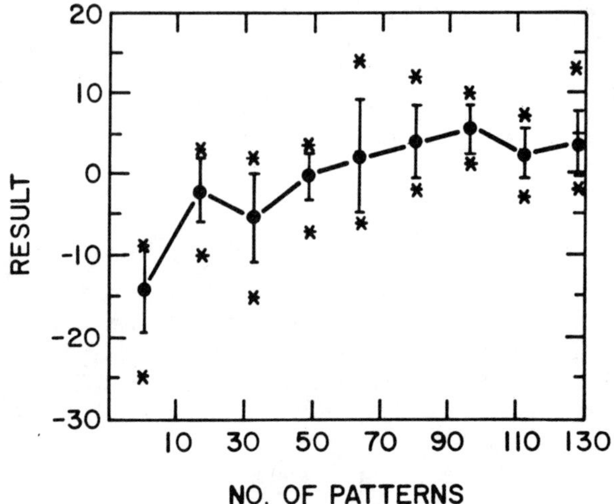

Figure 1. Results of Tournament "T-1."
Eight games per player at 40% pattern value; common opponent LP[64].

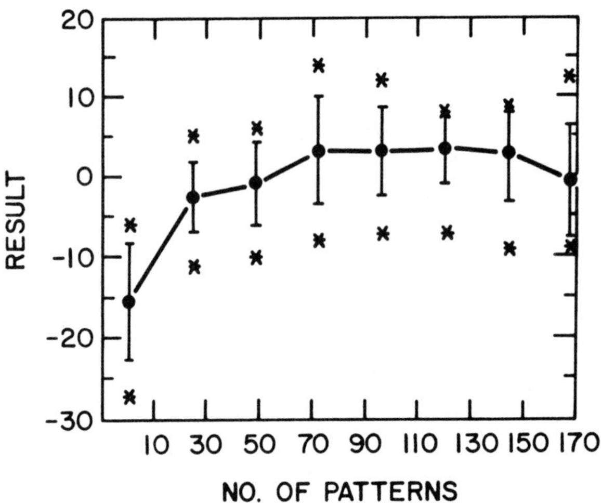

Figure 2. Results of Tournament "T-2."
Eight games per player at 40% pattern value; common opponent LP[64].

3.4 Limitations of static usage of knowledge

Research of the problem of deterioration in the level of play for "knowledgeable" players was carried out by a close study of the knowledge base and by a thorough analysis of the games played by LP[144] and LP[168] in "T-2." It was observed that the "knowledgeable" players very often played moves that created potentially valuable patterns -- but in many cases the variations associated with these patterns could not be carried out (most often the opponent could destroy the patterns as soon as they were created). The problem becomes more critical when patterns with longer variations (e.g., 3-ply and 5-ply) are known to the player. These patterns are generally very valuable (hold a large potential gain in the SEF) -- but they have a much smaller chance of being successfully carried out. It was therefore assumed that if the patterns (of the side that is considering the next move) would receive a lower initial value, the observed deterioration trend would shift to the right. Tournament "T-3" was set up in order to check this assumption.

Whereas in "T-1" and in "T-2" the initial value for the player's patterns was set at 40% of the full value, in "T-3" it was only 20%. Furthermore, the range of the players includes more knowledgeable players. The graph in Figure 3 displays the results of "T-3." As the graph shows, the assumption was validated, as the level of play stabilized from LP[144] to LP[192] and started to deteriorate only for LP[216]. Note that LP[168] had a +8 result versus LP[64], whereas in "T-2" LP[168] scored a −1 versus the same opponent.

An interesting question that arises from the previous discussion is the relative strength of a given player (e.g., LP[64]) when different weights are given to the patterns augmenting the SEF (e.g., 40% versus 20%). If the player with the 20% is stronger, then we may create even stronger players by decreasing that weight even more. To investigate this problem a tournament "T-4" of type "2" was set up.

In tournament "T-4," each player LP$[m]$ played against another LP$[m]$, with the difference between them being in the weight   that was given to the patterns -- the tested player scored 40% of the full value of the pattern and its opponent scored 20% of that value. The graph in Figure 4 shows the results of "T-4." The "40% player" was stronger than the "20% player" for all the cases that were tested. Initially, addition of new patterns increases the advantage of the "40% player" (as it actively creates and executes the patterns). However, when more patterns and patterns with a longer associated variation are added to the knowledge base, this advantage decreases rapidly because the "40% player" is drawn into creating patterns that cannot be executed to deliver the expected profit. Note that the big decrease in the advantage of the "40% player" appears when 5-ply variations are introduced into the knowledge base.

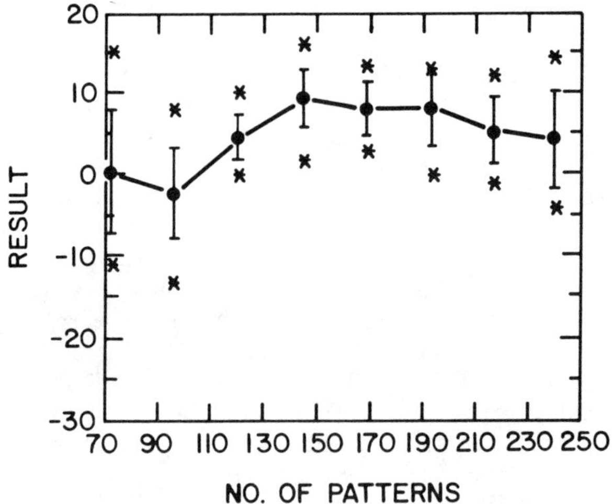

Figure 3. Results of Tournament "T-3."
Ten games per player at 20% pattern value; common opponent LP[64].

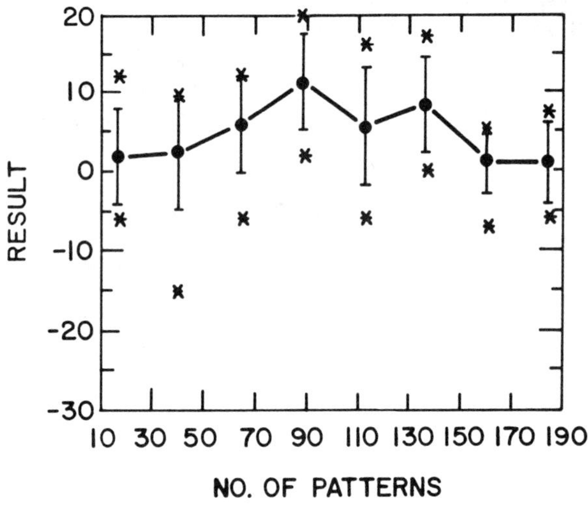

Figure 4. Results of Tournament "T-4."
Players LP[m] at 40% pattern value versus LP[m] at 20% pattern value.

The conclusion drawn from these experiments is that the static usage of the patterns improves the level of play significantly, but it suffers from some inherent limitations. The desire to create valuable patterns (which could be enhanced by giving the patterns a high value in the SEF) may lead to mistaken moves if these patterns cannot be played out. On the other hand, avoiding this problem by giving the patterns a low (or zero) value may prevent the player from recognizing profitable opportunities.

This problem is limited to the offensive usage of the patterns and does not apply to defensive usage, (enemy patterns are given their full value, because it is always desirable to recognize them and to try to destroy them).

In order to fully utilize the knowledge that is embodied in the patterns, the static usage should be complemented with a dynamic mechanism that checks out the feasibility of the "planned" variations before the SEF scores the value of the associated pattern.

3.5 Performance characteristics of the pattern matching algorithm

The performance characteristics of the pattern matching algorithm (measured in relation to the number of the patterns and their complexity) is important for evaluating the feasibility of the proposed model for more complex games. In order to study these characteristics, measurements of various parameters of the pattern matching algorithm were carried out. Generally, the results are satisfactory and show that as the pattern matching task becomes harder (more patterns and patterns of a more complex nature), the algorithm's efficiency decreases only marginally. It is expected that after the pattern matching tree reaches a certain size, further effective learning can be achieved with no effects on the response time of the system.

As the learning process is carried out, patterns with increasing complexity are extracted (i.e., more conditions and longer variations). However, since complex patterns are usually made up from simpler patterns, only a marginal addition of nodes to the pattern matching tree (PMT) is expected. The graph in Figure 5 shows the PMT size as a function of the number of patterns in the knowledge base. As expected, the size continues to grow in an approximately linear fashion as new (and more complex) patterns are added.

The graph in Figure 6 shows the average number of elements in the status list SL (i.e., the number of patterns found by algorithm A-4 to be currently active.) The result for the case of 240 patterns is an average of 80 games (played in tournament "T-4"). Each of the other results is an average of the values measured for the moves of one game (that was played during the learning process) representing approximately 90 measurements (moves per game).

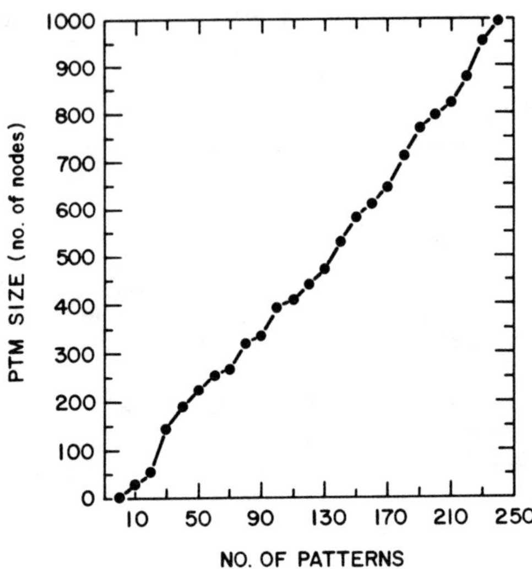

Figure 5. Number of nodes in the pattern matching tree (PMT).

Similar results have been observed in other experiments (not discussed in this paper) during the development of the model.

The size of the SL grows rapidly for the first acquired patterns (which are usually simple patterns and appear very often on the board) but levels out when a large enough KB has been accumulated. The reason for this (beneficial) behavior is that for the more complex patterns, if the SL reaches "deep" into the PMT in one area of that tree (i.e., a complex pattern appears on the board for a piece) it usually stays close to the root in other areas of the PMT (other complex patterns are not probable). The compactness of the PMT also contributes towards this behavior of the average length of the SL, because a single node of the tree may be holding the pattern matching process for a number of patterns.

The graph in Figure 7 shows experimental results for the average number of PMT nodes that were "visited" during the pattern matching process by A-4. This variable is a direct measure of the efficiency of this algorithm. The trend that is shown by this graph is very similar to the trend that appears in Figure 6 (the SL size); in fact, the ratio between the number of PMT nodes visited and the length of the SL (Figure 8) is quite constant and is approximately 2.2 (very close to the minimum possible value of 2.0 since A-4 must visit each node pointed to by an element in SL twice, when trying to go up and when trying to go down.)

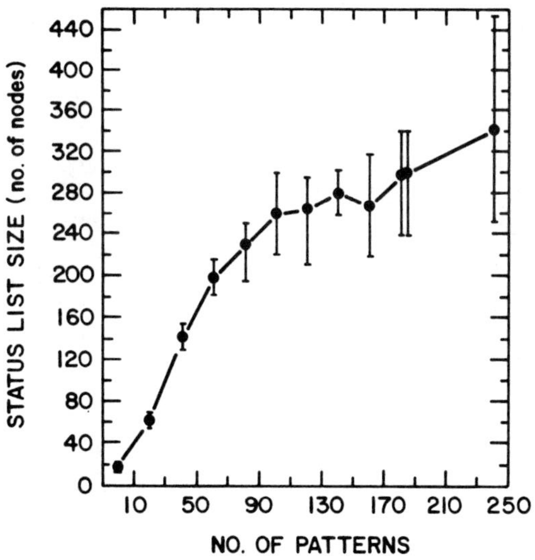

Figure 6. Average length of the status list in the PMT.

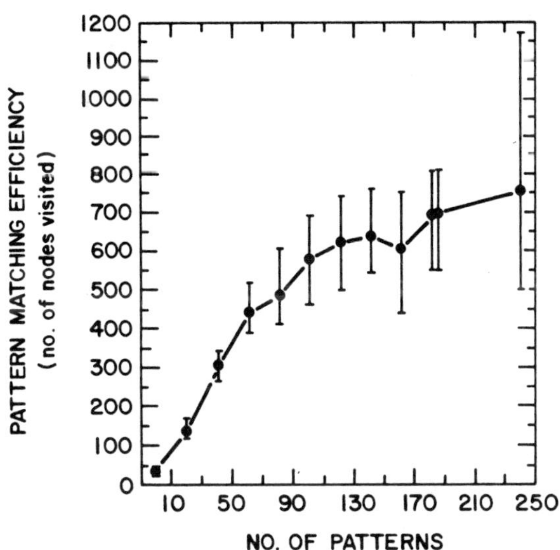

Figure 7. Average number of PMT nodes visited per move.

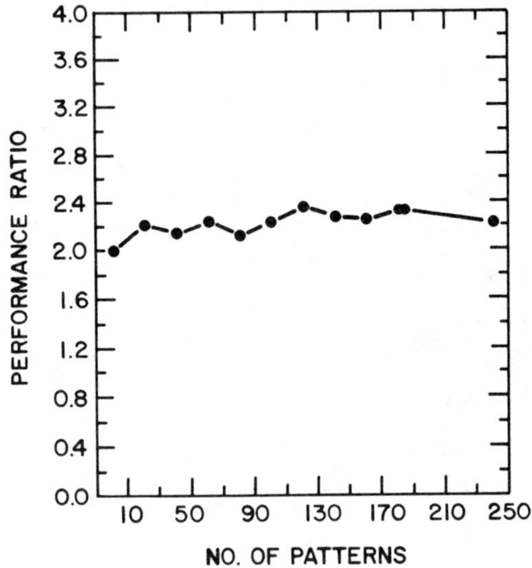

Figure 8. Ratio of nodes visited / status list length.

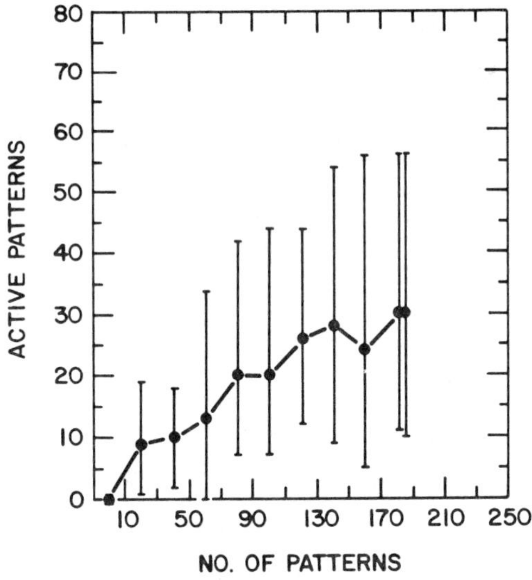

Figure 9. Average number of active patterns per move.

In addition to the efficiency of the pattern matching algorithm (A-4), it also seems reasonable to assume that the average number of PMT nodes visited by A-4 will reach a maximum level and will not rise above that maximum (regardless of any additions to the knowledge base). This means that from a certain point onwards, further learning does not affect the response time of the system (both for the learning and for the playing activities).

The graph in Figure 9 shows the average number of active (complete) patterns that are recognized by the system at each position during the game. This value increases rapidly at first, but is also expected to reach a maximum level at some stage (when the patterns become complex and rare enough).

4. Comparison of the LEFEX model to other AI learning systems

The central aim of a game playing system is *winning*. Most us some combination of "brute force" analysis of the game-tree, MINIMAX with α-β pruning and heuristic continuation, special purpose circuitry, and limited parallel processing to evaluate millions of possible future positions but without calculating complicated heuristics [1, 7, 8, 13, 14, 22]. Church [6] describes a program that is based on a goal oriented method of selecting moves, rather than the traditional massive tree search. The basic problem in any further development of Church's model stems from the need to describe and define to the system possibly thousands of different position-types (to which appropriate goals can be attached). As pointed out by Charness [5], a chess Grandmaster can recognize on the order of 50,000 patterns (piece-configurations) and knows the appropriate plan of action (production rules) for these patterns.[2] The system described by Church contains only three different (and very broad) types of positions and is not able to analyze board positions to recognize specific piece-patterns.

Schaeffer [20] describes a system PLANNER that implements and enhances the model proposed by Church. This program analyzes chess positions to determine a long-range strategical plan that suits the nature of the position. The selected plan is one of 13 pre-defined possible long-range plans) and is then used to influence the STATIC EVALUATOR towards selecting moves that enhance the achievement of the plan. The problems that were discussed above in connection with Church's model appear here again -- intricate analysis of the position is required to decide on the appropriate plan, and only a limited number of plans

---

[2] These rules specify the types of moves that are relevant to a given pattern on the board (thus reducing or eliminating the necessity of searching the game-tree.) This article provides a source of motivation for our work.

is available. Furthermore, this set of plans is externally given and constant and is specific to chess only.

The problems that are addressed by specific endgame programs for chess are somewhat different from those of other phases of the game. The number of possible continuations is not considerably smaller, but a "deeper" and "narrower" analysis, based on a specific plan of action, is necessary and possible. Several programs that deal specifically with different types of endgames have been developed, [2, 4, 15]. In these systems the learning is based on extensive analysis of all possibilities (or prototype positions) and the construction of libraries which store information that defines for a given position (or position-type) the proper playing strategy. Although a similar solution cannot be applied to the general problem of board-games, elements found in these systems (e.g., pattern recognition and the division of the board into manageable "chunks") appear in the LEFEX model.

4.1 Samuel's Checkers Program

Samuel's Checkers program [18, 19] (see description and extensions in Griffith [9]) is a classic application in AI learning systems. In one of its learning modes this program performs optimization of the coefficients of 31 positional elements, or *features*, that form the basis for an SEF for the game of Checkers. The optimization is performed in a way that will maximize the score given to positions that led to victory, and minimize the score of positions that led to a loss in a given set of games (learning instances). When the system was given a set of masters' games to learn from, it "learned" to play at a master's level. When playing against weak opponents, the system learned to beat them, but sometimes the system's level of play actually degraded (because bad positions often led to victory due to opponent's errors).

Studying the applicability of such a learning method to Chess, Hearst [10] concluded that it "would have to deal not with 31 component numbers but with 31 million or even more." Samuel's program differs from the LEFEX model in a number of ways:

1. **Learning Strategy** -- Samuel's program learns from given examples and not from experience, in the sense that it considers all positions leading to a win as good positions without any attempt of verifying this or understanding why such positions are good.
2. **Type of Acquired Knowledge** -- Samuel's program tunes the value of the coefficients in the static position evaluation function. It also handles certain prespecified nonlinear interactions (*signatures*) between features. In contrast, the proposed LEFEX model attempts to recognize new factors that should be incorporated in that function.

3. **Level of Complexity** -- Samuel's program learns a predefined (and small) number of values. It does not have to deal with the problems that arise when a large base of knowledge is to be created and managed efficiently, neither does it have the general applicability to more complicated board games.

4.2 Bayesian learning methods

Lee and Mahajan [12] present a Bayesian learning algorithm for combining features into a nonlinear evaluation function. This provides a significant improvement over both the linear combination and the signature table techniques of Samuel. Analyzing a large number of games played by experts, it automatically learns to recognize and classify feature patterns and assigns a probability that a position will lead to a winning outcome. Although their method also relies on a relatively small number of good features which are derived from expert knowledge, it considers and uses the correlation of *pairs of features* to obtain its evaluation function. This is a most essential contribution of their work since features are almost never mutually independent. Their method has been successfully used in the program BILL 3.0 for the game of Othello.

Whereas LEFEX learns all of its patterns from incremental "surprises" in the value of an SEF which it regards a "black box" in need of augmentation, BILL 3.0 assumes a given set of good features and learns how to correlate them into a quadratic SEF. LEFEX takes a local improvement approach and can learn good micro-patterns even from board positions that will eventually lose. BILL 3.0 takes a global approach treating each board position as either winning or losing and weighting its macro-features accordingly. This illustrates exactly why LEFEX will succeed on stable games and Bayesian BILL. will succeed on games which admit separation of positions into goal classes. BILL will recover from erroneous information during the Bayesian analysis of covariances between features, while LEFEX advocates a gradual forgetting mechanism. Thus, it would seem that the two approaches are somewhat orthogonal and successful game playing programs in the future could benefit from aspects of both.

4.3 SAGE

The SAGE system (described by Langley [11]) is a model of a learning strategy. The system learns by the following process:

- It tries to solve a given problem by a trial and error search of the tree of possibilities (full-width search in the worst case) using given production rules that define the elementary operations of the given problem domain.

- After a solution is found, the system assumes it is the correct one. At this stage the system tries to improve its performance (solve the problem more efficiently) by solving the problem again.
- Whenever the move suggested by the system differs from the move in the "correct" solution, the system recognizes this and searches for elements in the problem state (and solution history) that will differentiate between the proposed move and the correct one. A new production rule is created which adds restrictions and limitations to the **if** section of the original rule that was wrongly applied.
- After a sufficient number of such iterations, the program creates a set of production rules (with associated priority scheme) that will enable it to solve the problem with no backtracking.

This program has been tested (among other tests) on a game named JUMP-SLIDE (described in that paper). The rules that have been learned for the 4-pieces version of this game proved sufficient for the 6-pieces game (with no need of further learning).

The SAGE program resembles the LEFEX model in that it "discovers" new elements in the game states that influence the choice of moves. The basic difference between this program and our model is in the complexity of the problems with which it deals. SAGE's learning model is appropriate for solving problems that can be easily solved without the learning stage (or for which a solution is given to the system in advance). This is true because SAGE's learning mechanism depends on the availability of a correct solution at the outset of the learning phase. The applicability of rules learned from studying a simple problem to a more complicated problem cannot be guaranteed. Following Simon's objection to learning in AI [21] it can be argued that this model learns to solve a problem efficiently but only when it already knows the solution and so could simply remember that solution.

4.4 ID3 - A Program for Classification of Positions in Chess Endgames

The system ID3 described by Quinlan [16] learns to construct an effective decision tree for the classification of chess endings of the type KRKN (King and Rook vs. King and Knight) as lost-N-ply. The system receives as input a list of elements (predicates of the positions), creates a variety of random examples and analyzes these examples to see if they are lost-N-ply. According to the results it constructs a decision tree for the classification of the different possible positions in such endings.

This work differs considerably from the LEFEX model, but is mentioned here since it suggests a future development direction that fits well with its elements. It turns out that the major investment of work for the solution of problems of the type described above, as N grows bigger (as the problem grows more complex), is to recognize the appropriate predicates of the position that should be used in the decision tree.

The article reports that, "An attempt is currently under way as part of the 4-ply work to find some attributes automatically." Specifically this attempt concentrates on the automatic recognition of piece patterns that can be used as predicates for the decision tree. The techniques presented for such automatic discovery (as possible ideas) have been considered during the design of the proposed model and have affected the design of the LEFEX model.

5. Summary and conclusion

A complete model for a system that learns from experience in the realm of board games has been conceived, designed and verified experimentally. Learning in a completely autonomous fashion, a prototype implementation of the model has extracted valuable information (in the form of piece-patterns and associated variations) from its past experience and used that information to significantly improve its performance. An efficient pattern matching algorithm has been designed and implemented. The response time of this algorithm is expected to stay constant (after an initial period of knowledge acquisition) when more knowledge is acquired and used by the system.

The proposed model may help to explain complex human learning and playing characteristics. For example, it provides an explanation to the question of Grandmaster Blitz Chess capability posed by Charness [5]. It is clear that under the blitz conditions they cannot perform any lookahead, and they cannot even generate and examine all legal moves 1-ply ahead. To explain the fact that Grandmasters play excellent Chess moves in a "Blitz" situation, Charness proposes the general explanation that the *Grandmasters are doing some pattern matching process and performing only a minimal amount of lookahead.* It is estimated that a chess Grandmaster recognizes about 50,000 patterns (piece-configurations) and knows the appropriate plan of action (production rules) for these patterns. Knowing the types of moves relevant to a given pattern on the board, reduces or eliminates the necessity of searching the game-tree. The LEFEX model offers support for this proposition, and may also explain the correlated fact that Grandmasters sometimes make very bad mistakes during Blitz games. (The pattern matching process alone does not guarantee good performance, and some degree of lookahead is required in any case.)

Within the broad framework of this work only the initial design of the model has been accomplished. Many aspects of the model need to be further developed and researched, as discussed in [3], including full implementation of the learning algorithm, implementation for additional games, research into the effects of randomization, and dynamic usage of knowledge. Issues related to this model also merit further research. This model, with some appropriate modifications, may prove useful in areas that are not as structured as the realm of board games (e.g., economic games, war games, etc.)

ACKNOWLEGEMENTS

The authors would like to express their thanks to Jack Mostow for his helpful comments on this paper.

References

1. Adelson-Velsky, G.M., Arlazarov, V.L., and Donskoy, M.V., Algorithms of adaptive search, in *Machine Intelligence* 9 (Hayes, Michie, Mikulish, eds.) Chichester: Ellis Horwood, 1979.

2. Arlazarov, V.L. and Futer, A.L., Computer analysis of a rook endgame, in *Machine Intelligence* 9 (Hayes, Michie, and Mikulish, eds.), Chichester: Ellis Horwood, 1979.

3. Ben-Porat, Z. and Golumbic, M.C., "LEFEX" -- a General Model of Learning from Experience, IBM Israel Scientific Center, Technical Report 257, Dec. 1988.

4. Berliner, H.J. and Campbell, M.S., Using chunking to solve chess pawn endgames, *Artificial Intelligence* 23 (1984), 97-120.

5. Charness, N., Human chess skill, in *Chess Skill in Man and Machine* (Frey, ed.), New York: Springer-Verlag, 1977.

6. Church, R.M. and Church, K.W., Plans, goals and search strategies for the selection of a move in chess, in *Chess Skill in Man and Machine* (Frey, ed.), New York: Springler-Verlag, 1977.

7. Condon, J.H. and Thompson, K., Belle chess hardware, in *Advances in Computer Chess* (Clark, ed.) Oxford: Pergamon Press, 1982.

8. Frey, P.W., An introduction to computer chess, *Chess Skill in Man and Machine* (Frey, ed.), New York: Springler-Verlag, 1977.

9. Griffith, A.K., A comparison and evaluation of three machine learning procedures as applied to the game of Checkers, *Artificial Intelligence* 5 (1974), 137-148.

10. Hearst, E., Man and machine: Chess achievement and chess thinking, in *Chess Skill in Man and Machine* (Frey, ed.), New York: Springler-Verlag, 1977.

11. Langley, P., Learning search strategies through discrimination, *International Journal of Man-Machine Studies* 18 (1983), 513-541.

12. Lee, K-F. and Mahajan, S., A pattern classification approach to evaluation function learning, *Artificial Intelligence* 36 (1988), 1-25.

13. Newborn, M., *Computer Chess*, New York: Academic Press, 1975,

14. Newborn, M., Cray-Blitz wins world computer chess championship, *Abacus* vol. 1, no. 3, (Spring 1984), 58-61.

15. Newborn, M., PEASANT: An endgame program for kings and pawns, in *Chess Skill in Man and Machine* (Frey, ed.), New York: Springler-Verlag, 1977.

16. Quinlan, J.R., Learning efficient classification procedures and their application to chess endgames, in *Machine Learning* (Michalsky, Carbonell and Mitchell, eds.) Palo Alto: Tioga, 1983.

17. Rich, E., "Artificial Intelligence," McGraw Hill, 1983.

18. Samuel, A.L., Some studies in machine learning using the game of checkers, *IBM J. Res. Dev.* 3 (1959) 210-229.

19. Samuel, A.L., Some studies in machine learning using the game of checkers, II, *IBM J. Res. Dev.* 11 (1967) 601-617.

20. Schaeffer J., Long-range planning in computer chess, ACM, 0-89791-120-2/83/010/0170, 1983.

21. Simon, H.A., Why should machines learn?, in *Machine Learning* (Michalsky, Carbonell and Mitchell, eds.) Palo Alto: Tioga, 1983.

22. Slate, D.J. and Atkins, R.L., CHESS 4.5 - The Northwestern University chess program, in *Chess Skill in Man and Machine* (Frey, ed.), New York: Springler-Verlag, 1977.

PRODS: A Prototype Based Design Shell for Prototype Selection and Prototype Refinement

Rivka E. Oxman

Faculty of Architecture and Town Planning
Technion - Israel Institute of Technology
Haifa, Israel

1. Introduction : Prototype-Based Design Shells

The expert system shell is now considered to be one of the key concepts of AI. In this paper an application of the shell concept to design is described. This illustrates how a concept in artificial intelligence, the *shell*, can be adapted to fit the characteristics of design and the requirements of *knowledge-based design systems*. The early experiments with expert systems shells in design were simplistic adaptations of existing shells. They were developed to carry out diagnosis using classification concepts mainly for design analysis and evaluation tasks. They could make interpretations of properties and performances of design artifacts, where the theory by which interpretations are made is well understood. Expert systems for design analysis are now documented in the literature [2-6]. Most expert systems applications which have attempted to accommodate various synthesis processes of design lack general structures of design knowledge from which to derive and control other processes such as design generation. The limitation of current expert systems technology for design is due, among other things, to the lack of a comprehensive theoretical foundation including an epistemology of design knowledge. As opposed to the adaptive utilization of existing expert systems technology *for* design, the concept of the *design shell* as described here is proposed as a potential component of such a theoretical foundation for knowledge based design.

The design shell which is presented in this paper is based on the concept of the prototype. The notion of prototype has played a prominent role in linguistics, cognitive psychology and artificial intelligence [7-10]. In knowledge-based design systems, it shows promise as a useful representation schema for various kinds of generic knowledge which support design generation.

A design shell which accommodates design prototypes, termed *GPRS- Generative Prototype Refinement Schema* has been developed by the author [1,11]. The concept of the prototype provided a means to represent generative knowledge which supports an hierarchically structured, top-down refinement process of design. The shell is based on the employment of a design schema for pre-selected solution prototypes based on design precedents. The use of GPRS was limited to the generation and refinement of an existing *solution prototype*. The purpose of this paper is to demonstrate a broadening of the application of the concept of prototype in order to accommodate problem context as *situation prototypes*, in addition to solution space which is already accommodated as *solution prototypes*. We postulate that in the processes of selecting and fitting a prototypical solution to a prototypical situation both situation and solution type must be refined. GPRS is employed as part of a larger system for the representation of multiple situation prototypes and multiple solution prototypes. PRODS, a design system for the use of multiple prototypes, has been implemented. The paper describes its organization, implementation and operative characteristics.

2. Prototypes of Design Situations and Design Solutions

In this paper the prototype is expanded to include two kinds of prototypes: design solutions and design situations. The knowledge of design precedents is considered here as a deep form of knowledge which enables a designer to fit a solution type to a situation type.

Prototypes of Design Solutions

Prototyping, or generalizing the salient characteristics of past and known design solutions in a hierarchical schema, is one way in which design knowledge is conceptualized over years of the designer's experience. In design, terminology such as schema, schemata and design prototype derives from the cognitive significance of generic forms of knowledge. In the field of architecture, Hillier et al. [14] have postulated that it is the existence of knowledge in its generic forms, genotypes and phenotypes, in their terms, which makes design possible. The historical distinction between model as iconic source and the type as abstract model was explicated by Quartremere de Quincy (1832). He drew a distinction between a concrete model which is the source of exact copies and a generic type which can be a source for different variations all having in common the salient characteristics which characterize the class. Rowe [15] demonstrated how deep structural generic knowledge exists over centuries of architectural history. Current design theoretical literature [16] contains frequent references to architectural knowledge in the form of schemata and to its seminal role in the design process.

In knowledge-based systems, prototypes as solution types provide a basis for the generation of design [1,17]. During design, the prototype is localized and is made specific through modification within a refinement process, while preserving its salient characteristics as a member of a class.

Prototypes of Design Situations

Another form of knowledge in design enables the generalization of situations and constraints into typical contexts and problem classes. This provides a counter concept to that of design solutions, and one in which design solution classes may be considered as fits to typified contexts. The term, situation, is employed here in a broad sense for context, as well as problem characteristics and constraints. The typification of situations involves the recognition of the *typical and* recurrent types of constraint classes in a design domain. During design, the novelty of a new situation is accommodated to a cognitive situation-schemata in order that known principles can be applied. An experienced designer may be said *to know how to act* in certain kinds of situations. Direct mapping between sets of constraints, a set of requirements and a solution, hardly exists in design. According to Simon [18] there are two kinds of constraints: problem-oriented constraints and autonomous constraints. Similar kinds of constraints may be encountered in design. We have termed these as *intrinsic-design constraints* and *extrinsic-design constraints*. Intrinsic design constraints are part of the problem statement and traditionally associated with particular problem types. For example, a sloped site in a high density housing project, may be considered as an intrinsic constraint. Extrinsic design constraints are those associated with solution types because of a reason extrinsic to the problem. For example, design preferences of a designer such as a particular style may be considered as extrinsic constraints. Constraints typification may be institutionalized as a part of accepted design practice or part of a design tradition such as in the case of Ecole des Beaux Arts; or it may be personal and relate to the cognitive style of a particular designer. In both cases it is constraints typification which instantiate design solution typification and design generation.

Applying Design Constraints in the Process of Prototype Selection

Designers employ both intrinsic constraints and extrinsic constraints in order to guide processes of prototype selection, refinement and adaptation. A process of selection can be regarded as a reasoning process which leads from a current state situation to a desired state solution. The designer's situation typification enables him to define concepts which then condition a design solution. An intrinsic constraint such as 'narrow site' can cue several prototypical solutions depending upon preferred concepts of extrinsic constraints. For example, in residential design the designer knows that in order to provide external facades to as many dwelling units as possible he has to treat the frontage of the unit so that it will have a minimal width. The typification process develops a typical situation in the form of both prototypical constraints and typified context descriptions and enables the selection and refinement of prototypical solutions.

3. GPRS - Generative Prototype Refinement Schema

GPRS models the generative refinement process of design prototypes and implements the model computationally. The term *schema* is used to indicate the properties of a cognitive structure which specifies the general properties of the prototype and omits specifications irrelevant to the type. A hierarchy of subtypes is based on a classification of subtypes by specifying additional essential properties. A generative prototype contains generative knowledge in the form of a design description generator which derives the attributes of each subtype of the prototype. That is, it possesses the typological knowledge which defines and can generate by instantiation its subtype hierarchy. The generative prototype also has a set of intrinsic and extrinsic constraints which are associated with each subtype. It has the ability to use knowledge in order to relate these constraints to subtype instantiations and to activate design actions in a refinement process. *Prototype refinement* can be seen as a successive process of hierarchical instantiation in which typified design constraints are matched into typified subtype solutions.

Similar approaches [19] leave specific decisions about instantiations to the designer, while the meaning of a decision remains implicit. The proposed formalization makes these reasoning processes explicit in a single unified representation schema. At each stage of refinement, variables in the subtype are instantiated by reasoning about specific constraints. These then lead to a subtype instantiation. The following diagram describes this formalization in a successive prototype refinement process.

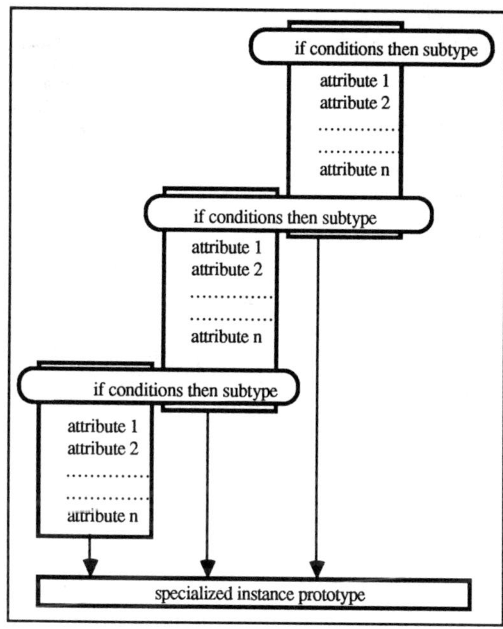

Figure 1 - The successive prototype refinement process of an instance-type

The refinement of prototypes includes an expanded model of GPRS for solution types as well as for situation types. This model also supports the selection of a prototype as well as its solution generation.

GPRS provides a formalism to encode the different kinds of knowledge which are involved in the processes of hierarchical refinement. GPRS provides means to generate solutions by reasoning from relevant knowledge bases. It was implemented in a *hybrid representation scheme* which combined different methods according to their suitability to specific kinds of knowledge. A specific method based on rule-frame-rule structure was developed. It combines the advantages of frames [20] as structured representations for objects, and classes of objects [21]; production rules as a formalism for describing generative patterns

[22]; and a rule-based formalism for describing causal heuristic knowledge [23]. Figure 2 is a diagram of the different kinds of knowledge represented as rules and frames. An interface module supports the flow of knowledge between the rules and the frames representation formalisms.

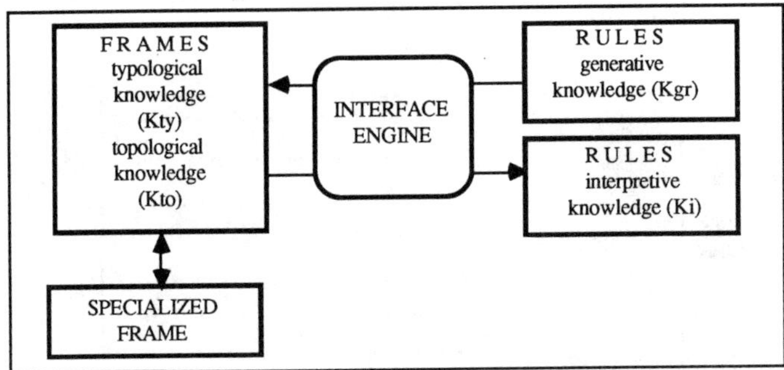

Figure 2 - Kinds of knowledge represented by rules and frames in GPRS

In the following section we briefly elaborate the knowledge, its representational method and the manner in which it is employed in GPRS.

Solution Prototypes in GPRS

Solution prototypes in GPRS include pre-defined elements, knowledge about relations between these elements, knowledge about the interpretations of related design constraints, and a design description generator which connects constraints to formal descriptions of solutions. The refinement process described above is based on activating the following kinds of knowledge.

1. Typological knowledge of the prototype, subtypes and their properties (Kty): This is the knowledge of the hierarchical relationship between the constituents of the prototype and its subtypes.

2. Topological knowledge of the type (Kto): Topological relations between components of the prototype. Each component can have its own typological hierarchy.

3. Interpretive knowledge of design constraints (Ki): Knowledge of typical constraints that effect decisions about refinement steps. These are typified constraints that consist of heuristic experiential knowledge related to their meanings in special cases.

4. Generative knowledge of the type (Kgr): Knowledge about sequential successive steps in a formal generative process. Each stage of refinement causes instantiation of subtype to the prototype in the typological hierarchy. The refinement process is executed by operations which produce parametrized design descriptions.

In the following section, the representational methods of GPRS which combine rules and frames in order to render this knowledge explicit will be presented. As an example, an architectural design prototype (a plan-type of a row-house application) is presented and illustrated.

Representation of Generative Knowledge by Rules

The generative knowledge of a prototype, (Kgr), may be represented by rules. A rule-chaining mechanism can provide a medium for a successive generative refinement process. This process can be guided and controlled by knowledge which provides the meanings of the refinement stages.

For example, the generative knowledge of a row house prototype is represented by rules which enable generation of a subtype through a succession of rule-chained design decisions. The first typological classification level of a row-house type is based on decisions about its number of floors, or sectional properties. The next level deals with the zonal partitioning of the plan. There are various options for zoning. The next decision level is stair location, and wet utilities location, etc. We thus proceed from a high-level generalization of the type through the successive levels of its detailed refinement. Figure 3 demonstrates a generative representation of a row-house plan-type in GPRS.

Representation of Typological and Topological Knowledge by Frames

Typological knowledge (Kty), and *topological knowledge (Kto)*, of a prototype can be described by frames in their traditional use. The frame provides a scheme which enables a generic description to support hierarchical inheritance of its typical attributes in the process of typological refinement. It also supports the notion of specifying default values in the frame. It describes its attributes and passes them, through the inheritance mechanism, to its sub-types. In this way, it is unnecessary to specify all the information at each level. It is assumed that in the level of an instance it inherits the properties of its superclass, unless it is purposely specified otherwise. This enables us to use abstraction levels as means of representation at each level of the typological generic class.

For example, a row house can be classified typologically by its number of floors, by its zoning etc. A double storey row house is then described as a subtype of a detached or semi-detached house plus a set of additional characteristic properties. At each typological level, the subtype is described by a set of properties that define its subtype-class. For example, attributes such as basic orientation of outside walls have been specified at the first level of the row house type, the number of floors have been specified to a double storey row house type at the next typological level, etc. In this way, each level contains the relevant attributes of its typological class. The properties of each typological level of a row house can be passed to its subtypes by inheritance.

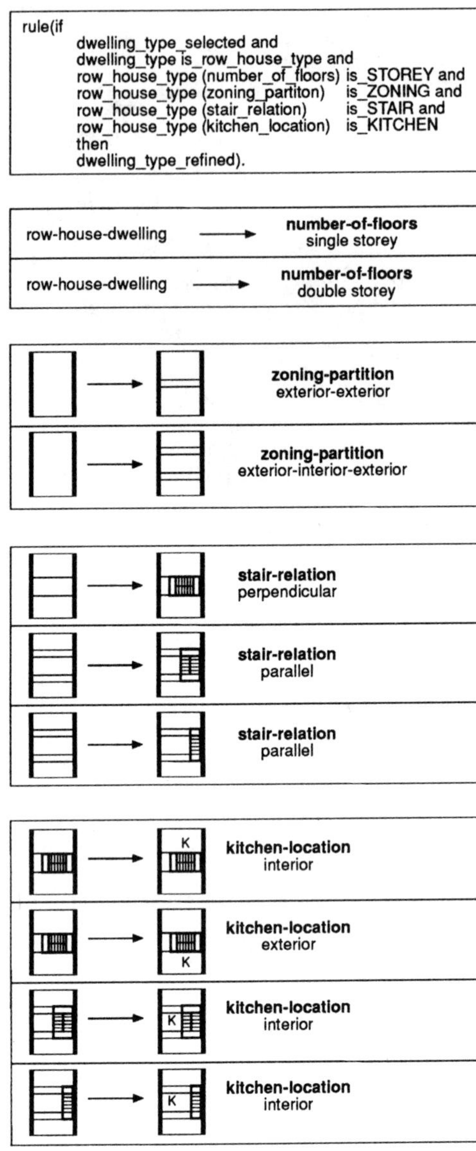

Figure 3 - A generative representation of a row house plan-type in GPRS

Rules Embedded in Frames for the Representation of Interpretive Knowledge

Most systems dealing with objects obtain their values by certain procedures which specify the attributes. The system must perform certain tasks in order to accomplish this. In design, these tasks are performed by reasoning from certain heuristics which are associated with decisions about attributes and formal acts, depending on design conditions. A method in the form of *rules* is proposed through which the system may consult relevant heuristic knowledge which provides reasons for formal decisions. The instance attributes are specified by consulting this knowledge base. The basic advantage of combining rules and frames in this case is that the frame structure provides explicit representation of the context in which relevant rules can be used for reasoning. In this way, each prototype represented in the frame formalism can direct the use of a set of rules in order to specialize its sub-type.

For example, in order to decide about the attribute of number of floors, a special reasoning process about the available width condition takes place by consulting a specific rule base by the name of 'knowledge-base-storey'. Figure 4 illustrates a frame representation of a row house plan-type with its relevant rule bases. The knowledge bases are activated by the frame inference engine which provides the 'if_needed' mechanism.

Rule Representation for Interpretive Knowledge

The knowledge bases which are embedded in the frames are, in fact, a specific collection of heuristic rules about refinement steps related to typical conditions. They represent *interpretive knowledge (Ki)* about meanings of typical formal refinement steps in a refinement process. For example, in order to decide about the number of floors in a row house the designer must consider the available width of the dwelling unit. Figure 4 presents the rule-frame-rule representation of a row house type in GPRS.

Frame Representation as a Model behind the Generative and Interpretive Knowledge Represented by Rules

Frames are used to describe a model of the prototype behind its generative rules. The frame offers a structured representation for providing and storing information associated with abstract refinement concepts reasoned by the rules. Interpretive knowledge is associated with the frame slots in a way that enables the frame to link relevant knowledge bases to its attributes. The knowledge bases invoked by the frame employ a rule mechanism and provide information back to the frame structure.

The row house frame is used to describe a model of the plan-type to which the generative rules are referring. The frame provides a representation for storing and retrieving information about the characteristics of the plan-type which is being reasoned about by the rules. The rules which are invoked by the frame provide information back to the frame structure. This formalism operates in a top-down fashion. Each hierarchical level is then related to a sub-type frame. For example a double storey row-house, a three-zone row-house type, etc., have their own plan characteristics. Each of them is described by a sub-type-frame. At any step, the instance type contains attributes which are added at each stage of the refinement process. Figure 5 demonstrates the flow of knowledge between rules and frames of a row-house prototype. The rules are activated according to the frame-model.

```
generative rule:
          (If
          dwelling type is row_house_type and
          row_house_type (number_of_floors) is_STOREY and
          row_house_type (zoning_partition) is_ZONING and
          row_house_type (stair_relation) is_STAIR and
          row_house_type (kitchen_location) is_KITCHEN and
          then
          dwelling_type_refined).


    prototype-frame:
          prototype_frame: row_house_type
          number_of_floors    if_needed          knowledge_base_storey
          zoning_partition     if_needed          knowledge_base_zoning
          stair_relation        if_needed          knowledge_base_stair
          kitchen_location     if_needed          knowledge_base_kitchen


    interpretive rule:
          knowledge_base_storey:
                if       dwelling frontage is_ narrow
                then    dwelling storey refinement is_ double storey.
```

Figure 4 - Row house plan-type representation in GPRS

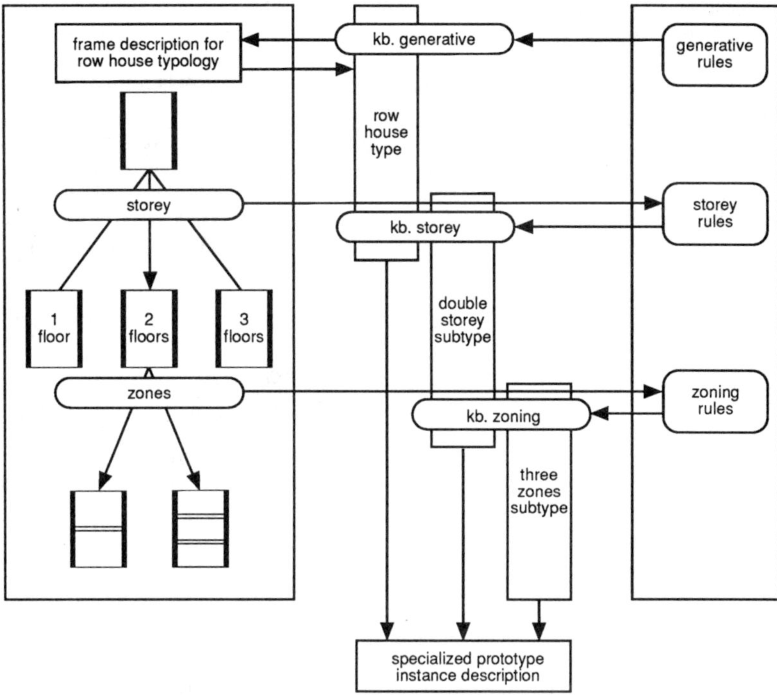

Figure 5 - Knowledge flow between rule bases and frame bases in GPRS

4. Situation Prototypes in GPRS

GPRS can be used to encode conceptual knowledge of a prototypical situation. A refinement process of a situation type starts with the typification of intrinsic constraints which are refined as extrinsic constraints. The GPRS formalism for a situation refinement process is presented below.

Rule Representation of Intrinsic Constraints

Intrinsic constraints are typified by activating rules on situation specifications. For example, twenty dwelling units per acre can be typified by an experienced designer as a typical high density site situation.

Generative Rules for a Refinement Process

Generative refinement knowledge of a situation indicates the order in which refinement design decisions are taken about extrinsic constraints. For example, in the case of a high density dwelling housing type the order might be: what kind of circulation system will be selected, what kind of access is preferable, etc.

Rules and Frames for the Representation of Extrinsic Constraints

The basic advantage of combining rules and frames is that the frame provides a generic model of a design situation, as well as the knowledge of its extrinsic constraints. The system consults relevant knowledge in the form of *rules* in order to specify the extrinsic constraints as instance attributes in the refinement process. For example, knowledge about types of movement and circulation is an integral part of the frame knowledge. In order to invoke that kind of knowledge, the 'if needed' formalism in a frame structure is activated.

Rules for the Representation of Interpretive Knowledge of Solution Features

Knowledge about the fit between extrinsic constraints and circulation types is represented by interpretive rules. For example, in order to achieve the quality of a street in a high-rise building an organizational scheme of horizontal circulation might be applied. Certain types of circulation such as horizontal corridors may characterize a solution prototype such as a horizontal corridor high-rise building type. These rules can be represented as follows:

```
kb. circulation-rules:

   if     'street like relation' in building

   then   dwelling circulation is horizontal corridor type
```

In this section, we have demonstrated how GPRS was employed as a medium to encode prototypical knowledge of both solution and situation prototypes within a design refinement schema. In the next section PRODS, a design shell system which is based on GPRS is described and its operation demonstrated.

5. PRODS: A Prototype-based Design Shell for Prototype Selection and Prototype Refinement

A session with PRODS begins with *context specification* through input of data in which conditions and requirements are specified. In the next stage *intrinsic constraints* of a *design situation* are typified by using knowledge about the meaning of the specifications. Typification of *extrinsic constraints*. starts with generative refinement process of a prototypical design situation. These enable the selection and the cueing of a solution prototype. After a prototype has been selected, its instantiation process commences with a *generative refinement* process until it reaches a final refinement. In the following section the operation of the system will be described. The domain of application is that of the selection and refinement of a multifamily dwelling prototype for a residential site.

Collecting Information and Specifying Attributes

The session starts with context definition by input data through graphical communication as coordinates or verbal specifications. Various site attributes such as geometry, proportions, topography and orientation which constitute general situation attributes in site analysis are specified.

Situation Typification: Domain Constraints Typification

Characterizing, or typifying, the situation is done through typified constraints which are intrinsic to the problem at hand. Attributes of a site such as *high degree of slope* or *narrow frontage* are specifically meaningful in the sub-domain of housing design. These attributes are typified through the range of their values as intrinsic design constraints.

Situation Typification: Typical Features as Extrinsic Constraints

Typification of the situation provides a frame description of a prototypical situation which contains its typical features. From a frame description of a prototypical situation such as 'narrow site' or a 'low density site' we can draw inferences and make assumptions. Assumptions made from typifications can be established as extrinsic constraints. For example, a typical situation such as 'low density site' is already a taxonomical expression of a site typification. Certain assumptions accompany this expression and which it inherits from the site typification. For example, one of the typical features of a low site density is that its dwelling units are commonly ground-attached, their exterior space is private, they have a private access, etc. In the following example the system inferred that on a 'low density' site, all 'units have private or semi private entrance' and on a 'narrow side site' 'main facades are oriented towards the street' . Figure 6 shows an example of a screen display of a refinement process of extrinsic constraints.

Prototype Selection

Extrinsic constraints are specialized features which direct the selection of a solution prototype. At this stage two strong categories of domain knowledge are related: the domain of the building-type, the morphological class of the grouping of the units; and the domain of the dwelling unit, the plan-type of the unit. The selection process in this case focuses on a row house prototype. The retrieval of the prototype is based on incremental specifications through which search is directed.

Prototype Refinement : A Row House Prototype

Once a prototype has been selected it carries with it its generative hierarchical refinement schema. In the following example we can consider the 'row house' as a prototype that is represented by its typological rules. The typological rules represents a solution space of all sub-types. Based on existing attempts to formalize prototypes in this domain [24, 25], a generative row house schema was presented earlier in figure 3. The order of specialization of attributes is shown in figure 7.

```
extrinsic constraints typified? - yes/no (how/why/explain)
The dwelling access of low density is_ enter value (how/why/explain)
the options for dwelling organization typification are:
1. private
2. semi private
? 1.
The dwelling orientation of narrow site is_ enter value (how/why/explain)
the options for dwelling orientation typification are:
1. side_facade
2. street_facade
? 2.
-----------------------------------------------------------------------------------
dwelling access is_ private
-----------------------------------------------------------------------------------
dwelling orientation is_ street_facade
-----------------------------------------------------------------------------------
*******************************************************************************
dwelling type is_ row house
*******************************************************************************
```

Figure 6 - A screen display of a refinement process of extrinsic constraints
which lead to the selection of a prototype

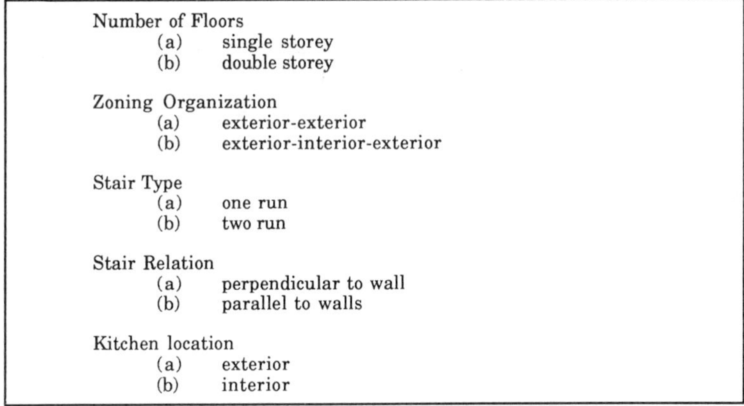

Figure 7 - The order of attributes specialization of a row house prototype

The process of refinement is controlled by interpretive knowledge at each stage of refinement. These knowledge bases are general and applicable to various kinds of design situations. The prototype is refined by the order of use of these knowledge bases which is specific to the prototype. An example of a design session in a refinement stage is shown in figure 8. It demonstrates a consultation with 'zoning knowledge base' which provides knowledge about zonal partitioning of the plan. It presents two options for making a decision about zoning: exterior-interior-exterior zoning, and exterior-exterior zoning. The first type of zoning, does not provide an outside access for the interior zone. The layout implications of such zoning is that the wet functions, such as toilets, are usually located in that zone. In the second type of zoning, the exterior-exterior type, the two zones have an outside access and it has its own typical layouts. In such housing types, these zoning patterns constitute the bases of sub-type classes.

```
The dwelling organization typification is_ ? - enter value (how/why/explain)

the options for dwelling organization typification are:

1. compact organization, wet core is not provided by outside orientation

2. loose organization, wet core is provided by outside orientation

? 1.
-------------------------------------------------------------------------------
dwelling organization typification is_ compact
-------------------------------------------------------------------------------
*******************************************************************************
dwelling zoning typification is_ exterior-interior-exterior
*******************************************************************************
zoning refinement is_true
*******************************************************************************
kb. zoning returned
```

Figure 8 - Design session in a refinement stage reasoning with
'zoning knowledge base'

PRODS Shell: System Architecture, Methods and Tools

PRODS (Prototype-Based Design System) is a system which utilizes GPRS rule-frame-rule structure in a design context. The implemented system which demonstrated these ideas consists of three basic components. An existing rule-based expert system [26], with an addition of a frame system, and an interface engine which controlled all system interactions. It passes control between the rule-based and the frame-based inference engines and provides communication between rule and frame representations. PRODS uses a system controller in the form of an expert system rather than an object oriented programming environment. It demonstrates how rule based systems and frame based systems can communicate kinds of knowledge during a design session. Each of the representational tools was selected because of its capability to represent and control the particular kind of knowledge in a way suitable to the design task. Figure 2 presented how frames and rules are activated in GPRS.

In order to facilitate the development of a design knowledge base, the shell provides the user with an acquisition facility which allows the user to modify and extend both rules and frames of GPRS design knowledge.

- KB. CS: Context Specifications.

    specification rules:
    rules for collecting information (data).
    rules for specifying attributes.

- KB. ST: Situation Typification

    intrinsic constraint typification rules

- GPRS: Generative Prototype Refinement of situation type

    generative rules
    prototype frames
    interpretive rules of extrinsic constraints

- KB. S: Selection

    prototype selection rules

- GPRS: Generative Prototype Refinement of a solution type

    generative rules
    prototype frames
    interpretive rules for a subtypes refinement

6. Summary and Conclusions

In order to accommodate generic knowledge in KBD systems, design knowledge must be well-formulated and structured. Design shells can accommodate generic knowledge and can be used as a design tool for developing applications.

Various research questions have been raised in the process of developing the pilot system, PRODS:

In addition to the concept of prototypes as top-down hierarchical knowledge structures, what other structures of knowledge can be employed to deepen the knowledge representational potential of knowledge based systems, and particularly of knowledge based design systems ? Can prototype based systems be used to integrate various types of knowledge behind the prototype ? What mechanisms are employed in making inferences with these knowledge structures and how do they operate in design?

The prototype is only one form of generic knowledge in design [12]. The design shell concept provides a framework for formulating generic design knowledge and work in the development of applications with such design shells should enhance the process of definition and formulation of other forms of knowledge in design.

Other significant future research implications of the work presented in this paper are related to the subject of creativity in knowledge-based design. The GPRS approach provides knowledge structures which support refinement and modification processes of design attributes. In creative design a knowledge-based design system must supports modifications of the knowledge structures themselves. In order to implement prototype based system for non-routine and creative design, a further range of theoretical questions must be addressed.

Acknowledgements

The research was carried out in the Design Computing Unit of the University of Sydney and in the Faculty of Architecture and Town Planning of the Technion. I wish to acknowledge the important contribution and support of Professor John Gero.

References

[1]   Oxman, R. E. "Architectural Knowledge Structures as Design Shells", *CAAD Futures* , MIT Press, Cambridge Mass., 1990 (in press).

[2]   Sriram, D. and Adey, R. (eds.) *Applications of Artificial Intelligence in Engineering Problems,* Springer-Verlag, Berlin, 1986.

[3]   Sriram, D. and Adey, R. (eds.) *Knowledge-Based Expert Systems in Engineering,* Computational Mechanics Publications, Southampton, England, 1987.

[4]   Gero, J. S. (ed.) *Expert Systems in Computer Aided Design,* North Holland, Amsterdam, Elsevier Science Publishers, 1987.

[5]   Gero, J. S. (ed.) *Artificial Intelligence in Engineering: Design,* Elsevier, Computational mechanics Publications, 1988.

[6]   Pham, D. T. (ed.) *Expert Systems in Engineering,* IFS Publications Springer-Verlag, Berlin 1988.

[7]   Schank, R. C. and Abelson, R. P. *Scripts, Plans, Goals and Understanding,* Lawrence Erlbaum Associates, New York, 1977.

[8]   Winograd, T. "On Primitives, Prototypes, and Other Semantic Anomalies", in *Proceedings Second Workshop on Theoretical Issues in Natural Languages Processing,* University of Illinois pp. 25-32. 1978.

[9]   Brachman, R. J. "Defaults and Definitions in Knowledge Representation", *AI Magazine,* vol. 6, pp. 80-93, 1985.

[10]   Sowa, J. F. *Conceptual Structures,* Addison-Wesley, Reading, Massachusetts 1984.

[11] Oxman, R. E. "Design Shells: A Formalism for Prototype Refinement in Knowledge-based Design", *Artificial Intelligence in Engineering*, Computational Mechanics Publications, 1990 (in press).

[12] Oxman, R. M. and Oxman, R. E. "The Computability of Architectural Knowledge", *CAAD Futures* MIT Press, Cambridge Mass., 1990 (in press).

[13] Oxman R. E. "Prior Knowledge in Design", *Design Studies* , 1990 (in press).

[14] Hillier, B., Musgrove, J. and O'Sullivan, P. "Knowledge and Design", *in EDRA* Mitchell, W. J (ed), *Environmental Design: Research and Practice*, pp. 29-33. Los Angeles, 1972.

[15] Rowe, C. and Koetter, F. *Collage City*, Cambridge, Mass., MIT Press 1978.

[16] Mitchell, W. J., *Logic of Architecture*, MIT Press, Cambridge, Mass., 1989.

[17] Gero, J. S. Prototypes: "A New Schema for Knowledge-Based Design", *Working Paper*, Architectural Computing Unit, Department of Architectural Science, University of Sydney, 1987.

[18] Simon, H. A. The Science of the Artificial, MIT Press, Cambridge,Mass., 1970.

[19] Mitchell, W. J. "The Top Down System and Its Use in Teaching", *in* P. J. Bancroft, (ed),*ACADIA* Workshop Proceedings, Ann Arbor, 1988.

[20] Minsky, M. "A Framework for Representing Knowledge", *in The Psychology of Computer Vision*, (ed. P. H. Winston) McGraw-Hill, New York, 1975.

[21] Fikes, R. and Kehler, T. "The Role of Frame-Based Representation in Reasoning", *Communication of the ACM*, Vol. 28, No. 9, pp. 904-920, 1985.

[22] Stiny, G. 'Introduction to Shape and Shape Grammar", *Environment and Planning B*, Vol. 7, pp. 343-351, 1980.

[23] Buchanan, B. G. and Shortliffe, E. H. (eds.) *Rule Based Expert Systems*, Addison Wesley, Reading, Massachusetts, 1984.

[24] Habraken, N. J., Boekholt, J. T., Thijssen, A. P., Dinjens, P. J. M.*Variations*, MIT Press, Cambridge, Mass., 1976.

[25] Sherwood, R. *Modern Housing Prototypes*. Harvard University Press, Cambridge, Mass., 1978.

[26] Rosenman, M. A. *The BUILD Manual*, Architectural Computing Unit, Department of Architectural Science, University of Sydney, Sydney, NSW, Australia, 1986.

What's in a Joke?

Michal Ephratt

Department of Hebrew Language
Haifa University
Haifa, Israel

1. The problem

When told a joke most of us recognize the sentence as a joke. What is it about
jokes that trigger this behavior? In this paper we shall try to analyse and
answer this question as regards a class of jokes which we term **linguistic jokes.**[1]

1.1 Linguistic jokes - ambiguities

Linguistic jokes are jokes that make use of properties of language to amuse the
listener (or reader). All these properties seem to come under ambiguities, i.e.,
more than one grammatical and meaningful reading of a sentence or discourse.
Linguists recognize different sorts of ambiguities:

* **Lexical ambiguity** occurs when a word stands for more than one lexical entry:
> *"What did the big chimney say to the small chimney?*
> *You are too young to smoke."*

Here there are two competing senses of 'smoke' (intransitive: "give off smoke or
steam", transitive: "draw into the mouth and puff out smoke of burning tobacco
or the like").

* **Structural ambiguity** occurs when one surface structure is interpretable as
originating from more than one deep structure:
> *"The girl: I don't speak with perfect strangers.*
> *The sailor: Don't worry, I am not perfect."*[2]

The structural ambiguity could be explained in terms of immediate constituents:
the girl meant 'people who are completely strangers to her' (((perfect

---

[1] We are not dealing here with non-linguistic jokes, such as social jokes: e.g.,
> *Old fellow A: "Do you remember how we chased girls in our good days?*
> *Old fellow B: "Of course, I do, but what did we want from them?"*

Raskin [8] does not distinguish between the two. Since most of the examples in his paper do not come
under the term "linguistic jokes", one needs more than command of language to understand them.

[2] Based on Jespersen [6, vol. 2, p. 287].

strange)r)s), whereas the sailor's answer refers to 'a person who is perfect and incidentally a stranger' (((perfect) (stranger))s).

* **Idiomatic vs. literal meaning** occurs when an utterance can be analysed according to its literal sense or interpreted as an idiom, as in
> *"Every time my wife is down in the dumps she buys a new hat.*
> *Oh, that's where she buys!"*

The ambiguity is in the interpretation of the phrase *down in the dumps* the literal interpretation is that 'the woman is physically standing (located) in an accumulation of refuse materials'. The idiomatic interpretation related to *down in the dumps* as a lexical entry, meaning 'a gloomy state of mind'.

1.2 Parsing ambiguities

Before we proceed to look at algorithms for parsing jokes, we should explain that ambiguity is not a property exclusive to jokes.

Much of the effort of the computational linguistic paradigm has been devoted to the issue of constructing theoretical models of parsers or implementing parsers, that handle computationally the issue of ambiguity.

By now, it is common practice for most parsers to identify ambiguities: some parsers do that by adding a stack to the grammatical component (see [1, pp. 178-185]); simple ones scan the output over and over (without a stack) until they exhaust all possible readings. Others, enable parallel grammatical processing within one scan of the output.

Now that the parser can supply all possible readings, the question arises as to how to handle these different readings. In most cases, only scholars interested in ambiguities as such might want to receive all the different possible readings of a string. Yet, for all other cases the user needs only one out of these possible readings.

Background parsers that by default provide the user with all possible readings (of every ambiguous string) were abandoned not only because they supplied too much information but also for the following reasons:

1. Such parsers are not efficient: they provide results that expand in storage and presentation. Such capacities could exceed the limits of the computer (usually memory, but also time that could slow down or even "paralyze" the system). They are, therefore, unsuitable for automated applications such as instructing a robot in industry, interacting with expert-systems, or even running machine translation software.

2. They were ruled out on theoretical grounds: the different parsings are all equal with respect to **grammaticality** i.e., they are all grammatical, but psycholinguists also incorporated **acceptability** into their theoretical and

empirical interest (see [7, pp. 15-16]). It turns out that not all grammatical readings are equally acceptable. In considering acceptability they account for variations in acceptability of the different grammatical parsings. It is then desirable that a parser will provide the user with the different readings in descending acceptability order.

The question then arose how to achieve a more efficient and strongly theoretically supported parser.

An easy way out was to leave the grammar unchanged and to modify the parser so that once a parse is successful, it is given as an output and no backtracking takes place. In this way the first answer is the only answer, but not necessarily the best one.

It was soon felt that strategies should be developed to arrive at the best parsing first. This demanded ordering the interpretations by **preference** from the most favored to the less favored, making explicit the criteria, so that preference rules could be formalized.

Strategies were developed to integrate preference into parsing (for an overview see [1, ch. 6] and [5]). These strategies differ from each other in their preference identification and implementation:

1. Some are strictly structural (ignoring semantic preferences, see for example [7] and [12]). The best known and the first (1973) to state preference rules was Kimball. He presented a set of seven structural principles. The most important one was **right association** - "terminal symbols optimally associate to the lower non-terminal node". This explains the attachment of e.g., - *for Mary* to *had selected* (rather than *bought)* in *John bought the book which I had selected for Mary.* Other researchers take the opposite extreme (see [13], but see Schubert's comments in [10] beginning of section 4 p. 603); and others integrate structural and semantic preferences (see [2, 4, 5, 9, 10]).

2. Some build deterministic parsers so that preference decisions are carried out before the entire sentence is parsed (see for example [4, 10, 11, 12]). Such parsing, if not combined with a look-ahead mechanism, could end in failure when a decision taken at a previous stage leads to a parse that is ruled out in a later stage (like in many 'garden path' sentences).
On the other hand, some preference parsers operate on top of the grammar parser. Each time they consider a node they have at hand full grammatical information. It seems to us that this is the only way for implementing a preference principle such as the **minimal attachment** resulting in minimizing the number of nodes in the tree. This principle accounts for the preference of e.g., *the horse fell* in the sentence *The horse raced past the barn fell.* This structural principle was introduced by Frazier and Fodor (in 1978, see [4]). Together with Kimball's right association principle (and not as in [5, p. 11]) they or their variants (see for example 'rule habituation effect' and 'graded

distance effect' in [10]) seem to be the two basic principles of structural preference.

3. Ways of implementation. The preference principles could be serial and ordered so that the first preference principle to fire is the decisive one (see for example [2, 5, 7, 12, 13]). A different way is a trade-off relation between the rules, so that each of the preference rules is weighed against the others (see [9] and [10]).

1.3 Choice of preference parser

Three stages are needed for resolving ambiguities: identifying the ambiguity, parsing all possible readings, and grading or choosing according to preference. These stages take place in all ambiguity parsing and are not unique to jokes. Yet, they were built (both as ordered principles and as a trade-off model) to reflect the assumption that the preferred reading is the most expected one, or cheapest in terms of the trade-off model.

It seems to us that here lies the crucial difference between a joke reading and a non-joke reading; unlike a non-joke reading, a joke reading does not choose the preferred reading (all being grammatical and meaningful) but chooses the unexpected. Clearly, preferring such a reading does not eliminate all other readings. By remaining as background, these readings give the joke its humor quality. It follows then that the essence is modifying the choice of a "general purpose" preference algorithm which is the key to understanding jokes and incorporating this issue in a preference model.

As we have seen, the preference strategies differ from each other in at least three major topics. The definition of an unexpected parsing varies for each of these implementations.

A preference parsing algorithm that seems to us most appealing (for all parsing purposes, including jokes) is a parser that

1. integrates all linguistic issues (structure, meaning, logical form, etc.),
2. operates on top of the grammatical component with no artificial limitations on deterministic decisions, and
3. is a trade-off parser, i.e., assigns equal weights to different linguistic criteria.

Requirements (1) and (3) seem to be fulfilled by Schubert's trade-off preference parsing algorithm (see [9] and [10]). Schubert has a set of six preference criteria, each accounting for a different source of possible ambiguity, three syntactic criteria and three semantic-pragmatic criteria.[3] Activating Schubert's criteria at each parsing step provides each node with its activation cost. This activation

---

3   We shall explain each of these criteria when we present our first example of joke parsing in section 3.1.

cost is obtained by the accumulative sum of costs according to each of the criteria when applied to that specific node. This sum is passed to the ancestors of that node to provide them with the transmitted cost. The transmitted cost added to the node's own cost provides the total cost of that node. According to the cost trade-off algorithm the preferred reading of a node is the reading with the lowest cost. We are then forced to modify this part of the algorithm to suit our theory of joke parsing.

2. Parsing jokes: partial reverse preference algorithm

We wish to maintain as much of Schubert's algorithm, allowing minimal modification of the final choice. Schubert's preferred reading is the reading with the lowest cost. We now suggest that the joke's unexpected reading requirement may be incorporated into this scheme, by what we shall term **partial reverse preferences.**

A (completely) reverse preference algorithm prefers the most costly reading. In a partial reverse algorithm, the preferred reading is partially reversed. Only one modification is made to the usual preference algorithm. It goes as follows:

- locate the one multiple parsing node with the largest numerical gap between its highest cost and its lowest cost

- define this node as the **punch node** and its highest cost as its **punch parsing**

- combine this punch parsing (of the node) with the lowest cost reading of the rest of the tree.

This combination results in the joke parsing.

Using Schubert's numerical preference algorithm means that we take the preference receiving the lowest cost for the whole tree except for the one punch node that receives the highest cost. In this paper we set all initial cost values to 0, i.e., we only increase costs and not decrease them.

The above algorithm defines linguistic jokes and should serve for parsing them. We should notice that just as the parsing algorithm is not binary but grades solutions from the most favored to the least favored, so does the joke algorithm. It follows that the node with the largest cost gap is the most unexpected, i.e., the best joke parse, but that successive gradings (smaller gaps) could still be jokes.

Although we chose Schubert's algorithm for the reasons stated above, we do not feel committed to his parser (as implicit in [11]) nor to his ambiguity limit. We use a top-down parser that accounts for gaps etc. We also feel that Schubert's three-phrase limit on successive ambiguous constituents, although fit for his parser and purposes, is not fit for our case. Either people know they are about to hear a joke, invoke the punch node parsing from the beginning, or they keep all parsings in parallel, choosing the favored parsing only at the end of the sentence (joke). If these are the possibilities, then using an algorithm that would force a deterministic decision on the fly will be inadequate. We also think that even within the general purpose algorithm (such as Schubert's) such a decision can lead to failure.

Finally, both Schubert's papers ([9, 10]) give a general description of each criterion, but do not supply an operative or formal decision procedure. The actual method of assigning costs is not indicated in these papers. To take a simple example, the sub-criterion **lexical preference** defined as a negative increment of the rule potential for the unusual rules (e.g., N -- > *fat*) should explicitly state how one decides (a) which rule is more usual than the other, and (b) what are the measures of the cost. Moreover, it should also indicate (c) how to deal with cases of multiple senses spread over different parts of speech. This is of crucial importance where the senses have different syntactic manifestations. For example, the word *box* is either a verb or a noun. As a verb it has two distinct senses and syntactic behavior: transitive 'to furnish with a container', and both transitive and intransitive 'to hit or fight with the fists'. As a noun *box* has two distinct senses: 'container' and 'a strike'.[4] When Schubert describes lexical preference he does not mention such possibilities of multiple senses and multiple syntactic structures (within one part of speech).

In order to make this algorithm operational we have tried to formulate the missing decision procedures according to the way we interpreted Schubert's intentions. We then are able to show the unique characteristics of parsing jokes. We wish to show that if one has a good steady general purpose preference parsing algorithm, only one well defined modification is needed for the joke's parsing.

3. Detailed illustration of preference parsing

We first look intuitively at one case, showing how each of Schubert's criteria (with our decision procedures) operates for determining the parsing of that joke. We then look in more detail at a more sophisticated case where we point out all multiple parsings (according to any of the six criteria). In both cases we do not provide all details of all rules that participate in the parsing unless they are the rules causing the multiple parsing. We also do not deal with parsings that later turn out to be ungrammatical - lead to failure. We end this paper with some more cases for the trial and enjoyment of the reader.

---

4   Throughout this paper we shall use *italics* to indicate words in the language, 'apostrophes' to indicate senses and **bold** to introduce terms.

3.1 First example

We all seem to manage to understand jokes, so, we shall first scan a joke intuitively.

      A.   *"A gold-miner is a person that has strong hands and boxes."*
We all feel that the whole weight of the joke is concentrated upon one ambiguous node *boxes,* where *boxes* can be either a plural noun, as in

      A1.   *"A gold-miner is a person that has strong hands and strong boxes".*
or a participle verb as in

      A2.   *"A gold-miner is a person that has strong hands and that boxes."*
Boxes can then mean either 'contain' as in *strong carton boxes* or 'strike' as in *strong painful boxes.*

Except for the reading of the last node: noun vs. verb and 'contain' sense vs. 'strike' sense (and parsings deriving from these readings, e.g., attachment of *and)* there seems to be no other possible ambiguity in this sentence.

When we hear this utterance, we first process the noun reading, (as in Fig. A1 - tree A1) which is the preferred reading for a non-joke reading. In order to grasp the joke, we replace this preferred reading with the least preferred, in our case, the verb (as in Fig A2 - tree A2). Also, as we shall soon see, we first process the 'contain' sense and then replace it with the 'strike' sense.

We now explore these intuitions through Schubert's six preference criteria, and our partial reversed algorithm. We should note that Schubert emphasizes the trade-off approach by activating each of the criteria independent of the rest, maintaining also separation between syntactic criteria and semantic ones.

Syntax

Rule habituation effect. This inhibits the use of phrase structure rules (including lexical rules) so that a parse tree using few and more usual rules would be preferred over one using more rules and less usual ones. This leads to a minimal attachment tendency for equal costs (see section 1.2). Schubert does not provide an operational description of this rule, and does not supply the costs attached to the different rules.

To procedurally define this criterion, we take the following steps:

1. We arrange grammar rules according to simplicity, regularity and parsimony

    a. we group all phrase structure rules (of our grammar)[5] which share the same sign on their left into one group. These rules are in fact competing rules. We grade them according to descending regularity or simplicity,

---

[5]   Although we consider only rules that might participate in parsing our sentence, it seems that our findings have wider validity.

where base rules precede transformations, transformations precede slash categories, etc.

b. We group all lexicon rules (rules having only terminal(s) on their right) which share the same terminal(s) on their right into one group. We then grade them according to descending frequency. This measure is easily found in any frequency lists reference book.

2. We then fix the costs of these competing rules so that the most regular (simple or frequent) rule in each such group will be free and the rest will collect costs negatively proportional to their grading.

Since we give meta-rules a special status within phrase structure rules, meta-rules such as conjunction will be graded right after the most regular phrase structure rule. To ensure parsimony we collect one code point from any phrase structure rule that results in a monadic branching.

We shall now demonstrate these statements with respect to the rules participating in parsing our sentence A. The following S rules might participate in parsing this sentence:

S --- > NP VP (e.g., *A gold-miner is a person*)

S --- > NP/NP VP (e.g *(that) has strong hands and {person} boxes*)

Also the meta-rule of the form

C --- > C' connective C''

(stating that any constituent might be a concatenation of members of that constituent) when assigned S as constituent, is competing with S rules.

Thus, we see three competing rules for rewriting S. No doubt the simplest is the base rule S --- > NP VP, as said we then grade the meta-rule, and finally the elliptic sentence of the form S --- > NP/NP VP (the elliptic sentence will later collect an additional code point because it results as a monadic branching).

The terminal *boxes* is ambiguous between a plural noun (N --- > box(es)) and participle (V --- > box(es)). We determine their regularity by looking-up their grading in a frequency list

We use [3] which is a recent and detailed frequency list (published in 1982, texts from 1961) that discriminates between parts of speech and their inflections. The frequency number indicates the number of occurrences of the form in the entire corpus (over a million words).

According to [3] the plural noun *boxes* occurs 14 times whereas the verb occurs only twice. *Boxes* splits semantically into two distinct senses: 'contain' and 'strike'. The two senses have different syntactic behavior: the 'strike' sense is both transitive and intransitive, whereas the 'contain' sense is only transitive. The two nouns act uniformly.

Since the distinction between the two noun senses of *box* does not have a bearing on syntax, the three phrase structure rules just described are appropriate for both senses. This is, however, not necessarily the case for the VP and S phrase structure rules. Both senses have transitive verb reading, but only the 'strike' sense allows an intransitive reading. Since in this paper we provide only parsings that terminate grammatically, the intransitive reading of the 'contain' verb sense is ruled out as ungrammatical.

The following table summarizes all groups participating in our current parsing:

group sign	No of members	rules	code point
S	2 + meta-rule	S ---> NP VP S ---> NP/NP VP	0 2
NP	4 + meta-rule	NP ---> N NP ---> det N NP ---> A N NP ---> NP that S NP ---> A/A N	0 2 3 4 5
VP	3 + meta-rule	VP ---> V NP VP ---> V VP ---> V/V NP	0 2 3
box(es)	2	N ---> box V ---> box	0 1

Table 1: Parse markers participating in sentence A, graded according to preference

The six successful parse trees for our sentence are presented in Figures A1 to A6, Attached to each node is its code points.

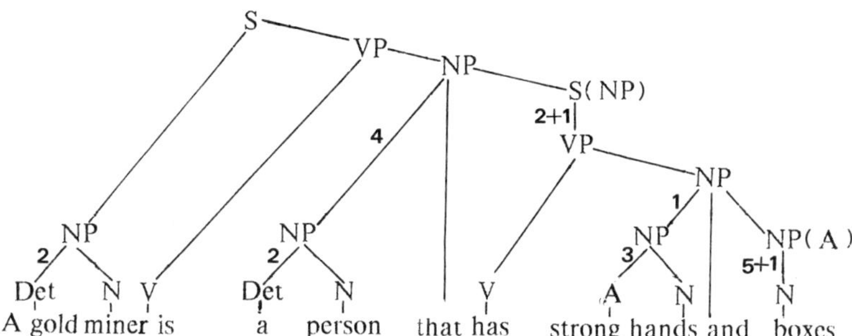

Figure A1: Parse tree and code points of sentence A1.

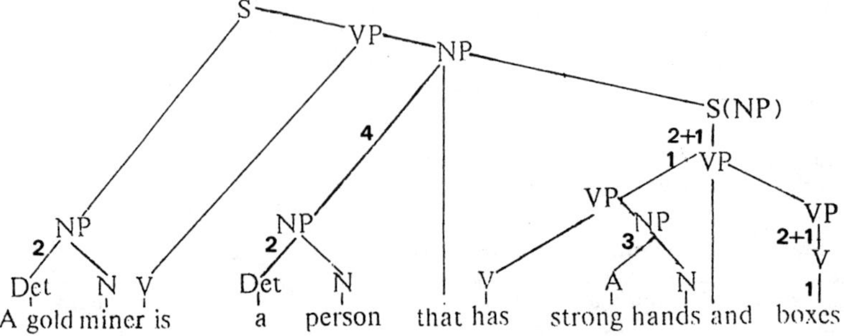

Figure A2: Parse tree and code points of sentence A2.

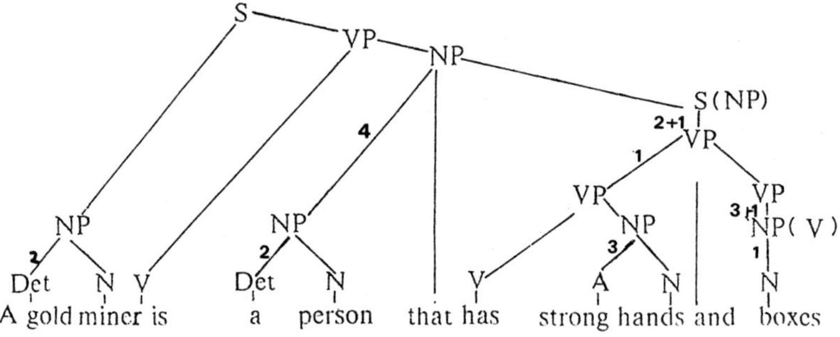

Figure A3: Parse tree and code points of sentence A3.

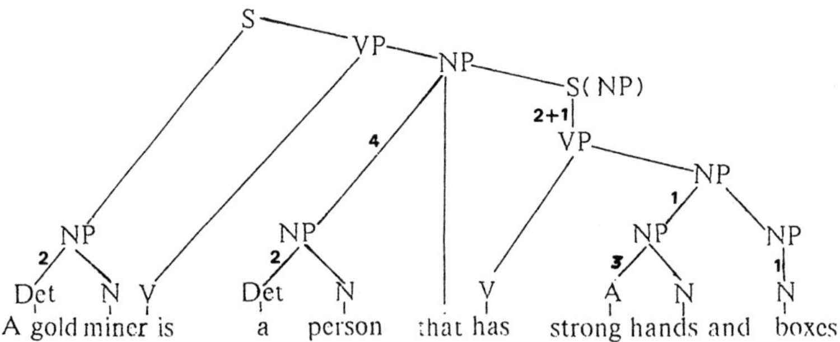

Figure A4: Parse tree and code points of sentence A4.

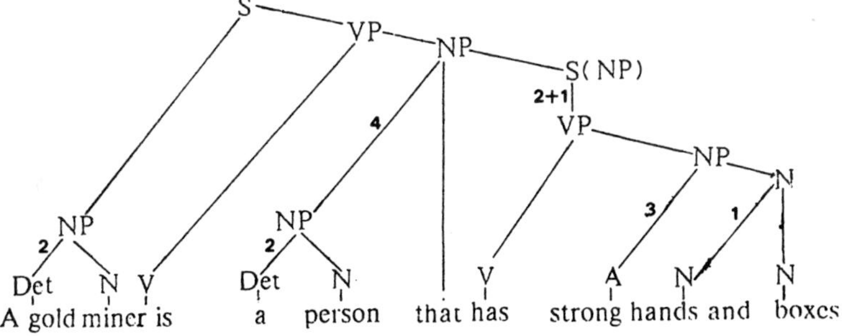

Figure A5: Parse tree and code points of sentence A5.

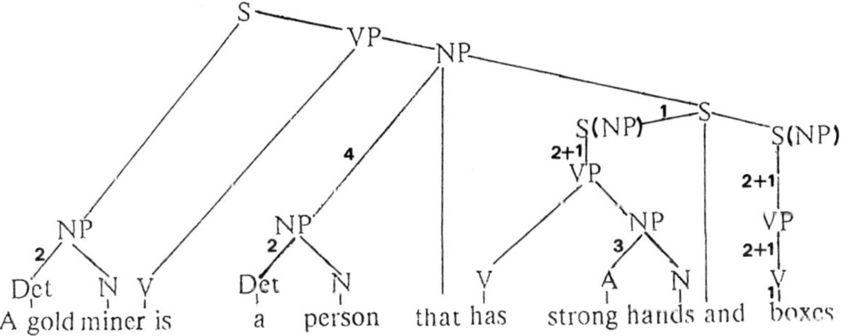

Figure A6: Parse tree and code points of sentence A6.

A note on our mode for calculating costs

As we shall see, Schubert's six criteria, when provided with an appropriate calculating function, might each result in different sorts of costs. Some result as ordinal numbers representing order of preference, others result as numbers representing quantities, others as real numbers of the fraction of the distance criterion, and others as three digit number for frequency of word occurrence in a frequency list.

In order to preserve the trade-off strategy, we have to ensure that the cost of one criterion will not override the rest. We allocate each of the six criteria with one sixth of the whole cost (100). We then calculate how this sixth (16.6) is broken-down within each criterion.

Each node in the parsing tree has as attribute the code points of the rule(s) it activates. These codes are dynamic in the sense that: for each tree (or subtree) we calculate the total of its codes, we then divide the relative cost of the criterion (16.6) by the highest sum (of codes in node) to yield the value of each code point. We then multiply the sum of each tree by the result of that fraction to obtain the final cost of the tree.

When we activate this method for the rule habituation criterion, we see that the tree with the highest sum of code points is tree A6 (22 code points). The value of each point is then 0.75 (16.6:22 = 0.75). The cost of tree A6 would then be 16.6. The tree with the lowest sum is tree A5 with 15 code points. Multiplying this sum by 0.75 would result as cost of 11.25. Tree A5 is then the preferred tree (reading) according to the rule habituation criterion, and tree A6 represents the least preferred reading according to this criterion.

Since we adopted a trade-off algorithm we shall have to check all other criteria before we could determine the final preferences results.

Graded distance effect. This effect prefers immediate constituents of a phrase to be close to the head lexeme of that phrase. Schubert states that since this potential is directly proportional to the number of words separating a constituent from the head lexeme and inversely proportional to the number of words of the constituent, larger constituents admit larger displacements from the head lexeme. This criterion usually accounts for the right association tendency (see section 1.2, but see [9] p. 249). Schubert does not provide the functions for calculating these values. Bearing in mind the properties listed above, we formulated a function for the graded distance cost. This function calculates for each possible parsing of the phrase ($\overline{P} = P_1, P_2, ..., P_n$) the fraction ($E_i$) of the number of words separating the constituent from the head lexeme (D_i) by the length of the constituent (W_i). These E_i values serve as code points for the weighed cost of each reading.

The word encountered just before *boxes* is *and* which is a diadic conjunctor. Such a conjunctor attaches two constituents of the same category

$$\text{Constituent-}C \text{ --} > \text{Constituent-}C_1 \text{ CONJ Constituent-}C_2.$$

We expect the two constituents attached by the *and* to be of the same category.

If we register all possible antecedent constituents of *and* and duplicate them for the *boxes* node,[6] we can then use the graded distance criterion (among others) to determine the preferred scope of *and* in our joke, i.e., which constituent does the *and* concatenate.[7] We duplicate the antecedent by adding subconstituents that

---

[6] In practice the actual choice can only be made after we encounter 'end of sentence'. But for methodological purposes and for simplicity we take a short-cut and provide the results on the fly.

[7] We eliminate the rules for which the second constituent will not be as expected or else will not terminate. We would comment that because of such cases we think there might be a major problem with Schubert's decision to set the preference to three-parse limit on successive ambiguous constituents. Picking a path that does not terminate or is later found to be ungrammatical leads the whole parse to failure instead of providing the most preferred grammatical reading.

were elided because of the recovery property of conjunctors (indicated by curled brackets). In Figure B, we present these different antecedents of *and*, by stretching a line along the antecedent (the word previous to it is the head lexeme) and the recovered *boxes* node. For each such reading we indicate the values of W_i (length of constituent) and D_i (number of words separating the constituent from the head lexeme), E_i fraction and the final result (F_i , the weighed cost) of the function.

					D	W	E	F
A	A gold-miner is a person that has strong hands and							
A5			N		boxes(N) 1	1	1	4.15
A4		NP ____			boxes(N) 2	1	2	8.3
A1	NP __________			{strong}	boxes(N) 3	2	1.5	6.22
A3	VP __________			{has}	boxes(N) 3	2	1.5	6.22
A2	VP __________				boxes(V) 4	1	4	16.6
A6	S __________			{he}	boxes(V) 4	2	2	8.3

Figure B: possible antecedents of *and* and recovery of *boxes* and their costs.

The last column (F_i) is the final (weighed) cost of each possible reading. This F_i value is obtained by dividing 16.6 by the highest E_i value (4 of A2) which yields point value 4.15, and then multiplying each of the E_i values by 4.15.

These costs show that according to the graded distance criterion the preferred scope of *and* is the minimal noun constituents: *boxes* and *hands* (A5 - costs 4.15). The least preferred scope is the conjunction of VPs: *boxes* and *has strong hands* (A2 - costs 16.6).

Inhibition by errors. This is the last syntactic criterion to consider. In Schubert's algorithm "mild errors" such as concord errors do not rule out the parsing (as ungrammatical) but rather contribute inhibitory potential (collects highest cost) to the phrases in which they occur. Concord errors are tracked at a further subconstituent of the phrase, thus, whenever we track such an error we collect the cost from that subconstituent.

Schubert does not supply any examples for this criterion. Two distinct cases could qualify for this criterion:

1. ungrammatical sentences that become grammatical by a mild correction, such as correction of concord,

2. grammatical sentences that could also be interpreted as ungrammatical either

    a. by choosing a part of speech or affixation that does not match the rest of the parse (e.g., *has* as auxiliary in *has boxes)* or
    b. by claiming that a certain letter or letters should be replaced by another letter, due to misprint (e.g., *boxes* as misprint of *boxed)*.

Clearly, our example does not meet the first case. Incorporating the possibility of parsing such cases might force a certain modification of our basic demand that all sentences be grammatical and meaningful. But such a modification might be beneficial for jokes that use alliterations and other phonetic means (see omission of capital B in 4.1 F.).

The second case seems to generate many possibilities that are not established by the text and that would demand an unjustified and superfluous grammar and algorithm. Such would also be the case with *strongboxes* as 'safe' which can not be recovered as grammatical.

Semantics

When we look at the semantic preference, the noun vs. verb distinction made for the syntactic preference becomes secondary to the conceptual distinction between *boxes* in the sense of 'contain(er)' and *boxes* in the sense of 'strike'. The 'contain' sense is ruled out in intransitive verbs, because the verbal reading (A2, A6) would be semantically unambiguous ('strike' sense).

Salience in context. Schubert says that "the potential of a word sense or a phrase is high to the extent that the denotation of the word sense or phrase is salience in the current context" ([10, p. 602]). When describing the same criterion (in [9, p. 249]) Schubert says that "possibly a spreading activation mechanism could account for the context-dependent part of the semantic potential". To operationally define 'salience in context' as the measure of the activation spreading in a semantic context we count distance between nodes as the number of nodes linking the intersection of the two concepts in a semantic net (for simplicity, we ignore here the nature of the links and other possible indices).

In our current node we consider the semantic relatedness of the concepts 'gold-miner' 'person' 'strong' and 'hand' (independently) to 'box' (as 'contain') and 'box' (as 'strike'). After we obtain such measures, we arrange them in descending order.

Any semantic network would link 'box' (as 'strike') and 'hand' directly to 'fist' (serves as intersection). No semantic network would have an intersection directly linking 'hand' and 'box' (as 'contain'). In fact, the relatedness of these two concepts is not stronger than the relatedness of any other two physical objects in the world. This means that for practical purposes we can consider them as maximally distant. It follows then that any measure of 'hand' and 'box' as 'contain' will exceed the measure of 'hand' and 'box' as 'strike'.

We now check the relatedness of 'box' senses to 'gold-miner'. 'Gold-miner' could be linked with 'box' as 'contain{er}' via SUBSTANCE node via INSTRUMENT node (manual) and via OCCUPATION node (at least three nodes). 'Gold-miner' is linked with the 'strike' sense of 'box' via a much longer chain which goes through the supernode PERSON to any ANIMATE or HUMAN concept (still, closer than the 'contain' - 'hand' relation). The concept 'person' is explicit in 'gold-miner' and is implicit in 'hand' (part of upper limb in man only). 'Strong' is not considered (independently) since it is a modifier (of *hands*).

We now grade these connections in descending order: 'strike' is immediately governed by 'hand': it collects no cost (code point 0); the next nodes' closeness (code point 1) is 'contain' sense with 'gold-miner' (three nodes); the extreme distance would be the 'contain' sense with 'hand' (code points 2) and in between will emerge 'strike' sense with 'gold-miner' (code points 3).

To determine using context the preferred sense of *box* we add the code points within each sense:
    'strike': 0 code points with 'hand' + 2 with 'gold-miner' = 2
    'contain': 1 code point with 'gold-miner' + 3 with 'hand' = 4
This in turn gives 4.14 as value point and the final cost of 16.6 (4.15 X 4) for the 'contain' sense and 8.3 (4.15 X 2) for the 'strike' sense.[8]

Familiarity of logical-form pattern. Schubert refers here to the logical translation instantiating a familiar pattern of function-argument combination (see [10, p. 602]). Logical-form (LF), like the previous criterion, is concerned with the whole phrase. We use here James Allen's translation and notation of LF (compare [1, ch. 7-10] with [11]). We operationally define the term "familiar LF" to be Allen's type translation which is also the most **general, coherent** and **complete.** By these characteristics we mean that the whole phrase is captured in one (=coherent) LF statement (=general), which has all arguments (operator, name, type and modifiers - especially inner-case roles) instantiated (=complete). Checking our case, we first identify the type of the LF, namely the verb action or event.

In readings A1, A3, and A5 the type is a HAVING-EVENT. HAVING-EVENT has two inner-cases THEME, and the object AT-POSS. The following are the LFs translations of these readings.

A1 and A5:
    (PRES h1 HAVE
        [THEME (INDEF/SING g1 PERSON "gold-miner")]
        [AT-POSS (AND (PL s1 HANDS (STRONG s1))
                    (PL b1 {CONTAINER,STRIKE} (STRONG b1))))])

A3 and A4:
    (PRES h1 HAVE
        [THEME (INDEF/SING g1 PERSON "gold-miner")]
        [AT-POSS (AND (PL s1 HANDS (STRONG s1))
                    (PL b1 {CONTAINER,STRIKE}))])

---

[8]   Because not all nodes are explicitly listed here (some are estimated), we do not collect the price per node.

In readings A2 and A6 there are two types, i.e., two LF statements joined as a conjuction. The first LF type is as before a HAVING-EVENT and the second STRIKE-ACTION. As discussed earlier *box* could be either a CONTAINING-EVENT or a STRIKE-ACTION, but since we ruled out the verb 'contain' reading, we skip this possibility. For the same reason we leave out the transitive reading of the STRIKE-ACTION:

A2 and A6:

```
(AND (PRES h1 HAVE
        [THEME (INDEF/SING g1 PERSON "gold-miner")]
        [AT-POSS (AND (PL s1 HANDS (STRONG s1))]])
     (PRES a1 STRIKE
        [AGENT (INDEF/SING g1 PERSON "gold-miner)]))
```

We now have to go back to our definition and decide which of the LFs is the preferred one. The sole HAVE-EVENT LF (which is not a conjunction of LFs and captures all in one LF statement) is more coherent than the STRIKE-ACTION which attaches two disjoint LFs. Since we rule out the intransitive verbal reading of *boxes* and since all inner cases expected for both HAVE-EVENT' and 'STRIKE-ACTION' are fully instantiated here, we claim that all forms suggested here are equally complete. We should notice however that the logical-form criterion does not determine the noun sense preference and adjective scope (i.e., 'strike' vs. 'contain' and *strong boxes* vs. *boxes)* such issues are solved elsewhere (we discuss these issues in the logical-form criterion for *can't* node in the next example 3.2.2).

To obtain the cost of the logical-form criterion from its two conditions (coherence and completeness) we split the total (16.6) collecting 8.3 for the 'STRIKE-ACTION' due to incoherence, and no cost for the sole 'HAVE-EVENT' (which is complete as the 'STRIKE-ACTION' but also coherent).

Conformity with scripts/frames. This criterion has to do with "familiar kinds of objects or situations (such as might be specified in a script or frame)" [10]. Scripts and frames are well defined entities in AI. No matter what particular description we use, they all cluster collections of knowledge about the world. Unlike the previous criterion (LF) that looks at linguistic data, the object of this criterion is the world.

Whereas conformity with scripts is one criterion out of six, and the least linguistic one, Raskin [8] uses scripts as sole criterion for interpreting jokes. As mentioned (footnote 1), Raskin includes under the term **linguistic jokes** many examples that demand **cotext** (rather than context), but then interpretation cannot be achieved by command of language alone (see [8, p. 38]).

To go back to our example, a crucial element in the script criterion is having a context - selecting a frame or script. We adopt the following key for choice of frame: look for the most specific noun or NP (in the context) and this will be the frame object.   The most specific noun in our context is no doubt 'gold-miner':

```
[FRAME : gold-miner
         IS-A : occupation          (* this entails 'person' etc.  *)
 SLOTS : object (gold)
         location (mine)
         uniform (helmet, working-cloth)
         instrument(drill, torch)
         mode(manual)
 ACT :   mine (quarry gold from mine)
         remove (gold to containers)].
```

We see that 'person', 'hand' and 'container' appear in the 'gold-miner' frame. Replacing the 'container' sense of *box* by the 'strike' sense (as noun and verb) forces us to switch frames: We start off with the 'gold-miner' frame, we ignore the 'container' meaning seen above using a new frame:

```
[FRAME:  boxer
 IS-A:  {sports, combat}  (* this entails 'person' *)
 SLOTS:  object(another boxer, drill-cushion)
         uniform(boxing-gloves, shorts,{})
         instrument(hands-fist)
         mode(manual)
 ACT: box(strike someone with fist for sports or combat)].
```

This frame maintains 'person' and 'hand'. It completely leaves out 'gold-miner' which is the core NP of our example (the two frames connect in a much higher level by sharing the 'person' property). It seems straightforward to claim that a sense that enables us to interpret the whole story within one frame is preferred over a choice of sense that forces us to use two frames (see [8] on this matter).

We then collect no cost from all 'contain' sense of *box* and 16.6 from all 'strike' senses (both noun and verb).

Searching such a frame we find that all three notions mentioned in our text: 'gold-miner', 'person' and 'contain{er}' appear in this frame. It is not difficult to see that the two latter notions would also appear in a 'strike' frame, but this will leave out 'gold-miner', apart from violating the demand for the most specific NP.

Summary

The following table summarizes the costs of all six criteria for the six syntactic readings and two sense readings:

reading	rule habituation	graded distance	mild errors		salience in context	logical form	frames	total
A1	15.75	6.22		'strike '	8.3	0	16.6	46.87
				'contain'	16.6		0	38.57
A2	14.25	16.6			8.3	8.3	16.6	*64.05*
A3	15	6.22		'strike '	8.3	0	16.6	46.12
				'contain'	16.6		0	37.82
A4	16	8.3		'strike '	8.3	0	16.6	49.2
				'contain'	16.6		0	40.9
A5	11.25	4.15		'strike '	8.3	0	16.6	40.3
				'contain'	16.6		0	*32*
A6	16.6	8.3			8.3	8.3	16.6	58.1

Table 2: Criteria costs for each of the possible readings of sentence A.

We started off with only one ambiguous node. As demonstrated by the different readings (see "rule habituation effect") expanding this node to its recovered different structures, and resolving the attachment of *and,* does in fact result in different nodes. It seems apparent from this table that different criteria prefer different readings: some prefer noun over verb (e.g., logical-form); some prefer 'strike' sense over 'contain' sense (e.g., salience in context); some prefer 'contain' sense over 'strike' (e.g., frames) etc..

According to the trade-off algorithm described here the preferred reading is the reading with the lowest cost: the lowest cost found in our table is 32 which is the cost for reading A5 with the 'contain' sense of *box*

> *"A gold-miner is a person that has strong hands and strong boxes."*
> (= 'containers').

Since we have located only one ambiguous node (the *boxes* node) this node is also the punch node. Thus the preferred reading A5 is replaced for the joke reading by the most costly reading A2 with the verbal 'strike' sense of *box* (cost of 64.05):

> *"A gold-miner is a person that has strong hands and he boxes."*
> (= 'strike').

3.2. Second example

The next example contains three ambiguous nodes (B1, B2 and B3). Having more than one ambiguous node will enable discussion of more aspects of the joke preference parsing algorithm and demonstrate the choice of a punch node.

B. *We eat what we can and what we can't we can.*

We parse this sentence node by node from left to right:

3.2.1 node B1 - Can {eat} NP1(V)

Syntax

Rule habituation effect. The first (from left to right) multiple parse we confront in B occurs when we have the competing phrase structure rules:

    NP rules: NP --- > PRO (code point 0)
                      NP --- > NP CONJ NP (meta-rule) (code point 1)
                      NP --- > COMP(wh) S (code point 2)
    VP rules: VP --- > AUX V {NP} (code point 0)
                      VP --- > V {NP} (code point 1).

Aux (Auxiliary) is obligatory for all modal verbs, future, perfect, negation (e.g., *can't* in the following node) etc. This is why VP --- > AUX V is more regular (no cost) than VP --- > V (code point 1).

As in the previous example, we collect one code point for each phrase structure rule resulting in a monadic branching (NP --- > PRO, VP --- > V).

The lexical lookup at the word *can* reveals two lexical readings that match *can* with the above mentioned phrase structure rules:

    AUX -- > *can*
    V -- > *can,*

i.e., *can* is ambiguous between auxiliary and verb (we leave out the N -- > *can* reading because, as said above, we ignore parsings that are later ruled out by the grammar). Checking [3] to determine the lexical preference of *can*, we find that *can* as auxiliary appears 2192 times (the forty-third most frequent word out of six thousand), as verb 14 times and as noun 7 times.

We do notice that the different gaps between the auxiliary frequency and the verb frequency, as well as between the verb frequency and the noun frequency, can not be ignored. We want to incorporate in our scaling an accurate representation of these gaps on the one hand, that on the other hand will result in costs small enough not to override the costs of the remaining criteria (to remain within 16.6). We therefore collect here one code point for every 1000 word gap:

We grade the lexical preference:

    AUX -- > *can* (code point 0)
    V -- > *can* (code point 3, 1-1000; 1001-2000; 2001-3000).

We now have two competing (partial) trees:

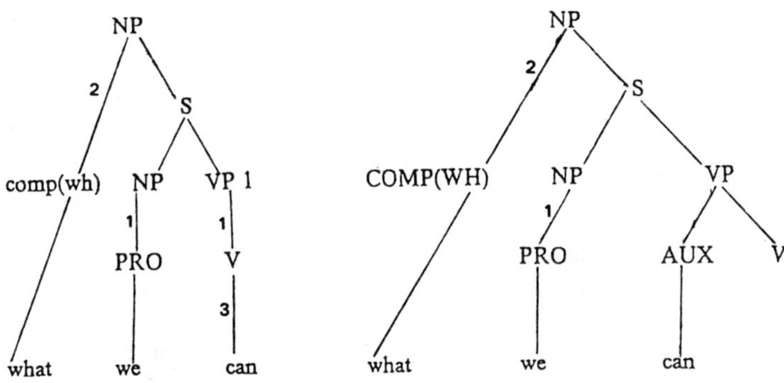

Figure C: Partial trees of node B1 of sentence B.

Since there are no other competing rules, the non-auxiliary reading costs 16.6 (16.6 : 8 = 2.07, 2.07 X 8 = 16.6), and the auxiliary reading costing 6.21 (3 code points) will be the preferred reading (for this criterion).

By a top-down parser we have traced a potential verb gap (in the first tree). A gap is a surface manifestation of a deletion (from a deep structure) permissible if the item deleted can be recovered. The most likely candidates for recovering such gaps are previously mentioned verbs. Looking at the trees that we have constructed so far, we find only one verb *eat* . We fill the gap with this verb:

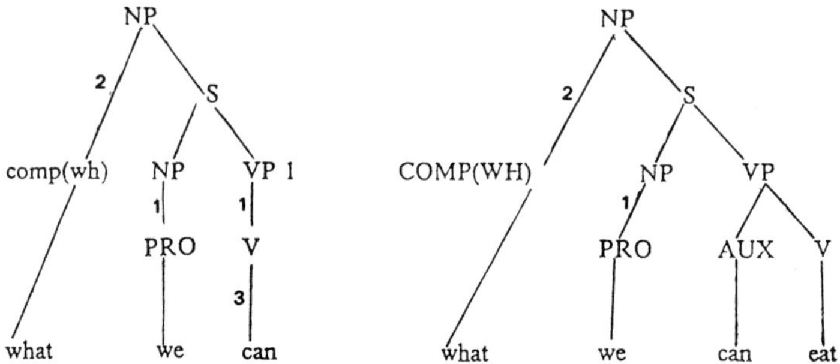

Figure D: Filling the gap of *can* in node B1 of sentence B.

It should be pointed out that Schubert's algorithm does not account for gaps.

Graded distance. The graded distance criterion served in the previous example to determine the scope of *and*. Since the scope of *and,* which might seem ambiguous during the parse process is uniquely determined at the end, it does not constitute a preference issue in this example.

We use this criterion to determine by preference of head lexeme whether we have a *can* or *can eat* reading. We claim that if we see *can* as a verb then NP1(V) would be a one word constituent, which is its own referential head lexeme (no distance, i.e., D = 0, W = 1 -- > E = 0). If we see *can* as an auxiliary of the main-verb *eat* then we shift to a two word constituent (W = 2) separated by two words (D = 2) from its referential head lexeme (main-verb S1(V) *eat*), which results in one code point (2:2 = 1).

These are the possibilities within the first node:

We eat (S1(V)) what we can (0, eat) (NP1(V)).

In principle we have to allow for the possibility of cataphor, i.e., the filling of NP1(V) by a verb which we have not yet encountered, i.e., the candidate for filling the gap is not previously mentioned but rather mentioned after the gap. Such cases seem to be grammatical and could be found in cases like:

What(ever,0) we can we sell
(= What(ever) we can sell we sell)

or

What you can't don't sell
(= What you can't sell don't sell).

The NP1(V) would then be either NP2(V)

and what we can't (can, eat) (NP2(V)),

or even more distant, or S2(V) the main-verb of the second S:

we can (0, eat,can) (S2(V)).

Yet, all psycholinguistic studies, syntax processing, logic based grammars, poetry parsing and even formal parser construction, indicate that resolving anaphor is much easier than cataphor; we therefore collect an additional code point for any cataphor.[9] Since S2(V) is *can {can, can can, can eat}* we will not deal here with any other possibility. We shall come back to this issue when looking at NP2(V).

The following are the measures of distance and their costs:

current node	possible recovery	cataphor/ anaphor	with	D	W	E	point value	F
	0 (verb)	itself		0	1	0		0
We eat what we can(NP1(V))	eat (AUX)	anaphor cataphor cataphor	S1(V) we eat NP2(V) can't eat S2(V) can eat	2 3 6	2 2 2	1 1.5 + 1 3 + 1	4.15	4.15 10.3 16.6

Table 3: Possible complements of *can* (node B1) and their costs.

Inhibition by errors. There do not seem to be any mild errors issues here.

---

9   Although it so happens that the final results of the trade-off algorithm would be the same no matter whether we collect this additional point or we do not collect it.

Semantics

We now examine the preferences according to the semantic criteria.

Salience in context.   One does not need a semantic net nor an elaborated dictionary to support the feeling that 'eat' (in *can eat)* is more salience in the context (as seen up till now) than *can* . 'Eat' is analytically present in the context and as Schubert states "The parser prefers phrases interpretable as references to previously introduced entities to phrases that introduce new entities" ([10, p. 602]). Because it is analytic in that context, 'eat' overrides any other contextual possibilities. Though, we should bear in mind that 'can' as a verb is not alien to our context. Entering a semantic net, via the main-verb *eat* we trigger spreading activation that would eventually get to 'can'.

Imagine a semantic net where 'food' is a physical object that is then broken down into substance types.   One of them is PRODUCT-STATE. PRODUCT-STATE has as subtypes FRESH, DEHYDRATED, FROZEN, PRESERVED, etc. In such a net we get by spreading activation from 'eat' to 'can'. But, as said, it is not self-evident as the analytic case (EAT - EAT) and as seen now, it is not directly triggered but via FOOD. These two operations are costly: We collect one code point for each node (in the semantic net) and that results in the following code points:

> 'eat' - 'eat' (*eat - can eat*): 0 code points,
> 'eat' - 'can': FOOD --- >
> > PRODUCT-STATE --- >
> > {dehydrated, frozen, preserved, ...}: 3 code points.

The actual cost would then be 16.6 for *can* as verb and 0 for *can* as auxiliary of *eat*.

Familiar LF pattern.   The *can* as auxiliary reading confronts us with a case where we can not even fix a type for the logical-form. The only information handy at this stage is a coherent and complete translation of the logical-form of the 'can' (as verb) sense:

> (PRES c1 CAN
> > [AGENT (PRO h1 HUMAN we)]
> > [THEME (WH w1 FOOD:PREPARED,PRESERVED)]])

The auxiliary reading will be incomplete when an AGENT or EXPERIENCER are instantiated ("we") but there are no explicit types. As shown, the most reasonable recovery verb of *can* here is 'eat':

> (MODAL C1 can
> > (PRES e1 EAT
> > > [AGENT (PRO h1 HUMAN we)]
> > > [THEME (WH w2 PHYS-OBJ)]])).[10]

which would collect 8.3 for its recovery (incompleteness in context).

Conformity with scripts/frames. As to conformity with scripts or frames, it seems the two trees differ in favor of the verbal reading of *can* . As stated earlier we enter any frame via the most specific NP: *what we can* . The 'preserve' ('can') sense is more specific than *what we can eat*. This seems straight forward since preserving is one (specific) way of keeping food (objects of 'eat'), or to put it differently, canned food is a subset of all edible products. Using Crain and Steedman's terms, we notice also that *can* as PRESERVE is much more loaded with presuppositions and previous conditions than CAN-EAT. The explicit 'preserve' can frame will have no cost. The implicit 'eat' frame will collect cost of 12.45 and not 16.6 since we can not ignore the frame relatedness of 'can' and 'food' = 'eat'.

Summation of can {eat}

The following table summarizes the different costs collected by each criterion for the *can* as verb reading and *can eat* reading. Braces indicate competing costs due to different scopes of distance (see Table 3).

criterion	can (as V)	can (as AUX) of eat
rule habituation	16.6	6.21
graded distance	0	{4.15} {10.3} {16.6}
salience in context	16.6	0
logical-form	0	8.3
frames	0	12.45
sum	33.2	{31.11} {37.26} {43.56}

Table 4: Criteria costs for each of the possible readings of *can {eat}* in node B1.

In cases of multiple costs for one criterion within one node reading, we always choose the lowest cost. It then follows that *can eat* costing 31.11 is preferred over *can* (as verb) costing 33.2 (gap of 2.09).

3.2.2 node B2 - can't VERB (NP2(V)): The next ambiguity in the sentence is the VP with *can't* as a daughter NP2(V). *can't* (in contrast to the previous *can)* is syntactically unambiguous: it can only be read as an auxiliary. The question now arises as to what is its verb? According to the heuristics that "one can delete only what can be recovered", we are looking for verbs that occur in the context, previously mentioned verbs (anaphor) or coming verbs (cataphor). The candidates are then *eat* and *can* .

---

[10]   It seems to us this way of incorporating modality is in the spirit of Allen's LF, see [1, p. 216.]

Syntax

Rule habituation. Having identical structures in all nodes enables us to use the same phrase structure rules and lexical rules used before. Although in our node there is no issue of preference of *can* as auxiliary or as verb (only the verb reading yields a grammatical parse) the choice between *can* and *eat* as the verb of the auxiliary, seems to justify collecting the lexical cost from *can* (3 code points). Notice, however, that *can* can stand as the missing verb only when it is the main-verb of the previous node (NP1(V)): *what we can.*

The following are two possible trees for this node (NP2(V)):

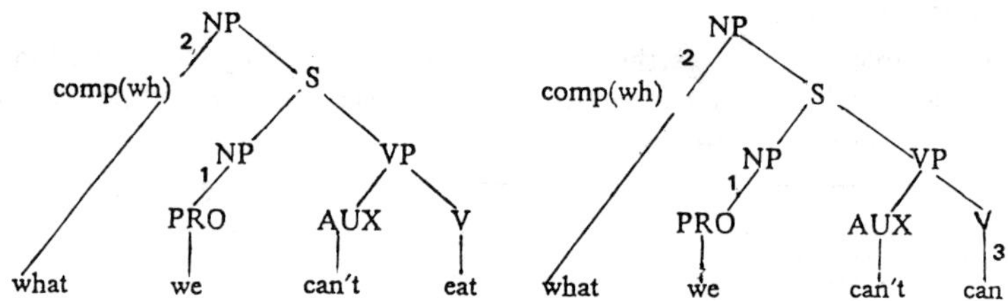

Figure E: Two possible trees for *can't,* in node B2.

The *can* tree collects 6 code points (16.6:6 = 2.76) which yields the cost of 16.6, and the *eat* tree collects 3 points, final cost 8.3.

Graded distance. We now use the "graded distance criterion" to determine the preference for recovery of the missing NP2(V). In the previous node the recovered verb of the auxiliary could only be *can eat. Can can* could not have been at that stage, yet this possibility (*can't can)* is grammatical now (if there is an explicit *can* verb elsewhere).

The following is the table of distance measures between the missing verb in our node and its possible anaphors or cataphors:

current node	possible recovery	cataphor/ anaphor	with	D	W	E	point value	F
what we can't NP2(V)	can't can	anaphor	NP1(V) we can	3	2	1.5		7.11
		cataphor	S1(V) we can	1	2	0.5 + 1		7.11
	can't eat	anaphor	NP1(V) we can eat	3	2	1.5		7.11
		anaphor	S1(V) we eat	7	2	3.5	4.74	16.6
		cataphor	S2(V) we can eat	1	2	0.5 + 1		7.11

Table 5: Possible complements of *can't* (node B2) and their costs.

Inhibition by errors. This criterion does not seem to be relevant here. We do not find concord or any other errors.

Semantics

Salience in context. As we have seen, when filling the first gap (NP1(V)), the choice of *eat* was supported by spreading activation. When checking for spreading activation in our current node (NP2(V)), there seems to be no doubt that the choice of *eat* is strongly supported (by a double source of activation, see [3, p. 94]) if both previous verbs are *eat - we eat what we can eat.* Since each repetition strengthens the activation of that sense, we calculate the code points as the sum of semantic net-nodes we traverse from S1(V) to NP2(V) and from NP1(V) to NP2(V):

parse node S1	parse node NP1	current node NP2	No. of semantic net-nodes	point value	final cost
eat	eat	can't eat	0 + 0 = 0		0
eat	eat	can't can	3 + 3 = 6	16.6:6 = 2.76	16.6
eat	can	can't eat	0 + 3 = 3		8.3
eat	can	can't can	3 + 0 = 3		8.3

Table 6: Costs of semantic connections between *can't* - node B2 and the reminder nodes.

Familiar LF pattern. Our current node is an argument of an independent proposition *(what we can't we can)*. Some considerations on LF have to be postponed until we reach the next node, where we parse the entire proposition. Our current parse stage, we consider the logical relation between NP2 and its parallel in the first proposition, namely NP1 *(what we can)*.

As we shall see when considering the next node, our example translates into two propositions connected by a conjunction. Each of these propositions has a proposition as an argument.

<pre>
        We eat
                what we can
        and
                what we can't
        we can.
</pre>

These propositions have identical structure. Also we notice that there is switch in order of presentation where the embedded proposition of the second proposition comes right after the embedded proposition of the first proposition. Although the two propositions are independent of each other, their structure, their content resemblance and the fact that by a conjunction they constitute a new proposition, lead to an expectation that they may be related.

what we can as an auxiliary verb is translated as:

```
    (MODAL C1 can
            (PRES G1 ACTION/EVENT TYPE
            [AGENT h1])) (* h1 being 'we' in the upper proposition
    *)
```

What we can't should then be translated as :
                    (NOT (MODAL C2 can
                              (PRES G2 ACTION/EVENT TYPE
                              [AGENT h1]))
By instantiating *eat* or *can* as action G1, G2 we obtain two possibilities:

1. negation, where G1 = G2 (G1 and G2 = *eat,* or G1 = G2 = *can*). e.g.,
    What we can eat and what we can't eat.
    What we can and what we can't can.
or

2. disjointness, where G1 is different than G2:
    What we can eat and what we can't can.
    What we can (as V) and what we can't eat.

This sort of relation is beyond form issues. Schubert indicating the LF preference of *met {someone} at a dance* over *married {someone} at a dance* does imply that LF does not only look at form structure but also looks at content combination (see [9, p. 250]). Still, from Schubert's "locomotion predicate" example it seems that content and thus selectional restrictions are secondary to LF preference. We therefore add to our operational definition a **content** characteristic which is activated after the type (and thus form) is set. The content characteristic looks at the relation between the type and the modifiers instantiations. Sometimes, as now, two logical forms seem equally preferred on coherence and completeness grounds, and yet one is preferred over the other due to such relations as content relations.

Thus, we add content as third condition for the "Familiar logical form" criterion. We propose two possible content relations: negation and disjointness. The negation here does not occur within the same proposition (see next node where it leads to contradiction) but in two conjuncted propositions. It seems to us that such cases complement each other, and so they are preferred over disjointness.

In order to sum the cost of this criterion for node NP2, we split 16.6 into three equal portions:

- 5.53 for incompleteness in all NP2 propositions - the action is missing and has to be recovered *(can't eat* or *can't can),*
- 5.53 for content relation between NP1 and NP2 of the disjoint type (the main-verb of NP2 and NP1 are not the same), and
- no cost for coherence, since we consider only the embedded proposition (the entire conjunction will be considered in the next node).

Conformity with scripts/frames. As for the first gap filling, the frame prefers the more specific. If the choice is between 'can' and 'eat', 'can' is preferred as being more specific. Yet, as in the previous node, here too we collect only 12.45 for the less specific reading ('eat') because of its close relateness to 'can'.

Summation of can't {eat, can}
The following table summarizes the costs of each of the six criteria for the
second node. Since some criteria (when applied to the current node) are
sensitive to choices made for the first or third node, costs are broken down
according to these choices (indicated under NP1, NP2 and S2).

NP1	NP2	S2	rule habituation	graded distance	salience in context	LF	frames	sum
eat	eat	can eat	8.3	7.11	0	5.53	12.45	33.39
eat	eat	can	8.3	7.11	0	5.53	12.45	33.39
eat	can	can	16.6	7.11	16.6	11.06	0	51.37
can	eat	can eat	8.3	7.11	8.3	11.06	12.45	47.22
can	eat	can	8.3	16.6	8.3	11.06	12.45	56.71
can	eat	can can	8.3	16.6	8.3	11.06	12.45	56.71
can	can	can eat	16.6	7.11	8.3	5.53	0	37.54
can	can	can	16.6	7.11	8.3	5.53	0	37.54
can	can	can can	16.6	7.11	8.3	5.53	0	37.54

Table 7: Criteria costs for each of the possible readings of *can't {eat}* in node B2.

Here too we choose the least of competing costs. Yet, we first insure that each
cost originates in the reading of that specific node (NP1, NP2 and S1). We can
now conclude that for NP2 the recovery verb *can't eat* (33.39) is preferred over
can't can (37.54) creating a gap of 4.15.

3.2.3 node B3 - Can {0, eat, can} (S2(V))

We now proceed to the last ambiguity: the main-verb of the second sentence
(S2(V)). Reaching this node we find that its surface is *can*. Considering this
node and encounting the end of our whole sentence with only two previously
mentioned verbs, we have three possibilities: AUX + V (*can eat* or *can can)*
and V *can.*

Syntax

Rule habituation effect. The rule habituation considerations in our current node
are very similar to those brought up in the first node (NP1(V)). The actual
phrase structure rules are identical, yet, our current sentence seems a
transformed form of the previous one:

"*we eat what we can*
what we can't we can."

In fact, we have here a case of another set of competing rules:
S rules: S --- > NP VP (code point 0)
                 S --- > S CONJ S (meta-rule) (code point 1)
         S(NPa V NPb) --- > NPb NPa S (transformation) (code point 2)
We shall then collect 2 additional code points from all parsings of S2.
As said we have here three possibilities:

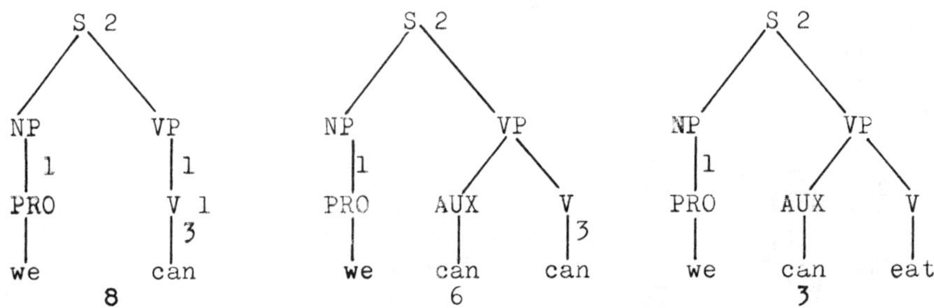

Figure F: Three possible readings of *can* in node B3.

We calculate point value (16.6:8) = 2.07 and grade the preferences as follows: *can eat* - 6.21; *can can* - 12.42 and *can* 16.6.

Graded distance. Here, as when considering this criterion for the previous nodes, we measure and grade the quantitative distance between the recovered verb and its referential head lexeme. Since we now discuss the last node, all references will be anaphors:

current node	possible recovery	with	D	W	E	point value	F
	can	itself (not anaphor)	0	1	0		0
we can S2(V)	can eat	NP2(V)we can't eat	1	2	0.5		1.66
		NP1(V)we can eat	6	2	3		9.96
		S1(V)we can eat	10	2	5	3.32	16.6
	can can	NP2(V)we can't can	1	2	0.5		1.66
		NP1(V)we can	6	2	3		9.96

Table 8: Possible complements of *can* (node B3) and their costs.

Inhibition by errors. Here too this criterion does not seem to apply.

semantics

Salience in context. Following is the table of costs of the repetition and recovery in the context of the last node:

parse node S1	parse node NP1	parse node NP2	current node S2	No. of semantic nodes	point value	costs
eat	eat	can't eat	can eat	$0+0+0=0$		0
eat	eat	can't eat	can	$3+3+3=9$	$16\text{-}6{:}9=1.84$	16.6
eat	eat	can't can	can	$3+3+0=6$		11.06
eat	can	can't eat	can eat	$0+3+0=3$		5.53
eat	can	can't eat	can	$3+0+3=6$		11.06
eat	can	can't eat	can can	$3+0+3=6$		11.06
eat	can	can't can	can eat	$0+3+3=6$		11.06
eat	can	can't can	can	$3+0+0=3$		5.53
eat	can	can't can	can can	$3+0+0=3$		5.53

Table 9: Costs of semantic connections between *can* - node B3 and the previous nodes.

Familiar LF pattern. At the current parsing stage (last node of example) we consider three issues:

1. preference of recovered action within the last node:
$$we\ can\ (S1(V)).$$

2. preference of the second proposition of the conjunction:
$$(and)\ what\ we\ can't\ we\ can.$$

3. preference of the relation between the two propositions that constitute the whole example :
$$We\ eat\ what\ we\ can$$
$$(and)\ what\ we\ can't\ we\ can.$$

1. The recovery of *can* as action or as modal for actions *can* or *eat* is very similar to the case discussed for the first node. All possible logical forms are equal as regards coherence (all translate to one proposition). As seen, only *can* as action is complete:
(PRES c2 CAN
    [AGENT (PRO h1 HUMAN we)] (* being the PRO h1 human "we")
    [THEME (WH w2 FOOD:PREPARED,PRESERVED)])

In all other cases (where *can* serves as modal of action 'eat' or 'can') the action type is incomplete (i.e., one must recover which action or event instantiate the type, e.g., EAT-ACTION or CAN-ACTION, etc.). We therefore collect one code point for the modal forms ('can eat' and 'can can').

2. We now check the content relation between these propositions and the NP2 propositions (embedded in them). Previously, we claimed that two propositions having the same action where one is the negation of the other, complement one another, e.g.,
$$'can\ eat' \qquad and \qquad 'can't\ eat'.$$

We hold this claim for two independent propositions. In a case like our current node the evaluation is different. Two such propositions where one is an argument of the other lead to contradiction , e.g.,

> What we can't eat we can eat.
> What we can't can we can (can).

We therefore collect content code points for all such forms.

3. The last logical form preference to consider is the content relations between the two independent propositions (connected by *and*). Since two independent propositions are at issue, we look for the most informative (contentwise) combination. It seems to us that such is the combination of 'eat-action' and 'can-action' (unlike 'eat' and 'can eat').

   We therefore collect content code points for all forms where 'eat' is the action of the second proposition (S2)).

We should explain here that all these points are collected within the S2(V) node, although they have to do with the whole constructed proposition, because all the relations checked here originate from this last node.

Conformity with scripts/frames. As seen before, conformity with scripts and frames would prefer 'can' to 'eat'. We go on collecting 12.45 for the 'eat' readings and no cost for the 'can' *(can, can can)* readings.

summation of can {0, eat, can} (S2)

NP1	NP2	S2	rule habituation	graded distance	salience in context	LF	frames	sum
eat	eat	can eat	6.21	1.66	0	16.6	12.45	36.92
eat	eat	can	16.6	0	16.6	0	0	33.2
eat	can	can	16.6	0	11.06	5.53	0	33.19
can	eat	can eat	6.21	1.66	5.53	16.6	12.45	42.45
can	eat	can	16.6	0	11.06	0	0	27.66
can	eat	can can	12.45	9.96	11.06	5.53	0	39
can	can	can eat	6.21	16.6	11.06	11.06	12.45	57.38
can	can	can	16.6	0	5.53	5.53	0	27.66
can	can	can can	12.45	1.66	5.53	11.06	0	30.7

Table 10: Criteria costs for each of the possible readings of *can* {*eat*} in node B3.

In this node we have three competing readings, we choose the least cost reading *can* (as V - costing 27.66). The most costly is *can eat* (costing 36.92), in between is *can can* (costing 30.7). The gap in this node is then 9.26.

3.2.4 Results for the joke reading: The parse of the phrase *We eat what we can and what we can't we can* reveals three ambiguous nodes. According to the partial reversed preference algorithm suggested here, we have to find the node with the largest gap (between costs) and designate this as our punch node. The gaps obtained during the parse are:

> NP1: 2.09 (table 4 - 3.2.1)
> NP2: 4.15 (table 7 - 3.2.2)

and

> S2: 9.26 (table 10 - 3.2.3).

The punch node is then S2 (node B3). We now follow the partial reversed preference algorithm and replace the cheapest reading in that node: *we can* with the most expensive one, namely *can eat*.

The joke reading would then be:

> *we eat what we can eat and what we can't eat we can eat.*

4. Summary

We hope to have convinced the reader that jokes parsing is a joke in terms of minimal adjustments needed when attempting to use a non-joke preference algorithm to successfully parse jokes. The only modification needed is the change of preferred reading of the punch-node. Yet, joke parsing is no joke in that it supplies serious support for preference issues in both natural language processing and parsing computer languages.

Our attempt to activate the algorithm presented here also for jokes in Hebrew (to appear in **Hebrew Linguistics,** 31 1990) seems to be successful: no modification is needed. We do expect similar results for other languages.

More examples

Meanwhile, as we promised, we supply the reader with additional examples both for his trial and his enjoyment:

C1. *"Do you serve crabs? Yes, we serve everybody."*
C2. *"Sorry, we don't serve women, you have to bring your own."*

D. [Someone turns to the Salvation Army] *"Do you save bad girls? Yes. Well, save two: one for me and one for my buddy."*

E. *"What did the horse-radish say to the frige? Keep me cool, I'll stay hot."*

F. [Ignore capital letters] *"Who is bigger, Mr. Bigger or his son? His son, because he is a little bigger."*

G. *"What did the Mayonnaise ask the frige? Close the door, I'm dressing."*

References

[1] Allen J. F., **Natural Language Understanding,** Benjamin / Cummins, 1987.

[2] Charniak E., "Passing markers: A theory of contextual influence in language comprehension", **Cognitive Science,** Vol. 7 (1983) pp. 171-190.

[3] Francis W. N. and Kucera H., **Frequency Analysis of English Usage,** Houghton Miffin, 1982.

[4] Frazier L. and Fodor J. D., "The sausage machine: A new two-stage parsing model", **Cognition,** Vol. 6 (1978) pp. 291-325.

[5] Hirst G. J., **Semantic Interpretation Against Ambiguity,** Ph.D thesis, Dept. of Computer Science, Brown University 1983.

[6] Jespersen O., **Modern English grammar,** 1914.

[7] Kimball J., "Seven principles of surface structure parsing in natural language", **Cognition,** Vol. 2 (1973) pp. 15-47.

[8] Raskin V., "Jokes", **Psychology Today,** October (1985) pp. 34-39.

[9] Schubert L. K., "On parsing preferences" **Proceedings of 10th International Conference on Computational Linguistics"** Stanford University (1984) pp. 247-250.

[10] Schubert L. K., "Are there preference trade-offs in attachment decisions?" **Proceedings AAAI86** (1986) pp. 601-605.

[11] Schubert L. K. and Pelletier F. J., "From English to logic: Context free computation of 'conventional' logical translation" **Journal of American Computational Linguistics (ACL)** Vol. 8 No. 1 Jan-March (1982) pp. 26-44.

[12] Shieber S. M., "Sentence disambiguation by a Shift-Reduce parsing technique" **Proceedings of the 21th Annual meeting of the ACL,** MIT Cambridge, June 15-17 (1983) pp. 113-118.

[13] Wilks Y., Huang X. and Fass D., "Syntax, preference and right attachment", **Proceedings of IJCAI-85,** Los-Angeles CA (1985) pp. 779-784.

Machinery for Hebrew Word Formation

Uzzi Ornan

Department of Computer Science
Technion - Israel Institute of Technology
Haifa, Israel

1. Introduction

As AI develops, Natural Languages Processing also develops. This phenomenon is quite natural: AI needs man-machine communication, and our desire is to use our daily language for this purpose. However, the main bulk of efforts in NL processing has been done by English speakers. As a consequence, there is an impression that English is "the natural language" for computers.

But AI development in countries with other languages, makes man-machine communication in other languages a necessity. Indeed, works devoted to processing other languages have been done and published in increasing numbers.

We as Israelis have a clear interest in developing man-machine communication in our natural language, Hebrew. The first obstacle seems to be the Hebrew script. The main reason is that essential factors of a word, such as most vowels, do not appear in writing. In order to enable reasonable processing of Hebrew, it has been suggested to introduce the Input by using a writing system which may be termed "a Phonemic Script". [1]

But this is not the sole obstacle. The Hebrew script has been the basis of the Hebrew grammar. The main points of the grammar have never been revised since it was established in the 11th-13th centuries C.E.. In order to achieve man-machine

---

† This project is being partially supported by the Ministry of Science and Technology

[1] Ornan-86a. By this writing, several projects have been accomplished within this approach, including most of the morphology (generating and analyzing) as described in what follows.

communication in Hebrew a new Hebrew grammar should be formulated. The following is an attempt to describe the structure of a part of this grammar: the morphology. Our attempt is to follow a formal approach as far as possible. Thus, we believe, processing Hebrew by computer may become possible. Still it is reasonable to assume that as the general approach and the particular demands that have been developed in computer science become accepted by the general public, our description would fit the needs of every Hebrew speaker for all their purposes.

2. Lexicon and Grammar

In all synthetic languages there are forms which are achieved by grammatic procedures. But in Hebrew, as well as in Arabic and other Semitic languages, even basic words, i.e. entries of the lexicon which have not been the result of concatenation, are also generated by the grammar. This is done by a special device, which we call "The Root-Pattern Array". All base forms of the verbs and most nouns could not have been introduced into the lexicon without having been generated in this grammatical device. If it is so, one could ask, why should you keep a lexicon ? But it has already been satisfactorily shown, that there are reasons to have a lexicon in our system, even when words can be generated by rules [2]. Another question might be asked: if you keep a lexicon of the entry-words, perhaps there is no need to keep the root-pattern array (in which entry-words are generated). We should explain here that the root-pattern array (which will be explored shortly) is not redundant, first of all, in order to enable us to generate new words which do not exist in our present lexicon. Generating such words should be done here according to a semantic component of the machinery (which is not described here, but see Ephratt-84). Another reason for keeping the root-pattern array in our system is to enable analysis of existing forms, where the root as well as the pattern are vital to establish semantic connections between given forms. We deal with these connections in section 4 below.

We assume that every speaker builds his or her own individual lexicon from the time he or she is a child, and many entries which exist in it have been generated by him/herself, i.e., not introduced from outer sources by way of imitation. In most cases, however, even words which have been generated inside the brain, exist also in the general, common lexicon.

This description seems to be true for many languages, but the amount of self-generated words in Hebrew is probably much higher than what is usual in Indo-European languages.

Our assumption is, then, that each individual has a grammatical machinery which includes both generating devices and a lexicon. Support for this assumption is the observation that in Hebrew a word may be ready for use without being listed before in the lexicon. Innovations are a daily phenomenon. They are made easily by many Hebrew speakers, sometimes unintentionally, and especially by children. A new word

---

[2] Aronoff-76, 22-23.

appears mostly in context, whether verbal context or circumstantial one. Under such conditions, its exact meaning is usually grasped without any difficulty. But it is not at all due to the context only: the ability to follow the generation of a new word is the main contributor to the clear understanding of its meaning by the listener. In what follows we describe such a machinery, which we assume is analogous to the device included in the brain of every speaker. What is more important is that our machinery can easily be programmed. We also assume, that it accounts for all possible Hebrew lexical forms as well as inflected forms of the Hebrew language.

Let us have a preliminary look on the machinery itself[3]. Fig. 1 shows the structure of the complete machine with all its components. We see the lexicon (no. [8]) in the center. Output of various components of the machine is gathered here. However, as we shall see later, entries in the lexicon may be used also as input to be processed again in other parts of the machine, in order to be transferred then back to the lexicon or ready for use elsewhere. The arrows which surround the lexicon are directed either inward or outward, to signify items which enter the lexicon or ones that are used as they are or ready for further processing. We now proceed in going over all components, and first of all - the Root-Pattern Array.

3. Root-Pattern Array

The most productive component of our morphological machinery is the "Root Pattern Array", which was mentioned above. If we look on it as an existing huge table, we could find in it the decisive majority of the entries which are listed in the Hebrew lexicon. Each line of this array (or table) contains words of the same "root". Root is an ordered group of consonants (usually three or four), which appear, in their original order, among other phonemes which are included in the word. The ordered group of p's'q' in the following words is their "root": pasaq, mapseq, psaq.

Each row in the array contains the other part of the word, namely, what remains from the word when we take the consonants of the root out of it. This part is called the "pattern". In other words, the pattern is a mould into which a root is poured. The result combines both root and pattern into one, integrated, word. The most important point for us here is that with this description of a word we can see how it is *generated* by the two factors: root and pattern. Fig. 2 is a picture of a small portion of the array. It is symbolized in Fig.1 as no.[4]. See Appendix for the Phonemic alphabet. A few points should be noted here concerning the array.

3.1. The word: Root and Pattern

Every word which exists in the array has two parameters. It belongs to both a root and a pattern. No word can belong to a root without being related at the same time to a pattern,

---

[3] Early Hebrew version of the machinery was published in Ornan-83.

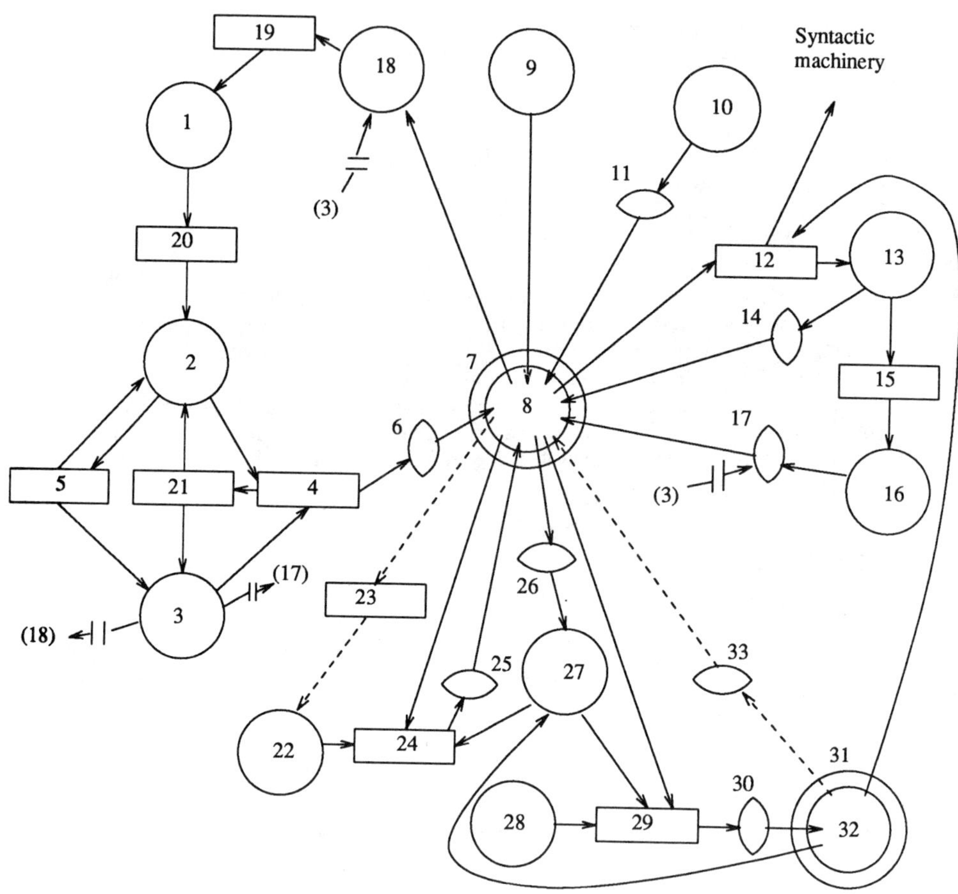

Fig. 1

legend for Fig. 1

1) list of roots
2) corrected roots' list
3) list of patterns
4) root-pattern array
5) "wandering" in the array
6) realization rules
7) socio-linguistic control
8) the lexicon
9) proto Semitic words
10) foreign words
11) phonetic control
12) concatenation of words
13) list of compound words
14) morpho-phonetic control
15) shortening of compound words
16) list of acronyms
17) morpho-phonetic control

17) morpho-phonetic control
18) bases candidate for squeezing
19) squeezing control
20) control for correct roots
21) (transferring root consonants)
22) lists of derivational affixes
23) control for new affixes
24) basis+affix derivational generator
25) morphophonemic control
26) rules for secondary bases
27) list of secondary bases
28) lists of inflectional affixes
29) basis+affix inflectional generator
30) morpho-phonetic control
31) socio-linguistic control
32) list of inflections
33) realization rules

pattern root	_A_A_-	_I__E_-	MA__E_	HIT_A__E_-	__A_	TA__U_A	HI$TA__E_-
p's'q'	pAsAq-	pIssEq-	MApsEq	-	psAq	-	-
g'm'r'	gAmAr-	gImmEr-	-	-	gmAr	-	-
x'b'r'	xAbAr-	xIbbEr-	MAxbEr	HITxAbbEr-	-	TAxbUrA	HI$TAxbEr-
&'b'd'	&AbAd-	&IbbEd-	-	-	-	-	HI$TA&bEd-
p'r's'm'-	-	pIrsEm-	-	-HITpArsEm-	-	-	-

Fig. 2

and vice versa: you cannot relate a word to a pattern without showing that it indeed can be related to a root. It is important to emphasize this point here, since the contrary may be implied from the writings of many grammarians.

3.2. Patterns Contain Both Vowels and Consonants

In our description we stick to the idea that there are only two elements in words which are generated in the root-pattern array: namely, root and pattern. Patterns contain vowels and may also contain consonants, as many of them do.[4] A few words should be added here . Chomsky-51, as well as other modern scholars, have another description. They separate what we consider one entity, namely a pattern, into two parts: 'prefix' - the first consonant, or consonants, of a pattern (such as 'M', 'HT','T','H$T' in Fig.2), and

---

[4] See e.g., rows 3,4,6,7 in the array at fig.2.

'vowel-pattern'. Thus Chomsky would analyze a word like *ha$pa&a* into (1) prefix 'h', (2) root '$p&', (3) vowel-pattern 'a--a' (p. 50). To remind the reader, we would say that this word is generated in the meeting box of the two factors 'HA__A_A' and $'p'&'.

Similarly, McCarthy-81 recognizes the same three parts of a word. He calls the 'vocalic pattern' a "melody" [5]. To justify this approach, he is compelled to show semantic connections among a series of words which share the same root. (In section 4 we discuss the matter.) This approach flourished during mediaeval times, when the grammarians considered roots to be the main part of a word since roots consist of consonants, and 'the consonants bear the main meaning', while 'vowels are unimportant in the Semitic languages'.

This idea is fallacious. It appeared only as a result of the ancient, awkward, alphabets used in most Semitic languages. But the reason why these alphabets have been accepted by the early Semites is not any linguistic feature of Semitic languages. It is only due to outward historical events that these languages have gotten into the situation in which vowels are scarcely signified in writing. The Canaanite (Hebrew) writing system was developed on the basis of the Egyptian simple syllabic script, when these nations were in contact. This is the reason why in the beginning Hebrew script did not contain any vowels; only during later generations were some signs for several vowels developed.[6] Linguists, especially in older times, were influenced by the writing system, and believed that since signs for vowels were scarcely found in writing, it was because they were not important from a linguistic point of view. Once we get rid of the influence of the script, as we should do, we easily come to the conclusion that there is no basis for the differentiation between a consonant and a vowel in Semitic languages. When we do not attribute less importance to vowels, Semitic morphology can be described much better, as we shall try to show here.

3.3. Equality of Verbs and Nouns

From the point of view of the root-pattern array, there is no difference between verbs and nouns. Both exist side by side in the same array, as we can observe in our example in Fig. 2. Though there are separate patterns for nouns and others for verbs, yet some of the patterns may be used for both, and the difference can be traced only when the word appears in a syntactic unit. We may take, however, special precautions to avoid confusion. Here verb patterns are signified by a dash at the end (such as _A_A_-, _I__E_- etc.).

3.4. Empty Boxes and Potential Words

There are empty boxes in the root-pattern array, as we can see even in our small example. These empty boxes should be divided into two groups: those which cannot be filled

---

[5] Martin Kay-87 accepted this assumption in his suggestion for processing Arabic by three tapes (instead of two).

[6] See Ornan-86a.

because of some phonetic and/or semantic restrictions, e.g., the last box in the first row: root p‘r‘s‘m‘ and pattern _A_A_-. The reason here is that four consonants are too many for a pattern with three slots. Other boxes have not yet been filled, but still may be filled. This last group may be called "Potential Words". If a potential word is needed for expressing a new idea, when the speaker does not know of any other way to express it, it is ready for use, and will easily be understood by the listener or reader. In the next paragraph we will see how. It might be more convenient to fill up all boxes of potential words, leaving empty boxes only where no potential word may be generated. When we do so, we must bear in mind that not every word in the array has also been transferred to the lexicon.[7] In our example we filled only those boxes which have been actually copied in the lexicon.

3.5. Common Meaning in a Line

Theoretically, there is a common meaning of all words along each line in the array, i.e., of all words of the same root. This rough meaning can be gathered by considering the common basic meaning of all the words of the same root. There is also a common semantic power of the pattern. Further investigation, however, should be carried out here,[8] especially when we take into consideration the vast phonetic and semantic changes during history.

3.6. Groups of Roots ('GZAROT')

The traditional dividing of roots into groups according to the phonetic behavior of the phonemes in words which are generated from the roots, is a trivial matter in the machinery. All generated forms which are transferred to the lexicon pass through realization rules, ([6] in Fig.1). Some rules apply to certain forms, other rules to others, as is the usual case with procedures. Existence of the glides /y/ and /w/ in a form is a common condition for changes when they appear in certain positions. Processes of monophthongization occur, or sometimes they simply become mute and disappear.

In fig. 3 we can see some examples of the realization rules. Note the position of the phonemes /y/ and /w/. In this connection the "group" of roots of four consonants should be mentioned. Its roots behave exactly as roots of three consonants when the pattern has four slots. In the latter case one of the consonants (by default, the second one) is used twice; when you have four consonants in the root, no doubling is needed, of course.

---

[7] This was suggested by Michal Ephratt, see Ephratt-84.

[8] See Ephratt-86, Ephratt-88.

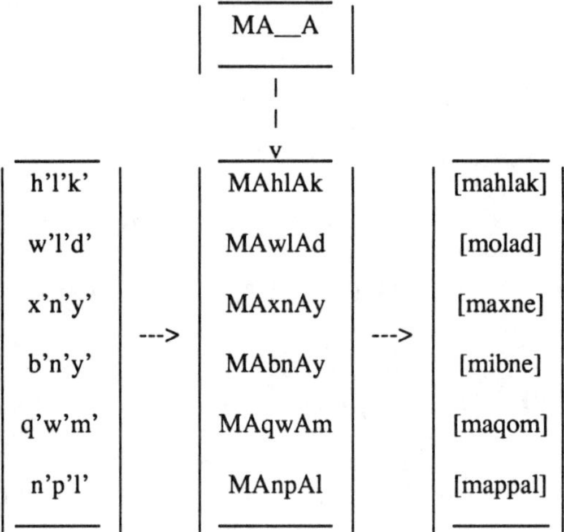

Fig.3

3.7. Morphological Analysis

The array is also very useful for analysis. One may grasp the meaning of an existing word which he or she meets for the first time, simply by tracing back the way of the word, from the lexicon through the reversed realization rules into the root-pattern array, and finding the box in which it was generated. This procedure reveals both the root and the pattern. By considering other words in the line and the impact of the pattern, one can grasp the meaning of the new word which he or she met for the first time. Of course, for automatic analysis we should write down the series of tests such as to be performed by the computer.

3.8. A Simpler Generator

A simplified and more practical way to describe the array would be to arrange it as two lists and a processor or a control unit: list of roots ([2] in Fig.1) , list of patterns ([3] in Fig.1) and the control unit ([4] in Fig. 1), where the consonants of the root are inserted into the slots of the pattern. From the control unit the generated word is transferred to the lexicon (through some realization rules ([6] in Fig.1). This description is valid mainly for generation.

3.9. The size of the array

What is the size of the array? There are more than 3000 roots in the existing Hebrew lexicon. Later we will see that the machinery contains a component in which new roots can be added ([18-19-1-20] in Fig.1). The number of patterns, however, is not so simple to determine. It depends on our linguistic approach. It seems to us that patterns are theoretical entities rather than observed ones. Only according to this approach are we able to consider words which differ on the surface, such as MAHLAK, MAPPAL, MOLAD, MAXNE, MIBNE, or MAQOM as belonging to the same pattern, namely MA--A-, as we did in Fig. 3. When we accept patterns as theoretical entities, there are approximately 120 of them.

4. Inflection and Derivation

4.1. Automatic vs. Non-Automatic Process

Before we proceed to describe other parts of the machinery, we should pose a question: what is the relation between words of the same line in the array, i.e., words which share the same root. In order to investigate possible relations between words, it will be convenient to start with an English example. We will look at the three words POSE - POSED - IMPOSE. Two kinds of relations can be revealed here: POSE - POSED is one thing; POSE - IMPOSE another:

(a) All three words share some common formal element: POSE.
(b) The difference in form between POSE and POSED as well as between
    POSE and IMPOSE can be formulated by general grammatic rules.
(c) Semantically, POSED differs from POSE in structural meaning
    only (here, in tense), while IMPOSE differs from POSE not in
    structural meaning, but in sense.
(d) Existence of POSE implies that also POSED does exist, while it does not
    imply that IMPOSE also exists.

One cannot write POSE in the dictionary, and let the grammar generate IMPOSE. This last item should be considered a separate entry. On the other hand, there is no need to write POSED in the lexicon. The grammar can handle it. Let us sum it up in the following way: words which share certain formal elements and their formal difference can be formulated, can relate to each other either in an AUTOMATIC relation, or in NON-AUTOMATIC one. Automatic relation means that the existence of word A implies the existence of word B, with semantic difference of structural (grammatical) meaning only; Non-automatic relation means that in spite of the shared formal element and the ability to formulate it, the existence of A does not imply the existence of B, and that the semantic difference is not in structural meaning, but in sense, i.e., they should be dealt with separately in the lexicon. For a non-automatic connection between words, let us see a "family" of verbs which share a common basis but differ in various prefixes, such as the "family" of POSE : IMPOSE, EXPOSE, COMPOSE, DEPOSE, DISPOSE,

SUPPOSE or PROPOSE (Fig. 4).

POSE	derivation:	compose	depose	dispose	impose	suppose
inflection:						
posed						
posing						
poses						

Fig. 4

Each of them will be either A or B in the following:

(a) A and B share some formal elements (here, POSE).
(b) B can be achieved through A by a rule.
(c) The semantic difference is not structural, but in sense.
(d) Existence of A does not imply the existence of B.

Automatic   relations   form   INFLECTION;   non-automatic   relations   form
DERIVATION.[9]

4.2. Where does the 'Conjugation' (BINYAN) stand?

Returning now to the root pattern array, we can pose a more accurate question: are the
relations between words of the same line in the array an inflection or a derivation?
 First, let us look at Hebrew words which decisively have inflectional relation with each
other. For example, PASAQ - PASAQTI (= he stopped - I stopped). [10]

(a) They share some formal elements: PASAQ.
(b) The difference in form between them can be formulated by grammatical rule.
(c) The semantic difference is in structural meaning only (here, person).
(d) Existence of PASAQ implies existence of PASAQTI.

What about the relations between two words in the array, such as PASAQ (=he stopped)
and PISSEQ (=he punctuated)?

(a) They share some formal elements: the root p's'q'.

---

[9] We believe that these characteristics could improve our understanding, and accomplish the efforts
to clearly distinguish between these two relations. See Halle-73, Aronoff-76, McCarthy-81, Selkirk-82.

[10] Note that a form like PASAQTI is not found in any box of the array. It is generated in another
component of the machinery ([28] - [32]), which we will soon see.

(b) The difference in form can be formulated by a rule,
but,
(c) The semantic difference between the two words is not a
structural one, but rather in sense. Therefore it can be predicted only
occasionally, provided it is in context.
(d) Existence of PASAQ does not imply existence of PISSEQ. Each of
these words may be a potential word only (in fact, they both exist).

The conclusion is that the two words are not related automatically to each other, although
they have some relation. They do not belong to the same inflection. They form a
derivation.

This conclusion is crucial for Semitic linguistics, since according to the conventional
approach, Semitic inflection of verbs includes not only changes in person, gender,
number and tense, but also changes in what is called "conjugation", which means mode
or verbal patterns (of the array in our description).

This prevailing approach compelled grammarians (and later modern linguists) to choose
one of the verbal patterns as the "bearer of the main meaning", - usually it was the "first
conjugation" (i.e. PA'AL,) - and to try to formulate its semantic connections with all
other verbal patterns as if they were related to the same inflection. The results are
catastrophic. In no other scientific field would such results have been accepted. Each
verbal pattern may change the so-called "basic, or main meaning" in several directions,
which in almost no instance can be predicted. Mediaeval grammarians copied selected
examples from each other, since there were scarcely other proper examples for use, while
modern linguists still make desperate efforts to save these unbased ideas.

4.3. 'Conjugation' in English

By formulating accurate differences between inflection and derivation, we can set the
verbal area free from the mystical complex of legends about the semantic connections
between various verbal patterns. They relate to each other as nouns may relate to each
other. An English equivalent to the "conjugations" of one verb would be a basic form
with several prefixes, such as the "family" of POSE that we mentioned above. An
equivalent to the "pattern" would be each of the prefixes, such as EN or CON. It has a
certain fixed influence on the meaning of the basis to which it is attached. Take
LARGE - ENLARGE, RICH - ENRICH and similar cases. But (a) it does not apply
automatically in all cases (e.g. SMALL), (b) even when it applies, one cannot predict
its meaning, e.g., GRAIN - ENGRAIN, GRAVE -- ENGRAVE.

4.4. Range of Inflection

It should be emphasized that the range of inflection may be different in various
languages. Aronoff-76 (p. 3) insisted that certain verbal forms in Hebrew and Syriac are
not part of the inflection, since they include a suffix which is a pronominal direct object

(or repeated pronominal subject, in Syriac). But these forms positively answer the four features mentioned above, i.e., they are received automatically. Therefore they should be considered part of the inflection, even though in English, as well as in other languages, there is nothing parallel to it.

5. Other Parts of The Machinery

5.1. Socio-Linguistic Control

The interim output of the root-pattern array, after it comes out of the phonetic rules of realization, enters ring [7] (of fig.1). This is a socio-linguistic control zone. Every potential word from the array (as well as other words which try to enter the lexicon from other sources) must be checked here before it is allowed to come into the lexicon.

It is significant to notice how this control zone develops: children use potential words very easily, with scarcely any restriction. They have not yet developed their control ability. They simply put together a root and a pattern, transfer the word through the phonetic rules (no. [6] in fig. 1), bring the result directly to their lexicon, and use it in their speech. The reactions of their listeners build the socio-linguistic control for the child machinery. Some people smile, others laugh or correct their words by repeating, and it happens that the listeners show that they don't understand what the child has said. Such reactions make the child erase this form from his or her lexicon, and build a list of items to be checked in the newly built control zone.

5.2. Proto-Semitic Words

We mentioned above "other sources" of words for the lexicon. There is a group of proto-Semitic words which have been inherited by Hebrew as well as by other Semitic languages. Mostly they are short prepositions and other grammatical expressions such as B- , L-, MIN-, HA-, or nouns such as 'AB (father), 'AX (brother), 'EMM (mother), YAD (hand), DAM (blood) etc.   These words have been changed when they passed from the Proto-Semitic into Hebrew. Linguists since the last century have written down the transition rules for these changes. But the present machinery of the speakers of Hebrew does not include these rules, simply because Proto-Semitic does not exist any more, and no words are now being taken from this source. There is no place for the transition rules in our system, since we try to reflect the actual machinery which exists in the brain of speakers of Hebrew. In other words, the transition rules should appear in an outer sphere of the machinery, such as above no. [9] (in Fig. 1).

5.3. Words from Foreign Languages

Another source of Hebrew words are foreign languages. As is the case in every society, Hebrew speakers who happen to know foreign languages use foreign words when they cannot find the proper Hebrew expression. These words (no. [10] in Fig.1) must pass through some phonetic control ([11] in Fig.1), which changes some phones if they do not exist in Hebrew. It seems that controls of this type exist in all linguistic societies[11]. The following words can easily be recognized: RAPPOR@ (traffic ticket), @EIPP (tape recorder), RADYO, @ELEWIZYA (television).

5.4. Compound Words

Compound words are generated by concatenating two (or more) words which are taken from the lexicon, whether or not their origin is in the root-pattern array. This process is done in rectangle [12] (in fig. 1), where the words are transferred from the lexicon. We should note, however, that taking words out of the lexicon is a procedure which is carried out for every expression, even when there is no intention to generate any compound word, but simply to generate any sentence. We take this possibility into account, and use the same schema as a source for the syntactic machinery. Rectangle no. [12] is thus the connecting point of the morphology and the syntax. A line from [12] is directed outward, to be connected with the syntactical machinery. Note that inflected forms can also go to the syntax. We allow it by drawing a path from [32] to [12].

However, in order to get a compound, the sequence of words remains in this machinery. More than one word is gathered in [12], and the sequence moves to [13], where it is connected, either by a hyphen or by erasing the blank. From here the compound goes into a series of checkings (no. [14]) which change it if necessary, or cut some small portions of it. From [13] the compound word returns to the lexicon as a new entry. Examples: MAXNE+NOP$ - MAXNOP$, YOM+HULEDT - YOMULEDT, &RAPELL+PIX -- &ARPIX.

In some cases, the concatenated sequence may take another route - [15-16-17](in fig. 1) - before it returns to the lexicon as a new entry. In this route some bigger parts of the words are cut, and what is left is an acronym, or an abbreviated form, either with the first letter only from each word or slightly larger parts of them. This practice goes back to ancient times, when writing letters was hard work.

Since Hebrew speakers are used to orally adding vowels to the written word, which is usually written without its vowels, they do so with acronyms as well. Scarcely an acronym is pronounced as a series of names of letters, as is done many times in English (UCLA, for example, is pronounced as YU SEE EL AI). It is interesting to look at the vocalization of an acronym in Hebrew. If there is a letter Y or W, or H at the end, they usually are interpreted as vowels, mostly I or E for Y, O or U for W, and A or E for H. Generally, speakers tend to insert such vowels so that the acronym will be identical with an existing word, especially if its meaning is not negative, and will be used as a name for an organization. This practice prevails in Arabic as well. FATH, e.g., is said to be an "inverted acronym" for an organization known as "the Movement for Liberation of Palestine", but it is also an Arabic word with the meaning of

---

[11] See Ornan-88

"conquering non-believers' land".

When no existing elegant word can be gathered from subsequent parts of the acronym, the sequence of letters is vocalized in such a way that the result will be similar to an existing word, or at least similar in shape to a pattern. (see the line from [3] directed to [17] in Fig.1.)

5.5. 'Squeezing'

We mentioned above that there are more than 3000 roots in Hebrew, but that the machinery includes a device for generating new roots. The need for new roots arises especially when we introduce foreign nouns into Hebrew, and here is the reason for it.

In order to express ideas, one needs both nouns and verbs. In English you have MINIMUM, and beside it you can use a grammatical device and get MINIMIZE; or vice versa, GOVERN - GOVERNMENT. As in English and other languages, such a technique also exists in Hebrew: in the root-pattern array there are both nominal and verbal patterns. Both a noun and a verb of the same root may be used, such as BANA (build) - BINYAN (building), $ALA@ (rule, govern) - $IL@ON (government, authorities). This is how we keep balance between verbal and nominal expressions.

But when a foreign noun enters into the language , it does not participate in the root-pattern array, since it does not have a root. Therefore no parallel verbal expression can be found in the array.

An easy way to regain a balance is to use a phrase which consists of a general-purpose verb of action and the noun. In English we find phrases like TAKE AN OATH, MAKE A CALL, RAISE A QUESTION etc. In Hebrew this is also possible, and there are idiomatic expressions which are considered pure Hebrew style: LHAQIM RA&$ (to make noise), LXOLEL MHUMA (to cause scandal), etc..

This is a good solution for verbal expressions of nouns taken from foreign languages. Vernacular expressions such as LHARIM @ELEPON (to raise a telephone receiver), LA&JOT SPONJA (to wash the floor with sponge), LNAHHEL ROMAN (to have an affair) appear also in writing.

But sometimes the form of a noun from a foreign source resembles a pattern of an original Hebrew word, e.g., BASIS (from the Greek, same meaning as in English) is similar to nouns from the root-pattern array, such as PAQID (clerk), or XALIL (flute). The speaker has no indication that BASIS does not stem from the array. Suppose that this word is quite new for a certain speaker. With no hesitation the speaker locates BASIS in a box where the root is b's's' and the pattern is -A-I-. By so doing, the speaker produces a whole line of potential words, some of which are verbs such as BISSES, HITBASSES, which may be used right away. What happened here was that a new root was introduced into the list of roots in the array.

It is more interesting to know that even if the noun from a foreign source does not have a form which makes it resemble a form of a Hebrew word, it is still possible to extract a new root from it. Simply by dropping its vowels. A word like @ELEPON (=telephone), which entered Hebrew when this instrument began to be used, is a good example. The word was "squeezed" of its vowels, leaving a sequence of consonants, @'L'P'N'. This sequence became a new root, and a new verb appeared: @ILPEN (same pattern as BISSES).

This device of extraction became so popular, that even an original Hebrew noun - if its pattern includes a consonant - may be extracted in order to enrich verbal expressions.

TIGBORT (reinforcement) is of pattern TI--O-T and root g'b'r'. The root is of words which denote 'power', 'force', but in order to have a verbal expression of 'bring reinforcement', a new root was extracted from TIGBORT : t'g'b'r' (the last T was dropped). Now we can say TIGBER, and we have both nominal and verbal expressions for the same meaning.

5.6. Basis and Affix

The last part of the machinery, which we describe now, consists of quite another way for generating forms. It is a whole basis to which an affix is concatenated. The affix may be either prefix or suffix. No infix is used in Hebrew.

Two separate parts work in this way. The division is whether the output should be considered an entry of the lexicon, or a new form of the inflection. There are clear cases where the output is definitely an inflectional form, such as PASAQTI, which was exemplified above (4.2). The basis, PASAQ, stems from the root-pattern array. It is a base of past tense verb. The entry is taken from the lexicon, and put in rectangle [29], to be used as the basis. A proper suffix arrives from the group of affixes' lists which are stored in [28]. A suffix TI has been chosen there, since it is a part of the list of suffixes entitled "past tense suffixes". The result of the concatenation of PASAQ + TI gives PASAQTI. After it passes through the realization rules of [30], it is checked in a socio-linguistic control zone [31] and enters [32]. From this place the form can move to [12] in order to be used in the syntactic machinery.

In some other cases of base + affix the base should take another shape in [27] before it can be used. A Boolean sign for such a need is attached to the entry in the lexicon, and it usually stems from a pattern in the root-pattern array. Such arrangements are common in existing dictionaries of many languages. In French, e.g., an indication of the gender is attached to a nominal entry; in Arabic an indication of the proper vowel in the inflection of future tense is attached to the verbal entry.

A secondary base is needed sometimes also for the other part of the basis + affix device, which is shown in [22-25]. The significant difference between [24] and [29] is that the output of [24] is transferred back to the lexicon, whereas the results of [29] are not.

Admittedly, sometimes it is not so easy to decide whether certain combination of a base and an affix takes place in [24] or in [29]. Still it seems to be clear that we need both components in our machinery. The question from where the affixes are inherited is very interesting, but it is out of our context. We would only say that affixes of the inflection are probably an inheritance from a previous phase of the language, or even from the Proto-Semitic, while most of the affixes for the derivation (which are gathered in [22]) have been developed in Hebrew during its history. One example will be sufficient. The pattern -A--AN signifies mostly 'a person who inclines to have a certain feature'. The feature is embodied in the root. The significant part of these words is of course its ending, which is always AN. When Hebrew speakers tried to give this signification to words which only as a whole embodied a certain feature, or to words which did not have any root, they began to use this ending AN as a suffix. This way words like TBUSTAN (defeatist) was innovated out of TBUSA (defeat) , with the theoretical structure TBUSAT and the new suffix AN.

6. A Universal Model

We have given a detailed description of the morphological machinery for Hebrew. From a more general point of view, we may come to the conclusion that behind the detailed, complicated description there is a model which may describe the morphology of many other languages, provided they are synthetic to some extent. In other words, every synthetic language may be described according to the shortened model which is drawn in Fig. 5. We will leave it for the reader to locate any morphological phenomena in a language that he or she is acquainted with, following the various parts of this universal model.

7. Concluding Reflections

We would like to conclude this description by expressing our belief that such a machinery is not only a sketch for building an algorithm and a program for generating Hebrew words which will be felt natural and accepted by Hebrew speakers.[12] This sketch seems to be analogous to what really happens in the Hebrew speaker's brain.

How does it grow there? It seems to develop when babies begin to have a vocabulary. They see similarities and common parts in words according to basis and affix as well as according to root and pattern. It brings them to what we may call "analysis" of the words of their vocabulary. Then they begin to build their own root-pattern array and fill its boxes with potential words, as well as gathering lists of affixes. We have mentioned above how children lack any socio-linguistic control in using their potential words. How otherwise did it happen that these words are in their access? They never had any chance of hearing them from adults, so it is not imitation, but generation according to the rules of grammar which they have formulated by themselves.

---

[12] Parts of such programs have already been prepared. See e.g. Ornan-86b, Goldstein-89.

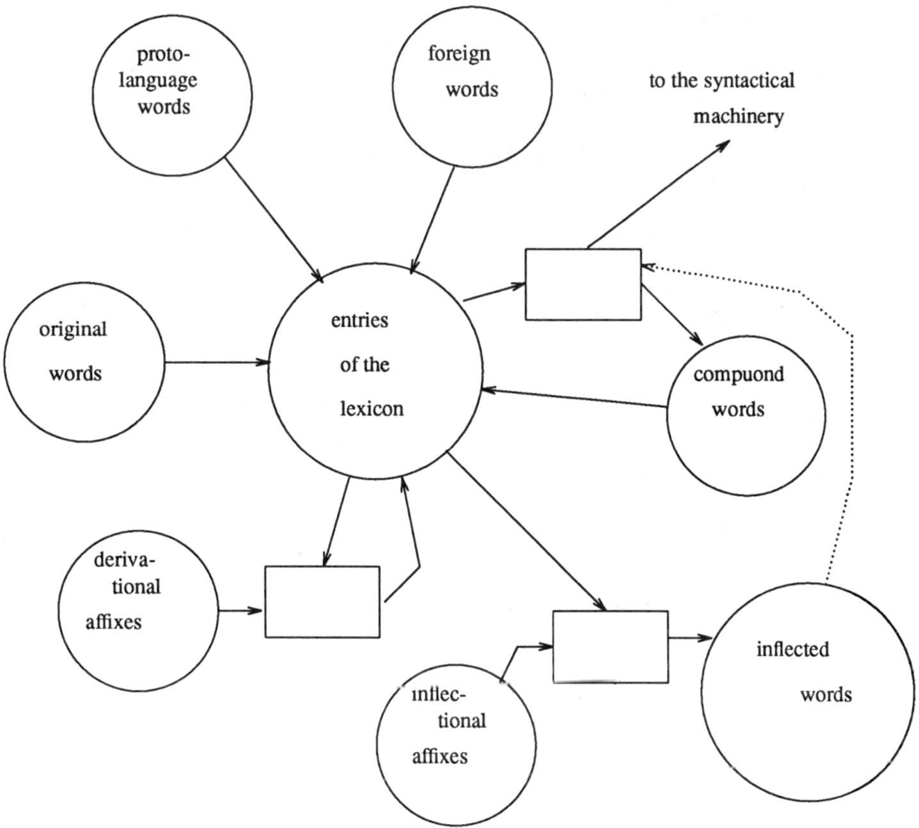

Fig. 5

Since the lexicon in Semitic languages is built out of grammar, it is much easier to come to the conclusion that the child is a self-supplier of his grammar, as Chomsky-59 suggested in his criticism of Skinner and the behaviorism school. This is indeed done at a very early stage, when the lexicon is small. Enlargement of the list of roots and adding some rare patterns or affixes occur later, but the main machinery is already there at a very early stage.

8. References

Aronoff-76 - Aronoff, Mark, *Word Formation in Generative Grammar*, Linguistic Inquiry Monograph 1, MIT Press, 1976

Chomsky-51 - Chomsky, Noam, *Morphophonemics of Modern Hebrew*, December 1951 (mimeograph)

Chomsky-59 - Chomsky, Noam, "Review of Skinner", *Language* vol. 35, 26-58

Ephratt-84 - Ephratt, Michal, *Root-Pattern Array: Main tool for Generating Hebrew Words*, Hebrew University, 1985 (1984), (in Hebrew, with English summary)

Ephratt-86 - _ _ , "Minimal Constituents of the Semantic Unit", *Proceedings of the 21th National Conference of IPA*, Jerusalem, 131-151, (in Hebrew)

Ephratt-88 - _ _ , "Semantic Properties of the Root-Pattern Array", *Computers and Translation*, Vol.3, Nos. 3/4, 215-236

Goldstein-89 - Goldstein Lyor, *Generation and Analysis of the Possession Inflection of Hebrew Nouns*, M.Sc. Thesis, The Technion, 1989 (in Hebrew, with English summary)

Halle-73 - Halle, Morris, "Prolegomena to a Theory of Word Formation", *Linguistic Inquiry*, vol. 4, 3-16

Kay-87 - Kay, Martin, "Nonconcatenative Finite-State Morphology", *Proceedings of the 3rd European ACL Conference, 2-10*

McCarthy-81 - McCarthy, John, "A Prosodic Theory of Nonconcatenative Morphology", *Linguistic Inquiry*, vol. 12, 373-418

Ornan-83 - Ornan, Uzzi, "How do we build a Hebrew Word", in Bar-Asher et al. (eds.) *Hebrew Language Studies presented to Zeev Ben-Hayyim*, Jerusalem, 13-42 (in Hebrew)

Ornan-86a - _ _ , "Phonemic Script: A Central Vehicle for Processing NL - The case of Hebrew", *Tech. Rep. 88.181*, IBM Scientific Center, Haifa, Israel

Ornan-86b - _ _ , "Processes of Analysis and Generation in Hebrew Morphology", *Proceedings of the 21st National Conference of IPA*, Jerusalem, 153-164, (in Hebrew)

Ornan-88 - _ _ , "Pronunciation of Words of Foreign Origin", in Abramson, S. and Luria, B.Z. (eds.) *Penina Sivan Memorial Volume*, Jerusalem, 71-76 (in Hebrew)

Selkirk-82 - Selkirk, E.O., *The Syntax of Words*, Linguistic Inquiry Monograph 7, MIT Press

Appendix

Each of the 23 Hebrew *consonantal phonemes* is transcribed in phonemic script by a single, separate, sign. The following is the list of special signs introduced for Hebrew phonemes that do not have equivalents in English.

    '   is a glottal stop (can be omitted in speech)

    x   is pronounced as a Scottish /ch/

    @   is another /t/

    &   is another glottal voice

    c   is pronounced as a cluster of /ts/ (e.g. cats)

    q   is another /k/

    $ is sh

    j   is another /s/

All other consonantal phonemes are approximately equivalent in realization to the English ones.

There are five *vowel phonemes* in Hebrew: /a/, /e/, /i/, /o/, /u/. They are pronounced as in Italian or Spanish. Length is not phonemic in Hebrew (it is in Arabic).

/b/, /k/ and /p/ has each *two realizations:* a plosive - as given, and a fricative - [v],[x],[f], respectively. Since we use a phonemic script, we do not use these realizations at all. Realization rules ("Reading Rules") are specified in Ornan-86a, p. 19-20.

The stress is on the last phonemic syllable, but verbal forms with a suffix beginning with a consonant, usually have the stress on the last-but-one syllable.

Theory Formation for Interpreting
an Unknown Language

Ephraim Nissan

Dept. of Mathematics and Computer Science
Ben Gurion University of the Negev
Beer-Sheva 84105, Israel

1. Introduction

Artificial intelligence concepts can be of help in trying to analyze very large processes
that would be unfeasible to simulate in detail, such as the development of certain
sciences, and of variants of expert behavior therein. Two centuries of failure in trying to
interpret Etruscan scientifically, have led to currently investigated avenues of research.
The example we are going to describe, is a *metamodel* of trial and error in linguistic
inquiry in the framework of *Etruscology,* that is, the study of the Etruscan civilization of
pre-Roman Italy.

This process calls for modeling patterns of principled investigation, as typical of the
specific research community. Domain analysis, as allowed by good protocols, is
challenging for AI: in a huge search space with too favorable odds for misleading partial
successes, variably cumulative learning is involved in two phases of interpretation trials.
The first, very fluid phase is the most dependent on the circumscribed linguistic
competence of the given Etruscologist, and tries to select a known language (or language
family) to be compared to. The second phase integrates island-driven interpretation of
documents belonging to the corpus of extant Etruscan inscriptions, with a linguistic-
description component being constructed by learning.

Archeological evidence, as well as the account of ancient non-Etruscan historians, have
allowed a partial reconstruction of the Etruscan civilization, but without understanding
its language, the picture cannot be complete. The core of *Etruria,* the ancient region in
North Western central Italy, corresponds to modern Tuscany — the region whose chief
town is Florence — and is delimited on the west by the Tyrrhenian Sea. Organized as a
loose confederation of 12 (later 15) city-states, they were at the zenith of their power in
the 7th century BC and lost their independence to the Romans in 283 BC. While the

earliest extant documents written in Etruscan date from the the 7th century BC, the latest documents in Etruscan date from the time of the Roman emperor Augustus (at the beginning of the Common Era). The Roman culture was influenced by Etruscans, to some extent. Some Roman or Greek authors explain single Etruscan terms, sometimes tentatively. Etruscan had long been forgotten, but inscriptions were found; attempts to understand this language started five centuries ago. However, it was only at the end of the 18th century, that a scientific foundation became available, once *comparative linguistics* entered its scientific phase.

Of the Etruscan language, hundreds of inscriptions are extant — Pallottino's corpus [10] lists about 950 inscriptions — in an alphabet that can be read. The lexicon and the grammar of the language are practically unknown. Besides, most often in inscriptions, words are separated by neither blanks, nor other separation marks; this causes the search space to be much larger, and certain aspects of interpretation trials are similar to speech-processing, because of the need to spot words inside continuous strings. In a monograph, [7], this author presents the relevant background and develops a knowledge analysis, intended to provide the basis for a metamodel of interpretation of Etruscan, based on protocols of principled interpretation trials, published in the literature of the domain. Protocols focused on are those of Bernardini Marzolla [1], as they are an instance of principled investigation according to modern criteria; it is peculiar not because of the method, but because of the direction of search — Etruscan is considered to be related to Sanskrit and Prakrits of India — and in that, it parallels other approaches that tried to relate Etruscan to other language families.

While my exposition in [7] addresses computer humanists and discusses various topics in linguistics and historical ethnography at length, presenting computing concepts tutorially, here we address people in AI, with the aim of pointing out the main ideas related to AI in the metatheory proposed. The presence of linguistic data and their discussion is deliberately minimal, so that the inclusion of background notions from linguistics will not lead the discussion out of focus, with respect to the AI concepts isolated from the metatheory.

This paper applies AI to epistemology. The goal is not the construction of practical AI tools for deciphering unknown languages, but rather the development of a computational account of the work of human experts in that domain. We are aware that this metatheory constitutes only a rough core; future research and further researchers are hopefully going to refine it in the direction of a cognitively more credible account. Attacking a problem of this degree of complexity, from a computational problem-solving viewpoint, is a contribution of its own.

2. Two Phases in Interpretation Trials

The corpus of knowledge needed to interpret an undeciphered dead language is necessarily vast, and the search process involved has an enormous associated search-space. In this space, odds are too favorable for having, misleadingly, partial matching satisfied for given lexical instances (or — all the more — substrings of a continuous string with no indication of word separation, as is frequent in Etruscan inscriptions). Moreover, this is dangerous ground for induction to reconstruct grammar, and for cultural analogy to hypothesize semantics. The enormity of the search-space stems from the fact that a relation is sought to one out of very many languages or language-families (known or also practically undeciphered), with conjectures ranging from phonetics and phonology, through morphology (sometimes, fanciful, unwarranted grammars were invented), to lexicography. Failing to have terms matched, led to loosening requirements, by allowing etymologies to be conjectured according to root resemblance and the admission of far-fetched semantic changes: a process that was rightfully condemned by several researchers, as it impairs the very ability to ascertain whether goal-states are being achieved or not.

It must be admitted that there is no intrinsic feature that could identify one approach to the interpretation of Etruscan, as being *the right one,* unless long bilingual texts become available, reliably identified as parallel, enabling point to point analysis of semantic equivalence. (A few bilingual, at least partly parallel inscriptions were found, but proved of little use, so far.) The metamodel of interpretation, outlined here, considers competing partial interpretations of Etruscan as trying to climb to *local optima* in a universe of paradigms being constructed by learning. Optimality criteria concern the relative amount of inscriptions completely interpreted, the absolute amount (as it can be proved that too little linguistic data are likelier to yield different interpretations), the robustness of the constructed paradigm *(post-optimality)* in front of trials to use it to interpret those inscriptions not tackled yet, the ability to dispense with emendations to inscriptions, and the ability to dispense with morphological conjectures that cannot be proved from the linguistic data available.

Two main phases are identified in the process of trying to interpret this dead language:

I) Attempts to select, among known languages, a candidate model with respect to which to reconstruct deviation. This is attempted by reduced runs of *Phase II.* Overall paradigm-shifts occur in *Phase I.* Promise-evaluation is hampered, in *Phase I,* by the cumulation of flaws in confidence-transmission among investigators.

II) Once a candidate model for deviation is selected (one language, or a family of phylogenetically or historically closely related languages), *Phase II* focuses search for relatively small discrepancies. A blackboard architecture is considered suitable for representation, if integrating *learning* methods. There are some analogies with speech-processing, e.g., the lack of word-separation motivates island-based word-hypothesizing (cf. [3]). By *islands,* as usual in speech-processing, we mean partial solutions in the framework of the Etruscan inscription considered as an input string; if corroborated, islands can be expanded. However, while English speech-processing refers to a description of English (a known language), for interpreting Etruscan, instead, *learning* has to bridge between two components:

- the model of interpretation of Etruscan itself; the description (lexicon and grammar) is the paradigm being constructed, in the partial-solution space, and is used as a constraint: coherence has to be maintained. Nevertheless, the paradigm is defeasible by a certain threshold of counterexamples. Induction is used only by strictly regulated comparison with:
- the description (lexicon and grammar) of a known language, selected by *Phase I* as a model of deviation. It is crucial that an established set of fixed rules of phonetic/phonologic or morphological correspondence would be maintained.

This two phased approach of speculation is supported by the analysis of protocols of interpretation, both in the case of Etruscan and in the case of other languages that had, or still have, to be deciphered. The first phase is a "browsing" phase, terminating with the selection of a language as a deviation model, while the second phase has detailed interpretation trials carried out confidently with respect to a given deviation-model.

The selection of one natural language, or a *linguistically coherent* family of languages, as a candidate model in *Phase I* may be based on *phylogenetic* relationship and *cultural proximity,* and, as the content of the textual corpus to be deciphered is initially unknown, such cultural proximity can be conjectured based on historical, geographical, or artifact-based archeological considerations. *Phase I* involves several attempts. The reduced runs of *Phase II* carry out partial-matching trials on sample inscriptions *(shortest first),* in order to classify and then decipher the Etruscan corpus. Directions of search are selected that are judged to deserve focus because of some successfully matched terms. The analyzing agent attempts partial matching with candidate model-languages, drawn from a set $\{\, L_i \mid i > 0 \,\}$, of descriptions (lexicons and grammars) of known languages. Coherent subsets (language families, e.g., $\{\, L_1 \,,\, L_2 \,\}$), or at least compatible subsets, are considered at each attempt. Considering L_1, or its family, $\{\, L_1 \,,\, L_2 \,\}$, rules out the admissibility of L_3 in the framework of the same attempt, if both of the following conditions hold: L_3 is linguistically unrelated to $\{\, L_1 \,,\, L_2 \,\}$ and those people that have been speaking respectively L_3 and L_1 or L_2 are very unlikely to have had contact. Ascertaining likely (in)compatibility involves another level of matching: against conditions reflecting basic knowledge on aggregation into language-families, and on general historical geography.

Early successes in interpreting words and short sentences, are likely to steadily increase the Etruscologist's confidence in the closeness of Etruscan to the model selected, e.g., in the case of Bernardini Marzolla [1], Sanskrit and Prakrits. Then, unless the paradigm crashes, the kind of search would remain in *Phase II*, immersed in partial matching and linguistic processing according to the model found. **Figure 1** shows a simplified sequence of macro-steps, according to the proper course of action: lexicon is checked before morphology. (Morphology is more important than syntax: indeed, *a priori* we could not rule out that the possibility that the unknown language has a free-order syntax.) **Figure 2** shows detail. Actions are explained in **Table 1.**

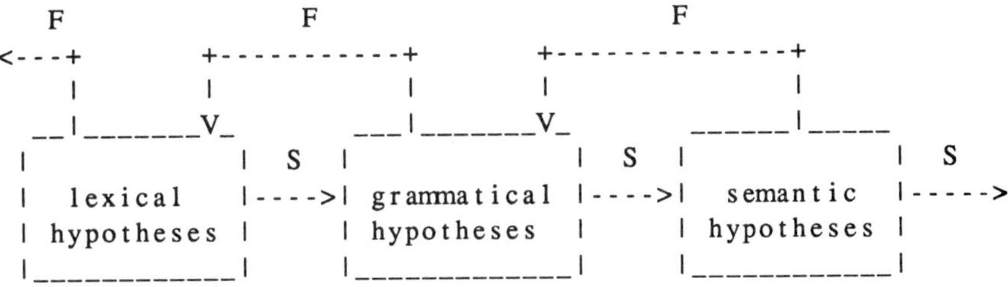

Figure 1 -- A simplified macro-schema of flow in Phase II.

A priori, we are not assured that Etruscan could prove close to any language to be found out of languages whose linguistic description is known. Bernardini Marzolla [1] in his pursuit of comparison to Sanskrit, was lucky, because the strategy of looking for just *small discrepancies* during *Phase II* seemed to succeed. Had Etruscan been Indo-European (and had this been a hypothesis to be validated), but not as close to any one particular Indo-European language, then the search strategy would have been unsuitable: looking for *loose relationships* could have been necessary with a set of very different Indo-European languages, such as Latin, Gothic, and Old Slavonic. This would have to have made up for the lack of supporting evidence by resorting to *induction* in morphology, and would have involved reckoning with conjectural etymologies, that can be neither proved nor disproved. Thus, the possibility for *loose-relationship* strategies to prove effective, has been questioned. For example, in 1915, Meillet [5], by scourging an attempt to relate Etruscan to Ugro-Finnic, observed: *"An unknown language cannot be deciphered by resorting to etymological comparisons. Nothing would be of lesser use than trying to understand a text in any given Indo-European language by comparison to other languages of the same family; a Sanskrit, Slavonic or Germanic dictionary is of no use to understand a Greek text."* (transl. from French).

The more successes interpretation can claim having pursued small-discrepancy matching trials in the framework of *Phase II,* the more it become confident, and tends to

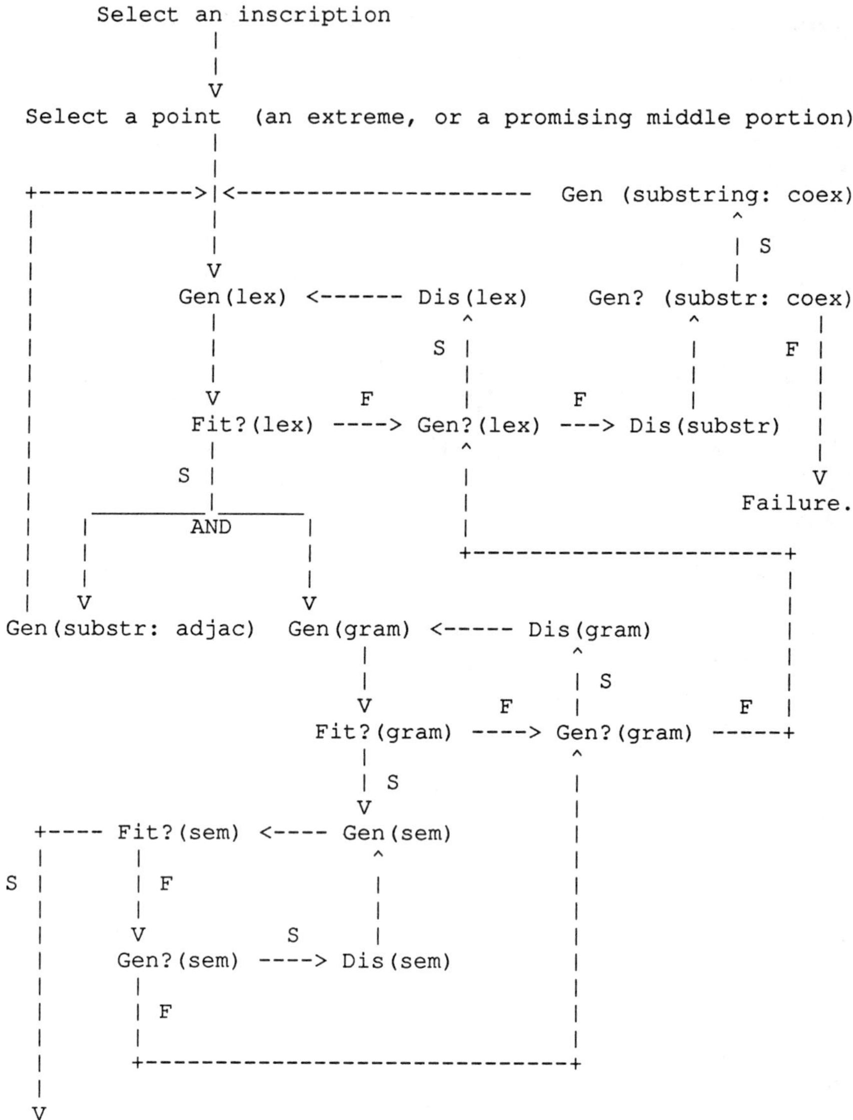

```
       Select an inscription
                   |
                   |
                   V
     Select a point   (an extreme, or a promising middle portion)
                   |
                   |
   +--------->|<--------------------- Gen (substring: coex)
   |          |                                  ^
   |          |                               | S
   |          V                               |
   |       Gen(lex) <------ Dis(lex)      Gen? (substr: coex)
   |          |             ^                ^          |
   |          |          S |              |        F |
   |          |             |                |          |
   |          V        F     |        F     |          |
   |       Fit?(lex) ----> Gen?(lex) ---> Dis(substr)  |
   |          |             ^                           |
   |       S |              |                         V
   |        ___|___         |                   Failure.
   |       |  AND   |       |
   |       |        |       |
   |       |        |    +---------------------+
   |       |        |    |                     |
   |  V     V       V    |                     |
 Gen(substr: adjac)  Gen(gram) <----- Dis(gram)         |
                       |          ^                     |
                       |       | S                    |
                       V    F     |        F          |
                   Fit?(gram) ----> Gen?(gram) -----+
                       |          ^
                     | S          |
                       V          |
   +---- Fit?(sem) <---- Gen(sem)          |
   |      |        ^                        |
 S |    | F       |                        |
   |      |        |                        |
   |      V     S   |                        |
   |    Gen?(sem) ----> Dis(sem)             |
   |      |                                  |
   |    | F                                 |
   |      |                                  |
   |      +---------------------------+      |
   |                                         |
   V
Handle other islands;  look for mutual
substantiation  through  consistence.
```

Figure 2 -- Detailed sequence of conjectures in Phase II.

```
Labels on arcs:              S              on success
----------------
                             F              on failure


Vertices:
---------

   Gen?(X)     Could further hypotheses of kind X
               be generated for the considered item?

   Gen(X)      Generate a new hypothesis of kind X.

   Fit?(X)     Do elements of kind X  fit?

   Dis(X)      Discard the current hypothesis of kind X.


where  X  is either:

     lex        lexical
     gram       grammatical  (of morphology and syntax)
     sem        semantic
     substr     substring


In particular, for inscriptions where
words are not separated:

Gen? (substr: coex)     Could a substring be selected
                        that is partly coextensive
                        with the one just discarded?

Gen (substr: coex)      Generate a hypothesis on the
                        substring:  as current candidate
                        substring, take such a substring
                        that is partly coextensive with
                        the last one that was discarded.

Gen (substr: adjac)     Consider a substring that
                        is adjacent to the last
                        one considered.
```

Table 1 -- Legend of Figure 2.

accomodate counterexamples in the prevailing paradigm, instead of discarding that paradigm because of them ("in panick"). In the case of Bernardini Marzolla's approach [1], attempts to handle counterexamples involve looking for presumed *loanwords* that Etruscan could have borrowed from the lexicons of a set of selected languages (Bernardini Marzolla selected Latin, Greek, Persian, and Semitic languages), belonging to a bordering area indicated by the first phase. *{Latin, Greek, Phoenician}* — where *Phoenician* is contained in *Semitic languages* — is such a subset identified according to available knowledge on historical contacts Etruscans are known to have had. *{Persian}* is a subset identified following the selection, by the first phase, of Sanskrit: beside Indo-Aryan affinity, this selection of the main model-language implies Etruscans had to migrate from regions in or close to India, to reach Etruria, and that then they had to traverse Persia. Indo-Aryan linguistic and cultural presence is documented among Indo-Europeans and others in Anatolia and Syria in the 2nd millennium BC. On the other hand, some researchers claim that Anatolia was the original fatherland of the Indo-European languages, according to a criterion of maximal diversity in the location considered of languages belonging to the family considered, and to contacts with other language families whose early area is known or conjectured. Bernardini Marzolla's original hypothesis [1] however, neither needs nor mentions this conjecture. Ethnographic considerations are discussed at length in [7].

Chance sometimes provides *pointers* that result in shortcuts; it is contingent on an itinerary of discovery that is *unobtrusive* in the laws of the paradigm. As we are focusing on Bernardini Marzolla's interpretation protocols [1], and since the language he selected as a model of deviation for Etruscan is Sanskrit, let us point out some relevant notions. In India, the earliest documented literary period of *Sanskrit* dates from about 1500 BC on. In particular, the period of *Vedic Sanskrit* ended in the 4th century BC, when the period of *Classic Sanskrit* entered, that in turn ended about the middle of the first millennium AD. Sanskrit survived as a literary language. Diversification between Sanskrit and the Indian languages in popular use termed *Prakrits* is documented from about 15 centuries ago, at a time when Etruscan in Italy had already been forgotten. However, Bernardini Marzolla [1] finds support in Prakrits for terms or grammatical forms for which Sanskrit — as documented — is not helpful, He assumes that ancient elements that were not accepted in literary Sanskrit, existed in popular varieties and were preserved in Prakrits, or even, later, in Hindī, a modern language that has been in use for a millennium, and whose lexicon has been influenced by Persian and Arabic. Now, even though such loanwords in Hindī *cannot* be *related* to Etruscan, they are, instead, *correlated:* Etruscan was credibly influenced by Punic, the Phoenician dialect of Carthage (thus Semitic, like Arabic); Carthage, as a power in the western Mediterranean, is known to have had frequent contacts with the Etruscans. Thus, the successful match with *Arabic* elements in Hindī, properly has to be rejected as evidence, as Arabic influences in India followed Islamization, far after the period of possible contacts with Etruscans. However, if *Phase II* is allowed short digressions for experimentations, it can discover that Semitic elements are relevant anyway as evidence, if found in Punic too. There is a qualitative difference between lexical and morphological influences: while loanwords are possible, morphological loan is not admitted, while autonomous morphological evolution (as well as dialectalisms) can be conceded.

3. A Related Domain: Inter-Intelligibility. An Example

A referee has pointed out that Ugaritic could be used as an example to show how dividing the assumption into two phases was vital in deciphering an ancient, unknown language. Ugaritic has been recognized to be a Northwest Semitic language, related to Canaanite and Hebrew, and successfully deciphered as being such. *Phase I* yields the choice of Canaanite as a candidate model. However, in the case of Ugaritic, there is a complication: the script is cuneiform, and resulted in a consonantal alphabet. Thus, upstream of lexical hypotheses, a conjecture on the interpretation of the script is necessary. This is not a major problem for Etruscan, since the identification of letters in the Etruscan alphabet (consonants or vowels) with letters having the same shape in other ancient alphabets from the Mediterranean was plausible. For Ugaritic, it is the properly linguistic hypotheses that proved simpler than for Etruscan. Once an interpretation of the script is assumed, then, had *Phase I* selected Greek, subsequent attempts to map Greek onto that interpretation of the script would have lexical hypothesis usually fail, as Greek is the wrong choice.

The example of Ugaritic raises a related, but simpler notion, called *inter-intelligibility*. In the late 1960's, about one generation after Ugaritic was interpreted, a small intellectual group published, in Israel, mythological Ugaritic texts without even translating them, claiming that Ugaritic, being a Canaanite dialect like Hebrew, should be understood by Hebrew-speakers. The texts were published in transliteration into the usual Hebrew script, with some orthographic adaptation to the way Modern Hebrew is normally written. In contrast to attempts to decipher totally unknown languages, *inter-intelligibility* facilitates understanding based on knowledge of a related known language. This is the kind of competence, for example, that allows a person familiar with Italian, Latin and French, as in the case of the author, to read and understand Spanish (at least in part) and Portuguese (with a bit more training), using knowledge of a few widely known native terms (or other features) and some expectation about the topic of the text.

The protocol of interpretation we are going to discuss on an example, indicates that the way kinds of hypothesis-generation are ordered according to **Figure 1**, and as stated in further detail in the previous section, should be considered tentative, not to be imposed rigidly. Rather, lexical, morphological, and semantic hypotheses could be conceived as being produced by the cooperation of several sources of knowledge in a blackboard architecture. The different sources correspond to the lexicon, morphology, orthography (the three of them, for various languages), semantics, and common sense concerning various cultural realities: ethnography, stylistics — e.g., the way a scientific paper is given a title, or is typeset — as well as some smattering of the domain.

Let us consider a simple example, drawn from a recent paper by Hasle [4], published in a Norwegian journal in computing and the humanities.

> *Fra præmisserne*
>   *(1)   Alle mennesker er dødelige*
>   *(2)   Sokrates er et menneske*
> *kan det konkluderes, at*
>   *(3)   Sokrates er dødelig*
> *Elementært.*

The protocol of interpretation considered is instantiated on a particular agent (the present author), who has a specific corpus of knowledge in natural languages; in particular, the present author knows no Germanic language other than English. The first clue we get, is that the text, that is not English, is drawn from a journal published in Norway. *Phase I* finds the language of the text somewhat similar to English and what German "should be", so it is likely to be a Germanic language. Since Norwegian, Swedish, and Danish are Germanic languages, and because of the country of origin of the journal, Norwegian is our guess. (This turns out to be wrong; both the author and the paper are Danish.) The journal is known to be in computing for the humanities. The title of the paper is *Fra sproganalyse til logikprogrammering*. Looking for the easiest point for lexical hypothesizing, *Logikprogrammering* yields two terms, that, because of their similarity to English and international Latinate terminology, are likely to mean, respectively, *"logic"*, and something related to *"programming"*. Then, grammatical hypotheses intervene: the ending *-ing* temptingly looks like the English ending, and we assume it means almost the same. Word-formation by composition occurs in English and is known to occur more massively, without hyphens, in German, so we assume that *Logikprogrammering* is a compound (*programmering* of *logik*). Then, our semantic knowledge tells us that *"logic-programming"* makes sense, in computing, the latter being one of the domains of the journal. The lexical hypothesis involves a hypothesis on the morphological category of the item we are considering: the English nominal compound *logic-programming* is a standard lexical entry in computing terminology; the Norwegian candidate-equivalent is constituted by the juxtaposition of two terms that we identified, and our guess about the morphological category is that it is the same as in English: a nominal compound.

Picking another word from the title of the paper, for the purposes of lexical hypothesizing: *sproganalyse* contains a substring that must mean something related to *"analysis"*. Assuming that the whole string is also a nominal compound, *sprog-* reminds us of a German term that even those who cannot understand German (as we assumed about the interpreting agent) often know: *Sprach,* that is, *"language";* the same lexical root is the one of the German verb for *"to speak"*. Linguistic data we are considering are not enough to check whether the assumptions about phonological correspondence can be coherently maintained. Semantically, the sense "must" be something like *"linguistic analysis"*, or, perhaps, *"speech-analysis"*, but by browsing the paper, no iconographic material was found of the kind one would usually expect in papers in speech-processing. So, let us assume the sense is *"linguistic analysis"*, or perhaps *"parsing"*. Now, two short words are left in the title: *Fra ... til ...* We take the risk, and, because of the parallelism of candidate wordsenses, as well as expected patterns of devising a title for a paper, we choose to rely on the similarity with the English terms *till* and *from,* so the title is considered to mean: *"From linguistic analysis to logic programming"*.

Now, let us analyze the passage extracted from the paper. In a paper about logic programming, it is hardly surprising to find a discussion on logic, so the fact we meet there *Sokrates* (lexical hypothesis: this must be Socrates), and the typographical layout, that reminds one of a syllogism, has us guessing the overall topic of the passage, perhaps the syllogism about the mortality of Socrates. And indeed: the first term, *Fra,* was already interpreted as *"from"* in the title; the second word, *præmisserne,* looks like a Latinate word; the term must be one that means *"premise"*, and the word is presumably in the plural, as two logical premises, (1) and (2), follow, and in turn are followed by a line where we recognize the Latinate and English lexical root of *"conclude"* in the word *konkluderes;* moreover, perhaps *kan* on the same line has the same lexical, syntactic and semantic role as English *can*. (3) is presumably the consequence of the syllogism; it reads *Sokrates er dødelig.* As we assume this is the syllogism about the mortality of Socrates (but have to prove this), the candidate meaning of the line is: *Socrates is mortal.* This is supported by the initial substring, that brings to mind the lexical root of English *dead* and *death,* while the remainder of the word looks like an adjectival ending in English *(-ly)* and, perhaps, in German (and other Germanic languages: see below). Word-formation would suggest English *deadly,* but semantics are not bound by the particular derivational-morphology choices instantiated in English, so semantics let us pick between *"mortal"* and *"deadly";* we pick *"mortal"*, because it suits our conjecture about the identity of the syllogism considered. The slashed *o,* looks like an *o* with a diacritic mark, so we presume it expresses some vowel related to *o*. We don't pretend we are able to pronounce the written strings.

Optionally, we may consider the case where the interpreter does not know German, but knows a few German terms. Some may remember one of the terms *tot* (for *"dead"*), *töten* (for *"to kill"*), *Tod* (for *"death"*), from the movies or some book on World War II. Many people who do not understand German, nevertheless know that German "rotates" certain consonants (with respect to Germanic consonants as still found, say, in English), or, at least, that *d,* a voiced consonant, becomes voiceless, that is, *t*. This further term of comparison, from fragmentary knowledge in German, provides supporting evidence (actually, indicators, not true evidence), for the interpretation of *dødelig* as meaning *"mortal"*. (The German suffix equivalent to the suffix instantiated in this term is *-lich,* as in the adjective *tödlich,* which is the exact equivalent from the viewpoint of word-formation. In Dutch, the adjective is *dodelijk.* Yiddish has *-lig* in the word *zelig,* that is, *"blessed", "[of] blessed [memory]",* also used as a proper name: *Zelig.* Let us suppose this information is unavailable, or not fully available, for the purposes of deciphering the passage considered). Under the hypothesis that the interpretation of *dødelig* is correct as stated, the previous word in the first premise, *er,* is likely to mean *"is".* (This should not be taken to apply indiscriminately for every language, as Hebrew and Hungarian do not employ a special word to mean *"is".*)

Now, let us go back to the premise of the syllogism. In (1), *Alle* looks like the English *all,* and, because of the title of the German anthem, the word *alles* has about the same meaning. The word *mennesker* presumably means *"men",* if the syllogism is actually about Socrates' mortality and (1) means *"All men are mortal":* the last word in (1) is *dødelige,* that exhibits a final *e* that did not occur in the word *dødelig,* as found in (3). As a consequence, the term must have been singular, while in (1), the plural is suitable. Hence the final *e* must be a plural ending at least in some situations, though not in *mennesker,* that must be a plural (cf. the irregular English plural *men,* not **mans).* In (1), we find again the word *er* that we considered to mean *"is"* in the singular as occurring in (1), and can still be singular as occurring in (2), but must be, instead, semantically in the plural, *"are",* as occurring in (1): this contradiction is not fatal, for our local hypothesis about the meaning of (1), as words often have more than one acceptation, and in morphology, it may well be that a certain language does not distinguish between the plural and the singular for a given verbal form (cf. the coalescence of verbal forms in English). We find the word *menneske* in (2), which we assume to mean — because of our global hypothesis about the syllogism — *"Socrates is a man* (or: *a human being)".* Then, *menneske* is seemingly the singular form of *mennesker.* As to *-sk-,* in certain Germanic languages this cluster, corresponds to the English *sh* and German *sch.* Without knowing German, Beethoven enthusiasts know that *Menschen* means *"men"* in that language, so it is hardly surprising to find *-sk-* inside the "Norwegian" (really Danish) word that, by our conjecture, means *"men".*

The word *et* is left in (2). By matching the meaning we assumed for (2), the word *et* is likely to be the indefinite article, *"a".* (Several languages, as disparate as Latin, Hebrew, Arabic, and Japanese, have no indefinite article, and moreover, Latin and Japanese have no definite article, so, again, such assumptions should not be considered to be universally valid. Dutch, however, another Germanic language, has the term *het* as an article. Actually, *het* is the neuter definite article; morphologically masculine or feminine nouns take the definite article *de.*)

We have analyzed the line between — *"kan det konkluderes, at"* — only partially. Even if we were not able to guess the sense of *et,* we would still have, thus far, a partial interpretation, for the whole passage, large enough for having us giving it a last touch, by integrating the line considered with the sense *"that"* (associated with the "Norwegian" word *at),* at the very end of the line considered, just before the conclusion (3). While not accounting for *det* on the same line, we have more or less made our point about the overall meaning of the passage.

The very last line remains: *Elementært.* It is safe to assume it means *"[It's] elementary.",* reminiscent of Sherlock Holmes (that the present author knows in Italian translation: *Elementare, Watson.*)

The advantage of having discussed a simple example from a Norwegian journal is that most comparisons with English should be easy to understand even for an audience of English-reading non-linguists. However, it is important to keep in mind that we had an almost straightforward hypothesis about the overall meaning (Socrates' mortality), which is similar to the way most Etruscologists reason about, say, an inscription found on a grave. Besides, *Phase I* has been far too easy; having speculated that the article is in Norwegian (because it comes from Norway), we immediately entered *Phase II,* relying on our knowledge that this language belongs to the same family as English and German. The fact that the article is really Danish might be discovered only after comparing several papers from the journal.

We have chosen not to present an example of an interpretation trial from Etruscan, since it would have been too long to include one in this paper, and inappropriate for AI experts unfamiliar with computational linguistics. Bernardini Marzolla's book [1] includes several very clear protocols of analysis of full sentences. They propose conjectures, but may not be the ultimate solution of the riddle. From the viewpoint of knowledge acquisition, the book is interesting because its protocols are ordered, fairly explicit, and readable (that is, if you read Italian). Thankfully, the literature of Etruscology abounds with interpretations, albeit their proposed interpretation is different from Bernardini Marzolla's. From the viewpoint of metatheorizing in terms of AI, such principled attempts would also do. Were we Etruscologists, it would have mattered choosing this solution instead of the other one, but as we are not concerned with the *object-level* as Etruscologists must be, but rather with the heuristics at the *meta-level,* the literature of the different schools of Etruscologists is a mine of material for the knowledge-engineer.

4. Variably Cumulative Learning

When constructing a model of reality, we have to hypothesize models and revise or discard them. *Knowledge revision* needs to be subjected to strategies defining and constraining it. For example, noisy data should be dealt with differently from meaningful new evidence, but assumptions are involved in devising insensitivity to noise. Discrimination among rules induced by machine-learning, if data are noisy, can be done by retaining only those rules for which a threshold value is exceeded based on the recurrence of successes or failures.

With reference to humans trying to decipher Etruscan, one notices that assumptions about how confident the partial model is, are crucial in causing the model to be revised thoroughly, once counterexamples or mismatches occur with new data, as opposed to trials to make exceptional data fit the model by minimizing revision.

In machine-learning, one possible heuristic is *conservatism* [2]. Induction, as performed there, excludes uncommon counterexamples, and — to rectify a theory that is being incrementally constructed — the smallest changes are chosen. Some amount of faithfulness to partial theories is necessary to allow one to survive, when data are liable to be noisy; however, conservatism has drawbacks: changes of mind should not always be minimal, in intelligent behavior, albeit in humans, they characterize doctrinarian inquiry. In machine-learning adopting conservatism, use of this approach is recommended together with the strategy of looking for confirmation rather than disconfirmation [2]. One of the drawbacks, is *convergence to local maxima (ibid.):* the partial theory is augmented through small changes, but then, a deadline is likely; better theories are ignored as it would take a major change to reach them. It is like climbing the wrong mountain. Then, a *non-cumulative* learning mode, that is, where the extent of modifications is not restricted by conservatism, is advisable as an option together with conservatism *(ibid.).* At the extreme end of the spectrum, as opposed to mere conservatism, there is *learning by scratch,* where knowledge is discarded and redeveloped all over again.

In protocols of interpreting Etruscan, the more confidence increases, the more conservatism we find. That notably happens in the second phase of the overall protocol, when a given language has already been adopted as a model for comparison with Etruscan, and details are being worked out. As a matter of fact, *non-cumulative* learning is general, but for a given task where much is unknown for the domain, such generality is a weakness, to the extent that it is difficult to find the extent to which knowledge should be discarded. Conservatism allows the investigator to proceed, and is justified by a long sequence of successes in matching trials. Yet, conservatism, with its coherence in choosing minimal changes, is to be blamed for the survival of erroneous directions in Etruscology, that sometimes have misled it for generations. Early superficial comparisons to Sanskrit had yielded mildly negative opinions, that, because of acritical strengthening based on relying on previous authorities, were gradually taken to be an extremely negative promise: this *confidence-avalanche* effect was deleterious in Etruscology, together with the acceptance as facts of provisional results due to *induction;* this effaced criteria for falsifying candidate partial theories. The more distant Etruscan seemed to be from the set of languages considered as candidate models, the more researchers were lured to induce, both in the lexicon and in grammar.

We can hypothesize that cumulativeness, low in *Phase I,* gradually increases. We model it as a *generally increasing* function where circumscribed oscillations are permitted (e.g., in the region between two exponentials, or a narrowing region), that correspond to minor hypotheses being discarded, to accomodate counterexamples. Then, we would still combine such a model with the possibility of major paradigm crashes (to zero, or to an intermediate level), then, with cumulativeness slowly increasing again, or crashing further. However, we can tentatively assume that the higher the cumulativeness, the lower the probability of crashes.

5. Assumptions on Analogy

Particular approaches to interpretation, when claiming success for certain inscriptions, can corroborate or refute general assumptions in the discipline. For example, **analogical reasoning** in Etruscology was based on an assumption that, if not admitting *cultural universals,* admits that neighboring cultures share attitudes. There is an approach — termed *bilinguistic* — that tries to understand Etruscan inscriptions found in graves in a certain context, or on artifacts of a certain kind, by means of analogical reasoning. This involved the assumption that inscriptions on objects left by Etruscans should mean something similar to what inscriptions are known to mean, as found on similar objects left by Romans, or on Greek objects. Instead, Bernardini Marzolla [1] found out that in several instances, such analogies provide no good clue to interpretation, as the way of thinking of Etruscans, when finishing the artifacts, was different from the Romans'. The analogical approach works when nearly universal phenomena in human culture *are* universal, as assumed, at least as concerning the culture investigated. Then, assumptions are just common-sense knowledge: for example, conjectures about what a grave or a cinerary stands for, about the fact there is a person involved — the dead one — that had a name and possibly relatives (especially parents), and about the role of death in the human collective, social cognition and undertakings. However, assumptions about analogy in different cultures happen to prove wrong, when a cultural phenomenon is not universal, and when affinity between neighboring peoples in cultural attitudes towards, say, artifacts, is unwarranted. For example, a Roman cup is likely to bear a votive dedication, while Bernardini Marzolla [1] found out that an inscription found on an Etruscan cup has a profane, convivial, jocular nature, as it means: *I am thirsty.* Free thoughts, small pieces of literature can be found on objects such as vessels, expressing concepts that would not belong, instead, in Greek or Roman vascular epigraphy (inscriptions on vessels).

6. Knowledge Macro-Systems and Their Simulation

The idea of studying patterns of research in the entire community of Etruscologists according to AI concepts, is related to three existing disciplines, that so far have belonged to the social sciences:

- **theories of research,** a sector of the mathematical social sciences that studies scientific careers; established in Poland since the Thirties, its main exponent today is Nowakowska (deceased in Columbus, Ohio, in 1989), who has investigated mathematical and computational properties [9], sometimes in relation to artificial intelligence;
- **cultural dynamics,** a sector of anthropology that studies dynamic processes in a given culture, out of a broad range of organic phenomena that can qualify as *cultures;*
- **knowledge systems,** a sector in sociology (and especially in social policy) that studies the evolution of social processes by effect of organic knowledge, and that investigates as well the impact of public funding on research.

There is an important potential in the investigation of *large-scale effects* for artificial intelligence, and for machine learning in particular. One approach to machine learning, is having small models gradually developed, as embodied in prototypes whose behavior is investigated. However, it is interesting to investigate *mass,* by tackling machine-learning the other way around: to be able to analyze a working large system, a program prototype cannot be suitable to begin with. Let us generalize *knowledge system* to include both computer programs or computational models, and large human systems, whose computational behavior we want to analyze. For *expertise,* an expert system based on the knowledge of one expert, or of few experts (in one domain or in domains related for the purposes of a given task), is just at one extreme of a range of knowledge systems; at the other extreme, there is the system represented by the entire research community in the domain. To be useful for the purposes of large-scale learning analysis, it is expedient to consider the research community (say, of Etruscologists) not just *synchronically* — that is, the way it behaves today — but *diachronically,* that is, historically.

Let us analyze patterns of scientific thought and major trends of behavior in the knowledge system that is the largest, for a given domain: the entire specific research community; then, let us formalize trends and phenomena spotted. Then, let us develop small, initially simple software prototypes that are very constrained, and rather deterministic. Certain phenomena could be initially imposed as direct, built-in constraints of the program: for example, predefined functions representing *(non)cumulativeness* in learning (how strong is the tendency to avoid discarding assumptions), or the propagation of opinions as promoted by credited authorities, and the like, as yielded by the manual analysis of the large human system. Then, let us increase the size of the search space, by introducing increasing amounts of indeterminacy, of factors, and of playing characters that learn. Initial constraints are relaxed, but still we would try to tune the program, so simulation would replicate the general phenomena that were individuated and formalized for the human system.

Simulation should not be necessarily *complete,* full-fledged with all details of the domain-knowledge through its evolution. **Selectivity** is a key to both *feasibility,* and *focus calibration* in the framework of inquiry as of interest to AI.

Simulating the spectrum of the specific expertise *models* of linguistic inquiry in Etruscology (as opposed to a general, undetailed schema of those models: the *metamodel*) looks unfeasible, unless a group of experts and knowledge engineers would be willing to devote a substantial portion of their professional life to the development of a running simulator of the various directions of research. Yet, once portable analyzers for a broad gamut of languages could be obtained, implementation could focus on the specific knowledge involved in trials to interpret Etruscan, whose detailed representation on its own would also require many man/years from Etruscologists and knowledge engineers. Indeed, the present status of Etruscology (which is not the same as extant results) developed from two centuries of work of researchers with certain competencies who pursued very different directions, especially in what we termed *Phase I.* The search-space was unmanageable not only for a single researcher to organize, but even for the trans-generational virtual community of all Etruscologists to coordinate: notwithstanding the existence of schools pursuing different avenues of investigation, there was no or little planning among the several agents. Limitations in terms of feasibility of exhaustive search even for Etruscology as a discipline, are reflected in its failures during several generations. Not only: the linguistic knowledge of the various researchers was, almost each time, an *unicum,* resulting from the cumulation of linguistic knowledge in one or more languages as an object of scientific inquiry, such knowledge was affected by given stresses, inexactitudes, and limitations, and presumably the linguist's competency exploited *synergies* between the domains learned. Not only linguists knew, each, a given set of languages (so partitions of the set of all languages involved should be accounted for), but knowledge was nuanced. Therefore, *detailed* implementation could be based just on simulated professional personalities of characters conceived as reflecting a "typical" set of Etruscologists. However, what we *are* interested in, is **partial metamodeling.** It is as such, that the study of entire research communities is of interest for AI: only certain classes of phenomena would be simulated.

7. Conclusion

Interpretation heuristics belong to a collection that may be conceived as being more or less "universal". It is hoped that readers that would not have liked to have to read a protocol of an interpretation trial for an Etruscan inscription — requiring the introduction of background notions in classical or exotic languages — have nevertheless been able to understand the procedure in general, by reading the protocol for "Norwegian"/Danish, a choice that has the advantage of relying on knowledge of English. The choice of the particular passage we have considered, for which, things were made easier by typographical features, Latinate words suggesting the passage is about a syllogism, and the mention of Socrates, is legitimate: Etruscologists trying to decipher an inscription are thematically oriented by the fact that, for example, the inscription was found on a grave. Actually, it is this kind of epigraphic material that used to yield lexical identifications about which the greatest number of Etruscologists tend to agree.

Allowing both working knowledge of a given language, and fragmentary, but somewhat justified, knowledge of another language, is a necessity for the sake of credibility that a realistic model should not ignore the fact that one person can have knowledge of just a limited number of languages, and that such knowledge is not a binary predicate. In humans — unlike present-day expert systems — the decline of competence (in linguistic expertise, as well as in any expertise domain) is often gradual, through degrees of tentative knowledge or of ignorance. In a monograph being completed [8], I discuss knowledge-engineering aspects of modeling linguistic-cum-cultural knowledge of a given language family, providing a unified architecture and representation schema that accounts for kinship (this is very different from the current paradigms of the lexicon in machine-translation projects). In my paper [6], I introduced the notion that *cultural fisheye* phenomena — culturally far phenomena are little known, and distorted — should also be accounted for, in computational models of cognition.

Acknowledgements

This paper is dedicated to the memory of Prof. Maria Nowakowska [9], who did not spare encouragement for my work, and in particular, espressed interest, in her last letter from Columbus before her decease in 1989, for the project on the metatheory of interpretation of Etruscan and on the cultural dynamics of Etruscologists.

Marty Golumbic provided careful suggestions and remarks on versions of this paper; in particular, his is the merit of having looked, *a posteriori,* for the exact identity of the Nordic language (Danish, not Norwegian) of the passage whose *Phase II* of interpretation is analyzed in Sec. 3.

References

[1]   Bernardini Marzolla, P., *L'etrusco. Una lingua ritrovata.* Mondadori, Milan, Italy, 1984.

[2]   Emde, W., "Non-Cumulative Learning in METAXA.3". *KIT Report 56,* Fachbereich Informatik, Technische Universität Berlin, West Germany, 1987. Extended version of a paper that appeared in: *Proceedings of the Tenth International Joint Conference on Artificial Intelligence (IJCAI-87),* Milan, Italy.

[3]   Erman, L.D., Hayes-Roth, F., Lesser, V.R. and Reddy, D.R., "The HEARSAY-II Speech-Understanding System: Integrating Knowledge to Resolve Uncertainty". *ACM Computing Surveys 12, 2,* 1980: pp. 213-253.

[4]   Hasle, P.F.V., "Fra sproganalyse til logikprogrammering". *Humanistiske Data 3-1989.* The Norwegian Computing Centre for the Humanities — NAVFs edb-senter for humanistisk forskning. Universitetet *(sic),* Bergen, Norway: pp. 66-82. (In Danish. We have used a paragraph from Sec. 2, p. 67, as linguistic data for a discussion on inter-intelligibility.)

[5]   Meillet, A., Review (in French) of *La langue étrusque. Affinités ougro-finnoises. Précis grammatical. Textes traduits et commentés. Dictionnaire étymologique* (by J. Martha. Leroux, Paris, 1913). *Bulletin de la Société de Linguistique de Paris,* Vol. XIX, 1915. Reprinted by Dawson France, Paris, 1966: pp. 150-151.

[6]   Nissan, E., "Exception-Admissibility and Typicality in Proto-Representations". In: Czap, H. and C. Galinski, Eds., *Terminology and Knowledge Engineering. (Proceedings of the International INFOTERM Conference,* Trier, West Germany, 1987.) Indeks Verlag, Frankfurt/M, 1987: pp. 253-267.

[7]   Nissan, E., "A Knowledge-Analysis of Bernardini Marzolla's Indoglottal Interpretation of Etruscan: For a Metamodel of Interpretation". ~ 100 p. To appear in *Advances in Computing and the Humanities 1.* JAI Press, Greenwich, Conn.

[8]   Nissan, E., *An Architecture and Representation for a Multilingual Knowledge-Base.* Vol. 1 in the SCCAC Monograph Series (K.M. Schmidt, E. Nissan and P. Mohler, Eds.; publisher to be determined). An earlier, shorter version of this book is going to appear as: Nissan, E., "Structure and Representation for a Multilingual Semitic Machine-Dictionary: Issues in Engineering a Lexicon Meant for Symbolic Manipulation" (~100 p.) To appear in Vol. 2 of: Schmidt, K.M., Ed., *Concepts, Content, Meaning.* (2 vols.) SCCAC Publications (The Society for Conceptual and Content Analysis by Computer), special volumes of *Advances in Computing and the Humanities,* JAI Press, Greenwich, Conn.

[9]   Nowakowska, M., *Theories of Research.* (2 vols.) Intersystems Publications, Seaside, California, 1984.

[10]   Pallottino, M., Ed., *Testimonia Linguae Etruscae.* La Nuova Italia, Florence, Italy, 1968. 1st Ed. is of 1954.

Ontology, Sublanguage, and Semantic Networks in Natural Language Processing

Victor Raskin

Natural Language Processing Laboratory
Purdue University
West Lafayette, Indiana 47907 U.S.A.

The main claim of the paper is that no significant progress in NLP semantics is possible without a comprehensive formal theory. It is demonstrated that, while having a great deal to offer to NLP semantics, linguistic semantics lacks such a theory. It is also argued that model-theoretical semantics, which is based on a formal theory, fails to reach any significant goals with regard to natural language semantics. It does, however, put forward the important idea of anchoring natural meaning representations in the real world. Such a direct anchoring, without the burden and constraints of truth values, is achieved by the ontologically-, sublanguage-, and semantic-network-based approach to NLPS, an approach in which theoretical needs and practical feasibility merge.

Significant progress in natural language processing (NLP), i.e., the development of fully automated systems capable of understanding human languages such as English, reasoning in them, and producing intelligent statements in them, is impossible without a breakthrough in meaning representation and analysis. Much of what has been achieved in NLP has been in the area of syntactic parsing and, while that problem can be considered largely solved, even the best syntactic parser provides only a few initial steps towards meaning analysis.

At the same time, much of what has been attempted in "semantic parsing," or computational semantics, or NLP semantics (NLPS), has not been done on a sound theoretical basis and has largely failed to solve the two crucial problems of meaning analysis in NLP, viz., resolution of ambiguity and selective inference. Such attempts, ranging from the enticingly impotent conceptual dependencies (see, for instance, Schank 1975) to diverse forms of feature representation (see, for instance, Pollard and Sag 1987 and also Rounds and Kasper 1986 and, especially, Kasper and Rounds 1986) to the much more promising semantic-network-based approaches (see, for instance, Quillian 1968, Bobrow and Winograd 1977, Brachman and Schmoltze 1985, Brachman et al.

1983), have all suffered from the lack of a comprehensive theory of meaning representation and, as a result, have been cripplingly *ad hoc.*

It has been argued elsewhere (Raskin 1987b) that NLPS must be based on the achievements of linguistic semantics (LS), whose declared goal is to present a formal model matching all the aspects of the native speaker's semantic competence, which includes the abilities to:

- interpret every utterance

- disambiguate any utterance

- paraphrase any utterance

- infer selectively from any utterance

- detect semantic anomaly, including inappropriateness.

Unlike linguistic syntax, however, LS has failed to develop a comprehensive formal theory on a sound logical foundation -- and simplistic attempts to base such a theory on truth values have proven unsuccessful (see below). The first and best known LS theory, Katz and Fodor's (1963) interpretive semantics (KF), was neatly compositional and based on the:

- presentation of each word meaning as a set of prepostulated semantic features and

- "amalgamation" of word meanings according to a couple of dozens of combinatorial rules fully determined by the syntactic type of the phrase made up by the words.

The effectiveness of the transparently simple KF formalism was, however, greatly undermined by the fact that each word meaning was represented only very partially, with only the most general part of the meaning captured by those semantic features which the theory "saw" and used in its "theorems." Thus, an application of each theorem would predict the semantic properties of a sentence listed above. At the same time, the most essential part of the meaning of the word was described by a pseudo-feature ignored by the theory. For instance, the theory captured the "man" part of the most obvious meaning of *bachelor* but ignored the "never married" part. Even so, KF could not avoid the problem of an unlimited proliferation of its primitives, i.e., the general semantic features.

Heavily attacked by the subsequently developed LS theories, most of which have never achieved the formal level of KF, it also came under serious fire from the philosophy of language. Most typically and memorably, D. Lewis (1972) accused it of simply translating a human language into another human language he called "Markerese" instead of relating linguistic entities to things outside of language and proceeded to claim that "semantics with no treatment of truth conditions is not semantics" (169). Lewis's alternative proposal is an archetypal approach in the tradition of truth-conditional, or referential, or model-theoretical semantics in the spirit of Tarski (1936), Carnap (1947, 1963), Kripke (1963), Kaplan (1964), Montague (1960, 1968, 1970a,b,c), and Scott (1970). More recent reverberations have not added much to the previously outlined positions, at least not in the aspect pertinent to this discussion.

Basing his syntax on the Ajdukiewicz (1935)-Bar-Hillel (1964) categorial grammar with the context-free phrase-structure rules of the form:

$$c \rightarrow (c/c_1...c_n) + c_1 + ... + c_n$$

Lewis attempts to reduce the meaning of each basic category (sentence, common noun, and name) to its intension, defined as a function, from a number of parameters, or coordinates, to the extension of the category, which is, of course, a truth value in the first case and an object in the other two (his coordinates range from possible worlds and sets of all individuals to speaker, audience, time, and space). The meaning of each derived category is similarly treated in terms of a fairly complex function taking basic intensions for arguments as well as values.

The resulting theory, an application of an intensional logic to natural language, finds it very hard to distinguish between the meanings of two sentences with the identical parameters (with the exception, say, of the time coordinate for two sentences uttered by the same speaker 2 seconds apart) and truth values, even though their meanings may be different. In other words, as an LS theory, the approach has a very large "grain size" (Hobbs 1985) equating the meanings of much larger sets of sentences than does the native speaker and ignoring numerous significant meaning differences.

Somewhat surprisingly, this is not what model-theoretical semantics is usually criticized for (cf., for instance, Wilson 1975). Instead, it is commonly faulted for difficulties with:

- "truth-valueless" sentences such as the notorious,

  The present king of France is bald.

- interrogative sentences

- hedging and fuzzy sentences,

even though important work on presupposition (Strawson 1950, Geach 1950), erotetic (Prior and Prior 1955, Åqvist 1965), modal (Hughes and Cresswell 1968 and Chellas 1980), conditional (Lewis 1973) and fuzzy logic (Zadeh 1965) can stave off some, if not most, of that less significant type of criticism.

Model-theoretical approaches to LS are still frequently professed though never practiced (in the sense of attempting serious full-scale descriptions of natural language material in these terms), especially in Europe, where they seem to take on an additional role of a declaration of freedom from the American dominance in the discipline. Ordinarily, a model-theoretical approach is assumed by an author dealing with an adjacent area, which presupposes natural meaning representation but does not actually do it (cf., for instance, Levinson 1983).

Even more to the point, the most sophisticated, seemingly versatile, and formally elegant model-theoretical approach, Montague grammars, turned out to be a source of bitter disappointment in NLP (see, for instance, Smith's 1979 criticism of Hobbs and Rosenschein 1977 as well as Friedman et al. 1978a,b, Gallin 1975, and Hirst 1983 and 1987). And it is NLPS which actually sheds interesting light on the otherwise inexplicable perseverance of truth-theoretical semantics in spite of a total lack of success beyond a limited number of preselected and predoctored examples travelling from one work to another.

Surely, the seductive power of axiomatic set theory and the desire to apply it in order to export its explicitness, transparency, and descriptive properties, if not explanatory capability is understandable. Nevertheless, the approach would not have survived so long without any significant nourishment if it had not been for a very serious and valid point, namely that **LS should anchor linguistic entities in non-linguistic ones**, or in other words, that **LS should indeed relate language to the world language describes**. The inconclusiveness of Carnap's seminal work in that direction, on the one hand, followed, of course, by a large number of successors and opponents in the philosophy of language, and KF's influential defeatism on the subject on the linguistic side (1963), on the other hand, have effectively removed this approach from the LS theoretical agenda, and this is where NLPS parts company with LS semantics in a dramatic -- and highly promising -- way.

It has been argued elsewhere that NLPS should, in fact, import from LS the sum total of all positive descriptions accumulated in the latter and covering the entire realm of natural semantic phenomena (Raskin 1987a,b). What is not there to import is a comprehensive and well-founded theory of meaning. Moreover, LS and NLPS have distinct goals:

- LS goals are:

    - to match the entire semantic competence of the native speaker (see (1))

- to deal with meaning in a natural language as a whole

- to deal with meaning in all possible detail

- to develop general and extrapolable principles of

- NLPS goals are:

  - to describe meaning in a way which will enable NLP systems to work by adequately handling specific and well-defined tasks

  - to deal with a limited, usually seriously constrained, sublanguage of a natural language

  - to deal with meaning to a certain depth of analysis, sufficient to do the work

  - to provide complete descriptions without any possibilities of the "etcetera" type of extrapolation widely used in LS.

It is precisely the sublanguage-oriented nature of NLPS and the ability, in fact the necessity, to predefine the grain size of the required meaning analysis which make it possible to put NLPS on a firm formal foundation, unavailable to LS. This is achieved by combining the ontological and semantic-network based approaches to NLP semantics. An example of such a description is given in the Appendix.

The approach is based on the following principles:

- NLP systems are typically developed for *limited subdomains served by limited sublanguages* of natural languages (e.g., the subdomain of computer software manuals) -- see Raskin (1971, 1974, 1987a), Kittredge (1987), Kittredge and Lehrberger (1982), Grishman and Kittredge (1986), and Nirenburg and Raskin (1989) for further discussion of the sublanguage approach and its formal and practical ramifications

- A limited subdomain is representable fully and practically in its ontology, or "theory" (cf. Hobbs 1986), i.e., it has a finite and feasibly restricted number of objects, actions, properties, etc.

- A semantic-network approach is used to capture the ontology in a "concept lexicon" (see Nirenburg and Raskin 1987b,c), which is a combination of a well-developed "isa" hierarchy with elaborate frames assigned to each node

- The meaning of natural-language expressions is represented with the help of "bilingual" dictionaries, natural language → concept for analysis purposes and concept → natural language for generation, (the Appendix example deals only with analysis.)

While generally powerful, outside of a limited sublanguage, the semantic-network approach presents major formal problems -- it:

- richly relates concepts to each other without defining any of them explicitly

- when used consistently for the purposes of a complete description is bound to lead to an uncontrolled proliferation of the concepts in the frames

- muddles the formal nature of its slot- and filler names, which are those concepts.

Often billed, including by this author, as a primeless approach, semantic networks, in fact, smuggle each and every slot and filler name as an undefined prime and cannot control their number -- all that with regard to a natural language as a whole. **In a sublanguage, however, each such prime is directly ontologically anchored in an object, action, or property** finitely and feasibly prepostulated for the subdomain, and the **anchoring is achieved without the crippling narrow constraints imposed by truth values.** In other words, anchoring is fine and necessary, truth values as the anchors arc not good for meaning representation in natural language.

Whether some of those ontological anchors can be conveniently related to each other and thus their number reduced becomes a somewhat secondary matter of elegance and compactness of the description rather than of the conceptual essence. It is clear, nevertheless, that an anchoring which does not miss all the generalizations which are there in the domain will be more effective. It is precisely the absence -- in fact, the impossibility -- of such anchoring which rendered Chomsky's ill-fated formal measure of "simplicity," i.e., for all practical purposes, brevity of his formal grammars, totally devoid of sense as a measure of explanatory adequacy -- see Chomsky (1965:37-47).

Also importantly, while LS has to distinguish clearly between linguistic and encyclopedic information (see, for instance, Raskin 1985a,b), NLP semantics has to use both of these types of information for reasoning, mainly for the resolution of ambiguity and selective inference, because humans, whose activities NLP systems attempt to match and exceed, do the same. The sublanguage meaning available to these humans is firmly rooted in their knowledge of the subdomain. The ontologically-based approach proposed here captures this in its formal foundation.

We will not go here into an interesting and dangerous discussion of the fact that the formal model of NLPS proposed here is not in principle extrapolable into LS semantics because of the qualitative difference between constrained sublanguages and a natural language as a whole. Nor will we bring up the increasingly important issue of **constrained linguistics** which can and must be developed for many practical applications of the science of language, not just for NLP. What will suffice here is a firm statement that practical work in NLP semantics, as it should have been conducted and as it bound to develop in the foreseeable future, can be based on a firm formal foundation. It can be tentatively suggested that the same principle can be extended to adjacent areas of AI, for instance, automatic reasoning, machine learning, and even certain aspects of robotics (in particular, in its spatial aspect -- cf. Nirenburg and Raskin 1987a).

ACKNOWLEDGEMENTS

The work on this project has been supported in part by the NSF research grant #8803733. The author would also like to acknowledge Sergei Nirenburg's significant contribution to the coauthored works in which the framework for the general approach has been laid out. He also owes a debt of gratitude to his associates in the NLP Lab, especially Salvatore Attardo, Donalee Hughes, and Kevin Kuehl.

References

1. Ajdukiewicz, K. 1935. Die syntaktische Konnexität. *Studia Philosophica* 1, pp. 1-27. Translated as: Syntactic connection. In: S. McCall (ed.), **Polish Logic**. London-New York: Oxford University Press, pp. 207-231.

2. Åqvist, L. 1965. **A New Approach to the Logic of Questions**. Uppsala: University of Uppsala Press.

3. Bar-Hillel, Y. 1964. **Language and Information**. Reading, MA: Addison-Wesley.

4. Bobrow, D. and T. Winograd 1977. An overview of KRL, a knowledge representation language. *Cognitive Science* 1, pp. 3-46.

5. Brachman, R. J., R. E. Fikes, and H. J. Levesque 1983. KRYPTON: A functional approach to knowledge representation. *IEEE Computer* 16:10, pp. 67-73.

6. Brachman, R. J. and J. Schmolze 1985. An overview of the KL-ONE knowledge representation system. *Cognitive Science* 9, pp. 171-216.

7. Carnap, R. 1947. **Meaning and Necessity**. Chicago: University of Chicago Press.

8. Carnap, R. 1963. Replies and systemetic expositions. In: P. Schilpp (ed.), **The Philosophy of Rudolf Carnap**. La Salle, IL: Open Court.

9. Chellas, B. F. 1980. **Modal Logic**. Cambridge: Cambridge University Press.

10. Chomsky, N. 1965. **Aspects of the Theory of Syntax**. Cambridge, MA: M.I.T. Press.

11. Friedman, J., D. B. Moran, and D. S. Warren 1978a. An interpretation system for Montague grammar. *American Journal of Computational Linguistics* 1978:1, Microfiche 74, pp. 23-96. Also: Paper N-4, Computer Studies in Formal Linguistics, Department of Computer and Communication Sciences, University of Michigan, Ann Arbor, MI.

12. Friedman, J., D. B. Moran, and D. S. Warren 1978b. Evaluating English sentences in a logical model: A process version of Montague grammar. **Proceedings of COLING '78**. Bergen, Norway. Also: Paper N-15, Computer Studies in Formal Linguistics, Department of Computer and Communication Sciences, University of Michigan, Ann Arbor, MI.

13. Gallin, D. 1975. **Intensional and Higher-Order Modal Logic with Applications to Montague Semantics**. Amsterdam: North-Holland.

14. Geach, P. 1950. Russell's theory of descriptions. *Analysis* X, pp. 84-88.

15. Hirst, G. 1983. Semantic interpretation against ambiguity. Providence, R.I.: Brown University TR CS-83-25.

16. Hirst, G. 1987. **Semantic Interpretation and the Resolution of Ambiguity**. Cambridge: Cambridge University Press.

17. Hobbs, J. R. 1985. Granularity. **Proceedings of IJCAI '85**. Los Angeles, CA, pp. 432-435.

18. Hobbs, J. R. 1986. Overview of the Tacitus project. *Computational Linguistics* 12:3, pp. 220-222.

19. Hobbs, J. R.] and S. J. Rosenschein 1977. Making computational sense of Montague's intensional logic. *Artificial Intelligence* 9:3, pp. 287-306.

20. Hughes, G. E. and M. J. Cresswell 1968. **An Introduction to Modal Logic**. London: Methuen.

21. Kaplan, D. 1964. Foundations of Intensional Logic, Ph.D. thesis. Ann Arbor, MI: University Microfilms.

22. Kasper, R. and W. Rounds 1986. A logical semantics for feature structures. In: **Proceedings of the 24th Annual Meeting of the Association for Computational Linguistics**. New York: Columbia University, pp. 257-266.

23. Katz, J. J. and J. A. Fodor 1963. The structure of a semantic theory. *Language* 39:1, pp. 170-210.

24. Kripke, S. 1963. Semantic considerations on modal logic. *Acta Philosophica Fennica* 16, pp. 83-94.

25. Levinson, S. 1983. **Pragmatics**. Cambridge: Cambridge University Press.

26. Lewis, D. 1972. General semantics. In: D. Davidson and G. Harman (eds.), **Semantics of Natural Language**. Dordrecht-Boston: D. Reidel, pp. 169-218.

27. Lewis, D. 1973. **Counterfactuals**. Cambridge, MA: Harvard University Press.

28. Montague, R. 1960. Logical necessity, physical necessity, ethics, and quantifiers. *Inquiry* 3, pp. 259-269.

29. Montague, R. 1968. Pragmatics. In: R. Klibansky (ed.), **Contemporary Philosophy -- La Philosophie Contemporaine**. Florence: La Nuova Italia Editrice.

30. Montague, R. 1970a. English as a formal language I. In: **Linguaggi nella società e nella tecnica**. Milan: Edizioni di Comunità.

31. Montague, R. 1970b. Universal grammar. *Theoria* 36.

32. Montague, R. 1970c. Pragmatics and intensional logic. *Synthese* 22, pp. 68-94.

33. Nirenburg, S. and V. Raskin 1987a. Dealing with space in natural language processing. In: A. Kak and S. Chen (eds.), **Spatial Reasoning and Multi-Sensor Fusion. Proceedings of the 1987 Workshop**. Los Altos, CA: Morgan Kaufmann, pp. 361-370.

34. Nirenburg, S. and V. Raskin 1987b. The analysis lexicon and the lexicon management system. *Computers and Translation* 2, pp. 177-188.

35. Nirenburg, S. and V. Raskin 1987c. The subworld concept lexicon and the knowledge base management system. *Computational Linguistics* 13:3-4, pp. 276-289.

36. Nirenburg, S. and V. Raskin 1990. **Sublanguages and Minitheories**. Dordrecht: Kluwer (forthcoming).

37. Pollard, C. and I. A. Sag 1987. **Information-Based Syntax and Semantics. Volume 1. Fundamentals**. Stanford, CA: Center for the Study of Language and Information.

38. Prior, A. N. and M. Prior 1955. Erotetic logic. *Philosophical Review* 64, pp. 43-59.

39. Quillian, M. R. 1968. Semantic memory. M. Minsky (ed.), **Semantic Information Processing**. Cambridge, MA: MIT Press, pp. 216-70.

40. Raskin, V. 1971. **K teorii jazykovyx podsistem** /Towards a Theory of Linguistic Subsystems/. Moscow: Moscow State University Press.

41. Raskin, V. 1974. On the feasibility of fully automatic high quality machine translation. *American Journal of Computational Linguistics* 1974:3, Microfiche 9.

42. Raskin, V. 1985a. Linguistic and encyclopedic knowledge in text processing. *Quaderni di Semantica* VI:1, pp. 92-101.

43. Raskin, V. 1985b. Once again on linguistic and encyclopedic knowledge. *Quaderni di Semantica* VI:2, pp. 377-383.

44. Raskin, V. 1987a. Linguistics and natural language processing. In: S. Nirenburg (ed.), **Machine Translation**. Cambridge: Cambridge University Press, pp. 42-58.

45. Raskin, V. 1987b. What is there in linguistic semantics for natural language processing? In: **Presentations from the 1987 Natural Language Planning Workshop: "Planning for Future Research: Directions for the Next Decade."** Blue Mountain Lake, N.Y.: Northeast Artificial Intelligence Consortium, WR-8703, pp. 78-96.

46. Rounds, W. and R. Kasper 1986. A complete logical calculus for record structures representing linguistic information. In: **Proceedings of the IEEE Symposium on Logic in Computer Science**, June 1986.

47. Schank, R. C. 1975. **Conceptual Information Processing**. Amsterdam: North Holland.

48. Scott, D. 1970. Advice on modal logic. In: K. Lambert (ed.), **Philosophical Problems in Logic: Recent Developments**. Dordrecht: D. Reidel, pp. 143-173.

49. Strawson, P. 1950. On referring. *Mind* 59, pp. 320-344.

50. Tarski, A. 1936. Der Wahrheitsbegriff in den formalisierten Sprachen. *Studia Philosophica* 1, pp. 261-405. Translated as: The concept of truth in formalized languages. In: A. Tarski, **Logic, Semantics, Metamathematics**. London-New York: Oxford University Press, 1956.

51. Wilson, D. 1975. **Presuppositions and Non-Truth-Conditional Semantics**. New York: Academic Press.

52. Zadeh, L. 1965. Fuzzy sets. *Information and Control* 8, pp. 338-353.

Appendix A.

A typical sentence from the computer sublanguage has been selected for the illustrative analysis of the ontologically- and semantic-network-based approach to NLPS. The sentence is:

- *Data such as the above, that are stored more or less permanently in a computer, we term a database.*

What follows is the result of the analysis of the example sentence.

```
(object
    (id object1)
    (is-token-of data) *
    (subworld computerworld) *
    (quantifier (type all) (scope (and clause1 clause2))))

(object
    (id object2)
    (is-token-of computer)
    (subworld computerworld)
    (quantifier any))

(object
    (id object3)
    (is-token-of database)
    (subworld computerworld))

(state
    (id state1)
    (is-token-of be-equivalent)
    (phase static)
    (patient1 object1)
    (patient2 (antecedent-of above))
    (time always)
    (space none)
    (subworld computerworld))

(state
    (id state2)
    (is-token-of in)
    (phase static)
    (patient1 object1)
    (patient2 object2)
    (time always)
    (space none)
    (subworld computerworld))

(state
    (id state3)
    (is-token-of  be-a-name-of)
    (phase static)
```

```
        (patient1 object3)
        (patient2 object1)
        (time always)
        (space none)
        (subworld computerworld))

  (clause
        (id clause1)
        (discourse-structure ( + expan clause1 clause3))
        (event state1)
        (focus state1.patient2)
        (modality conditional)
        (subworld computerworld)
        (time always)
        (space none))

  (clause
        (id clause2)
        (discourse-structure ( + expan clause2 clause3))
        (event state2)
        (focus time)
        (modality conditional)
        (subworld computerworld)
        (time always)
        (space (in object1 object2)))

  (clause
        (id clause3)
        (discourse-structure none)
        (event state3)
        (focus object3)
        (modality real)
        (subworld computerworld)
        (time always)
        (space none))

  (sentence
        (id sentence1)
        (main-clause clause3)
        (clauses clause1 clause2)
        (subworld computerworld)
        (modality real)
        (focus object3)
        (speech-act (type definition)
                (performative direct)
                (speaker author)
                (hearer reader)))
```

Obviously, this analysis must be based on an analysis lexicon. What follows is the entries for all the words of the example sentence in the English → concept dictionary of the computer sublanguage. These entries will indeed lead to the analysis results presented above.

Since the analysis lexicon is preceded and largely determined by the concept lexicon, we will first present a fragment of the corresponding concept lexicon containing the entries for the concept nodes used in the example sentence:

```
(data
  (isa information)
  (subworld computerworld officeworld world)
  (object-of computer-mental-action)
  (instrument-of mental-action)
  (belongs-to user)
  (consists-of file record byte)
  (part-of database))

(store
  (isa operate)
  (subworld computerworld)
  (consists-of (locate agent destination)
          (send agent object destination))
  (part-of computer-mental-action)
  (precondition (thereexists object destination)
          (controls agent object))
  (effect (in object destination))
  (tempor computer-mental-action)
  (agent user)
  (object data)
  (instrument operating-system DBMS)
  (destination computer-memory database))

(computer        ;the physical object computer
  (isa device)
  (subworld computerworld)
  (consists-of (box board cable peripherals)
          (in board box)
          (connect cable box peripheral))
  (belongs-to organization person)
  (object-of use)
  (size size-set)
  (shape shape-set)
  (color color-set)
  (mass integer))

(define
  (isa mental-action)
  (subworld computerworld scienceworld)
  (precondition (thereexists patient1)) ;patient1 = definiendum
  (effect (be-a-name-of patient2 patient1))
  (agent author)
  (patient1 mental-object)
  (patient2 mental-object)
  (source author))

(program
  (isa information)
  (subworld computerworld)
```

```
  (part-of system)
  (consists-of code)
  (object-of computer-mental-action)
  (instrument-of computer-mental-action))

(database
  (isa data)
  (subworld computerworld)
  (consists-of data)
  (belongs-to user)
  (object-of manage-database))

(to-be-a-subset-of
  (isa mental-state)
  (subworld computerworld world)
  (patient1 all)
  (patient2 all)
  (precondition  ;patient1 is a member or a subset of patient1;
              ;there is a certain defining property for all
              ;members of patient2 (cf. all people such as
              ;Peter) )

(author
  (isa person)
  (subworld computerworld scienceworld cultureworld world)
  (source text))
```

What follows now is a fragment of the English → concept dictionary for the example sentence. The marker # stands for an empty string, which in this case means that no concept has been found to correspond to the SL lexical unit in question. The lexical units in parentheses show that there are additional meanings (not given in the sample dictionary) for the lexical units involved.

DATA data

SUCH to-be-a-subset-of; the task of looking for fillers of patient1 and patient2 is triggered by the unfilled slots in the instantiated frame for this state

AS #; test whether SUCH precedes; if so, AS precedes patient1 of 'to-be-a-subset-of'

THE #; an NP follows; this NP is coreferential with an object already instantiated

[THE #; an NP follows; set the value of the slot 'quantifier' of this NP to 'every']

ABOVE #; if a noun, then look for the appropriate instance of NP to which ABOVE refers (deixis resolution)

[ABOVE #; if a preposition, insert the value (above actant1 actant2) in the instances of both actant1 and actant2]

THAT #; if a relative conjunction, then instantiate a clause and insert the proper NP into an appropriate actant slot of the clause event

[THAT]

BE #; if an auxiliary in passive then signal that the clause event is the state which is the effect of the IL correlate of the main verb

[BE]

STORE store

[STORE]

MORE OR LESS #; a value of quantifier2; makes the concept or property value it modifies fuzzy; belongs to the same class as VERY, ALMOST, APPROXIMATELY...

PERMANENTLY #; insert the value 'always' in the time property slot of the event which this word modifies

IN #; insert the meaning of the modified NP in the
     'space' of the clause event

[IN]

A #; an NP follows; it should be represented with a newly in- stantiated object frame, with 'any' as the value of the quantifier slot

COMPUTER program

[COMPUTER]

WE author

TERM define

DATABASE database

An Incremental Conceptual Clustering Algorithm that Reduces Input-Ordering Bias

Yoëlle S. Maarek

IBM Thomas J.Watson Research Center
Computer Science Department
Yorktown Heights, NY

1   Introduction

Cluster analysis has been of long-standing interest in statistics. It can be traced to the work of Adanson in 1757 [Adanson 1757] who used numerical clustering for classifying botanic species. Statisticians and more particularly taxonomists have widely developed the field since then. Cluster analysis offers now a large range of techniques for identifying underlying structures in large sets of objects.

Two major trends can be distinguished in cluster analysis, *numerical taxonomy* [Sokal 83], also termed numerical, statistical or regular clustering, and the more recent *conceptual clustering* [Michalski 80] which has been introduced as an extension to numerical taxonomy. The goal of both numerical and conceptual clustering is to determine a set of clusters, a *clustering*, over a given set of objects, such that inter-cluster similarity is low and intra-cluster similarity is high. The structure of the set of clusters as well as the internal structure of each cluster varies with the clustering technique which must be carefully chosen according to the context of application. In this work, we concentrate on conceptual clustering. We present an incremental conceptual clustering algorithm, GCC, that reduces the input-ordering bias which exists in most incremental clustering techniques.

The GCC algorithm has been originally developed for classification purposes in the context of GURU, a tool for building software library systems [Maarek 87], [Maarek 89], but can be seen independently as a general conceptual clustering algorithm.

The key characteristics of GCC algorithm are the following:

- It is a *hierarchical* conceptual clustering algorithm. It automatically constructs a hierarchy of concepts, where each concept is associated to a cluster of objects implementing that particular concept. The hierarchy thus produced is conceptually organized, *i.e.*, physical closeness of nodes reflects conceptual similarity.

- It is an *overlapping* technique. Clusters are not necessarily disjoint and may share components.

- It is an *incremental* technique with correction of the insertion-order bias. Clusters are dynamically created as new objects are added. The hierarchy is incrementally built and regularly rearranged to correct the bias.

These three features are all desirable for structuring a software library. First, a hierarchical technique allows to generate a hierarchy of concepts/clusters. Each cluster corresponds to a sub-library of software components that implement a specific concept. The fact that similar concepts are physically close in the library eases the browsing among conceptually similar sub-libraries. Second, an overlapping technique is desirable since the same component may implement different concepts and therefore should be allowed to belong to several sub-libraries. Third, an incremental technique allows continuous evolution of the library, which is necessary for large long-living libraries.

The application of GCC to the construction of software libraries is described in [Maarek 89]. This paper rather concentrates on a formal description of GCC as a conceptual clustering algorithm. We first define the basic terminology in conceptual clustering, briefly review some classical conceptual clustering techniques, and then present the GCC algorithm and an analysis of its time complexity.

2 Conceptual clustering

Originating from machine learning research, conceptual clustering has been introduced by Michalski [Michalski 80] and Michalski and Stepp [Michalski 83] as an extension to numerical clustering as well as a method of learning by observation.

The goal of a clustering method, whether conceptual or numerical, can be abstracted as the task of finding clusters over a set of objects such that the set of clusters identified is (possibly locally) optimal according to a quality measure. In addition, conceptual clustering not only identifies a cluster as a group of objects, but also determines its implicit conceptual structure. A cluster is then defined both extensively and intensively, that is, by the enumeration of its elements as well as by a set of rules or properties defining membership. Another difference between numerical and conceptual clustering concerns the type of arguments of the quality measure. In numerical clustering, the quality measure is a numerical function of the objects on which the clustering is performed, whereas, in conceptual clustering, the quality measure depends also on other parameters. Fisher in [Fisher 87] defines the quality function as depending also on the concepts which may be used for describing the clusters, and Stepp in [Stepp 87] is more general and defines it as depending on the environment. The key feature in both definitions is that the quality function in conceptual clustering is not based exclusively on quantitative criteria on clusters but also on qualitative criteria on the nature of the clusters/concepts identified. Before presenting our algorithm, let us first precise the terminology on the notions of objects and concepts.

2.1 Objects and concepts

Conceptual clustering methods allow objects to be described in terms of *nominal* or *categorical* variables, *i.e.*, discrete-value variables. Each variable takes values on a finite set of values, called the *domain* of the considered variable. Examples of pairs *(variable,domain)* are (color,{yellow, blue, red}) or (size,{small, medium, large}). To facilitate the process of generating concepts from such sets of objects, concepts are also represented by a set of (variable,value-set) pairs. An object can be seen as a concept for which the value set is a singleton.[1] Then, the relations between concepts and objects are expressed in terms of *generalization* as follows:

Definition 1 *Let* $K = \{(v_1, V_1), (v_2, V_2), \ldots, (v_n, V_n)\}$ *where* v_i *is a variable and* V_i *its value set, for* $i = 1, \ldots, n$. *Let* $O = \{o_1, o_2, \ldots, o_m\}$ *be a set of objects, K is a* **generalization** *of O if and only if,*

$$\forall i = 1, \ldots, n \quad \forall j = 1, \ldots, m \quad v_i(o_j) \in V_i \tag{1}$$

If a concept K is a generalization of a singleton object set $\{o\}$, *i.e.*, if $v_i(o) \in V_i$, for all $i = 1, \ldots, n$, then the object o is called a *member* of the concept K. In the above definition, it is implicitly assumed that concepts and variables are described by the same variables.

Concepts can then be partially ordered by the relation *more general than* as follows:

Definition 2 *Let D_i be the domain of the variable v_i, for $i = 1, \ldots, n$. Let K and K' be two concepts such that: $K = \{(v_1, V_1), (v_2, V_2), \ldots, (v_n, V_n)\}$, and $K' = \{(v_1', V_1'), (v_2', V_2'), \ldots, (v_n', V_n')\}$.*
K is said to be **more general than** *K' if and only if,*

$$\forall i = 1, n \quad V_i' \neq D_i \Rightarrow V_i' \subset V_i \tag{2}$$

---

[1] Any object is a concept, but the converse is not necessarily true.

*It can also be said that K' is **less general** than K.*

In this relation, the least general concepts are said to be of *maximal specificity*.

Definition 3 *A concept K is a maximally-specific concept of an object set O, if K is a generalization of O and if there does not exist any other generalization of O which is less general than K.*

The principles and terminology presented above are derived from [Fisher 86][2].

2.2 Previous conceptual clustering techniques

Two classes of techniques are distinguished according to the structure of the clustering produced, hierarchical techniques and flat techniques.

The most representative flat clustering system is the *Partitioning Module* of CLUSTER/2 due to Michalski and Stepp [Michalski 83]. The Partitioning Module attempts to build an optimal k-partition, where k is a user-given parameter, over a set of objects described in terms of categorical variables as well as integers or structured variables. The Partitioning Module algorithm is based on a flat numerical clustering algorithm: the Dynamic Cluster method [Diday 73], [Diday 82].

Hierarchical conceptual clustering techniques are more numerous than flat techniques. Most of them are divisive rather than agglomerative, that is, they construct a classification tree top-down over a set of objects. Thus, the *Hierarchy-building Module* of CLUSTER/2 constructs such a tree level by level. Each level is generated by calling the Partition Module on the nodes of the previous level. Siblings in the tree are distinguished by a conjunction of values across several variables. Other algorithms such as RUMMAGE [Fisher 84] and DISCON [Langley 84] construct a different kind of tree where the edges are labeled by a single variable value.

A sub-class of hierarchical algorithms gathers incremental algorithms, *e.g.*, UNIMEM [Lebowitz 86] and COBWEB [Fisher 87]. Incremental techniques are highly desirable for applications in which the context constantly evolves. However, incremental algorithms such as UNIMEM are very sensitive to the ordering of initial input. Like COBWEB, GCC is a hierarchical clustering algorithm derived from UNIMEM that proposes to reduce the bias introduced by input ordering. However, unlike COBWEB, GCC is an overlapping technique and therefore the ordering bias is of a different nature. COBWEB deals with the ordering bias at every insertion of a new object in the hierarchy (via the *merging* and *splitting* operators). This is not

---

[2][Fisher 86] should be consulted for a more detailed introduction to conceptual clustering.

feasible in GCC context due to computational complexity problems. Indeed, GCC being an overlapping technique, the insertion process involves many more nodes, and it would be computationally expensive to try to correct the bias at every insertion. As an alternative, the whole hierarchy is regularly upgraded for reducing the input-ordering bias. In the following, we present both the insertion and upgrading stages in detail as well as a formal analysis of their time complexity.

3 The GCC algorithm

The basic mechanism of the algorithm is the following. New objects are added one at a time to a (originally empty) hierarchy *via* the **GCC** procedure. The **GCC** procedure takes the following two input parameters: the new object described by a set of attributes, and the whole hierarchy. Starting with the most general node, *i.e.*, the root of the hierarchy that corresponds to the whole universe of concepts, **GCC** performs a search to find the concepts that are of maximal specificity for the input object. The new object is then added to these most specific nodes and becomes a member of the associated sub-clusters. Then, the object is compared to other members of these sub-clusters in order to determine if new clusters can be created. When instances of the considered node are similar enough, an abstraction is made in order to identify a new concept, and a new sub-cluster is created.

3.1 The GCC procedure

Let H be the current hierarchy, each node of H corresponds to a distinct concept and is defined by a set of attributes. To each node n, is associated a cluster $cl(n)$ that gathers the objects from which the concept has been extracted through abstraction.

The hierarchy H is created incrementally by successive calls to the procedure **GCC**. The procedure $\mathbf{GCC}(o, H)$ inserts the object o into the hierarchy H. The object o is described by a set of categorical variables $\{(v_1, V_1), \ldots, (v_p, V_p)\}$ where V_i is the value-set of the variable v_i. The V_is are not necessarily finite, but their number, *i.e.*, the number of attributes, is bounded by a constant p.

First, the function **find-best-concepts** is called on the set of attributes $v_1(o)$, $v_2(o)$, $\ldots, v_p(o)$ that describe o. Note that in case the object is described by fewer attributes than p, some of the attributes might be not instantiated. The function returns the concepts that are the most specific to o. Then, for every returned concept, the procedure **abstract** is called. The latter makes an abstraction for creating a new concept when possible. Otherwise, the object o is simply added to the associated cluster.

The procedure **GCC** is at the top-level and works as follows.

GCC(o, H)

- **Let** $A_o = \{a_1, \ldots, a_p\}$ be the set of attributes of o.

- $N \leftarrow$ **find-best-concepts**(A_o, r_H), where r_H is the root of H.
  Return to N the set of nodes in the hierarchy H whose concepts are the maximally specific of o.

- $\forall \nu \in N$, **abstract**(o, ν)
  if possible, make an abstraction, (i.e., create a new cluster), otherwise add the object o to the cluster associated to ν.

The function **find-best-concepts** takes two arguments, a list of attributes A and a node describing recursively a hierarchy, ν. It looks recursively in the subtree under ν, for the concepts of maximal specificity for the set of attributes A and returns those nodes. In fact, while looking for maximally specific nodes, "partial" membership of objects is considered rather than membership criterion as defined in Definition 1.

Partial membership is defined as follows. Given a certain compatibility threshold τ, where $\tau \geq 1$, we say that an object o defined by list of attributes A is a *partial* member of a concept C if and only if:

$$\text{card}(\{i \in \{1, \ldots, p\} \mid v_i(o) \in A \text{ and } v_i(o) = v_i(C)\}) \geq \tau \tag{3}$$

where τ is a given threshold of compatibility between an object and a concept. We also say that a concept C *explains* an attribute $a_i = v_i(o)$ if and only if:

$$v_i(C) = a_i \tag{4}$$

Thus, an object is a partial member of a concept if this concept explains a sufficient number of the attributes describing the object.

The attributes of the instance to process are considered to be *unexplained attributes* at the beginning of the search since the object they describe is not a member[3] of any concept. As the hierarchy is searched down, these attributes are removed from the unexplained list. The search performed by **find-best-concept** returns the most specific nodes, such as defined in Definition 3, but considering

---

[3]In the rest of this paper, we will omit the "partial" qualification for members and membership when there is no ambiguity.

"partial" membership, and by immediate extrapolation "partial" generalization, instead of the membership and generalization defined in Definition 1. The returned concepts are those for which the unexplained list is minimal. Once they are found, the instance is stored in all the corresponding sub-libraries.

The function **find-best-concepts** works as follows:

---

find-best-concepts(A, ν)

- **Let** C be the concept associated to ν, and
  Let $\{v_1(C), \ldots, v_p(C)\}$ be the attributes defining ν.

- **If** ν explains the list of attributes A, *i.e.*, if

$$\mathrm{card}(\{i \in \{1, \ldots, p\} \mid v_i(o) \in A \text{ and } v_i(o) = v_i(C)\}) \geq \tau \qquad (5)$$

  then

    - **Let** UA be $A - \{v_i(C)\}_i$, *i.e.*, the set of attributes unexplained by C.
    - **Let** S be the set of sub-nodes of ν,
      $\forall s \in S,\ N(s) \leftarrow$ **find-best-concepts**(UA, s)
    - **If** $\bigcup_{s \in S} N(s) = \emptyset$
        * **then return** ν
        * **else return** $\bigcup_{s \in S} N(s)$

- **Else return** $\emptyset$.

Let us notice that the function **find-best-concepts** is recursively called with the list of unexplained attributes, which contains at least τ attributes less than the list of attributes A. At least τ attributes are dropped at each recursion, and the number of attributes with which **find-best-concepts** is originally called is finite, therefore the number of recursions is also finite. More precisely, in the worst case, if $\tau = 1$, the number of recursions is bounded by the maximal number of attributes, *i.e.*, p.

Once the most specific concepts/clusters in the hierarchy have been identified, the new object is compared to the other members of these clusters in order to determine if new clusters can be created. This is the case when some of the objects of the considered cluster have enough attributes in common to constitute a separate cluster. The criterion for deciding the minimum allowable number of attributes in common, among the attributes which are not already explained by the considered concept, is fixed by a parameter α, the abstraction threshold. An abstraction is then made that identifies a new concept/cluster as a new descendant of the considered node. Like the compatibility threshold, the abstraction threshold can be either user-given or defined according to the indexing scheme that identify the list of attributes.

The procedure **abstract** works as follows:

---

abstract(o, ν)

- **Let** $cl(\nu) = \{o_1, o_2, \ldots, o_p\}$ be the cluster of objects associated to ν, and C the concept associated to ν.

- **Let** UA_{o_i} be be the set of attributes of o_i which are not explained by the concept C.

- **Let** UA_o be the set of attributes of o which are not explained by the concept C.

- **If** $\forall o_i$, $card(UA_o \cap UA_{o_i}) < \alpha$
  α *is the abstraction threshold.*
  then add o to $cl(\nu)$
  no possible new abstraction.
  else
  $\forall o_i$ such that $card(UA_o \cap UA_{o_i}) \geq \alpha$

  - **Create** μ a new descendant of ν.
  - **Associate** to μ the cluster $\{o_i, o\}$.
  - **Associate** to μ the concept defined by the set of attributes $UA_o \cap UA_{o_i}$.

3.2   The time complexity of GCC

In this section, we evaluate the worst case time complexity of the insertion of a new object, o, into a GURU hierarchy already containing n objects. The expected time complexity should be much smaller but it cannot be computed without more information on the input distribution.

Let us first define our notation.

- Let p be maximum number[4] of attributes allowed to describe an object or a concept.

- Let $\nu(n)$ be the number of nodes in the hierarchy.

- Let $\mu(n)$ the maximum number of objects that have been stored in a node. Both $\nu(n)$ and $\mu(n)$ are functions of n as demonstrated later.

As the function **GCC** calls two sub-functions, **find-best-concepts** and **abstract**, we first evaluate the time complexity of the two sub-functions.

Proposition 1 *The worst case time complexity of the operation* **find-best-concepts** *is $O(\nu(n) \times p^2)$.*

Proof: When calling **find-best-concepts** with the object o, in the worst case, o is compared to *each* node of the hierarchy. Each comparison takes at most p^2 time since the maximum number of attributes allowed is p and the attributes are compared pairwise. Therefore, the execution of **find-best-concepts** takes at most $\nu(n) \times p^2$. $\square$

Proposition 2 *The worst case time complexity of* **abstract** *is $O(\mu(n) \times p^2)$.*

Proof: There are at most $\mu(n)$ objects in the node for which **abstract** is called. Each of these objects is compared with o, in at most p^2 time. Therefore, the execution of **abstract** takes at most $\mu(n) \times p^2$. $\square$

Proposition 3 *The worst case time complexity of* **GCC** *is $O(\nu(n) \times \mu(n))$.*

Proof: For each node selected by **find-best-concepts**, the function **abstract** is called. In the worst case, all the nodes of the hierarchy, *i.e.*, $\nu(n)$ nodes, are selected. Therefore, $\nu(n)$ abstractions are made. These take $\nu(n) \times \mu(n) \times p^2$ time, according to Proposition 2. We know from Proposition 1 that one call to **find-best-concepts** requires $O(\nu(n) \times p^2)$ time. Therefore, we deduce that **GCC** is done in $O(\nu(n) \times \mu(n) \times p^2)$ time, which is equivalent to $O(\nu(n) \times \mu(n))$. $\square$

Let us now evaluate an upper bound of $\mu(n)$ and $\nu(n)$ as functions of n. The evaluation of an upper bound for $\mu(n)$ is trivial. Given a hierarchy in which n objects have been stored, the maximum number of objects stored in any node, $\mu(n)$, is at most equal to n. In other words, $O(\mu(n)) = O(n)$. Thus, we now determine an upper bound of $\nu(n)$.

---

[4]This parameter depends on the indexing scheme, classically it must be fixed so as no two components have the same set of attributes. In our implementation of GURU, it is set to 10.

Proposition 4 *The total number of nodes, $\nu(n)$, in a hierarchy into which n objects have already been inserted is bounded by $O(n^p)$.*

Lemma 1 *The depth of a* GURU *hierarchy into which n objects have been inserted is at most equal to p.*

Proof: Each time the object to be inserted compares successfully with a node, a certain number of the object's attributes are explained by the node attributes. These explained attributes are removed from the list of unexplained attributes, and the object is transferred to the descendants of the considered node. Each time an object goes down a level, at least one attribute is removed from this list. Consequently, an object can go down at most p levels until its unexplained list becomes empty, therefore the depth of the tree is at most p. $\square$

Lemma 2 *The branching factor in a* GURU *hierarchy, into which n objects have been inserted, is bounded by n.*

Proof: We assume that n objects have already been inserted into the hierarchy. For any node in the hierarchy, we note b_n, its number of descendants, and c_n, the number of objects it contains. Let us demonstrate by induction that,

$$\text{for } n \geq 1, \text{ if the hierarchy contains } n \text{ objects, then } b_n + c_n \leq n. \qquad (6)$$

First, consider the case in which $n = 1$. When only one object has been inserted into the hierarchy, this object is necessarily stored into the root cluster which has no descendant. Therefore, $b_1 = 0$ and $c_1 = 1$, and (6) is satisfied for $n = 1$. Assuming that the inequality (6) is satisfied for $n = i$, we want to demonstrate that it is also true for $n = i + 1$. Given a hierarchy containing i objects, a new object is inserted and transferred to the considered node which contains already c_i objects and has b_i descendants. Then two cases are possible. Either the new objects is stored into the node and no new abstractions are made, or new sub-concepts are formed. In the first case, the number of objects in the node becomes $c_{i+1} = c_i + 1$ and $b_{i+1} = b_i$. Therefore, by the inductive hypothesis, we obtain $b_{i+1} + c_{i+1} = b_i + c_i + 1 \leq i + 1$.

In the second case, the new objects can form new concepts with k different objects of the node, where $k < c_i$. Then, k new descendants are formed, and $b_{i+1} = b_i + k$. At the same time, when an object belonging to the node forms a new cluster with the new object, it is removed from this node in order to be put in the new node. Therefore, the k objects that lead to the creation of new clusters have been removed from the node, and we have $c_{i+1} = c_i - k$. Then, we have $b_{i+1} + c_{i+1} = (b_i + k) + (c_i - k) = b_i + c_i$. By using the inductive hypothesis, we obtain $b_{i+1} + c_{i+1} \leq i < i + 1$. Therefore, (6) is satisfied for $i + 1$.

From this inductive proof, we deduce that the inequality (6) is satisfied for all $n \geq 1$. Therefore, as $c_n \geq 0$ for $n \geq 1$, we obtain, $b_n \leq n$, for $n \geq 1$. We thus know that any node in the hierarchy has at most n descendants. Therefore the branching factor of the hierarchy is bounded by n. $\square$

From Lemma 1 and Lemma 2, we deduce Proposition 4, which gives an upper bound of $\nu(n)$. Given the upper bounds of $\mu(n)$ and $\nu(n)$ evaluated above and Proposition 3, we deduce that the time complexity of **GCC** is $O(n^p)$, where n is the number of objects already stored in the hierarchy and p the maximum number of attributes allowed per object.

3.3   Upgrading the hierarchy

Most incremental learning techniques are insertion-order dependent. This is also the case for the **abstract** procedure of GCC, where the generated hierarchy takes a different form according to the order in which the objects have been inserted. This is not always desirable. A particular sequence of object insertion may lead to the identification of new concepts, whereas some other may not, only because of the order of insertion. As a very simple example, let us assume that the objects considered are boxes described by a set of attributes such as *color, size, weight,* etc. If only red boxes of different size, weight, etc. have been inserted from the beginning of the hierarchy construction, there are very strong probabilities that the distinction on the concepts is made on the size of boxes. For instance, we might have identified a concept **big red** (for big red boxes) and a concept **small red** (for small red boxes). If then blue boxes are to be processed, they will lead to the creation of sibling of **big red** and **small red**, the new sibling concepts might be for example **big blue** (for big blue boxes) and **small blue** (for small blue boxes). See Figure 1. However, it will be impossible to identify the concept **blue** box, as opposed to **red** box, simply because this new information came too late. It would not have been the case if, for instance, a blue box would have been processed right after the first red box.

To reduce this order dependency, we regularly upgrade the hierarchy by reprocessing sibling concepts – still using the same conceptual clustering algorithm –in order to detect conceptual relationships between the concepts themselves. More precisely, the **GCC** procedure is called taking as arguments concepts rather than objects.

The basic principle of the upgrading method is the following. For each node in the hierarchy from the root to the leaves, not inclusive, the **upgrade** procedure is called recursively. The direct descendants of the processed node are then considered as objects whose attributes are the concept attributes. These objects are then processed by **GCC** and a small hierarchy is built. The resulting hierarchy is a

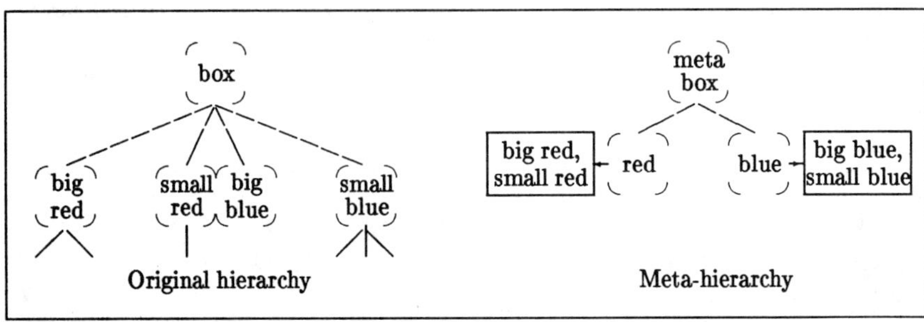

Figure 1: Examples of original and meta hierarchies

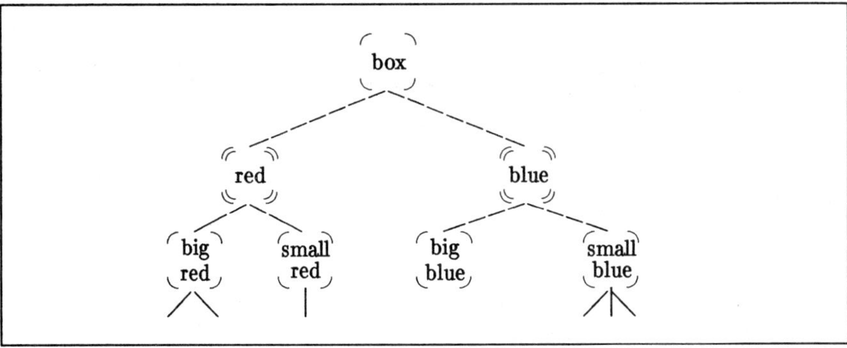

Figure 2: Example of derived upgraded hierarchy

meta-hierarchy organizing concepts among themselves. Thus, in the previously cited example, a small meta-hierarchy is built that contains two nodes: the meta-concept **red** whose associated cluster contains **big red** and **small red**, and the meta-concept **blue** which contains **big blue** and **small blue**. See Figure 1. The existence of meta-concepts is then reflected into the original hierarchy by inserting them as intermediate super-concepts with no associated members. Thus in Figure 2, the upgraded hierarchy contains two new concepts: **red** and **blue**. They may receive members later, as new components are inserted. The members of the original concepts are still attached to the same concepts.

The **upgrade** procedure is presented more precisely below. For the purposes of this presentation, hierarchies are represented by a recursive data structure, *node*, defined as follows.

$$node \begin{bmatrix} node.attributes & = & \text{list of attributes} \\ node.cluster & = & \text{list of objects} \\ node.descendants & = & \text{list of elements of type } node \end{bmatrix}$$

The primary elements of type *node* are elements with an empty *descendants* field. The procedure **upgrade** is a recursive procedure which takes as argument an element of type *node*. In order to upgrade a given hierarchy, **upgrade** is called on its root which defines the whole hierarchy recursively.

upgrade(r)

1. **If** $r.descendants = \emptyset$, *i.e.*, if r is a leaf, **then STOP**.

2. **Set** *list-of-descendants* $\leftarrow$ *r.descendants*
   Store the list of descendants before modifying them.

3. **Initialize** M as an empty *node*, *i.e.*, a node satisfying
   - $M.attributes \leftarrow \emptyset$
   - $M.descendants \leftarrow \emptyset$
   - $M.cluster \leftarrow \emptyset$

   M *will be holding the meta-hierarchy for* r.

4. **For** each $s \in$ *list-of-descendants* **do**
   $$GCC(s, M)$$
   Each descendant s of r is then considered as an object, rather than a node, whose associated list of attributes is s.attributes. The successive insertions create a hierarchy storing the descendants of r.

5. **Explore** recursively M a in depth-first-search,
   for each node m encountered **do**

   - $m.descendants \leftarrow m.descendants \cup m.cluster$
     Associate to each element m of the meta-hierarchy M, the members of its associated cluster as direct descendants.

   - $m.cluster \leftarrow \emptyset$

6. **Set**

   - $M.descendants \leftarrow M.descendants \cup M.cluster$

   - $M.cluster \leftarrow r.cluster$

   - $r \leftarrow M$

   As a side-effect, because of the recursive structure of node, the meta-hierarchy is merged into the original one originating in r.

7. **For** each $s \in$ *list-of-descendants* **do**
   $$\textbf{upgrade}(s_i)$$
   Recursive call of **upgrade** *on the original descendants of* r.

3.4   The time complexity of upgrade

We evaluate here the worst case time complexity of **upgrade** on a hierarchy holding n objects.

The first three steps can obviously be performed in constant time. The fourth step consists of inserting the descendants of r into an originally empty hierarchy. According to Lemma 2, we know that the branching factor of a hierarchy storing n elements is at most n. Therefore, at most n **GCC** operations are performed. As we know that an **GCC** in a hierarchy holding i elements is done in at most $O(i^p)$ time, and since $O(\sum_{i=0}^{n-1} i^p) = O(n^p)$, all the **GCC** operations, and therefore the whole fourth step, are done in $O(n^p)$ time.

The fifth step of the **upgrade** procedure consists of exploring the hierarchy built in Step 4 in a depth first search and performing two operations on each node encountered. Both of these operations can be done in constant time. Since the hierarchy built in Step 4 holds at most n objects, we know that it counts at most $O(n^p)$ nodes (See Proposition 4). Therefore, Step 5 requires $O(n^p)$ time. Moreover, Step 6 is performed in constant time. From the above paragraphs, we deduce that the six first steps of the **upgrade** procedure are done in $O(n^p)$ time.

The six first steps of **upgrade** are performed on all the nodes of the original hierarchy, originating in r, through the recursive call of **upgrade** in Step 6. Since we know by Proposition 4 that the original hierarchy counts at most $O(n^p)$ nodes, the whole recursive **upgrade** operation takes at most $O(n^{2p})$ time.

4   Conclusion

Cluster analysis offers a wide range of techniques that allow recovering underlying structures in a set of objects. In particular, conceptual clustering allows identifying conceptual structures without the user's intervention. In this paper, we have presented a hierarchical conceptual clustering algorithm, GCC, that assembles incrementally objects into a hierarchy of concepts. GCC improves the incremental conceptual clustering algorithm from which it is derived by regularly upgrading the hierarchy of clusters it produces so as to reduce the insertion-order dependency. In contrast to most previous work in conceptual clustering, a formal computational complexity analysis of both the basic GCC algorithm and the upgrading algorithm is also presented.

The GCC technique has been implemented in the framework of GURU [Maarek 87], [Maarek 89]. GURU is a tool for automatically generating large software libraries organized conceptually. It has been used for building such a library from the set of UNIX[1] tools that form the first section of the UNIX manual. Part of GURU is currently being integrated to RPDE [Harrison 86], a programming and design development environment developed at the IBM T.J. Watson Research Center.

Acknowledgements

Gail Kaiser first suggested to apply conceptual clustering to software classification. Marty Golumbic, Dan Berry, William Harrison and Peter Sweeney read earlier versions of this paper and made useful criticisms and suggestions.

References

[Adanson 1757] M. Adanson, *Histoire Naturelle du Sénégal. Coquillages. Avec la relation abrégée d'un voyage fait en ce pays, pendant les années 1749,50,51,52 et 53*. Bauche, Paris, France, 1757.

[Diday 73] E. Diday, *The Dynamic Clusters Method and Sequentialization in Non Hierarchical Clustering*. Research Report IRIA, Rocquencourt, France, August 1973.

[Diday 82] E. Diday, J. Lemaire, J. Pouget and F.Testu, *Eléments d'Analyse des Données*. Dunod, Paris 1982.

[Fisher 84] D. Fisher, *A Hierarchical Conceptual Clustering Algorithm*. Technical Report, Department of Information and Computer Science, University of California, Irvine, 1984.

[Fisher 85] D. Fisher and P. Langley, *Approaches to Conceptual Clustering*. In Proceedings of IJCAI'85, pp. 691-697, Los Angeles, CA, August 1985.

[Fisher 86] D. Fisher and P. Langley, *Methods of Conceptual Clustering and their Relation to Numerical Taxonomy*. In Artificial Intelligence and Statistics, 1986.

[Fisher 87] D.H. Fisher, *Knowledge Acquisition via Incremental Conceptual Clustering*. In Machine Learning 2:139-172, Kluwer Academic Publishers, Boston, 1987.

[Harrison 86] W. Harrison, *A Program Development Environment for Programming by Refinement and Reuse*. In the Proceedings of the 19th Annual Hawaii International Conference on System Sciences, pp 459-469, CS Press, Los Alamitos, CA, 1986.

---

[1] UNIX is a trademark of the AT&T Bell Laboratories.

[Langley 84] P. Langley and S. Sage, *Conceptual Clustering as Discrimination Learning*. In Proceedings of the Fifth Biennal Conference of the Canadian Society for Computational Studies of Intelligence, 1984.

[Lebowitz 86] M. Lebowitz, *Concept Learning in a Rich Input Domain: Generalization-Based Memory*. In R.S. Michalski, J.G. Carbonell and T. M. Mitchell, Machine Learning: An Artificial Intelligence Approach, Volume II, pp. 193-214, Morgan Kaufman, Los Altos, CA, 1986.

[Maarek 87] Y.S. Maarek and G.E. Kaiser, *On the Use of Conceptual Clustering for Classifying Reusable Ada Code*. Ada Letters, Using Ada: ACM SIGAda International Conference, ACM Press, pp 208-215, Boston, MA, December 1987.

[Maarek 89] Y.S. Maarek, D.M. Berry and G.E. Kaiser, *Automatically generating software libraries without pre-encoded knowledge*, Research Report RC 14990, IBM Research Division, August 1989. Submitted for publication.

[Michalski 80] R.S. Michalski, *Knowledge Acquisition through Conceptual Clustering: A Theoretical Framework and Algorithm for Partitioning Data into Conjunctive Concepts*. In International Journal of Policy Analysis and Information Systems, 4:3, pp. 219-244, 1980.

[Michalski 83] R. Michalski and R. Stepp, *Automated Constructions of Classifications: Conceptual Clustering versus Numerical taxonomy*. In IEEE Transactions on Pattern Analysis and Machine Intelligence 5:4, pp 396-409, 1983.

[Sokal 83] R.R. Sokal and P.H. Sneath, *Principles of Numerical Taxonomy*. W. H. Freeman, San Francisco, CA, 1973.

[Stepp 87] R.E. Stepp, *Concepts in Conceptual Clustering*. In Proceedings of IJCAI'87, pp 211-213, Milan, Italy, August 1987.

Anticipating a Listener's Response in Text Planning

Ingrid Zukerman

Department of Computer Science
Monash University
Clayton, Victoria, Australia

1. Introduction

In the process of generating text, competent speakers/writers take into consideration the effect their utterances are likely to have on listeners/readers[†]. In other words, speakers try to generate utterances which are best suited to attain their communicative goals with respect to a particular audience [Hovy 1987].

In the traditional approach to text planning, text is generated to directly reflect a speaker's communicative intent, under the implicit assumption that a listener will immediately acquire the presented information [Appelt 1982, Kukich 1983, McKeown 1985, Hovy 1988, Paris 1988]. In particular, several of these researchers have adopted the hierarchical planning paradigm [Sacerdoti 1977], where rhetorical structures are proposed to satisfy preconditions in a hierarchy of communicative goals. In addition, Mann and Thompson [1987] provide a descriptive account of rhetorical structures, and McKeown [1985] offers a schema-based approach for the generation of rhetorical predicates. Finally, Paris [1988] presents a mechanism for generating explanations, where the viewpoint of an explanation is influenced by a user's level of expertise, and Moore and Swartout [1989] change the content of an explanation based on the user, in order to produce a suitable context for follow-up questions.

In this paper, we follow the hierarchical planning paradigm for the generation of *Rhetorical Devices (RDs)* to satisfy a communicative goal. However, we depart from the traditional text planning approach, by presenting a view of text planning based on the interaction between a listener's conjectured beliefs and a communicative goal. That is, given a communicative goal to transfer an *Intended Message (IM)* to a particular listener, our mechanism generates rhetorical devices to overcome likely impairments to the fulfillment of this goal. These impairments are caused by some discrepancy between the intended message and a listener's beliefs. In this paper, we confine our discussion to one type of communicative goal, namely *KNOW*, whereby the speaker wants the listener to fully comprehend and believe what is being said, as opposed to merely *being aware of* or *knowing about* the concepts in question. The fulfillment of this goal is essential in educational settings.

[†] The terms speaker/writer and listener/reader are used interchangeably in this paper.

Revision	1 2	We have seen in Chapter 1 that in arithmetic, brackets must always be calculated first.	
	3 4 5 6	E.g., $2 \times (5 + 3) / 4$ $\quad 2 \times 8 / 4$ (brackets) $\quad 16 / 4$ (multiplication) $\quad 4$ (division)	*(Procedure Desc. and Inst.)* *(Object Inst.)*
Contradiction	7	However, in algebra, brackets cannot always be simplified.	*(Causality)*
	8	E.g., in $2(x+y)$, $x+y$ cannot be simplified	*(Procedure Inst.)* *(Object Inst.)*
Intended *Message*	9	but can anything be done with an expression such as this?	*(Implicit Goal)*
	10 11	Consider, if we have 2 bags each containing 3 apples and 4 bananas, how many apples and bananas do we have? [DIAGRAM]	
	12 13	$2 \times (3 \text{ apples} + 4 \text{ bananas}) = 2 \times 3 \text{ apples} + 2 \times 4 \text{ bananas}$ $\qquad\qquad\qquad = 6 \text{ apples} + 8 \text{ bananas}$	*(Correctness)* *(Simile)*
	14 15 16	Using pronumerals $2 \times (3a + 4b) = 2 \times 3a + 2 \times 4b$ $\qquad\qquad = 6a + 8b$	
	17 18	This is called multiplying out or expanding brackets using the distributive law.	*(Identification)*
	19 20	The distributive law states that *each* term in the brackets is to be multiplied by the term outside the brackets.	*(Identification and Procedure Desc.)*
	21	E.g., $4(a + 3) = 4 \times a + 4 \times 3 = 4a + 12$	*(Procedure Inst.)* *(Object Inst.)*

Fig. 1: Distributive Law Sample Text

This approach affects the text planning process in two ways: firstly, it determines the choice of *Supportive RDs*, such as *Descriptions*, *Instantiations* and *Similes*, which are necessary to directly satisfy a communicative goal; and, secondly, it supports the generation of *Peripheral RDs*, such as *Contradictions* and *Revisions*, pertaining to other beliefs which may be affected by an IM. For instance, in the sample text in Figure 1 (from [Lynch, Parr and Keating 1979]), the communicative goal is *KNOW* with respect to the IM [Distributive-Law apply-to Algebraic-Terms has-goal Bracket-Elimination]. In this text, the authors have generated a Simile between distributive law and a "real life" situation (lines 10-16), and a Description (lines 19-20) and an Instantiation (line 21) of distributive law, to cater for an "average" student who has no previous knowledge of this procedure. In addition, prior to discussing distributive law, the authors present a Revision of the bracket simplification procedure (lines 1-6) and a Contradiction to the applicability of this procedure to Algebraic Terms (lines 7-8).

We postulate that these rhetorical devices are generated in order to prevent possible comprehension problems which may be triggered by the discourse. Similarly, given a communicative goal with respect to an IM, our mechanism anticipates the effect of this IM on a model of a listener's beliefs, and proposes rhetorical devices to preclude possible adverse effects. We represent a listener's beliefs by means of a network, and characterize in terms of this network several types of impairments which bring about undesirable effects commonly encountered in a knowledge acquisition setting[†]. Examples of these effects are: Confusion, Loss of Interest and Misunderstanding. Their detection prompts the generation of remedial rhetorical devices. At present, we are concerned with avoiding undesirable effects rather than with fostering desirable ones, because the absence of undesirable effects is a necessary condition for knowledge acquisition.

In the following section, we discuss a model of a student's beliefs capable of predicting inferences commonly drawn in a learning environment. We then describe our mechanism for the generation of rhetorical devices, discussing possible impairments to the knowledge acquisition process and rhetorical devices generated for their invalidation.

2. Model of a Student's Knowledge

In order to address beliefs presumably entertained by a particular student, we maintain an epistemological model which represents a student's beliefs as a function of the presented material [Zukerman and Cheong 1988], as opposed to traditional models which represent a student's knowledge in terms of the material known by the teacher [Goldstein 1982, Burton and Brown 1982]. Such a function must portray both direct and indirect inferences drawn from presented messages. The latter are generated by means of *Common-sense Inference Rules* (see Section 2.2).

2.1 The Network Model

We represent a student's beliefs by means of a network whose nodes contain individual information items and whose links contain the relationships between the nodes (see Figure 2). The information in the network is represented at a level of detail which is consistent with the level of expertise required to learn the subject at hand, e.g., for a high-school student learning algebra, well-known concepts, such as numerical addition and subtraction, are primitive, whereas relatively new or complex concepts, such as bracket simplification, are represented in terms of more primitive concepts.

The links in the Student Network are labeled according to the manner in which they were acquired, i.e., they can either be Inferred, Told or previously Known, where Inferred links are generated by means of generally applicable Common-sense Inference

---

[†] The term *knowledge acquisition setting* is used liberally in this paper to describe a situation in which transfer of knowledge from one agent to another takes place.

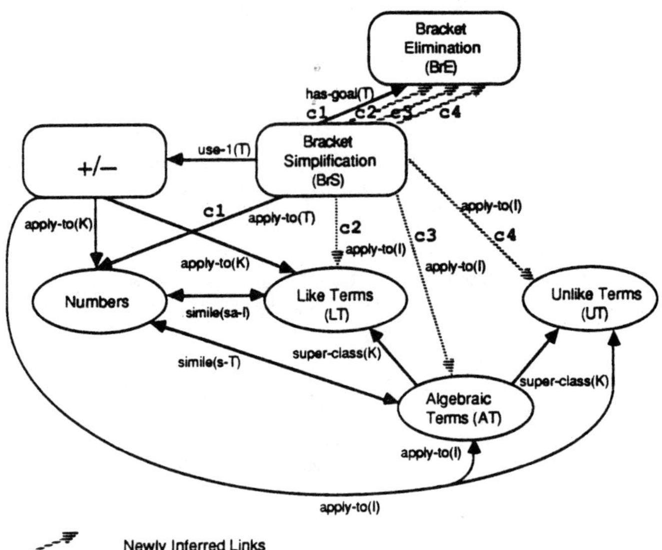

Fig. 2: Network Model of a Student's Beliefs in High-School Algebra[†]

Rules. A simile link is also labeled according to the type of the similarity, namely, *structural simile* between two objects (**s**), or *simile through the applicability of several operators* to two objects (**a**). In addition, each link is accompanied by a *Measure of Belief (MB)* between -1 and 1, akin to Certainty Factors [Buchanan and Shortliffe 1985]. A Measure of Belief with a value close to 0 represents mere awareness of the existence of a link, whereas a Measure of Belief with an absolute value close to 1 reflects a strong belief (+1) or disbelief (-1) and is typically attached to a link supported by extensive information. Notice, however, that this information is not necessarily correct, e.g., a student may have a very detailed albeit erroneous account describing how s/he can simplify Unlike Algebraic Terms. Finally, our model explicitly stores a disbelief in *L*, represented by *L* with *MB* <0, if the student believes *L* to be false, however, at the same time *L* is readily derivable from the student's beliefs. Such a derivation is possible if the rules of inference activated by the student are unsound or if s/he maintains inconsistent beliefs.

The nodes in the Student Network are labeled according to their complexity, **p** for primitive concepts and **c** for complex ones. In addition, like links, nodes may be Inferred, Told or previously Known[‡]. Finally, each node has a *Degree of Expertise (DE)* between 0 and 1. The DE of a c-node is a function of the DEs and MBs of its constituent nodes and links, respectively. At present, the following naive heuristic

---

[†] In the actual network each link may have a counterpart representing the inverse relationship. However, for clarity of presentation, only links which are relevant to our discussion are shown here.

[‡] The issues related to inferred nodes and their effect on the Student Model and on the generation of RDs are the subject of future research.

function is being considered:

$$DE(N) = \underset{i \in constituent-nodes}{Min} \{Max(0, MB(link(i,N))) \cdot DE(i)\}$$

According to this function, a person's expertise with respect of a concept is as low as his/her expertise with respect to the least known constituent of this concept. A low DE value prompts further examination of a concept to determine which of its constituents demands further explanation. The suitability of such a simple function for the generation of rhetorical devices still remains to be tested.

In this paper, we focus on technical domains featuring *procedures* which achieve certain *goals* when applied to particular *objects*. In many cases, one procedure will achieve the same goal to different extents when applied to different objects, e.g., factoring out a common factor will only partially factorize a quadratic trinomial such as $3x^2+5x-2$, while it will completely factorize a binomial such as $3x^2+5x$. This prompts us to define a *context* as a triple composed of a procedure, an object to which it is applied, and the goal accomplished by this procedure when applied to this object (labeled c1-c4 in Figure 2).

2.2 The Inference Mechanism

Our inference mechanism generates plausible inferences from links in the network by means of generally applicable Common-sense Inference Rules (see Figure 3). These rules are inspired by rule adaptations commonly performed by students which were studied by Matz [1982], Brown and Van Lehn [1980], Van Lehn [1983] and Sleeman [1984]. In order to account for the deductive abilities of a particular type of student, we annotate each rule with a measure of uncertainty, denoted ρ, which represents a student's belief in the validity of a conclusion given that the evidence is certain. This measure resembles the rule strength used in ACT* [Anderson 1983].

The application of the rules in Figure 3 to the solid links of the network in Figure 2 yields the correct context c2, [BrS apply-to LT has-goal BrE], and the erroneous contexts c3 and c4, [BrS apply-to AT has-goal BrE] and [BrS apply-to UT has-goal BrE], respectively. In particular, context c3 may be obtained from the combination of three different sources: (1) Generalization — by applying R3 to context c2 and link [AT super-class LT], (2) Similarity — by applying R2 to context c1, [BrS apply-to Numbers has-goal BrE], and link [Numbers simile(s) AT] (this link is usually created from information explicitly mentioned by the teacher), and (3) Causality — by applying R1 to the link [BrS use-1 +/−] and the wrongly believed link [+/− apply-to AT] (this rule application actually yields the link [BrS apply-to AT] and not the entire context). For experts, a causal rule, such as R1, generally has a larger contribution to a conclusion than rules based on surface similarities, while for novices, less sound rules may have a stronger effect.

In the current implementation, a strictly numerical method is used to represent and combine MBs. Although the RDs proposed so far based on this method are generally appropriate for several network instances, two main problems still have to be addressed: (1) Providing and modifying the different measures of belief (MBs, DEs

R1
; *If procedure $PROC_a$ initially uses a given set of procedures and these procedures apply to*
; *disjoint parts of a given object OBJ_m then, with likelihood ρ_1, $PROC_a$ is applicable to OBJ_m*
IF [for $i=1,\cdots,n$ $\exists$ a use-1 link between $PROC_a$ and $PROC_i$ with MB k_{ai}
    AND for $i=1,\cdots,n$ $\exists$ an apply-to link between $PROC_i$ and OBJ_m with MB k_{im}]
    THEN (with certainty ρ_1)

        Add an apply-to link of type I between $PROC_a$ and OBJ_m with MB $k_{am}=\dfrac{\rho_1}{n}\sum_{i=1}^{n}k_{ai}k_{im}$

R2
; *If two objects are identified as similar, the applicability of a procedure to one of the*
; *objects may be inferred from its applicability to the other, accomplishing the same goal*
IF [$\exists$ a simile link between OBJ_m and OBJ_n with MB k_{mn}
    AND $\exists$ a context between $PROC_a$, OBJ_m and $GOAL_l$
        with an apply-to link between $PROC_a$ and OBJ_m with MB k_{am}
        and a has-goal link between $PROC_a$ and $GOAL_l$ with MB k_{lam}]
        THEN (with certainty ρ_2)
        Add a context between $PROC_a$, OBJ_n and $GOAL_l$
        with an apply-to link of type I between $PROC_a$ and OBJ_n with MB $k_{an}=\rho_2 k_{mn}k_{am}$
        and a has-goal link of type I between $PROC_a$ and $GOAL_l$ with MB $k_{lan}=\rho_2 k_{mn}k_{lam}$

R3
; *Generalization — If a procedure applies to an object accomplishing a certain goal,*
; *then it may be applicable to a superclass of this object accomplishing the same goal,*
; *where the applicability of this procedure to the superclass is inversely proportional*
; *to the number and type of constraints applied to the superclass to form this object*
IF [$\exists$ a super-class link from OBJ_n to OBJ_m with constraints c_{nm}
    AND $\exists$ a context between $PROC_a$, OBJ_m and $GOAL_l$
    with an apply-to link between $PROC_a$ and OBJ_m with MB k_{am}
    and a has-goal link between $PROC_a$ and $GOAL_l$ with MB k_{lam}]
    THEN (with certainty ρ_3)
    Add a context between $PROC_a$, OBJ_n and $GOAL_l$

    with an apply-to link of type I between $PROC_a$ and OBJ_n with MB $k_{an}=\dfrac{\rho_3 k_{am}}{|c_{nm}|}$

    and a has-goal link of type I between $PROC_a$ and $GOAL_l$ with MB $k_{lan}=\dfrac{\rho_3 k_{lam}}{|c_{nm}|}$

R4
; *Specialization — If a procedure applies to an object accomplishing a certain goal,*
; *then it may be applicable to a subclass of this object accomplishing the same goal*
IF [$\exists$ a super-class link from OBJ_m to OBJ_n with constraints c_{mn}
    AND $\exists$ a context between $PROC_a$, OBJ_m and $GOAL_l$
    with an apply-to link between $PROC_a$ and OBJ_m with MB k_{am}
    and a has-goal link between $PROC_a$ and $GOAL_l$ with MB k_{lam}]
    THEN (with certainty ρ_4)
        Add a context between $PROC_a$, OBJ_n and $GOAL_l$
        with an apply-to link of type I between $PROC_a$ and OBJ_n with MB $k_{an}=\rho_4 k_{am}$
        and a has-goal link of type I between $PROC_a$ and $GOAL_l$ with MB $k_{lan}=\rho_4 k_{lam}$

Fig. 3: Sample Common-sense Inference Rules[†]

[†] From [Zukerman 1989].

and ρs) to adequately reflect the expertise of a particular student or type of student; and (2) Blocking undesirable persistent inferences, e.g., how do we prevent a later statement about [BrS apply-to Numbers] from affecting the link [BrS ¬apply-to AT]? To solve the second problem, we envision complementing our representation by means of justifications in a manner similar to Truth Maintenance Systems (TMS) [Doyle 1979].

3. Generating Rhetorical Devices

In order to determine a sequence of rhetorical devices required to achieve $KNOW(IM)$, we apply the following procedure:

Message:Plan (IM)

1 Generate *Peripheral RDs* to invalidate impairments caused by the *IM*
2 For each message $m \in \{Peripheral\ RDs,\ IM\}$
      Generate *Supportive RDs* to satisfy $KNOW(m)$
3 Sort the *RDs* and the *IM* according to rhetorical considerations

In the first step, our procedure evaluates the global impact of an IM on a student's beliefs, and generates Peripheral RDs to counteract any undesirable effects which are likely to take place. To this effect, we temporarily assume that the goal $KNOW(m)$ for $m \in \{Peripheral\ RDs,\ IM\}$ is attained by merely stating the message in question. This assumption is eliminated in step 2, where Supportive RDs are generated for each of these messages to ensure its acquisition by the student. Finally, focusing principles are applied to sort the proposed RDs and the IM. In the following subsections, we describe the steps of procedure *Message:Plan*.

3.1 Generating Peripheral RDs

In this step, we simulate the alterations taking effect in the Student Network due to the presentation of an IM, and generate Peripheral RDs to overcome undesirable effects. This is performed by means of the procedure described in [Zukerman 1989]: the simulation is initiated by adding a network representing the IM to the Student Network (see Figure 4). Next, a *Recognition-Selection* mechanism proposes Peripheral RDs if the acquisition of this message is likely to be inhibited due to interactions with a listener's intended or existing beliefs. A *Propagation* mechanism then draws inferences from the proposed RDs and the IM by activating Common-sense Inference Rules. The Recognition-Selection-Propagation cycle is repeated with respect to the newly drawn inferences until no impairments remain, i.e., no Peripheral RDs are proposed.

During the Recognition-Selection phase, our mechanism identifies impairments which lead to the following undesirable effects: *Loss of Interest, Confusion, Mislearning, Insufficient Learning* and *Insignificant Change* in a listener's knowledge status. These effects are characterized in terms of our network model as follows (Table 1 summarizes the RDs which are suitable for the invalidation of each type of impairment).

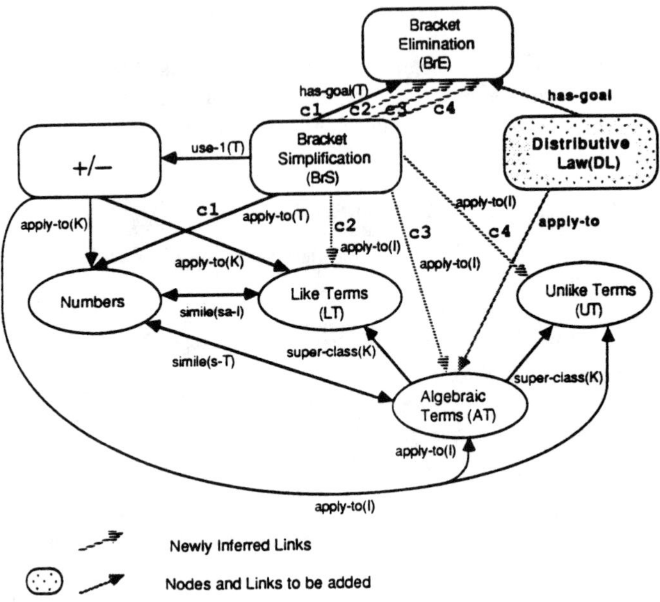

Fig. 4: Updated Network Model of a Student's Beliefs

Loss of Interest takes place when a listener believes that the information in an IM is redundant, i.e., there exists a sub-net in the Student Network which subsumes the network corresponding to the IM. If the IM pertains to a procedure, Loss of Interest takes place if there exists a procedure in the network which obtains the same goal with respect to the same object. For instance, in Figure 4, the student believes that distributive law is redundant, due to his/her incorrect belief that bracket simplification eliminates brackets when applied to Algebraic Terms (context c3). If Loss of Interest is caused by a link representing an incorrect belief, a Contradiction to this belief must be generated, e.g., "In algebra, brackets cannot always be simplified" (line 7 in Figure 1). If, however, all the relevant links in the network are correct, the listener must be motivated to acquire the IM by adding to it nodes and links which render it unique. A special case of this situation occurs when the IM repeats existing information. In this case, the generated Motivation may be extended to appeal to other goals of the listener, such as mastering the subject matter or passing an exam [Zukerman 1987].

Confusion occurs when an inference decreases a listener's confidence in a previous belief, i.e., the absolute value of the MB of a link in the Student Network is significantly lowered due to the effect of the inference. If this impairment occurs due to the interaction between a correct link and an incorrect inference, a Revision of the correct link is called for, e.g., " ... in arithmetic, brackets must always be calculated first" (lines 1-2). If, however, the impairment has occurred due to an incorrect link and a correct inference, a Contradiction to the link must be generated.

Mislearning takes place when an incorrect inference yields an erroneous belief with a relatively high degree of confidence, i.e., the link in question acquires a high MB with a wrong sign. In this case, a Contradiction to the inference must be generated.

Insufficient Learning takes place when a correct inference fails to achieve a desired MB, representative of proficiency, in a link. This impairment is invalidated by a Revision of the inference.

Finally, an *Insignificant Change* occurs when an inference produces a rather inconsequential change in a link with an MB representative of insufficient proficiency.

<table>
<tr><td colspan="4">Table 1: Peripheral RDs as a Function of Impairments, Message Types and Link Values</td></tr>
<tr><td>Impairment</td><td>Message Type</td><td>Link Value</td><td>Peripheral RD</td></tr>
<tr><td rowspan="2">Loss of Interest</td><td rowspan="2">IM</td><td>Correct</td><td>Motivation (add links)</td></tr>
<tr><td>Incorrect</td><td>Contradiction of link</td></tr>
<tr><td rowspan="2">Confusion</td><td rowspan="2">Inference</td><td>Correct</td><td>Revision of link</td></tr>
<tr><td>Incorrect</td><td>Contradiction of link</td></tr>
<tr><td>Mislearning</td><td>Inference</td><td>—</td><td>Contradiction of inference</td></tr>
<tr><td>Insufficient Learning</td><td>Inference</td><td>—</td><td>Revision of inference</td></tr>
<tr><td rowspan="2">Insignificant Change</td><td rowspan="2">Inference</td><td>Correct</td><td>Revision of link</td></tr>
<tr><td>Incorrect</td><td>Contradiction of link</td></tr>
</table>

The IM and the proposed Peripheral RDs may in turn cause other impairments due to inferences drawn by the listener, calling for the generation of additional Peripheral RDs. This process is modeled by the Propagation phase, where Common-sense Inference Rules are activated with respect to the links modified by the IM and the Peripheral RDs. For example, the Contradiction [BrS ¬apply-to AT] may weaken the link [BrS apply-to LT] due to the application of the specialization rule R4 (see Figure 3). Recognition-Selection is then applied to links affected by these rules.

Finally, if, during the Recognition-Selection process, a number of impairments are detected concurrently, our mechanism first proposes a Peripheral RD for the link with the highest ranking impairment, and then propagates the effect of this RD. The ranking of an impairment depends on two factors: (1) its type, where Confusion and Loss of Interest are ranked higher than the other impairments, and (2) its strength, which for Confusion is defined as the distance between the MB of a link and its previous MB, and for the rest of the impairments as the distance between the MB of a link and an MB considered satisfactory. According to this policy, impairments which inhibit the attainment of the goal *KNOW(IM)* or affect adversely a listener's beliefs are given a high ranking, i.e., the invalidation of Insufficient Learning has a lower priority than the invalidation of Confusion, Loss of Interest and Mislearning. This process is repeated until all the impairments discovered at this stage are invalidated. The application of this ranking policy attempts to minimize the number of Peripheral RDs, since relatively weak impairments may be spontaneously corrected as a result of inferences drawn from the Peripheral RDs generated to correct the stronger impairments.

Let us now illustrate this process by describing the behaviour of our mechanism when the IM [DL apply-to AT has-goal BrE] is added to the Student Network in Figure 2: Loss of Interest sets in due to the presence of context c3. Since this context features the incorrect link [BrS apply-to AT], a Contradiction is required. The propagation of the IM and the Contradiction yields the inferences in Table 2. All these inferences, except [BrS ¬apply-to Numbers] and [BrS ¬apply-to LT], are correct. Depending on the values of the MBs of the links in the Student Network and the uncertainty measures of the Common-sense Inference Rules, any of these inferences may lead to an impairment.

Table 2: Inferences and Possible Impairments after Propagation in the Sample Network			
Message	*Rule*	*Inference*	*Possible Impairment*
Intended Message [DL apply-to AT has-goal BrE]	R2 R4 R4	[DL apply-to Numbers has-goal BrE] [DL apply-to LT has-goal BrE] [DL apply-to UT has-goal BrE]	*Insufficient Learning*
Contradiction [BrS ¬apply-to AT]	R2 R4 R4 R1	[BrS ¬apply-to Numbers] [BrS ¬apply-to LT] [BrS ¬apply-to UT] [+/− ¬apply-to AT]	*Confusion/Mislearning/ Insignificant Change* *Confusion/Insuf. Learning/ Insignificant Change*

In order to focus the rest of our discussion, we assume that the only impairments which take place in the network at hand are the ones which lead to Confusion in the links [BrS apply-to Numbers] and [BrS apply-to LT]. According to our heuristic, we first propose an RD for the invalidation of the highest ranking impairment. In this case, this results in a Revision of [BrS apply-to Numbers has-goal BrE]. The propagation of this RD invalidates the impairment in the context [BrS apply-to LT has-goal BrE]. This process yields the following messages:

IM	[DL apply-to AT has-goal BrE]
Contradiction	[BrS ¬apply-to AT]
Revision	[BrS apply-to Numbers has-goal BrE]

Notice that in general the Revision of a link restricts the incidence of impairments, since existing beliefs are reinforced, whereas the Contradiction of a link typically fosters the occurrence of further impairments. For instance, in our sample network, the propagation process terminates after one iteration with the generation of a Revision. If, however, impairments had taken place in the erroneous links [+/− apply-to AT] and/or [BrS apply-to UT], Contradictions of these links or, equivalently, Revisions of the inferences responsible for these impairments would be called for. The Propagation of these RDs through the application of rules R4 and R1, respectively, may have resulted in an impairment in the link [+/− apply-to UT].

3.2 Generating Supportive RDs

Until now, we have generated RDs assuming that the propositions expressed by these RDs and the IM will be acquired by the listener. However, it is seldom the case that the mere statement of a proposition causes a listener to understand it and believe in it. We therefore consider each message separately, in order to ascertain whether impairments are likely to occur with respect to the listener's acquisition of this message, i.e., whether the goal *KNOW (message)* is being satisfied. If the occurrence of impairments threatens the satisfaction of this goal, RDs which are local to the message in question are proposed to invalidate these impairments.

We have found it useful to separate the process of acquiring a message into three parts: *Access, Construction* and *Acceptance.* The first two sub-processes deal with the comprehension of a message: Access attempts to reconcile lexical items mentioned in a message with nodes in the Student Network, and Construction builds a network by linking the nodes referred to in a message. The third sub-process, Acceptance, determines the need for additional information to foster belief in a message once its contents are understood by the listener. In general, messages generated by competent speakers contain one or more concepts already known by a listener. Hence, the activation of Access and Construction typically results in the incorporation of a network representing a message into the network representing a listener's beliefs. For instance, in our example, the nodes BrE and AT of the IM already exist in the Student Network, linking the IM [DL apply-to AT has-goal BrE] to the network.

We now consider impairments which may take place with respect to each of these sub-processes, and account for the generation of Supportive RDs for their invalidation[†]. We distinguish between three types of Supportive RDs according to their function: *Creative, Indicative* and *Explanatory.* Creative RDs are generated to build or reinforce a mental representation of a concept, Indicative RDs are generated to identify an existing concept in memory, and Explanatory RDs are produced to foster belief in a proposition. Our distinction between the different types of RDs is one of function and not of structure, since RDs with the same structure may accomplish a number functions depending on the type of the message in question, the contents of the listener's memory and his/her ability. For example, a Description of an object is often used as a Creative RD, however, it may also be used as an Indicative RD, if the nodes participating in the Description are unique and accessible in memory.

3.2.1 Access

To understand a concept correctly, the following conditions must be satisfied: (1) A listener must reconcile a lexical item mentioned by a speaker with a node in memory which is intended by the speaker, and (2) The goal *KNOW* must be fulfilled with respect to the intended node. Failure of the first condition results in a connection-related impairment, such as *Lack of Connection* or *Misunderstanding*, whereas failure

---

† We assume that the meaning of links, e.g., apply-to and subclass, is understood by a listener, and concentrate on nodes as possible sources of impairments.

of the second condition results in a content-related impairment, such as *Lack of Understanding* or *Insufficient Understanding*. These impairments are characterized in terms of our network model as follows.

Lack of Connection occurs when one of the following conditions is satisfied: (1) the lexical item used by a speaker to refer to an intended node does not exist in the Student Network, (2) the lexical item exists in the network, but it is not connected to a concept node, (3) it is weakly connected to the intended node (and no other node), or (4) it is connected to the intended node (and no other node), but this node is not primed in the Student Network. Condition (1) characterizes a situation where a listener is unfamiliar with the terminology used by the speaker. Conditions (2) and (3) characterize a situation where a listener is familiar with the terminology but does not connect between it and the intended concept. These conditions are illustrated by the following exchange:

> S1: Have you heard of Fermat's Last Theorem?
> S2: Yes, but I don't know which one it is.
> S1: $\exists n>2 \quad s.t. \quad x^n+y^n = z^n$.
> S2: Ah! that one ... .

The fourth condition, where the intended node is not primed in the Student Network, depicts a situation where the node intended by the speaker is outside the listener's *attentional state*[†], i.e., the discourse has diverged both in time and place from the intended node, inhibiting the listener's ability to access it, even if its name has been mentioned. Note that the attentional state in this context is influenced by the listener's expertise in the subject matter, i.e., an expert listener may be able to bridge attentional gaps which cannot be overcome by a novice.

The invalidation of this impairment requires an Indicative RD to identify the node in question. This RD is generated by selecting a set of nodes which are linked to the intended node and are sufficient to uniquely identify it. The types of the selected nodes and their relationship to the intended node determine the type of an Indicative RD. For example, in the text "So far we have studied two methods for solving quadratic equations: factorization and completion to square," the goal node solving-quadratic-equations is identified by means of a *Perspective* in terms of procedure nodes which accomplish this goal, namely factorization and completion-to-square. The level of detail of an Indicative RD has to be sufficient to enable access to the nodes mentioned in it, i.e., the fulfillment of the goal *KNOW* may not be necessary, rather, the goal *KNOW–ABOUT* may be preferred. The determination of a communicative goal in this context is influenced by possibly conflicting considerations, such as the time we have to achieve our main goal *KNOW* (*IM*), the listener's attention span, the extent of the departure from our main focus, and the potential benefits to the listener from achieving the different subgoals. As said before, at present, we cater only for the goal *KNOW*, leaving for future research issues of goal determination and generation of RDs for the attainment of other goals.

---

† The term *attentional state* is due to Grosz and Sidner [1986].

Misunderstanding occurs when a lexical item mentioned by a speaker is connected to a node which is not the intended node. This may be due to a true mis-connection or due to the fact that there is more than one concept with the same name, and the 'wrong' one is primed. A common example of the latter case is a scenario where two people are discussing another person, let's call her Mary, but each participant in the dialogue has a different Mary in mind. Like for Lack of Connection, the invalidation of this impairment is accomplished by means of an Indicative RD which delivers sufficient information to discriminate between the nodes in question.

Lack of Understanding takes place when there does not exist in the Student Network a node which corresponds to an intended concept, and the listener is unable to build such a node from his/her existing knowledge. It entails a connection-related impairment, since a lexical item cannot point to an absent node. At first glance, it appears that this impairment may be invalidated simply by creating a node. However, the creation of a node alone is not sufficient, since it would result in mere awareness of the concept and would not fulfill the goal *KNOW (concept)*. Hence, in order to satisfy this goal, our mechanism generates a Creative RD which presents the nodes which constitute this concept. The following Description is an example of such an RD: "[The distributive law states that] each term in the brackets must be multiplied by the term outside the brackets" (lines 19-20 in Figure 1). If the goal *KNOW* is not fulfilled for a constituent node, then an RD has to be generated for this node as well. However, in discourse generated by competent speakers, the constituent nodes are usually known by the listener.

Finally, *Insufficient Understanding* takes place when there exists a node which corresponds to an intended concept, but the Degree of Expertise associated with this node indicates insufficient proficiency. This impairment may occur in conjunction with a connection-related impairment or by itself. Like for Lack of Understanding, a Creative RD is required to invalidate this impairment. However, if the lack of expertise is localized to some missing or erroneous constituents, the RD may be focused on this aspect of the impairment. Note that the requirement for expertise is essential in educational settings, where the communicative goal is *KNOW*, but may be waived in settings where different goals prevail.

In the above discussion, we assumed that the name of a concept is initially used to refer to it. Therefore, the recognition of an impairment calls for the generation of an *Identification* which associates RDs proposed as explained above with this name. For instance, in the statement "*The distributive law states that* each term in brackets must be multiplied by the term outside the brackets," the text in italics identifies the Procedure Description with its technical name. The generation of an Identification may result in other impairments, such as Confusion or Mislearning, if the intended node is connected (either correctly or incorrectly) to another lexical item, i.e., it is identified with another name, or if the lexical item is connected (either correctly or incorrectly) to another node, i.e., there is more than one node with the same name. Both cases call for the generation of a Revision of the link in question, if it is correct, and a Contradiction, otherwise, as explained in Section 3.1. This situation is illustrated by the

158

following dialogue:

> S1: A crook is a shepherd's staff.
> S2: I thought it was a bad person.   (*Confusion*)
> S1: Yes, that too.   (*Revision*)

Notice, however, that there are situations where a speaker is unable or unwilling to reference a concept by means of a lexical item. In such cases, Lack of Connection takes place, calling for the generation of an Indicative RD to enable the listener to access the node in question. In addition, as stated above, a Creative RD may be required if the listener's expertise with respect to this concept is insufficient.

These observations yield the following rather simple procedure for the generation of Supportive RDs for the Access phase. This procedure is activated with respect to each node mentioned in the messages generated so far, receiving two parameters: an intended node, N, and a lexical item, L. It returns an expression which represents the manner in which N is to be presented. This expression may range from a single lexical item to a number of RDs, and must be positioned either before or immediately after the first mention of N in the final message sequence.

Access-RDs:Plan (N,L)[†]

```
1  RD ← nil
;  Lack of Understanding or Insufficient Understanding
2  If { ∄node = N } ∨ { DE(N) < Threshold } Then
       RD ← Creative-RD(N)
;  Misunderstanding
3  If { L ∧ [ ∃lexical item = L ] ∧ [ L is-name-of N' ] ∧ [ N' ≠ N ] ∧
        { ¬[L is-name-of N] ∨ primed(N') } } ∨
;  Lack of Connection
       { ¬L } ∨ { ∄lexical item = L } ∨ { L is-name-of NIL }
       { MB(L is-name-of N) < Threshold } ∨
       { [ L is-name-of N ] ∧ ¬primed(N) }
    Then Do
       If RD Then RD ← Join (RD, Indicative-RD(N))
       Else RD ← Indicative-RD(N)
    end
4  If { L ∧ RD } Then Do
       RD ← Cons (Identification(L,N), RD)
       RD ← Append (RD, Recognition-Selection-Propagation(L is-name-of N))
    end
    Elseif L Then L
    Else RD
```

[†] The semantics of the boolean connectives are as in Lisp.

According to this procedure, Insufficient Understanding is considered only if the detection of Lack of Understanding has failed, and Lack of Connection is examined only if the recognition of Misunderstanding has been unsuccessful. In addition, if both a content-related and a connection-related impairment are detected, the procedure *Join* is activated to determine whether both a Creative and an Indicative RD are required, or whether a Creative RD alone is sufficient to perform both functions. Finally, if the lexical item L is null, only the proposed RDs are returned. If, on the other hand, L is non-null and one or more RDs were proposed, an Identification is generated and the impairment invalidation mechanism presented in Section 3.1 is activated to invalidate impairments which may be triggered by it. If no RDs were proposed, i.e., no impairments were anticipated, L is deemed sufficient to access the intended node.

The application of procedure *Access-RDs:Plan* to the nodes in the message [BrS apply-to Numbers has-goal BrE] may result in the detection of Insufficient Understanding with respect to the node BrS, and in the recognition of Misunderstanding or Lack of Connection with respect to the lexical item 'bracket calculation'. This prompts the generation of a Creative RD for the node BrS, and an Identification linking the lexical item 'bracket calculation' with this node:

Identification (BrS, 'bracket calculation')
Creative RD (BrS)

The above discussion characterizes Supportive RDs according to their function, however, it does not present a strategy for the selection of a particular form of RD, such as a Description, an Instantiation or a Simile. At present, we offer some observations with respect to this process which is the subject of ongoing research. We postulate that a Supportive RD must satisfy three requirements: Minimality, Sufficiency and Coherency. Minimality and Sufficiency constitute the conditions of Grice's Maxim of Quantity [Grice 1975]. They guide the selection of a set of nodes to perform a supportive role, demanding that this set contain a minimal number of nodes which is still sufficient to accomplish this role. Coherency constrains the presentation of these nodes.

For Creative RDs, where the goal is to establish a concept in a listener's memory, the requirements posed by Sufficiency and Minimality are objective, in the sense that the set of nodes required to satisfy the goal *KNOW* with respect to a concept is relatively well defined by the speaker. Hence, the contents of Creative RDs may be specified by schemas such as the ones proposed by McKeown [1985]. For example, the statement "A chair is a piece of furniture *which has a seat, a back and usually four legs*, and is used for sitting," is composed of a subclass link, has-part links (in italics) and a has-goal link, respectively. These links correspond to McKeown's Identification Schema. The subclass and has-goal links are used to link the chair node to the rest of a listener's network, whereas the has-part links constitute a Creative RD, representing the distinctive features of a chair. Analogies and Similes may also be used as Creative RDs, e.g., "The atom is like the solar system" (from [Gentner 1983]), however, they need to be augmented by statements which assert key similarities and discrepancies between the source and target concepts. Notice, however, that a selected Creative RD may still be insufficient to overcome a content-related impairment, if the concept in question is rather abstract relative to a listener's ability. In this case, Illustrations and/or Instantiations are usually called for. For instance, in our above example, a Description of the bracket simplification procedure may be selected, and then complemented by an Instantiation, yielding the following RDs:

> *Identification*   (BrS, 'bracket calculation')
> *Description*   (BrS)
> *[Instantiation* (BrS)] $\rightarrow$ *Instantiation* (BrS apply-to *?x1*)

As illustrated in our sample text in Figure 1, a Procedure Instantiation always requires an Object Instantiation. In addition, Descriptions and Instantiations may be combined in a variety of ways, i.e., a Description may be followed by an Instantiation (lines 19-21), they may appear interleaved (lines 3-6), or an Instantiation may be followed by a Description. In any case, when a Description and an Instantiation of a procedure are proposed, each step in the Description is usually instantiated. The effect of each of these combinations on the comprehension process still remains to be ascertained.

For Indicative RDs, where the goal is to uniquely identify an intended node, there may be several sets of nodes which satisfy the Sufficiency and Minimality requirements. In this case, some specialized forms of RDs provide Coherency constraints for the nodes in each set, i.e., an Illustration requires a diagram, an Instantiation demands one or more specific instances of the node in question, and a Perspective requires nodes which have the same type of link with the intended node. For instance, the text "So far we have discussed a number of pieces of furniture, namely chairs, beds and tables" provides a Perspective to the node furniture by means of objects which have a subclass link to this node. In addition, any uniquely identifying subset of the nodes used in Creative RDs, such as the nodes composing a partial Description, may be presented to identify a concept.

3.2.2 Construction

Construction links the nodes mentioned in a message to create a structure which represents the knowledge to be acquired by the listener. The impairments which may take place during Construction may be expressed as a listener's inability to build an explanation to answer implicit *HOW* questions, e.g., How does DL apply-to AT? How does it achieve the goal BrE?

The occurrence of a content-related impairment in the Access phase is a sufficient condition for a comprehension-related impairment in the Construction phase, i.e., if a concept is not readily understood, its relationship with other concepts is not likely to be understood either. For example, if a student is experiencing difficulty in understanding the workings of the bracket simplification procedure, s/he is also likely to have difficulty with respect to its application to Algebraic Terms. In this case, the

Construction phase can either complement the output of the Access phase by forcing an Instantiation if none has been proposed, or it can constrain this output by grounding an *instantiation variable*. In the above example, this is performed by resolving the proposed Instantiation of [BrS apply-to *?x1*] with the current message, [BrS apply-to Numbers has-goal BrE], yielding the following Supportive RDs:

Identification	(BrS, 'bracket calculation')
Description	(BrS)
Instantiation	(BrS apply-to Numbers)

Notice, however, that although the occurrence of a content-related impairment during the Access phase is a sufficient condition for a comprehension-related impairment during the Construction phase, once RDs have been proposed to invalidate the former, it is possible that the latter will no longer take place. This is due to the fact that the generated RDs may be sufficient to allow a listener to successfully complete the Construction phase. The adequacy of RDs generated during the Access phase to accomplish this task depends on the ability of the student and on the relationship between these RDs and the message in question.

Furthermore, a content-related impairment in the Access phase is not the only sufficient condition for an impairment in the Construction phase. This is due to the fact that a concept may be understood in isolation at a level of abstraction which is not the appropriate level to link it to other concepts in a message. For instance, the node DL may have an acceptable Degree of Expertise, despite the fact that the student is not proficient with respect to all the applications of its constituents, e.g., s/he may not know how to multiply Unlike Algebraic Terms. In this case, a comprehension-related impairment may take place with respect to the message [DL apply-to UT].

So far, we have not characterized additional sufficiency conditions for the occurrence of impairments during the Construction phase. However, for messages pertaining to the application of a procedure to an object, the likelihood of an impairment may be ascertained by checking whether the links between the constituents of the procedure node and the object node have an MB indicative of proficiency. If an impairment is detected, the procedure must be instantiated with respect to the object in question, and the constituent responsible for the impairment must be described. This policy proposes RDs which are compatible with the text planned by Paris under similar circumstances [Paris 1988]. Finally, if an Indicative RD for the procedure node was already proposed in the Access phase, it is joined with the RDs generated during the Construction phase, thereby eliminating redundancy and, at the same time, ensuring that the conditions for the completion of both phases are fulfilled.

3.2.3 Acceptance

Once a message has been understood, its acceptance hinges upon a listener's capability to reconcile its contents with his/her beliefs. The impairments which may take place during Acceptance may be expressed as a listener's inability to construct an explanation to answer implicit *WHY* questions, e.g., Why doesn't BrS apply-to AT? Why does BrS apply-to LT?

At present, we do not provide a formal characterization of the conditions which require Explanatory RDs to foster the acceptance of a message. However, we offer a schema-based approach which accounts for commonly encountered Explanatory RDs. In particular, we consider two important factors which affect their generation: (1) the type of a message (new, contradicting or revising) affects the need for an Explanatory RD, and (2) the type of the link being addressed affects the type of a proposed RD.

Any link in a constructed network may cause an acceptance-related impairment, if a listener is unable to accept at face value a statement representing this link. Contradictions, IMs which contradict existing beliefs and IMs which present new beliefs generally require Explanatory RDs[†], whereas Revisions and IMs which reinforce existing beliefs may dispense with Explanatory RDs, if the MBs of the corresponding links are sufficiently high. We now discuss Explanatory RDs which are often presented to convince a listener of the correctness of a particular type of link. Note that forms of RDs which are commonly used in a Creative or Indicative role may also be used in an Explanatory role.

i. [A subclass B] and [A inst-of B] — A causal justification of these types of links may be given by presenting attributes of A which are sufficient attributes of B, while an evidential justification presents necessary attributes. A common explanation pattern which uses sufficient attributes is "A is a B because A has all the sufficient attributes of B [and although A lacks some of B's attributes, they are not sufficient ones]." To contradict a subclass link, the negation of one necessary attribute constitutes a causal support, while the negation of sufficient attributes constitutes an evidential support. In addition, one may contradict a subclass link by showing membership in another class.

ii. [A is-similar-to B] — If the nodes A and B are children of the same parent node in a network representing a speaker's beliefs, the speaker can substantiate this link by presenting the attributes of the parent node, since they are common to both A and B. To show lack of similarity, a sufficient number of significant[‡] attributes which have incompatible values must be presented. Still, if enough common attributes are left, the listener may remain unconvinced.

iii. [A has-goal B] — This link may be explained by following the same pattern as the subclass explanation above, i.e., stating how the goal accomplished by A has the

---

† Flowers [1982] discusses conditions for the applicability of several types of supports for contradictions.

‡ The significance of different attributes still remains to be assessed.

attributes of the goal pattern B, or by stating how A leads to the satisfaction of sufficient conditions of B, e.g., "Factoring out x completely factorizes this expression, since we obtain a product of factors." The negation of this link may be accomplished in a similar way to the negation of a subclass link.

iv. [A has-part B] and [A has-attribute B] — These types of links may be explained by showing how B satisfies a necessary condition of the goal or function of A, e.g., "Tweety has wings. It can't fly without wings." If B is a part or an attribute of a super-class node of A, then these links may be explained by means of this node, e.g., "Cats nurse their young, because cats are mammals [and mammals nurse their young]." Evidential reasoning and Instantiations may also be used to support these links, however, they do not constitute sound arguments. To justify the negation of these links, one may show that the existence of B entails a function or a subclass link which is not true for A, e.g., "Canaries don't have fins. If they had fins, they would be fish [not birds]."

v. [A apply-to B] — This link may be explained along two main parameters:

Correctness (Why is this procedure correct with respect to some theory?) — This parameter may be independent of a particular object. For instance, when studying distributive law, a student may want to know why it is correct to multiply the terms as prescribed by this procedure. In addition, s/he may want to know why the multiplication of Algebraic Terms is correct. The soundest way to show correctness is by means of a formal proof, however, this may be too abstract for some students, requiring the use of other less conclusive RDs, such as a Simile (as in the sample text in Figure 1), an Analogy, an Illustration or an Instantiation. To show incorrectness, a contradicting example is often used as a causal support, or a proof may be presented.

Enablement (Why is this procedure applicable to this object?) — This parameter requires an explanation of how the attributes of an object match the applicability conditions of a procedure. In this case, explanations which are similar to the ones used for subclass links may be generated. In addition, Enablement may be causally explained by showing the procedure to be applicable to a super-class of the object. A causal explanation for Disablement may be generated by showing lack of applicability with respect to a subclass of the object in question, or by directly demonstrating that this object does not fulfill necessary conditions for the application of the procedure. This may be accomplished by means of a counter-example, such as "E.g., in $2(x+y)$, $x+y$ cannot be simplified" (line 8 in Figure 1).

These explanations are by no means exhaustive, rather, they represent often used explanation patterns which are supported by our network model. However, as seen above, not all the explanations with respect to a given proposition are equally sound. Since our goal is to teach or transfer information, and not to convince by any possible means, we must give preference to sound Explanatory RDs. This preference, however, is constrained by a listener's ability to comprehend our arguments and also by his/her other beliefs, i.e., a proposition may be used to substantiate an assertion only if the listener's beliefs do not contradict this proposition. If the listener does not believe in a link which is required for an explanation, then a chain of Explanatory RDs needs to be generated, e.g., "You cannot always simplify brackets in algebra because you cannot always add the terms inside the brackets. For example, you cannot add $x+y$." In this example, the chain is formed because [BrS ¬apply-to AT] is initially explained by means of rule R1 (see Figure 3) and the link [+/− ¬apply-to AT] in the speaker's network, but since this link contradicts the link [+/− apply-to AT] in our sample network, it must be justified as well. This is done by means of a counter-example. Finally, inferences from the links used for Explanatory RDs may in turn cause impairments. At present, we assume that this process will converge, since in an effective educational setting, misconceptions are not allowed to pile up. The effects of the relaxation of this assumption on the proposed RDs will be tested once the system is fully operational.

3.3 Sorting Messages

In order to sort the proposed RDs and the IM, we consider the application of the focusing principles specified by Sidner [1979] and extended by McKeown [1985]. These principles are:

1. Shift focus to a member of the potential focus list.
2. Maintain focus.
3. Return to a topic of previous discussion.
4. Select a proposition with the greatest number of
   implicit links to the potential focus list.

Unfortunately, existing focusing algorithms [McKeown 1985, McCoy and Cheng 1988] cannot be directly used to order our message list, since our messages are not constrained by schemas, as required by McKeown, and our IM and Peripheral RDs do not form a hierarchical structure in the sense assumed by McCoy and Cheng. Hence, a different type of focusing algorithm is required. In this section, we offer some preliminary insights into the envisioned focusing process.

In addition to the above mentioned focusing principles, this process must take into consideration the question of prevention vs. correction. That is, if an RD is generated before a message responsible for a likely impairment, it precludes this impairment, whereas if it is generated after this message, the impairment is invalidated after it takes place. The impact of this effect on the learning process depends on the type of the impairment. For instance, the preventive invalidation of Loss of Interest is crucial to the acquisition of an IM which may cause this impairment, while the preventive invalidation of other types of impairments appears to be less critical. In our example, this constraint yields two possible configurations for the IM and the Peripheral RDs: (1) Revision-Contradiction-IM, which may result in text similar to the one in Figure 1, and (2) Contradiction-IM-Revision.

The need for Supportive RDs for an IM and its Peripheral RDs depends on the order of these messages. This is due to the fact that Supportive RDs modify a listener's level of expertise with respect to the concepts they refer to, thereby affecting the need for Supportive RDs for subsequent messages featuring these concepts. For instance, it is possible that a Supportive RD proposed to invalidate an impairment during the Construction phase of the message [BrS apply-to Numbers] will prevent a similar impairment for a subsequent message involving the application of BrS, such as [BrS apply-to LT]. Therefore, at first glance, it appears that an ordering of the IM and the Peripheral RDs should be determined first, and then Supportive RDs should be proposed to satisfy the goal *KNOW* locally with respect to each message. This policy entails that the subjects which are local to each message are discussed prior to proceeding to the next message, i.e., it directly implements the first focusing principle given above, whereby subjects which appear in the potential focus list of an item currently in focus are mentioned before other items in the current focus. However, for this policy to generate coherent text from the messages proposed by our mechanism, we must restrict the meaning of the term *local Supportive RD* as follows: a Supportive RD is local to a given message, if it does not contain any nodes which are mentioned in another message and are not mentioned in this message. Typically, Descriptions and Instantiations are local to the messages they support.

If one or more of the proposed Supportive RDs are not local to the messages they support, the above policy does not guarantee the generation of coherent text. For example, given the IM [DL apply-to AT has-goal BrE] and the Contradiction [BrS ¬apply-to AT], a connection-related impairment with respect to the node BrE during the Access phase may prompt the generation of a Perspective such as [BrE is-goal-of BrS]. This Supportive RD is not local to the IM, since it contains the node BrS which is mentioned in the Contradiction. Sorting the IM and the Contradiction first supports the generation of text such as the following: "Bracket simplification does not always apply to Algebraic Terms. It is a method for eliminating brackets. In algebra, we can eliminate brackets by applying distributive law." Clearly, this text is less coherent than the following text, which may be produced by placing the Perspective to BrE before the IM and the Contradiction: "So far we have studied one method for eliminating brackets, namely bracket simplification. However, this method does not always apply to Algebraic Terms. In algebra, we can eliminate brackets by applying distributive law."

In addition, although the need for Supportive RDs depends on the ordering of the IM and the Peripheral RDs, the generation process of Supportive RDs for the Access phase is not influenced by this ordering. This is due to the fact that the nodes mentioned in all the messages may be independently inspected to anticipate connection-related and content-related impairments. If a Supportive RD has been proposed for a particular node, it is constrained to be presented either before or immediately after the first message featuring this node. Supportive RDs for the Construction and Acceptance phases, on the other hand, pertain to entire messages rather than single nodes. Hence, their generation cannot be divorced from the messages requiring support.

According to these considerations, we postulate that a preliminary ordering should be obtained after the Access phase has been completed for all the messages. At present, a sorting algorithm to accomplish this task has not been developed, however, we envisage that it should be based on a procedure which calculates the shortest path between the nodes to be mentioned. The Construction and Acceptance phases will then have to be performed for each message, and if a non-local Supportive RD is generated, the entire message sequence should be examined to eliminate redundant messages. For instance, if Confusion had been anticipated with respect to the erroneous link [+/– apply-to AT] in the sample network in Figure 4, a Contradiction of this link would have been proposed. Now, if the Explanatory RD [+/– ¬apply-to AT] had been generated to support the Contradiction [BrS ¬apply-to AT], yielding a statement such as "You cannot always simplify brackets in algebraic expressions, because your cannot always add algebraic expressions," the Contradiction to the link [+/– apply-to AT] would become superfluous.

3.4 A Worked Example

In this section, we describe a possible behaviour of our mechanism with respect to the following messages proposed after the activation of step 1 of procedure *Message:Plan*:

IM	[DL apply-to AT has-goal BrE]
Contradiction	[BrS ¬apply-to AT]
Revision	[BrS apply-to Numbers has-goal BrE]

In the Access phase, the nodes mentioned in these messages are considered, and the following impairments are anticipated: (1) Insufficient Understanding and Lack of Connection with respect to the node BrS, (2) Lack of Connection with respect to AT, and (3) Lack of Understanding with respect to DL, since the concept of distributive law is new to the student. The generation of Supportive RDs for BrS is performed as explained in Section 3.2.1; an Indicative RD is proposed to identify AT, and a Creative RD, such as a Description, is suggested for node DL. However, this Description may be too abstract for our student, requiring the generation of an Instantiation. Thus, upon completion of this phase, the following Supportive RDs may be proposed:

Identification	(BrS, 'bracket calculation')
Description	(BrS)
Instantiation	(BrS apply-to *?x1*)
Identification	(DL, 'distributive law')
Description	(DL)
Instantiation	(DL apply-to *?x2*)
Identification	(AT, 'algebraic terms')
Instantiation	(AT)

Table 3: RDs Proposed for the Intended Message [DL apply-to AT has-goal BrE]		
RD Type	*RD Contents*	*Possible Text*
Revision *Identification* *Description (partial)* *Instantiation*	[BrS apply-to Numbers has-goal BrE] (BrS, 'bracket calculation') (BrS) (BrS apply-to Numbers)	In arithmetic, we can eliminate brackets by performing bracket calculation. E.g., (brackets) (multiplication) $2\times(5+3) = 2\times8 = 16$.
Contradiction *Causality* *(Instantiation)*	[BrS ¬apply-to AT] (BrS ¬apply-to AT)	However, in algebra, we cannot always calculate brackets. E.g., we cannot calculate brackets in $2(x+y)$.
Intended Message *Identification* *Description* *Instantiation*	[DL apply-to AT has-goal BrE] (DL, 'distributive law') (DL) (DL apply-to AT)	In algebra, we can eliminate brackets by applying distributive law: We multiply each term inside the brackets by the term outside the brackets. For example, $2(x+y) = 2x + 2y$.

Prior to proceeding to the Construction phase, the proposed messages are provisionally sorted. Since all the Supportive RDs generated so far are local to their messages, the IM and the Peripheral RDs may be sorted separately from the Supportive RDs. Each Supportive RD may then be positioned either prior or immediately after the first message containing the node addressed by it. As stated in the previous section, a possible configuration of the IM and the Peripheral RDs is Revision-Contradiction-IM, yielding the ordering featured in Table 3.

As explained in Section 3.2.2, during the Construction phase, the instantiation variable $x1$, used in the Instantiation of BrS, is ground to Numbers. Note that the problem instance in the sample text in Figure 1 is unnecessarily complex, and the one proposed in the text in Table 3 is sufficient to concretize the message. (A module for the generation of examples from specifications is currently being developed.) Similarly, the instantiation variable $x2$, used in the Instantiation of DL, is ground to AT. Now, in general, impairments may occur during the Construction phase with respect to Contradictions, e.g., a listener may not understand at which point in the application of a procedure a failure occurred. However, in our example, the application of bracket simplification to Algebraic Terms fails in the first step of the procedure, hence, no further explanations for the Construction phase can be generated. Nevertheless, since this message contradicts a listener's belief, the need for an Explanatory RD is detected during the Acceptance phase. In this case, a counter-example is proposed as a causal explanation for Disablement, calling for an Instantiation of the node AT. Since an Instantiation of this node has been proposed previously as an Indicative RD, it just needs to be constrained to comply with the requirements of the counter-example. Finally, note that since an Instantiation of AT is required for both the IM and the Contradiction, and the constraints placed by these messages on this instantiation are compatible, the same problem instance may be generated for both messages.

4. Summary and Discussion

This paper offers a text planning mechanism which proposes explanations tailored to particular types of users. Our mechanism generates sufficient information to convey an intended message by anticipating and preventing potential impairments to a listener's comprehension process. It relies on a model of a listener's beliefs and inferences to characterize these impairments, and simulates a listener's comprehension process on this model. Our mechanism characterizes and invalidates two types of impairments: (1) Impairments with respect to beliefs which are related to an intended message — invalidated by means of Peripheral RDs; and (2) Impairments to a listener's ability to comprehend and believe a message — invalidated by means of Supportive RDs. In particular, the presented mechanism distinguishes between three different functions performed by Supportive RDs, namely Creative, Indicative and Explanatory.

Our mechanism proposes rhetorical devices under the assumption that after it has done "its best" a listener will understand and believe an intended message. This is a valid assumption for discourse generation, since one can not say more than one knows. However, after the planned discourse has been generated, the model of the listener's beliefs must be updated by an independent assessment of the listener's understanding. Otherwise, the listener's model will eventually diverge from the true state of affairs, and the rhetorical devices proposed based on it will be ineffective.

Our mechanism has been successfully applied as an analytical tool with respect to texts in a variety of domains, ranging from expert domains (Cognitive Science, Linguistics and Telecommunications) through intermediate ones (Data Structures and Algebra) to novice ones (*Childcraft Encyclopedia* and Dr. Spock's *Baby and Child Care*). At present, the generation of Peripheral RDs has been implemented, and produces various combinations of these rhetorical devices for different instances of the Student Network in Figure 4. In addition, the generation of Supportive RDs for the Access phase is in initial stages of implementation. Finally, investigation towards a formal characterization of Supportive RDs for the Construction and Acceptance phases is still in progress, however, valuable insights have been obtained with respect to the generation of these rhetorical devices.

References

Anderson, J.R. (1983), *The Architecture of Cognition*, Harvard University Press, Cambridge, Massachusetts.

Appelt, D.E. (1982), *Planning Natural Language Utterances to Satisfy Multiple Goals*. Technical Note 259, SRI International, March 1982.

Brown, J.S., and Van Lehn, K. (1980), Repair Theory: A Generative Theory of Bugs in Procedural Skills. In *Cognitive Science* 4, pp. 379-426.

Buchanan, B.G. and Shortliffe, E.H. (1985), *Rule-Based Expert Systems — The MYCIN Experiments of the Stanford Heuristic Programming Project*, Addison-Wesley Publishing Company.

Burton, R.R. and Brown, J.S. (1982), An Investigation of Computer Coaching for Informal Learning Activities. In D. Sleeman and J.S. Brown (Eds.), *Intelligent Tutoring Systems*, London: Academic Press, pp. 79-98.

Doyle, J. (1979), A Truth Maintenance System. In *Artificial Intelligence* 12, pp. 231-272.

Flowers, M. (1982), On Being Contradictory. In *AAAI-82 Proceedings, American Association for Artificial Intelligence*, pp. 269-272.

Gentner, D. (1983), Structure-Mapping: A Theoretical Framework for Analogy. In *Cognitive Science* 7, pp. 155-170.

Goldstein, I.P. (1982), The Genetic Graph: A Representation for the Evolution of Procedural Knowledge. In D. Sleeman and J.S. Brown (Eds.), *Intelligent Tutoring Systems*, London: Academic Press, pp. 51-77.

Grice, H.P. (1975), Logic and Conversation. In P.J. Cole and J.L. Morgan (Eds.), *Syntax and Semantics, Volume 3: Speech Acts*, Academic Press, pp. 41-58.

Grosz, B.J. and Sidner, C.L. (1986), Attention, Intentions, and the Structure of Discourse. In *Computational Linguistics*, Volume 12, Number 3, pp. 175-204.

Hovy, E.H. (1987), *Generating Natural Language under Pragmatic Constraints*. Doctoral Dissertation, Computer Science Department, Yale University, New Haven, Connecticut.

Hovy, E.H. (1988), Planning Coherent Multisentential Text. In *Proceedings of the Twenty-Sixth Annual Meeting of the Association for Computational Linguistics*, State University of New York, Buffalo, New York.

Kukich, K. (1983), *Knowledge-Based Report Generation: A Knowledge-Engineering Approach to Natural Language Report Generation*. Doctoral Dissertation, The Interdisciplinary Department of Information Science, University of Pittsburgh, Pennsylvania.

Lynch, B.J., Parr, R.E. and Keating, H.M. (1979), *Maths 8*, Sorrett Publishing.

McCoy, K.F. and Cheng, J. (1988), Focus of Attention: Constraining What Can Be Said Next. Presented at the *4th International Workshop on Text Generation*, Los Angeles.

McKeown, K.R. (1985), Discourse Strategies for Generating Natural Language Text. In *Artificial Intelligence* 27, pp. 1-41.

Mann, W.C. and Thompson, S.A. (1987), Rhetorical Structure Theory: A Theory of Text Organization. Report No. ISI/RS-87-190, Information Sciences Institute, Los Angeles, June 1987.

Matz, M. (1982), Towards a Process Model for High School Algebra Errors. In D. Sleeman and J.S. Brown (Eds.), *Intelligent Tutoring Systems*, London: Academic Press, pp. 25-50.

Moore, J.D. and Swartout, W.R. (1989), A Reactive Approach to Explanation. In *IJCAI-11 Proceedings, International Joint Conference on Artificial Intelligence*, pp. 1504-1510.

Paris, C.L. (1988), Tailoring Object Descriptions to a User's Level of Expertise. In *Computational Linguistics*, Volume 14, Number 3, pp. 64-78.

Sacerdoti, E.D. (1977), *A Structure of Plans and Behavior*, Elsevier-North Holland Publishing Company, Amsterdam.

Sidner, C.L. (1979), *Towards a Computational Theory of Definite Anaphora Comprehension in English Discourse*. Doctoral Dissertation, MIT, Cambridge, Massachusetts.

Sleeman, D. (1984), Mis-Generalization: An Explanation of Observed Mal-rules. In *Proceedings of the Sixth Annual Conference of the Cognitive Science Society*, pp. 51-56.

Van Lehn, K. (1983), Human Procedural Skill Acquisition: Theory, Model and Psychological Validation. In *AAAI-83 Proceedings, American Association for Artificial Intelligence*, pp. 420-423.

Zukerman, I. (1987), Goal-based Generation of Motivational Expressions in a Learning Environment. In *AAAI-87 Proceedings, American Association for Artificial Intelligence*, pp. 327-331.

Zukerman, I. and Cheong, Y.H. (1988), Impairment Invalidation: A Computational Model for the Generation of Rhetorical Devices. In *Proceedings of the International Computer Science Conference '88: Artificial Intelligence, Theory and Applications*, pp. 294-300.

Zukerman, I. (1989), A Predictive Approach for the Generation of Rhetorical Devices. Submitted for publication.

Towards an Intelligent Finite Element Training System

Alex Bykat

Center for Computer Applications
University of Tennessee at Chattanooga
Chattanooga, TN

1. Introduction.

Intimate knowledge of a sophisticated package requires a great deal of training, and many hours of practice coupled with the constant availability of a patient expert. Unfortunately, the expert is frequently not available and often not at all patient.

Manuals, be it on-line or not, are valuable but only as one of training options; they are of little merit when available as the only training tool. Using the on-line, or the hard copy, reference manual, the novice user is faced with masses of information to scan through. (For example, NASTRAN documentation has already over 8,500 pages!) Yet, frequently, the same information could be offered in 'no time' by an expert consultant. Furthermore, to avail himself even of this avalanche of facts, he must be sufficiently trained to be able to index his query with a correct keyword; incorrect keyword might at best retrieve no information at all, though more frequently it will simply swamp the user with irrelevant facts.

This situation can be alleviated by provision of an automated knowledge-based system capable of training, answering, and explaining its answers to questions about the usage of the underlying system (and its domain).

The capabilities of training functions to be investigated fall within the area of open problems in design of Intelligent Tutoring Systems. Much of the work in this field concentrates on construction of student models. Notable examples are GUIDON [Clancey, 1982], WUMPUS [Goldstein, 1982], SOPHIE I,II,III [Brown, 1982], and BUGGY [Burton, 1978]. Our work differs in the theories proposed, in mechanism of knowledge collection and the calculus adopted for evaluation of the students knowledge and misconceptions.

This paper describes a project concerned with construction of a knowledge based finite element applications consulting and training system (FEATS). FEATS communicates with the user and with the Finite Element Package (FEP). Through its capabilities, FEATS offers intelligent features for control and interrogation of the underlying finite element system. FEATS is intended to provide facilities for use of the FEP, and for effective training of personnel in the use of the system resources. Further, it is a step towards elimination of the demand for an FEP user to possess knowledge of the FEP internal implementation detail.

This paper, presents briefly the overall design of FEATS, but concentrates on the natural language communication aspects of the project.

2. The FEATS project.

FEATS environment consists of a TI Explorer LX with components specified in Fig.1. This computer is a dual processor in which the Explorer processor (Lisp machine) is coupled with a M68020 processor (LX).

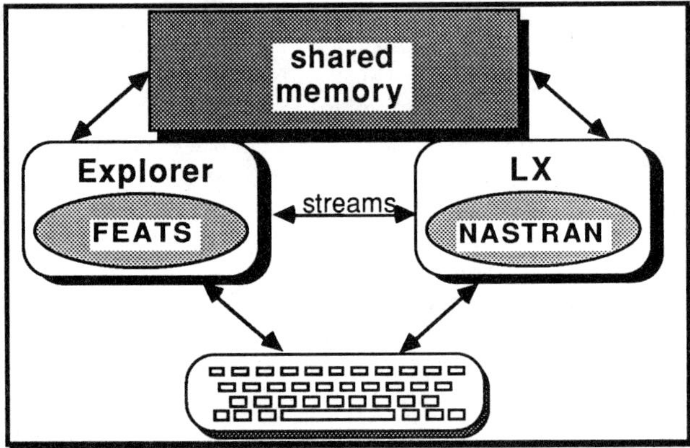

Fig.1 FEATS environment

The bulk of FEATS resides on the Explorer processor, whereas the Nastran finite element package (FEP) resides on the LX processor.

FEATS unifies a number of cooperating modules including:
A.   communication module for input of user utterances and presentation of systems conclusions,
B.   control module for rule construction, conflict resolution and rule invocation,
C.   reasoning module for interpretation of user utterances, selection of appropriate rules, and explanation of conclusions reached,
D.   model construction module for collection of facts and rules describing the user, his machine, and his conversation,
E.   teacher module for instruction and training of concepts and facilities available under the underlying FEP system,

Figure 2 shows FEATS's architecture; brief descriptions of some of the shown modules are presented in subsequent sections.

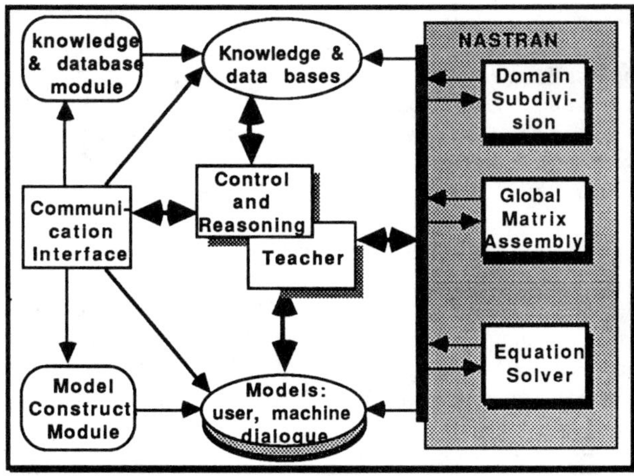

Fig.2 Major components of FEATS

3. Communication interface.

The OSCAT's NL interface prototype, [Bykat, 1986], was adapted for FEATS project, see fig.3. This interface performs as an expectation driven parser. The sentences are parsed by

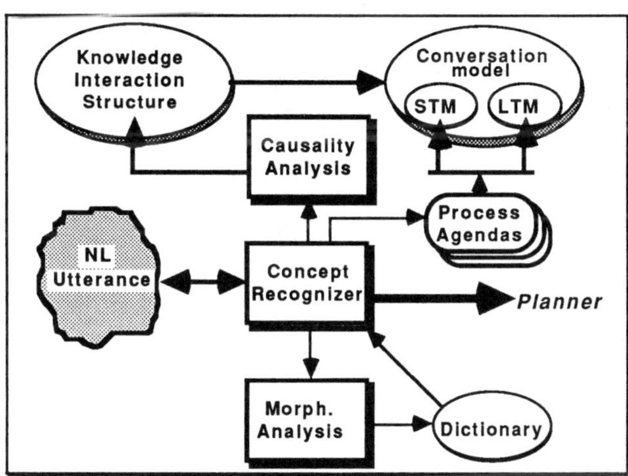

Fig.3. FEATS natural language interface.

using a dictionary of predefined words. Each word defines the expectation of other words and concepts which either precede it or follow it. The structure of the word definitions is fashioned after the Conceptual Dependency theory, [Schank & Abelson, 1977].

Parsing of sentences is effected in short term memory (STM). While parsing, the meaning of the sentences is formulated as a graph of linked concept frames. Once the parse of a sentence has been completed, the final semantic representation of the sentence is then memorized by moving it to the long term memory (LTM). The information thus acquired is then passed on to appropriate modules for further processing (identify goals, plan actions, generate response, etc).

The knowledge structures and their interactions are shown in Fig.4. The 'surface meaning' presented by the sentence identifies actions and objects of actions. This surface meaning is complemented with knowledge hinted at by the various concepts involved in a sentence. The additional knowledge identifies situations in which various actors possess goals which are achieved and enabled by execution of plans. FEATS will realize the plans, thus creating events which alter states of objects and actors. A consequence of realizing plans may be creation of new goals, etc.

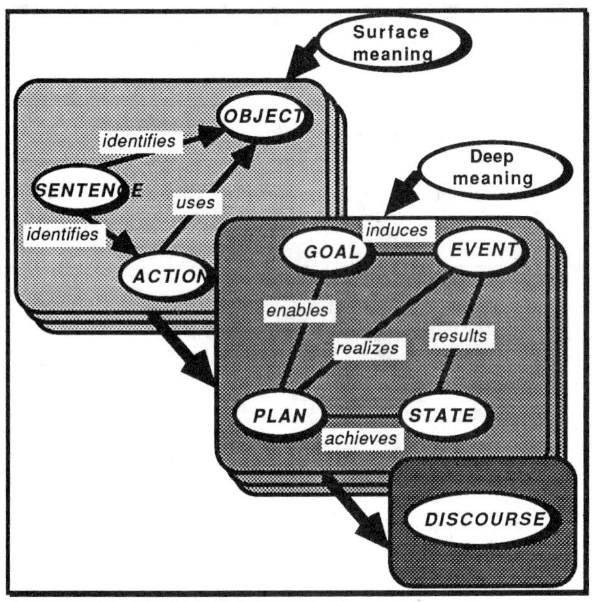

Fig 4. Knowledge interaction in FEATS

The following dialogue (Fig.5) serves as an example of the recognition of the surface meaning and its amplification into the deeper meaning necessary for FEATS functioning. In the dialogue **U:** precedes user's utterances, while *F:* precedes FEATS utterances.

U: **A concrete gravity dam is placed across a river. It's cross-section is of trapezoidal shape. The dam rests upon bedrock and is 500 ft high, 500 ft wide at the base, and 300 ft wide at the top.**

      I want to determine the maximum tensile stress for a typical cross-section.

F: *Your problem requires calculation of 2-D plane strain. Shall I proceed?*

U: **Wait. Why 2-D plane strain?**

F: *Your goal is to calculate tensile stress in a cross-section of the dam. Since a cross-section is 2-D, a 2-D analysis is sufficient. Further, since the dam is a long structure, therefore a plane strain calculation is appropriate.*

U: **OK, proceed.**

F: *The shape of the cross-section is trapezoidal. This suggest a trapezoidal, linear stiffness element. Division of the trapezoid into such elements can be uniform.*

      How many nodes along the basis do you want?

U: **5 will do.**

F: *and along the height?*

U: **5 again.**

F: ......

Fig.5. FEATS dialogue

The first three slices of Fig.6 show the state of the LTM after the first three sentences, i.e. after:

A concrete gravity dam is placed across a river. It's cross-section is of trapezoidal shape. The dam rests upon bedrock and is 500 ft high, 500 ft wide at the base, and 300 ft wide at the top.

have been uttered by the user. Notice the separation of the utterance into a number of concepts. Each of these concepts can be manipulated appropriately as the current focus of conversation warrants. Further, since these concepts are preserved in the LTM, they can be referred to in subsequent conversation too.

The fourth sentence, with its resulting structure, is shown in the fourth slice of Fig.6. This sentence identifies the user's goal which identifies a 'compute situation' (M-Compute) and results in creation of an appropriate plan for the achievement of this goal.

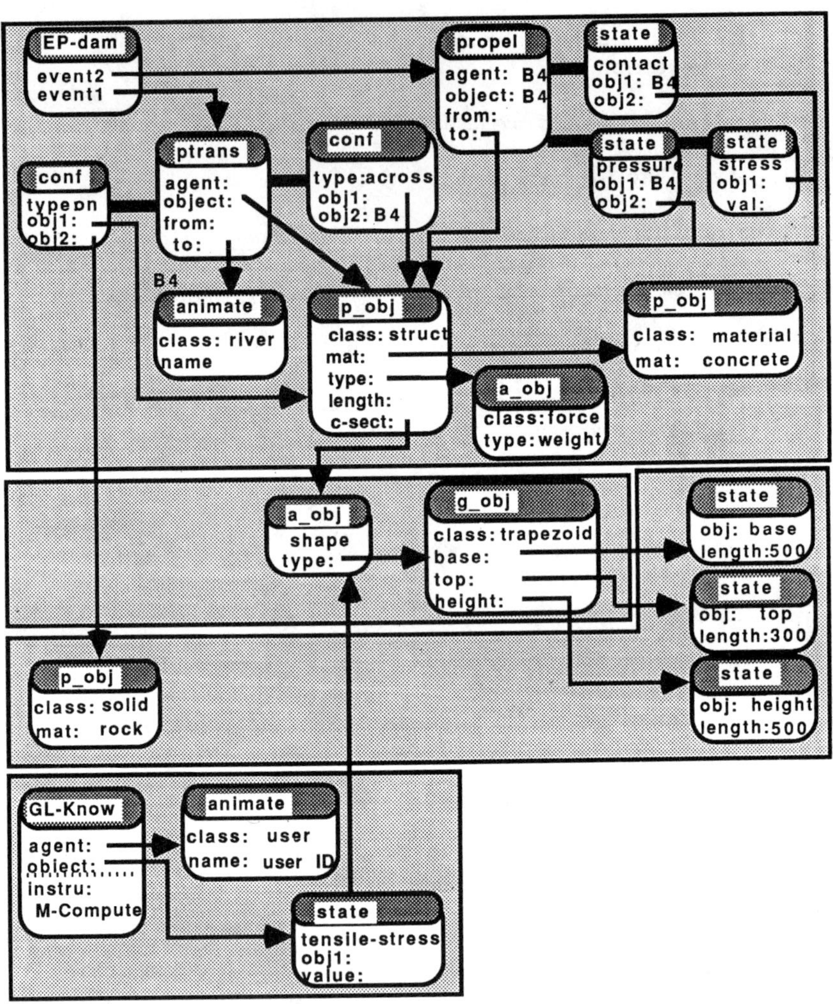

Fig. 6. Representation of meaning.

The plan, as shown in Fig.7, is in fact a sequence of plans motivated by goals which arise from satisfaction of the sequence of plans. The final plan, when realized, achieves the goal GL-Know (Fig.6) and results in the first FEATS response (see Fig.5). The knowledge needed for this response is extracted from the appropriate FEATS knowledge bases.

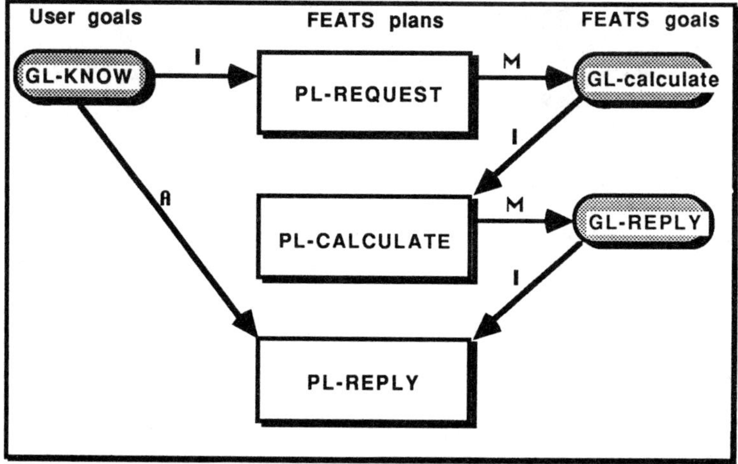

Fig.7. M-Compute situation.

4. Reasoning and control module.

The functions of the reasoning module are concerned with selection of rules which are appropriate for firing (invoking) in the current context. There are frequently a number of rules suitable for selection in any given situation. Conflicts can arise due to, the origin of two categories of rules, which are candidates for selection: (1) general rules inherited from the initial model of the FEATS world, and (2) specific rules selected by the pending goals as implied by the user's utterance. The reasoning module resolves all conflicts that arise.

A major control function is the selection of rules applicable within the current context. Since the knowledge base is expected to grow into a considerable size, a crucial pragmatic concern for this module is its search efficiency.

To reduce the number of rules to be searched in any given instance, the knowledge base is structured into classes of rules with each class declared as separate module. The search can then be restricted to a class of rules, subject to a particular set of goals, then within the class for a subclass of rules, subject to a particular subset of goals, etc.

5. Planner module.

Some of the more salient functions of this module are: goal extraction and plan formation. For example, the control module uses the internal representation of the conversation, to extract the goals and to create plans to satisfy these goals. Thus in the above example, the following goals will be extracted:

> *Calculate tensile stress.*
> *Obtain results of calculation.*
> *Explain these results.*

The training and the consulting aspects of FEATS require plan building. In the current prototype we employ a hierarchical plan construction. Once the goal of the utterance is understood, the first level of the plan is established. The first level is then refined to produce a second level, the second level is refined to produce a level third, and so on.

Refinement of plans proceeds by invoking plan fragments which are pre-defined. On the other hand, composition of the plan fragments into subplans and whole plans depends entirely on the particular goal that is extracted from the utterance.

Thus, for example, for the goal "create Object", FEATS produces the following plan (indentation shows plan refinement):

```
create(Object)
     precond(create,Object)
          exists(Object,new)
               identify(Object)
                    search(KB)
               identify(Depository)
                    search(KB)
               search(Object,Depository)
          material(Object,Qty)
               in_stock(Qty)
                    search(KB)
     use_tool(create,Object)
          identify_tool(create,Object,Tool)
               . . . . . . . . . .
          exists_tool(Tool,Id)
               . . . . . . . . . .
     apply_tool(Id,create,Object)
          use_method(Tool,create,Object,Method)
          call(Method)
```

Fig.8. Hierarchical planning

The interesting fact about the above plan is its generality. Thus, given an operation (eg. create), and the object 'Object', it requires only general search routines for the predicate exists and material to form a general model for performing the Operation on the Object. The dependence on the domain of FEATS is thus isolated to specification of the Tool (looked up by the identify_tool predicate), discovery of the particular Tool's Id (in exists_tool predicate), and the specification of the method for using the tool (found by the use_method predicate). In the case of "create file" goal, these are specified in the knowledge base as:

> *file(create,editor).*   *% to create a file use editor*
> *editor('VI').*   *% 'VI' is an editor*
> *'VI'(create,file,[vi,FID]).*   *% to create a file using VI*
>   *% specify command: vi <file id>*

6.   Teaching module.

FEATS will be designed to perform its evaluation actions unobtrusively. To achieve this we shall investigate an approach to gathering as much information for the user model as possible in a supervisory manner. That is, as the user interacts with the system, FEATS will gather information for the user model by carefully evaluating the user actions, much as a human supervisor would. This supervisory function will coexist with the test-and-grade (TAG) approach.

The supervisory function will extract (mainly negative) evaluation information from communication failures which attempt to violate the system model or the pragmatic beliefs of the system. The TAG function will yield (positive and negative) evaluation information by observing the effect of actions performed by the user under direction of FEATS.

Thus, two sources will supply data for the user model: the omnipotent supervisory function, and the training TAG function. Information gathered in this model will then be used to select appropriate interaction level with the user.

Our metrics and training theory is based on viewing the student model as a subset of the Cartesian set TM=ODxID, where OD is the FEATS set of operators and ID is the set of information points obtained by the TAG and supervisory functions described above. The TAG and supervisory functions will gather the information by essentially mapping elements of TM into a set of values V. By redefining TM as a space of vectors along the dimension ID students knowledge can be classified with respect to points in TM. This can be achieved by establishing an equivalence relation which partitions the redefined TM into a set of classes identifying the level of knowledge application in problems tackled by the student. Similarly, the knowledge of FEATS in answering the same questions can be partitioned by the same equivalence relation.

Using the equivalence relation, we can utilize the concept of 'rough understandability', [Pawlak, 1982; Rambally, 1986] to measure the apprenticeship level of the student. As a further extension of the latter work we shall then employ this measure to formulate a training (remedial) strategy (for the TAG function) based on the principle of 'maximum improvement with minimum effort'. This is achieved by (dynamic) classification of unmastered concepts with respect to this principle, and then teaching of concepts in the order discovered by this classification.

7.   Conclusion.

This paper describes natural language understanding and planning aspects of the FEATS project. FEATS offers intelligent features for control and interrogation of the underlying finite element system, as well as facilities for effective training of personnel in the use of the system resources.

A prototype of FEATS is written in Prolog on a Texas Instruments Explorer LX. The latter is a dual processor machine consisting of a lisp machine (EXPLORER) and an M68020 based computing engine (LX) running a Unix System V. This provides therefore an ideal environment for cooperation between AI type of a system and an engineering type of a system. In our case, the AI system is FEATS, whereas the engineering system is NASTRAN.

References.

1.   Anderson J.R. "Acquisition of proof skills in geometry" Michalski, Carbonell & Mitchell, 1983

2.   Brown, J.S, Burton, R.R, "Diagnostic models for procedural bugs in basic mathematical skills", Cognitive Science, 2,1978

3.   Burton, R.R, Brown, J.S. "An investigation of computer coaching for informal learning activities" in Sleeman and Brown, 1982

4.   Bykat, A. "Implementation of the finite element method" Univ. of London, UK 1974

5.   Bykat, A. "Automatic generation of triangular grids." International J.Num.Meth.Engng 10(6) 1976

6.   Bykat, A. "A note on an element ordering scheme." International J. Num.Meth.Engng 11(1)1977

7.   Bykat, A. "Design of a recursive shape controlling mesh generator." International J.Num.Meth.Engng, 19(9)1983

8.   Bykat, A. "Designing an intelligent operating system consultant and teacher" Proc.IEEE-PCCC-86, pp.572-578 3,1986

9.   Dyer, M.G. "In-depth understanding.", The MIT Press, 1983

10.   Pawlak, Z., "Rough sets", IJCIS, 11(5)1982

11.   Rambally G.K., "A theory of student modelling in instructional expert systems", Conf.ACM, Feb. 1986

12.   Schank R., Abelson R. "Scripts, Plans, Goals and understanding.", LEA, 1977

13.   Sleeman D., Brown J.S. "Intelligent tutoring systems", Academic Press,1982

14.   Wilensky, R. "Planning and understanding", Addison-Wesley, 1983

Bayesian Inference in an Expert System without Assuming Independence

Alex Gammerman

Computer Science Department
Heriot-Watt University
Edinburgh, Scotland

A. R. Thatcher

129 Thetford Road
New Malden
Surrey, U.K.

1. Objectives

In many expert systems, estimates are made of probabilities and use is made of Bayes' Theorem; but in applying the theorem it is often assumed that some of the probabilities are independent. These are sometimes known as "simple Bayes" models. One reason for assuming independence is that it is believed that without this assumption, the complexity of the calculations would become totally unmanageable as the number of pieces of evidence increases.

However, it was pointed out by Thatcher [13, 14] that in principle it is possible to apply Bayes' Theorem without assuming independence and without an unmanageable increase in complexity (see also Cumberbatch et al [3]). Consider, for example, the problem of estimating from past data the probabilities that patients have certain diseases, given their symptoms. If we apply Bayes' Theorem strictly without assuming independence, the argument leads to a simple, indeed obvious, result: if we can identify the past patients who had the same combination of symptoms as the new patient, and see what happened to them, then we can estimate probabilities for the new patient.

For simplicity of exposition, and to avoid confusion with the existing "simple Bayes" method, we shall describe the method described in the last paragraph as the "proper Bayes" method, because it is based on a strict application of Bayes' Theorem. The difference is simply that "simple Bayes" assumes independence whereas "proper Bayes" does not.

The reason why the complexity of the "proper Bayes" calculation does not increase exponentially as the number of symptoms increases - why there is no "combinatorial explosion" - is that the calculations only involve those combinations of symptoms which actually occur in the database, and this cannot exceed the number of past patients.

With a very large database, the method would, in principle, be very simple indeed. However, with a limited database it is necessary to use selected combinations of those symptoms which are most relevant to the diagnosis of each disease. A method is given for selecting such combinations. The method also gives upper and lower confidence limits for each probability, to provide a measure of the precision of the estimates.

A major question is how large a database is needed in order to obtain useful results. The main objective of the present report is to test the "proper Bayes" method in a particular practical application. For this purpose we use data on 2,000 patients with acute abdominal pain. Experts provided qualitative advice on the design of the model and on the relevance of symptoms to diseases, and in this sense the system is an expert system. However, the experts were not asked to supply numerical estimates of probabilities: these were estimated entirely from the database, using also technique of pattern recognition.

The "proper Bayes" method and the method of constructing selected combinations of relevant symptoms are used to calculate nine probabilities for each patient - one for each possible disease - with corresponding confidence limits. This was the original object of the exercise and it shows that the "proper Bayes" approach can indeed be used to estimate probabilities with a database of 2,000 patients.

The paper goes on to compare the results with the "simple Bayes" method. Both methods were found to be subject to various types of error, though in the "proper Bayes" case the errors will eventually tend to zero as the size of the database increases.

The conclusions of the investigation are summarised in Section 11.

2. Relationship to Existing Methods

The "simple Bayes" method has been widely applied in a number of statistical systems for computer-aided diagnosis. It has been used in hospitals and has been the subject of many papers since the early 1970's, many by De Dombal and his collaborators [4]. It has been applied to the same problem, viz. patients with acute abdominal pain, as is discussed in the present paper. For the latest references, see Adams et al [1].

Another method which makes the "simple Bayes" assumptions, though it applies them differently, is the Glasgow Dyspepsia System (GLADYS) which has been described by Spiegelhalter and Knill-Jones [11]. In this, a logistic regression model is applied to weights of evidence in order to estimate numerical scores which can be attached to each symptom.

More recently there is the method of causal networks which has been developed by Lauritzen and Spiegelhalter [7]. This assumes that some, but not all, of the causes or symptoms or diseases are independent. However, the method also assumes that experts can supply a very closely- specified structure for the problem and can provide, on request, subjective estimates of an extremely large number of conditional probabilities. These conditions are not satisfied in the problem considered in the present paper.

There are also a number of expert systems which have been developed using the "simple" Bayes assumptions. Among them one of the first expert systems, called Prospector, was developed by Duda et al [5] as a consultant system for mineral exploration. Since then several other Prospector-like systems have been developed using the same assumption (see, for example, Cox and Broughton, [2]).

The present work is also related to an approach developed by Gammerman and Lanin [6].

3. Bayes' Theorem Without Assuming Independence

In order to show the theory behind the "proper Bayes" method, let us begin with the simplest case, in which there are two possible symptoms (which we denote by A and B) and one possible disease (which we denote by D).

Let P(D) be the prior probability that a new patient has the disease D. Here, "prior" means "before we know his symptoms", and at that stage all we know is that he is a patient: so on this information, P(D) can be estimated as the proportion of all past patients who were found to have the disease D. Using a bar over a letter to denote negation, the prior probability that the new patient does not have the disease D is

$$P(\overline{D}) = 1 - P(D)$$

Now, let P(A/D) be the probability that a patient has the symptom A, given that he has the disease D. Similarly, let P(A,B/D) be the probability that he has both the symptoms A and B, given that he has the disease D, and without assuming that A and B are independent.

Now suppose that we observe the patient and find that he has both the symptoms A and B. The likelihood that a patient chosen at random will have both these symptoms is P(A,B/D) if he has the disease and P(A,B/$\overline{D}$) if he does not. Then by Bayes' Theorem we have

$$
\begin{aligned}
P(D/A,B) &= k.P(D).P(A,B/D) \\
P(\overline{D}/A,B) &= k.P(\overline{D}).P(A,B/\overline{D})
\end{aligned}
$$
(1)

where k is a constant of proportionality. Therefore the odds in favour of D are given by

$$O(D/A,B) = \frac{P(D/A,B)}{P(\overline{D}/A,B)}$$
(2)

$$= \frac{P(D).P(A,B/D)}{P(\overline{D}).P(A,B/\overline{D})}$$
(3)

$$= \frac{P(A,B,D)}{P(A,B,\overline{D})}$$
(4)

Here (2) is the definition of the odds; (3) follows from (2) on substituting (1); and (4) follows from (3) since by definition the conditional probability P(A,B/D) is equal to P(A,B,D)/P(D), where P(A,B,D) is the probability that a patient chosen at random will have both A and B and D. From (4) it follows that

$$P(D/A,B) = \frac{P(A,B,D)}{P(A,B,D)+P(A,B,\overline{D})}$$
(5)

Alternatively, if both symptoms are not known simultaneously, but are known one after the other, then Bayes' Theorem can be applied in two stages. After we have observed the symptom A, the theorem gives a posterior probability for D. This can then be used as a prior probability for the second stage, when we observe the symptom B. Equation (3) now involves more complicated conditional probabilities like P(B/A,D); but the important point is that (4) and hence (5) remain the same. For the full formulae for the two-stage method, see Thatcher [13].

If we have the records of previous patients, (5) can be evaluated by using the proportion of all past patients who had A and B and D as an estimate of P(A,B,D), and the proportion who had A and B but not D as an estimate of P(A,B,$\overline{D}$).

If we now consider cases with more than two symptoms and more than one disease, we find that the equation (3) becomes more and more complicated, but (4) and (5) remain simple. If D_k denotes the k-th possible disease and if $\underline{S}$ denotes the combination of symptoms for a given patient, then the generalisation of (5) is

$$P(D_k/\underline{S}) = \frac{P(D_k,\underline{S})}{\sum\limits_{k} P(D_k,\underline{S})} \tag{6}$$

Again, if we can identify past patients who had the combination of symptoms $\underline{S}$, and find the proportion of them who had the disease D_k, then this proportion will give an estimate of the right hand side of (6). What (6) then tells us is that this proportion will also give an estimate of the probability that a new patient with symptoms $\underline{S}$ will have the disease D_k. Put this way, the conclusion is perhaps rather obvious. We may note that (6) also follows immediately from one of the text book results on Bayes' Theorem - see, for example, Stuart and Ord [12], page 280.

We describe (6) as the "proper Bayes" formula for $P(D_k/\underline{S})$ because it results from a strict application of Bayes' Theorem, without any artificial assumptions. In contrast, the "simple Bayes" method fails to take the step from (3) to (4). Instead it <u>assumes</u> that A and B are independent, so that

$$P(A,B/D) = P(A/D).P(B/D) \tag{7a}$$
$$P(A,B/\overline{D}) = P(A/\overline{D}).P(B)\overline{D}) \tag{7b}$$

The methods also differ, at least superficially, in the form of the information which is needed to operate them. Thus "simple Bayes" requires the prior probability P(D) and conditional probabilities like P(A/D) etc. In the "proper Bayes" method these are subsumed in the joint probabilities P(A,B,D) etc.

4. Confidence Limits

If we wish to estimate the probability p that a new patient will have a certain disease, given his symptoms, then (6) shows that one way to do this is to identify the records of previous patients who had the same symptoms and see how many of them proved to have the disease. Suppose that there were n past patients with the symptoms and that of these a number d had the disease. A simple estimate of the probability p is given by d/n and we now wish to have a measure of the precision of this estimate.

One such measure is provided by what are known as the "95 per cent confidence limits". For any given observed values of n and d we can say that d/n is our best estimate of p, but we can accompany this estimate with both a lower limit L and an upper limit U. These are determined in such a way that if we always use the same formula to calculate U and L as functions of n and d, and if we always assume that the true value of the probability p lies somewhere between L and U, so that

$$L \leq p \leq U, \tag{8}$$

then we shall be right at least 95 per cent of the time.

Confidence limits are derived in the frequency theory of probability and it may perhaps seem odd to use them in conjunction with Bayes' Theorem. The justification is that for this particular problem it is known that there is only a small numerical difference between confidence limits calculated by the frequency method and alternative limits calculated by the Bayesian method. This difference is, in fact, no larger than the effect of one extra patient in the past data - see

Thatcher [15]. Given this small difference, it is convenient to use the standard formulae for confidence limits.

It raises an interesting point on the "necessity" of some theories of uncertainty in expert systems which operate with two-probabilities values' - the low and upper bounds: so-called "two-values scheme" approaches (Quinlan, [9]; Shortliffe et al, [10]). The standard formulae for calculating the confidence limits are reproduced in Appendix J. They are used later in this report to calculate explicit upper and lower confidence limits for many estimated probabilities (see Appendices B and D).

5. A Particular Example: Patients With Acute Abdominal Pain

As a particular example, the methods described above have been tried out on the data for 2,000 patients who were admitted to hospital suffering from acute abdominal pain.

When the patients were admitted, their symptoms were recorded in the form listed in Appendix A. A word of explanation is necessary because the terminology is not entirely standard. The term "symptom" is used to include not only symptoms which are directly caused by the disease, but also other signs or indications which may be relevant to the diagnosis. According to one usage, there are 33 main symptoms (sex, age, etc.) and for each of these there are several possible states or values (coded in Appendix A as 1/0, 1/1, etc.). In this terminology we can use S_{ij} to denote the j-th state of the i-th symptom, where i = 1, 2, ... , 33. In the Appendix there are 135 lines showing states, so the average number of states per symptom is $\dfrac{135}{33}$.

However, the word "symptom" can also be used to refer to a particular state like "pain in the lower half of the abdomen". In this terminology there are 135 symptoms (= states) and we may use S_i to denote the i-th symptom on this definition, where in this case i = 1, 2, ... , 135.

When the symptoms have been recorded, a preliminary diagnosis is made by a doctor, who provisionally allocates the patient to one of the nine diseases or "Diagnostic Groups" listed in Appendix A. Another word of explanation is needed here. Patients who are not diagnosed as in Groups 1- 3 or 5-9 are placed in Group 4 (= unspecified abdominal pain), which is therefore a residual group.

In many hospitals a preliminary diagnosis is also made by a computer, using the "simple Bayes" method. The computer calculates nine probabilities, one for each of the diagnostic groups, and the "computer diagnosis" is taken as the group with the highest probability.

Later on, the patient will be given a "final diagnosis" which takes into account all further information since the preliminary diagnosis, including the results of surgical operations which will show whether the preliminary diagnosis was correct.

6. Relevant Symptoms and the Selection of Combinations

Equation (6) gives the probability that a patient with the combination of symptoms $\underline{S}$ will have the disease D_k, but it does not tell us which symptoms need to be included in $\underline{S}$. If we are trying to diagnose a particular disease, and if we include in $\underline{S}$ some symptom which has no relevance whatever to that disease, then we will have made the problem more difficult than it need have been. For example, estimates of $P(D_k/\underline{S})$ from past data will have to be based on smaller numbers, and so will be less precise, than was necessary.

Let us begin, then, by regarding a particular symptom S_i as being "relevant" to the diagnosis of a particular disease D_k if the probability of having the disease depends on whether Si is present or absent. In other words, if S_i is "relevant" then we shall expect to find that $P(D_k/S_i)$ is different from $P(D_k/\bar{S_i})$. Of course it can be argued in theory that all symptoms may be relevant; but nevertheless, some symptoms will be much more relevant than others. At least we can begin by identifying symptoms which are visibly relevant.

Whether $P(D_k/S_i)$ is different from $P(D_k/\bar{S_i})$ can be tested by looking at the 2 x 2 table with rows S_i, $\bar{S_i}$ and columns D_k, $\bar{D_k}$ and with cells showing the numbers of past patients in each category. For the disease D_1 = appendicitis there are 135 such 2 x 2 tables, for i = 1, 2, ... , 135. For each such table we can calculate χ^2. The highest value of χ^2 was 448.2, for one degree of freedom. Even allowing for the fact that this was the best out of 135, it was clearly significant by any standard. The symptom S_i concerned was "tenderness in the right lower quadrant (of the abdomen)". Thus, this purely statistical method succeeds in identifying a genuine symptom of appendicitis!

Of course, if S_i is a relevant symptom then so is $\bar{S_i}$.

We now seek a second symptom S_j which will further improve the diagnosis for those patients who are already known to have S_i. We therefore need to test whether $P(D_K/S_i \, S_j)$ is different from $P(D_K/S_i \, \bar{S_j})$. This can be done by constructing a 2 x 2 table with rows S_j, $\bar{S_j}$ and columns D_K, $\bar{D_K}$ and with the cells containing the numbers of past patients who were in the categories concerned and who all had the symptom S_i. We can now find the S_j which gives the highest value of χ^2 in these tables. If this is significant - at some level of significance χ_0^2, to be discussed later - then we conclude that the combination $S_i \, S_j$ will be relevant to the diagnosis of D_K. So will $S_i \, \bar{S_j}$.

Next, we seek a symptom S_k which will be relevant for those patients who are in the category $\bar{S_i}$, that is, those who do <u>not</u> have the symptom S_i. We will then have identified four relevant combinations of symptoms, namely

$$S_i S_j \quad S_i \bar{S_j} \quad \bar{S_i} S_k \quad \bar{S_i} \bar{S_k}$$

We can continue in this way, adding further symptoms one at a time, until the process comes to a natural end. This will certainly happen eventually, because as each new symptom is added, the number of patients in the next 2 x 2 tables becomes smaller. The procedure will certainly halt when this number falls to one, or it may end much sooner, when the maximum value of χ^2 (for a potential new symptom) falls below χ_0^2.

As regards the level of χ_0^2, a provisional value was chosen as follows. If we were considering only a single symptom, the conventional level of significance would normally be taken as 1 in 20 or 1 in 100. The latter would give a significance level, for 1 degree of freedom, of $\chi_0^2 = 6.6$. However, we are actually testing 135 symptoms and then taking the one which gives the highest level of χ^2. This extreme value of χ^2 out of 135 cases will be significant at the 1 in 100 level in the same way as a single value at the 1 in 100 x 135 level, and for this the threshold level is $\chi_0^2 = 14.4$.

When the combinations are complete, the number of patients in each combination, and the numbers of these who had the disease D_k, can be found. A best estimate for $P(D_k/\underline{S})$ and the upper and lower confidence limits for this estimate can then be found by the method described in Section 4.

At this point the reader will find it helpful to look at the specimen set of combinations which is given in Appendix B. He may also care to read the comments in Appendix C and see the confidence limits in Appendix D. It will be noted that every patient will fall into one and only one combination for each disease.

The specimen combinations in Appendix B are based on those found by the method above taking $\chi_0^2 = 14.4$, but they were slightly condensed for ease of presentation and discussion, for example by introducing the grouped symptom 26/2* defined in Appendix C.

It will be seen from the comments in Appendix C that the method gave useful results for all the diseases except one, namely pancreatitis. For this, the reason for failure was that the most relevant symptoms for diagnosis were not recorded in the database.

It will be seen that the problem of selecting relevant symptoms is rather similar to that of deciding which variables to include in a multiple regression, except that here we are dealing with attributes instead of continuous variables. The advantages and disadvantages of this particular method of selecting relevant symptoms and combinations will be discussed thoroughly later in this paper. It is not claimed that this particular method is optimal. What is shown, though, by the results in Appendices B - D is that it is possible (at least for these diseases) to construct combinations of relevant symptoms in a way which enables us to use the "proper Bayes" formula (6) in a practical situation. Moreover, the results are medically sensible and the confidence limits for the probabilities are not unduly wide, even when based on a database of only 2,000 past patients for 9 diagnostic groups.

7. Computational Model

In the course of this work, computer programmes have been written which will select the relevant symptoms and combinations in the way described, and which will then calculate the resulting probabilities and their confidence limits.

The system called "PROB" has been written in the language C using UNIX operating environment on a VAX 11/750. It includes 3 major procedures:
-     for finding combinations of symptoms with the best estimation of probability, and the associated confidence limits, for each diagnostic group ('Find_Combinations');
-     for assigning probabilities to each patient for each diagnostic group ('Assign_Probabilities'). The output is a table for all 2000 patients with nine probabilities for each;
-     for classifying correct diagnoses ('Find_Matrix'). The output is a matrix of correct diagnosis versus final diagnoses which characterize the classification rate.

The major procedure 'Find_Combinations' operates by taking an initial file of patient records and creating a frequency table from this data. The chi- squared of each 2 x 2 table is then calculated, and the table sorted in order of decreasing value of chi-squared. The most significant symptom/state is then taken (i.e. the one with the largest value of chi- squared), and a secondary frequency table calculated consisting of all the patients with this symptom, the process then repeating itself until a termination condition occurs (that corresponds to a certain threshold χ_0^2). The program then repeats the process, this time taking all the patients who do not have each significant symptom, creating the frequency tables, etcetera. The procedure as it can be seen is recursive.

Further details including semi-formal descriptions of these main procedures are given in Appendix I.

8. Comparisons Between "simple Bayes" and "proper Bayes"

Some examples of probabilities calculated by the "proper Bayes" method using selected combinations of symptoms are given in Appendix E, for a sample of 20 patients. The corresponding probabilities calculated by the "simple Bayes" method for the same sample of patients are given in Appendix F. These figures are given solely for purposes of illustration. The following comments take account of results found in a much wider comparison than just the small sample in Appendices E and F.

The first point which calls for comment, in a critical examination of the "proper Bayes" method, is a difficulty which arises from the fact that in practical applications the database is bound to be of limited size. In our particular application we are trying to do a very difficult thing, estimating nine probabilities simultaneously from a database of 2,000 patients with 135 symptoms each. Eight of these probabilities are estimated independently, but the probability for the residual group D_4 = non-specific abdominal pain is calculated by subtracting the sum of the other eight from unity. If the database had been infinite this would have given accurate results, but with a finite database there is no guarantee that the estimated value of $P(D_4/\underline{S})$ will be positive.

Each of the eight estimates is subject to what are, in effect, sampling errors, in the sense that they would all disappear if we had an infinite data base. The confidence limits in Appendix D show the width of the margins of error for individual estimates. The sum of eight such estimates will necessarily have a wider margin still, so we must not be taken aback if their sum sometimes exceeds 1, with the result that the estimates of $P(D_4/\underline{S})$ is negative. In fact, although in calculations using the specimen combinations in Appendix B some 12 per cent of the estimates $P(D_4/\underline{S})$ were negative, only 2 per cent were less than -0.4 and only 0.1 per cent were less than -0.8.

The extreme cases are very instructive. In general terms, the patient concerned falls in one of the combinations of symptoms $\underline{S}_i$ which are relevant to the diagnosis of D_i. He also falls in one of the combinations $\underline{S}_j$ which are relevant to the diagnosis of D_j, and these particular combinations happen to be such that

$$P(D_i/\underline{S}_i) + p(D_j/\underline{S}_j) > 1.$$

This can happen when there is a particular symptom Sk which is relevant to the diagnosis of both D_i and D_j but which was not quite included in the selected combination $\underline{S}_i$, and/or which was not quite included in $\underline{S}_j$, because the relevant value of χ^2 fell below the threshold χ_0^2. This would not have happened if we had had a larger database.

The next point which calls for comment is that Appendix F contains more zeros and ones than Appendix E. One of the reasons for this is that if there is no past patient in the database who had both the particular symptom S_i and the particular disease D_k, then the "simple Bayes" method automatically takes the likelihood $P(S_i/D_k)$ as zero and so will calculate $P(D_k/\underline{S}) = 0$ for all those patients whose combination of symptoms $\underline{S}$ includes the particular symptom S_i. However, the "proper Bayes" method will only do this if the particular symptom S_i appears explicitly in one of the selected combinations.

This is another case where there would be no discrepancy if the database were infinite. With a finite database, the "simple Bayes" method will be right if there is a genuine medical reason why S_i cannot happen in conjunction with D_k, but it will be wrong if the conjunction of S_i and D_k has not happened <u>so far</u> but will happen if the database is increased. Conversely, the "proper Bayes" method will be wrong in the first case but right in the second. Which method will give the best results in a particular application is not obvious <u>a priori</u> , at least unless there is expert advice.

The wider comparisons show that a similar effect can occur not only when $P(S_i/D_k) = 0$ but also when the ratio $P(S_i/\overline{D}_k)/P(S_i/D_k)$ is either very large or very small. Such symptoms can of course be identified and it would be possible to add them to the list of "relevant symptoms" in the "proper Bayes" method. This might perhaps get the best of both worlds.

Finally, we come to the most obvious reason for differences between the two methods, when the basic assumption of the "simple Bayes" method, that the symptoms are independent, is not valid. There are plenty of cases. For example, there are patients with the symptoms A = "rebound" and B = "guarding"; these are conditions or reactions of the abdomen which are well-known symptoms of the disease D = appendicitis. From the data we find $P(D/A,B) = .676$ on the "simple Bayes" method but only .476 on the "proper Bayes" method. The latter estimate is based on the simple fact that there were 231 past patients who had both rebound and guarding, and of these 110 had appendicitis. The resulting estimate of the probability of appendicits, on a strict application of Bayes' Theorem, is $110/231 = .476$, and it seems incontrovertible that the "simple Bayes" estimate is too high.

Whether this clear disadvantage of the "simple Bayes" method will outweigh, or will be outweighed by, the disadvantages of the "proper Bayes" method when the database is limited, is a question which can only be decided by experiment. In time, as the database grows, the errors in the "proper Bayes" method will eventually disappear but those in the "simple Bayes" method will not.

9. Computer Diagnoses and Decision Theory

The method described in Sections 3-6 was designed to estimate probabilities. However, such methods are also judged by how well they make diagnoses.

On the basis of decision theory, it might be argued that treatment for the disease D_k should be followed if the probability that the patient has that disease exceeds some threshold level t_k: that is, if

$$P(D_k/\underline{S}) > t_k \tag{9}$$

The reason why the threshold may not be the same for each disease is that the penalties for making wrong decisions may not be the same for each disease. However, in hospitals where preliminary diagnoses are made by computers as well as by doctors, the "computer diagnoses" do not use (9) but simply choose the disease with the highest probability, as calculated by the "simple Bayes" method.

Choosing the disease with the highest probability has the merit that it is the method which maximises the expected total number of correct diagnoses. This can be seen as follows. If a patient with the combination of symptoms $\underline{S}$ is diagnosed as having the disease D_i, then the expected number of correct diagnoses (per patient with symptoms $\underline{S}$) will be $P(D_i/\underline{S})$. This expected number will clearly be maximised if we choose the diagnosis D_i as the disease with the highest probability $P(D_i/\underline{S})$. (In the special case where two diseases D_i and D_j happen to have equal probabilities, then changing the diagnosis from one to the other will make no difference to the expected number of correct diagnoses).

We may note in passing that in order to find the disease with the highest probability - if that is all one wants to do - it may not be necessary to calculate nine probabilities for each combination of symptoms. We need only look at the past patients who had that combination of symptoms and see which was the commonest disease amongst them. This requires less calculation than finding nine separate probabilities.

10. Numbers of Correct Diagnoses

It is not easy to distinguish accurately between nine diseases which have many similar symptoms. Of the preliminary diagnoses made by doctors on these diseases, an estimated 76 per cent are correct in the sense that they agree with the final diagnosis(see appendices G and H). If for each of the 2,000 patients in the data base we calculate the nine probabilities by the "simple Bayes" method, and take as the "computer diagnosis" the disease with the highest probability, then 74 per cent of these diagnoses are correct. If we calculate probabilities by the "proper Bayes" method using just the specimen combinations in Appendix B, then only 65 per cent of the diagnoses are correct. The full details of these comparisons will be found in Appendices G and H.

Thus the specimen combinations can be used to make estimates of individual probabilities in a very simple way which illustrates how the "proper Bayes" method works, but they are not sufficiently elaborate or precise to improve on the "simple Bayes" method for the purpose of making computer diagnoses. The next task is therefore to see whether the specimen combinations can be improved. We also need to remember that in the comparisons described above, the methods have been tested on the same data to which they were fitted. If they were fitted to one set of data and tested on another, the results might be different.

In principle there are several ways in which the specimen combinations could be elaborated:

(a)   The selection of combinations depends on the choice of the value of χ_0^2. The calculation could be repeated using smaller values of χ_0^2.

(b)   The list of relevant symptoms could be topped up by adding the further symptoms suggested by the experts (see the end of Appendix C).

(c)   Following the findings in Section 8, the relevant symptoms could be topped up by adding those for which the ratio $P(S_i/D_k)/P(S_i/\bar{D}_k)$ is either very large or very small.

Course (a) could reasonably be expected to pick up many of the extra symptoms in (b) and (c). It could also be tried out immediately using the general computer programmes described in Section 7. When applied to the 2,000 patients in the database, the results were as follows:

per cent	Number of combinations	Correct diagnoses
Specimen combinations	49	65.0
$\chi_0^2 = 14.4$	81	66.2
$\chi_0^2 = 10.5$	103	66.8
$\chi_0^2 = 6.6$	178	70.0
$\chi_0^2 = 2.7$	584	85.8

Thus lower values of χ_0^2 appear at first sight to increase the number of correct diagnoses. However, this effect could be partly artificial:
 increasing the number of combinations is bound to improve the fit to the database, and so will tend to increase the percentage of diagnoses which are correct when tested <u>on the same data</u>. At the same time, increasing the number of combinations will reduce their average size (in terms of past patients per combination) and so will reduce the precision of the resulting estimates of probabilities; in other words, the confidence limits will widen.

It is not obvious, before one tries it, whether increasing the number of combinations will make the computer diagnoses better or worse when tested on different data.

At this stage of the investigation, it became possible to make use of a second database. This consisted of 6,387 past patients and included the original 2,000 patients, though these could not be identified separately because patient reference numbers had not been coded. It was therefore decided to select a new set of 2,000 patients at random from the 6,387 for testing purposes, and to refit the combinations afresh to the other 4,387 patients.

The following table shows the results when combinations were fitted to 4,387 patients for various values of χ_0^2 and then tested on 2,000 different patients. It also shows the corresponding result for the "simple Bayes" method, when the probabilities (for any given combination of symptoms in the 2,000 patients) were calculated from the date for the 4,387 patients.

	Correct diagnoses (per cent)
Specimen combinations	62.4
$\chi_0^2 = 16.5$	63.7
$\chi_0^2 = 14.4$	64.4
$\chi_0^2 = 13.5$	64.8
$\chi_0^2 = 12.5$	64.8
$\chi_0^2 = 12.0$	65.0
$\chi_0^2 = 11.5$	65.1
$\chi_0^2 = 11.0$	64.7
$\chi_0^2 = 10.5$	64.7
$\chi_0^2 = 8.5$	64.2
$\chi_0^2 = 6.6$	64.2
$\chi_0^2 = 2.7$	61.8
"Simple Bayes"	73.8

Thus course (a), i.e. reducing the value of χ_0^2 below 14.4, improves the predictive power of the combinations only slightly. The percentage of correct diagnoses reaches a maximum of just over 65 per cent when $\chi_0^2 = 11.5$. This remains below the 74 per cent achieved be "simple Bayes" method.

It is still possible that courses (b) and (c) might perhaps improve the combinations more efficiently than course (a). This remains untested.

11. Conclusions

Although the predictive power of the method developed in this report is not quite as good as that of the present method in this particular application, nevertheless there are some positive results. From a very complicated database it proved possible to identify, by a purely statistical method, a selection of symptoms which were immediately recognised by doctors as being relevant to the diagnosis of the diseases concerned. Using combinations of these symptoms it was possible to estimate probabilities by a strict application of Bayes' Theorem, without assuming independence. These probabilities were estimated entirely from the database and did not require experts to make subjective estimates of large numbers of conditional probabilities. The only complete failure in this particular exercise was for a disease (pancreatitis) for which the most relevant symptoms were not recorded in the database.

Conceptually, the method is extremely straightforward and easy to explain. Users can see immediately how the probabilities are derived from the past data. Upper and lower confidence limits are given for every estimate. General computer programmes have been written which could be applied to any database.

Acknowledgements

We wish to thank Mr. S.J. Nixon MB, ChB, BSc, FRCS of the General Surgical Unit, Western General Hospital, Edinburgh, and Mr. A.A. Gunn, MB, ChM, FRCS, formerly of the Bangour Hospital and Dr. C.G.G. Aitken of Edinburgh University, for their expert advice and for making available data originally collected at Bangour Hospital. We are greatly indebted to Miss Yiqun Gu of Heriot-Watt University for writing the computer programs. We also wish to thank Joyce Smith and Susan Donachie for typesetting and formatting this paper.

References

1. Adams, I.D. et al. (1986) Computer Aided Diagnoses of Acute Abdominal Pain: a multicentre study, British Medical Journal, 293 , pp. 800-804

2. Cox,P.R., Broughton, R.K. (1981) Micro Expert Users Manual. Version 2.1, ISIS Systems Ltd.

3. Cumberbatch,J. and Heaps,H.S. (1976) A Disease-conscious method for sequential diagnosis by use of disease probabilities without assumption of symptom independence. Int.J.Bio-Medical Computing, 7 ,pp. 61-78

4. de Dombal, F.T. et al. (1972) Computer-aided Diagnosis of Acute Abdominal Pain. British Medical Journal, 2 ,pp. 9-13

5. Duda, R.O., Gasching, J., Hart, P.E. (1979) Model Design in the Prospector Consultant System for Mineral Exploration Expert Systems in Micro Electronic Age Edinburgh University Press.

6. Gammerman, A.and Lanin, M. (1978) Multivariate Information Analysis of Qualitative Factors. Bulletin of Mathematical Genetics, 61 ,pp.99-104

7. Lauritzen, S.L. and Spiegelhalter, D.J. (1988) Local computations with probabilities on graphical structures and their application to expert systems. Journal of the Royal Statistical Society, Series B; 50 ,pp.157-224.

8. Pearson, E.S. and Hartley, H.I. (1954) Biometrika Tables for Statisticians, Vol.1, Cambridge University Press.

9. Quinlan,J.R. (1983) INFERNO: A Cautious Approach to Uncertain Inference. The Computer Journal, 26 ,No.3

10. Shortilffe,E.H., Buchanan,B.G. (1975) A model of inexact reasoning in medicine. Mathematical Biosciences, 23 ,pp.351-379

11. Spiegelhalter, D.J. and Knill-Jones, R.P. (1984); Statistical and knowledge-based approaches to clinical decision-support systems with an application in gastro-enterology (with discussion). Journal of the Royal Statistical Society, Series A; 147 :35-77.

12. Stuart, A. and Ord, J.K. (1987) Kendall's Advanced Theory of Statistics, Vol.1 Griffin, London.

13. Thatcher, A.R. (1988) Computer Models of Probabilistic Reasoning: Bayes' Theorem Without Assumming Independence. Techical Report No. 88/1 Heriot-Watt University, Edinburgh.

14. Thatcher, A.R. (1988) Local computations with probabilities on graphical structures Contribution to the discussion on a paper by the Journal of the Royal Statistical Society, Series B $\underline{50}$, pp.196

15. Thatcher, A.R. (1964) Relationships between Bayesian and Confidence Limits for Predictions. Journal of the Royal Statistical Society (B), Vol.26, 176-192.

List of Diagnostic Groups and Symptoms*

Diagnostic Groups	
Group	Diagnosis
D=1	Appendicitis (APP)
D=2	Diverticulitis (DIV)
D=3	Perforated Peptic Ulcer (PPU)
D=4	Non-Specific Abdominal Pain (NAP)
D=5	Cholisistitis (CHO)
D=6	Intestinal Obstruction (INO)
D=7	Pancreatitis (PAN)
D=8	Renal Colic (RCO)
D=9	Dyspepsia (DYS)

Symptom 1	
Value	Sex
1/0	male
1/1	female

Symptom 2	
Value	Age
2/0	0-9
2/1	10-19
2/2	20-29
2/3	30-39
2/4	40-49
2/5	50-59
2/6	60-69
2/7	70+

Symptom 3	
Value	Pain-site Onset
3/0	right upper quadrant
3/1	left upper quadrant
3/2	right lower quadrant
3/3	left lower quadrant
3/4	upper half
3/5	lower half
3/6	right half
3/7	left half
3/8	central
3/9	general
3/10	right loin
3/11	left loin
3/12	epigastric

---

* For each symptom in this list, there are two more values coded 88 for multiple observations and 99 for missing observations.

Symptom 4	
Value	Pain-site Present
4/0	right upper quadrant
4/1	left upper quadrant
4/2	right lower quadrant
4/3	left lower quadrant
4/4	upper half
4/5	lower half
4/6	right half
4/7	left half
4/8	central
4/9	general
4/10	right loin
4/11	left loin
4/12	epigastric
4/13	pain settled

Symptom 5	
Value	Aggravating Factors
5/0	movement
5/1	coughing
5/2	inspiration
5/3	food
5/4	other
5/5	nil

Symptom 6	
Value	Relieving Factors
6/0	lying still
6/1	vomiting
6/2	antacids
6/3	milk/food
6/4	other
6/5	nil

Symptom 7	
Value	Progress of Pain
7/0	getting better
7/1	no change
7/2	getting worse

Symptom 8	
Value	Duration of Pain
8/0	under 12 hours
8/1	12-24 hours
8/2	24-48 hours
8/3	over 48 hours

Symptom 9	
Value	Type of Pain
8/0	steady
8/1	intermittent
8/2	colicky
8/3	sharp

Symptom 10	
Value	Severity of Pain
10/0	moderate
10/1	severe

Symptom 11	
Value	Nausea
11/0	nausea present
11/1	no nausea

Symptom 12	
Value	Vomiting
12/0	present
12/1	no vomiting

Symptom 13	
Value	Anorexia
13/0	present
13/1	normal appetite

Symptom 14	
Value	Indigestion
14/0	history of dyspepsia
14/1	no history of dyspepsia

Symptom 15	
Value	Jaundice
15/0	history of jaundice
15/1	no history of jaundice

Symptom 16	
Value	Bowel Habit
16/0	no change
16/1	constipated
16/2	diarrhoea
16/3	blood
16/4	mucus

Symptom 17	
Value	Micturition
17/0	normal
17/1	frequent
17/2	dysuria
17/3	haematuria
17/4	dark urine

Symptom 18	
Value	Previous Pain
18/0	similar pain before
18/1	no similar pain before

Symptom 19	
Value	Previous Surgery
19/0	yes
19/1	none

Symptom 20	
Value	Drugs
20/0	being taken
20/1	not being taken

Symptom 21	
Value	Mood
21/0	normal
21/1	distressed
21/2	anxious

Symptom 22	
Value	Colour
22/0	normal
22/1	pale
22/2	flushed
22/3	jaundiced
22/4	cyanosed

Symptom 23	
Value	Abdominal Movements
23/0	normal
23/1	poor/nil
23/2	visible peristalsis

Symptom 24	
Value	Abdominal Scar
24/0	present
24/1	absent

Symptom 25	
Value	Abdominal Distension
25/0	present
25/1	absent

Symptom 26	
Value	Site of Tenderness
26/0	right upper quadrant
26/1	left upper quadrant
26/2	right lower quadrant
26/3	left lower quadrant
26/4	upper half
26/5	lower half
26/6	right half
26/7	left half
26/8	central
26/9	general
26/10	right loin
26/11	left loin
26/12	epigastric
26/13	none

Symptom 27	
Value	Rebound
27/0	present
27/1	absent

Symptom 28	
Value	Guarding
28/0	present
28/1	absent

Symptom 29	
Value	Rigidity
29/0	present
29/1	absent

Symptom 30	
Value	Abdominal Masses
30/0	present
30/1	absent

Symptom 31	
Value	Murphy's Test
31/0	positive
31/1	negative

Symptom 32	
Value	Bowel Sounds
32/0	normal
32/1	decreased/absent
32/2	increased

Symptom 33	
Value	Rectal Examination
33/0	tender left side
33/1	tender right side
33/2	generally tender
33/3	mass felt
33/4	normal

Specimen Set of Combinations

Explanation

The following specimen combinations of symptoms were constructed by the method described in Section 6. For brevity, the symptoms are represented by reference numbers; their meanings are given in plain language in Appendix C, together with some comments.

Each symptom may be either present or absent and we use a bar or line over the reference number to denote absence, so that the bar stands for "not". For example, 27/0 is the reference number for the symptom "rebound present" and $\overline{27/0}$ means "does not have rebound present".

For each disease there is a table with lines numbered (1), (2), (3), etc., and these line numbers are followed by the reference numbers of a combination of symptoms. Every patient falls in one, and only one, of the combinations.

The column headed N gives the number of past patients (out of the 2,000 in the data base) who had this combination of symptoms. The column headed D shows how many of them had the disease. The column headed P shows the ratio D/N, which can be used as an estimate of the probability p that a new patient with this combination of symptoms will have the disease. Some of these estimates are based on small numbers, but the upper and lower confidence limits for p are given in Appendix D.

D1 = Appendicitis

					N	D	P
(1)	26/2*	27/0	28/0		120	94	.783
(2)	26/2*	27/0	$\overline{28/0}$		98	53	.541
(3)	26/2*	$\overline{27/0}$	28/0		97	50	.515
(4)	26/2*	$\overline{27/0}$	$\overline{28/0}$	33/1	44	18	.408
(5)	26/2*	$\overline{27/0}$	$\overline{28/0}$	$\overline{33/1}$	273	26	.095
(6)	$\overline{26/2}*$	27/0	2/1		28	11	.393
(7)	$\overline{26/2}*$	27/0	$\overline{2/1}$		148	16	.108
(8)	$\overline{26/2}*$	$\overline{27/0}$	2/1		229	8	.035
(9)	$\overline{26/2}*$	$\overline{27/0}$	$\overline{2/1}$		963	10	.010
Total					2000	286	.143

D2 = Diverticulitis					N	D	P
(1)	26/3	8/3	2/6 or 2/7		12	9	.750
(2)	26/3	8/3	$\overline{2/6}$	2/7	15	6	.400
(3)	26/3	$\overline{8/3}$	2/6 or 2/7		6	2	.333
(4)	$\overline{26/3}$	$\overline{8/3}$	$\overline{2/6}$	2/7	44	2	.045
(5)	$\overline{26/3}$	2/7	3/3		7	5	.714
(6)	$\overline{26/3}$	2/7	$\overline{3/3}$		204	16	.078
(7)	$\overline{26/3}$	$\overline{2/7}$			1712	16	.009
Total					2000	56	.028

D3 = Perforated Peptic Ulcer				N	D	P
(1)	29/0	32/1	8/0	31	26	.839
(2)	29/0	32/1	$\overline{8/0}$	14	4	.286
(3)	29/0	$\overline{32/1}$		35	3	.086
(4)	$\overline{29/0}$	23/1		110	5	.045
(5)	$\overline{29/0}$	$\overline{23/1}$		1810	10	.006
Total				2000	48	.024

D4 = Non-Specific Abdominal Pain

This Diagnostic Group consists of all those patients who have not been diagnosed to one of the other Groups. The probability that a particular patient will fall in Group 4 can therefore be found by estimating his separate probabilities for each of the groups 1-3 and 5-9 and then subtracting their sum from unity.

D5 = Cholecystitis				N	D	P
(1)	31/0	26/0		73	64	.877
(2)	31/0	26/0	1/1	58	40	.690
(3)	31/0	26/0	1/0	33	7	.212
(4)	$\overline{31/0}$	22/3		24	18	.750
(5)	$\overline{31/0}$	$\overline{22/3}$	26/0	39	16	.410
(6)	$\overline{31/0}$	$\overline{22/3}$	$\overline{26/0}$	1773	47	.028
Total				2000	192	.096

D6 = Intestinal Obstruction						N	D	P
(1)	25/0	9/2	12/0			37	30	.811
(2)	25/0	9/2	12/1			11	4	.364
(3)	25/0	9/2	30/0			27	19	.704
(4)	25/0	9/2	30/0			80	20	.250
(5)	25/0	19/0	4/8			40	16	.400
(6)	25/0	19/0	4/8	32/2		59	13	.220
(7)	25/0	19/0	4/8	32/2	30/0	28	7	.250
(8)	25/0	19/0	4/8	32/3	30/0	382	13	.034
(9)	25/0	19/1	32/2			124	6	.048
(10)	25/0	19/1	32/2			1212	10	.008
Total						2000	138	.069

D7 = Pancreatitis

The relevant symptoms for pancreatitis were not recorded in the data base - see Appendix C. The best that could be done was therefore to give all the patients the average score P = .014 for pancreatitis.

D8 = Renal Colic					N	D	P
(1)	3/10	5/5			23	20	.870
(2)	3/10	5/5			12	5	.417
(3)	3/10	3/11	5/5		22	18	.818
(4)	3/10	3/11	5/5		9	4	.444
(5)	3/10	3/11	17/3		10	8	.800
(6)	3/10	3/11	17/3	5/5	764	65	.085
(7)	3/10	3/11	17/3	5/5	1160	134	.012
Total					2000	134	.067

D9 = Dyspepsia					N	D	P
(1)	26/12				143	109	.762
(2)	26/12	4/12			80	41	.513
(3)	26/12	4/12	4/4		128	46	.359
(4)	26/12	4/12	4/4	14/0	332	47	.142
(5)	26/12	4/12	4/4	14/0	1317	45	.034
Total					2000	288	.144

Relevant Symptoms

Group 1: Appendicitis

In the statistical analysis described in Section 6, the symptom most closely associated with appendicitis was found to be

26/2 Site of tenderness - right lower quadrant.

This was closely followed by

4/2   Site of present pain - right lower quadrant

and later by

3/2   Pain - site onset - right lower quadrant.

There were 467 patients who had tenderness in the right lower quadrant and another 165 who were recorded as having pain onset or pain present there, but no tenderness. The various combinations of these similar symptoms greatly confuse the analysis, so to simplify we have used in Appendix B the combined symptom

26/2*Tenderness or pain present or pain onset in right lower quadrant.

For those patients who had 26/2*, the further symptoms which appeared relevant included

27/0   Rebound present
28/0   Guarding present
33/1   Rectal examination - tender right side
7/2   Progress of pain - getting worse
8/2   Duration of pain - 24-28 hours
13/1   Absence of normal appetite

For those patients who did not have 26/2*, the most relevant symptoms were

27/0   Rebound present
2/1   Age - 10-19 years
33/1   Rectal examination - tender right side
8/1   Duration of pain - 12-24 hours

A great many combinations of the above symptoms are potentially possible, but for the purpose of estimating probabilities we confine ourselves in Appendix B to the combinations which have occurred sufficiently often (among 2,000 patients) to provide a reasonably reliable basis for estimation.

Group 2: Diverticulitis

The combination of symptoms most closely associated with Diverticulitis was

    26/3   Tenderness in left lower quadrant
    8/3   Duration of pain over 48 hours
    2/6   Age 60-69
    or 2/7   Age 70 and over

For those who did not have tenderness in the left lower quadrant, the most closely associated symptoms were

    2/7   Age 70 and over
    3/3   Pain onset in left lower quadrant
    4/3   Pain present in left lower quadrant
    33/2   Rectal examination - generally tender

There was also some association with pain or tenderness in the lower half (symptoms 3/5, 4/5 and 26/5) but this was much less marked than for the left lower quadrant.

Group 3: Perforated Peptic Ulcer

The symptoms most closely associated with Perforated Peptic Ulcer were

    29/0   Rigidity present
    32/1   Bowel sounds decreased/absent
    26/9   Site of tenderness - general
    8/0   Duration of pain - under 12 hours
    23/1   Abdominal movements poor/nil

Group 5: Cholecystitis

The symptoms most closely associated with Cholecystitis were

    31/0   Murphy's test positive
    26/0   Tenderness in right upper quadrant
    22/3   Colour - jaundiced
    1/0 or 1/1   Male or female

Group 6: Intestinal Obstruction

The symptoms most closely associated with Intestinal Obstruction were

    25/0   Abdominal distension
    9/2   Pain colicky
    12/0   Vomiting present
    12/1   Vomiting absent
    30/0   Abdominal masses present
    19/0   Previous surgery

19/1   No previous surgery
4/8   Pain - - site present - central
32/2   Bowel sounds increased
2/7   Age 70 or over

Group 7: Pancreatitis

Pancreatitis is generally diagnosed when patients with gallstones, or who are suspected alcoholics, are given blood tests. These symptoms and tests are not recorded in the data base and combinations of the recorded symptoms did not give useful results.

Group 8: Renal Colic

The symptoms most closely associated with Renal Colic were:

3/10   Pain onset in right loin
3/11   Pain onset in left loin
17/3   Micturation - haematuria
5/5   Aggravating factors - nil

Group 9: Dyspepsia

The four symptoms most closely associated with dyspepsia were

26/12 Site of tenderness - epigastric
4/12   Pain - site present - epigastric
4/4   Pain - site present - upper half
14/0   History of dyspepsia

Other symptoms, less closely associated, included sex (1/0 or 1/1) and rectal examination normal (33/4).

Comments by Medical Experts

The relevant symptoms listed above and used in the specimen set of combinations in Appendix B were obtained by the purely statistical method described in Section 6 and were then discussed with medical experts. In the light of their comments some minor changes were made. (Three symptoms were omitted from the original list, two were added, and some unsuccessful combinations for pancreatitis were abandoned.) All the other symptoms on the list were immediately recognised by the experts as being relevant to the diagnosis of the diseases concerned.

The experts also suggested some further symptoms which might prove to be worth testing for relevance. These included the following:

APPENDICITIS	5/0	5/1	3/8	6/0	6/5			
DIVERTICULITIS	16/1	16/2	18/1					
PERFORATED PEPTIC ULCER	3/4	3/12	7/1	7/2	10/1	9/0	4/12	23/1
CHOLECYSTITIS	3/0	3/12	4/0	4/12	17/4	28/0		
INTESTINAL OBSTRUCTION	4/5	5/5	16/1					
RENAL COLIC	9/2	10/1	27/1	28/1	6/4	6/5		
DYSPEPSIA	6/2	6/3						

Appendix D

Confidence Limits

The following tables show the 95 per cent confidence limits for each of the estimated probabilities given by the combinations in Appendix B.

For each disease, the lines numbered (1), (2), (3) etc. relate to the combinations with the same reference numbers in Appendix B. For example, under Appendicitis the line (1) relates to the combination of symptoms 26/2*, 27/0 ,28/0.

Appendix B showed that patients with this combination of symptoms have an estimated probability P = .783 of having appendicitis, and the following table shows (in the columns headed L and U) that the lower and upper confidence limits for this particular estimate are .69 and .86 respectively.

Appendicitis					
	N	D	P	L	U
(1)	120	94	.783	.69	.86
(2)	98	53	.541	.43	.65
(3)	97	50	.515	.41	.62
(4)	44	18	.408	.26	.57
(5)	273	26	.095	.06	.14
(6)	28	11	.393	.21	.60
(7)	148	16	.108	.05	.17
(8)	229	8	.035	.01	.07
(9)	963	10	.010	.00	.02

Diverticulitis					
	N	D	P	L	U
(1)	12	9	.750	.42	.95
(2)	15	6	.400	.16	.68
(3)	6	2	.333	.04	.78
(4)	44	2	.045	.00	.16
(5)	7	5	.714	.29	.97
(6)	204	16	.078	.04	.13
(7)	1712	16	.009	.00	.02

Perforated Peptic Ulcer					
	N	D	P	L	U
(1)	31	26	.839	.66	.95
(2)	14	4	.286	.08	.59
(3)	35	3	.086	.01	.24
(4)	110	5	.045	.01	.11
(5)	1810	10	.006	.00	.01

Cholecystitis					
	N	D	P	L	U
(1)	73	64	.877	.77	.95
(2)	58	40	.690	.55	.81
(3)	33	7	.212	.08	.39
(4)	24	18	.750	.53	.91
(5)	39	16	.410	.25	.58
(6)	1773	47	.027	.01	.04

Intestinal Obstruction					
	N	D	P	L	U
(1)	37	30	.811	.64	.93
(2)	11	4	.364	.10	.70
(3)	27	19	.704	.49	.87
(4)	80	20	.250	.15	.36
(5)	40	16	.400	.24	.57
(6)	59	13	.220	.12	.35
(7)	28	7	.250	.10	.45
(8)	382	13	.034	.01	.06
(9)	124	6	.048	.01	.11
(10)	1212	10	.008	.00	.02

Renal Colic					
	N	D	P	L	U
(1)	23	20	.870	.66	.98
(2)	12	5	.417	.15	.73
(3)	22	18	.818	.59	.95
(4)	9	4	.444	.13	.79
(5)	10	8	.800	.44	.98
(6)	764	65	.085	.06	.11
(7)	1160	14	.012	.00	.02

Dyspepsia					
	N	D	P	L	U
(1)	143	109	.762	.68	.83
(2)	80	41	.513	.39	.63
(3)	128	46	.359	.27	.45
(4)	332	47	.142	.10	.19
(5)	1317	45	.034	.02	.05

Specimen of Output: Nine Probabilities for a Sample of Patients

9 probabilities for a sample of patients ("Specimen" Combinations)								
Patient No.	APP	DIV	PPU	NAP	CHO	INO	PAN	RCO	DYS
2	0.783	0.009	0.006	0.107	0.027	0.008	0.014	0.012	0.034
23	0.515	0.009	0.006	0.375	0.027	0.008	0.014	0.012	0.034
69	0.108	0.009	0.006	0.782	0.027	0.008	0.014	0.012	0.034
96	0.108	0.009	0.006	0.199	0.212	0.008	0.014	0.085	0.359
287	0.010	0.078	0.006	0.008	0.027	0.811	0.014	0.012	0.034
292	0.108	0.750	0.045	-0.20	0.027	0.034	0.014	0.085	0.142
307	0.108	0.078	0.045	-0.13	0.027	0.704	0.014	0.012	0.142
486	0.010	0.009	0.006	0.030	0.877	0.008	0.014	0.012	0.034
744	0.035	0.009	0.006	0.423	0.027	0.008	0.014	0.444	0.034
864	0.095	0.009	0.006	-0.06	0.027	0.008	0.014	0.870	0.034
1224	0.010	0.009	0.006	-0.08	0.877	0.008	0.014	0.012	0.142
1248	0.010	0.009	0.006	0.216	0.212	0.008	0.014	0.012	0.513
1347	0.010	0.009	0.006	-0.14	0.027	0.704	0.014	0.012	0.359
1412	0.010	0.078	0.006	0.604	0.027	0.034	0.014	0.085	0.142
1536	0.010	0.078	0.006	0.382	0.027	0.364	0.014	0.085	0.034
1671	0.010	0.009	0.006	0.807	0.027	0.008	0.014	0.085	0.034
1680	0.010	0.009	0.006	0.807	0.027	0.008	0.014	0.085	0.034
1769	0.010	0.078	0.006	0.010	0.027	0.008	0.014	0.085	0.762
1811	0.010	0.009	0.006	0.401	0.027	0.008	0.014	0.012	0.513
1938	0.010	0.009	0.045	0.274	0.027	0.250	0.014	0.012	0.359

Nine Probabilities for the Same Patients by "Simple" Bayes

9 probabilities for a sample of patients ("Simple" Bayes)								
Patient No.	APP	DIV	PPU	NAP	CHO	INO	PAN	RCO	DYS
2	0.997	0.000	0.000	0.003	0.000	0.000	0.000	0.000	0.000
23	0.913	0.004	0.000	0.080	0.000	0.002	0.000	0.000	0.000
69	0.915	0.000	0.000	0.085	0.000	0.000	0.000	0.000	0.000
96	0.002	0.000	0.001	0.067	0.187	0.002	0.001	0.000	0.739
287	0.000	0.315	0.000	0.000	0.000	0.685	0.000	0.000	0.000
292	0.000	0.994	0.000	0.000	0.000	0.006	0.000	0.000	0.000
307	0.000	0.076	0.000	0.000	0.000	0.924	0.000	0.000	0.000
486	0.000	0.000	0.000	0.000	0.999	0.000	0.000	0.000	0.000
744	0.000	0.000	0.000	0.766	0.000	0.000	0.000	0.229	0.005
864	0.000	0.000	0.000	0.105	0.000	0.000	0.000	0.895	0.000
1224	0.000	0.000	0.000	0.000	1.000	0.000	0.000	0.000	0.000
1248	0.000	0.000	0.000	0.000	1.000	0.000	0.000	0.000	0.000
1347	0.000	0.000	0.000	0.014	0.060	0.000	0.123	0.000	0.803
1412	0.000	0.000	0.000	0.001	0.000	0.995	0.000	0.000	0.003
1536	0.000	0.000	0.000	0.000	0.000	1.000	0.000	0.000	0.000
1671	0.000	0.037	0.000	0.136	0.000	0.004	0.000	0.822	0.000
1680	0.004	0.000	0.000	0.079	0.163	0.002	0.000	0.739	0.014
1769	0.000	0.000	0.000	0.000	0.020	0.000	0.002	0.000	0.979
1811	0.000	0.000	0.000	0.001	0.003	0.000	0.000	0.000	0.997
1938	0.000	0.000	0.000	0.000	0.093	0.681	0.174	0.000	0.052

Appendix G

Number of Correct Diagnoses

	Final Diagnosis (actual)	Specimen Combinations	Correct Computer Diagnoses $\chi_0^2 =$				"Simple" Bayes	Doctors Diagnoses*
			14.4	10.5	6.6	2.7		
APP	286	201	192	192	169	256	224	243
DIV	56	16	23	24	34	41	38	31
PPU	48	27	29	28	30	41	37	33
NAP	829	666	650	638	695	767	616	591
CHO	192	129	126	132	133	153	142	136
INO	138	59	62	68	79	116	96	113
PAN	29	0	0	0	3	15	9	16
RCO	134	49	69	69	62	101	102	125
DYS	288	153	173	186	196	226	224	225
Total	2000	1300	1324	1337	1401	1716	1488	1513

* This column has been derived from Appendix H and "normalised" to 2000 patients.

Comparisons between Preliminary and Final Diagnoses

Matrix 1

Computer Diagnosis vs Final Diagnosis ("Specimen Combinations")										
	Computer Diagnosis									
Final Diagnosis	APP	DIV	PPU	NAP	CHO	INO	PAN	RCO	DYS	Total
APP	201	0	2	73	3	0	0	0	7	286
DIV	2	16	1	33	0	4	0	0	0	56
PPU	2	0	27	11	5	1	0	0	2	48
NAP	108	5	0	666	9	13	0	11	17	829
CHO	0	0	1	32	129	3	0	1	26	192
INO	6	6	0	55	2	59	0	0	10	138
PAN	0	0	0	21	3	0	0	0	5	29
RCO	4	1	0	80	0	0	0	49	0	134
DYS	3	0	2	108	14	5	0	3	153	288
Total	326	28	33	1079	165	85	0	64	220	2000

Matrix 2

Computer Diagnosis vs Final Diagnosis (Threshold 14.4)										
	Computer Diagnosis									
Final Diagnosis	APP	DIV	PPU	NAP	CHO	INO	PAN	RCO	DYS	Total
APP	192	1	4	77	3	0	0	1	8	286
DIV	3	23	2	19	0	6	0	1	2	56
PPU	1	2	29	6	7	0	0	0	3	48
NAP	95	10	0	650	10	14	0	23	27	829
CHO	0	1	1	30	126	2	0	1	31	192
INO	7	5	0	51	2	62	0	1	10	138
PAN	0	0	1	17	4	0	0	0	7	29
RCO	4	2	0	58	0	1	0	69	0	134
DYS	0	0	2	93	13	3	0	4	173	288
Total	302	44	39	1001	165	88	0	100	261	2000

Matrix 3

| Computer Diagnosis vs Final Diagnosis (Threshold 10.5) | | | | | | | | | |
| Final Diagnosis | Computer Diagnosis | | | | | | | | |
	APP	DIV	PPU	NAP	CHO	INO	PAN	RCO	DYS	Total
APP	192	1	2	79	3	1	0	1	7	286
DIV	3	24	2	18	0	6	0	1	2	56
PPU	1	1	28	11	5	0	0	0	2	48
NAP	99	10	0	638	11	17	0	23	31	829
CHO	0	0	1	33	132	2	0	1	23	192
INO	7	5	0	48	2	68	0	1	7	138
PAN	0	0	0	18	3	0	0	0	8	29
RCO	4	1	0	58	0	2	0	69	0	134
DYS	1	0	2	78	14	3	0	4	186	288
Total	302	44	39	1001	165	88	0	100	261	2000

Matrix 4

| Computer Diagnosis vs Final Diagnosis (Threshold 6.6) | | | | | | | | | |
| Final Diagnosis | Computer Diagnosis | | | | | | | | |
	APP	DIV	PPU	NAP	CHO	INO	PAN	RCO	DYS	Total
APP	169	0	2	105	2	1	0	0	7	286
DIV	1	34	2	14	0	2	0	0	3	56
PPU	1	1	30	9	5	0	0	0	2	48
NAP	63	12	1	695	10	14	0	5	29	829
CHO	0	1	1	35	133	2	0	1	19	192
INO	5	3	0	41	3	79	0	0	7	138
PAN	0	1	0	16	3	0	3	0	6	29
RCO	2	1	0	67	0	2	0	62	0	134
DYS	2	0	2	74	12	1	0	1	196	288
Total	243	53	38	1056	168	101	3	69	269	2000

Matrix 5

Computer Diagnosis vs Final Diagnosis (Threshold 2.7)									
	Computer Diagnosis								
Final Diagnosis	APP	DIV	PPU	NAP	CHO	INO	PAN	RCO	DYS	Total
APP	256	0	0	29	1	0	0	0	0	286
DIV	0	41	1	13	0	1	0	0	0	56
PPU	1	0	40	5	2	0	0	0	0	48
NAP	32	1	1	768	4	10	1	3	9	829
CHO	0	0	1	29	153	1	0	0	8	192
INO	1	0	0	17	3	115	0	1	1	138
PAN	0	1	0	11	1	0	15	0	1	29
RCO	1	0	0	33	0	0	0	100	0	134
DYS	2	0	3	53	5	0	0	0	225	288
Total	293	43	46	958	169	127	16	104	244	2000

Matrix 6

Computer Diagnosis vs Final Diagnosis ("Simple Bayes")									
	Computer Diagnosis								
Final Diagnosis	APP	DIV	PPU	NAP	CHO	INO	PAN	RCO	DYS	Total
APP	224	1	5	47	1	3	0	0	5	286
DIV	2	38	2	6	0	6	1	0	1	56
PPU	1	0	37	1	4	1	1	1	2	48
NAP	104	19	1	616	15	25	0	16	33	829
CHO	1	1	4	5	142	9	2	1	27	192
INO	4	7	1	18	3	96	3	0	6	138
PAN	2	0	2	2	4	1	9	0	9	29
RCO	3	3	1	16	1	2	0	102	6	134
DYS	5	0	2	26	12	13	6	0	224	288
Total	346	69	55	737	182	156	22	120	313	2000

Matrix 7*

Doctor's Diagnosis -vs- Final Diagnosis									
	Doctor's Diagnosis								
Final Diagnosis	APP	DIV	PPU	NAP	CHO	INO	PAN	RCO	DYS	Total
APP	430	2	2	49	6	7	4	2	4	506
DIV	4	56	3	16	1	16	0	1	3	100
PPU	4	1	60	8	6	2	1	1	3	86
NAP	299	12	7	1169	9	48	7	49	30	1640
CHO	3	1	12	11	256	12	11	2	33	341
INO	8	1	2	24	4	222	1	1	8	271
PAN	0	0	3	4	8	3	33	0	8	59
RCO	5	1	1	8	2	1	0	268	1	287
DYS	6	5	11	35	43	9	12	3	443	567
Total	759	89	101	1324	335	320	69	327	533	3837

* The table shows the results of 3,837 preliminary diagnoses by doctors at Bangour hospital (reproduced with permission of Mr. S. Nixon and Mr. A. Gunn)

Appendix I

Description of Computer Programs

The 'Find_Combination' procedure performs all the tasks necessary to produce the final combination of symptoms. Its basic operation is as follows:

```
            PROCEDURE 'FIND_COMBINATION';
        MAKE_TABLE; {omitting those with insignificant symptoms}
         IF( there are patients in the table )
         BEGIN
          CALCULATE CHI-SQUARED FOR EACH ENTRY IN TABLE;
           SORT TABLE ENTRIES IN ORDER OF DECREASING CHI SQUARED;
            ADD MOST SIGNIFICANT SYMPTOM TO LIST OF SIGNIFICANT SYMPTOMS;
            CALL CHI_FIND WITH NEW LIST OF SIG' SYMPTOMS;
             NEGATE SYMPTOM AT HEAD OF LIST;
             CALL CHI_FIND WITH NEW LIST OF SIG' SYMPTOMS;
              REMOVE SYMPTOM FROM HEAD OF LIST;
           END;
         ELSE
           BEGIN
             IF( there are patients in the table )
              BEGIN
                 CALCULATE THE BEST ESTIMATE OF PROBABILITY
                CALCULATE THE CONFIDENCE LIMITS;
                 DISPLAY THE ENTRY;
              END;
           END;
         END.
```

The main output of the 'Assign_Probabilities' procedure is a table with 9 probabilities corresponding to each of the 9 possible diagnostic group for each patient. It basically operates by using the following procedure:

```
            PROCEDURE 'ASSIGN_PROBABILITIES'
         READ THE ORIGINAL FILE OF PATIENT'S RECORDS
          IF (file is not empty);
           BEGIN
            FOR EACH PATIENT i
                FOR EACH DIAGNOSTIC GROUP j
                 BEGIN
                MATCH THE PATIENT'S RECORD WITH COMBINATIONS;
                    RECORD THE PROBABILITY P:
                P(patient i, diagnostic group j)=PROBABILITY (of the
                coincidence) OF COMBINATION;
           END;
```

PRINT OUT 9 PROBABILITIES FOR ALL PATIENTS;
END

The output of 'Find_Matrix' procedure is a matrix to characterise misclassification rate. It follows the routine:

```
    PROCEDURE 'FIND_MATRIX'
BEGIN
  FOR EACH PATIENT;
    BEGIN
      SELECT THE DISEASE i WITH THE HIGHEST PROBABILITY (as
      the diagnosis);
      READ THE FINAL DIAGNOSIS (disease j) OF THIS PATIENT;
       MAKE MATRIX (by counting):
          MATRIX (i,j)++;
          /* Count each coincidence with final diagnosis */
    END;
  PRINT OUT MATRIX;
END
```

Appendix J

Exact Formulae for Confidence Limits

Full derivations and proofs of the exact formulae for confidence limits will be found in textbooks on the advanced theory of statistics. Pearson and Hartley (1954) give both the proof and some tables (pages 74-8 and Tables 16 and 41). In this Appendix we give just the formulae.

In the problem considered in this report, there is an (unknown) probability p that a patient with certain symptoms will have a certain disease. We know that d our of n past patients with the same symptoms had the disease. We choose a desired level of confidence C and define such that C = 1 - 2α . (Thus for 95 per cent confidence limits we have C = .95 and α = .025.) The upper and lower confidence limits for p are functions of d, n and α. We call these limits U and L respectively.

U and L can be expressed in terms of two integrals. These are the beta- function, which is defined by

$$B(a,b) = \int_0^1 x^{a-1}(1-x)^{b-1}\, dx = \frac{(a-1)!(b-1)!}{(a+b0-1)!} \tag{1}$$

and the incomplete beta-function, which is defined by

$$I_x(a,b) = \frac{\int_0^x x^{a-1}(a-x)^{b-1}dx}{B(a,b)} \tag{2}$$

With this notation, the upper confidence limit is the value of U which satisfies

$$I_{1-U}(n\text{-}d,\, d+1) = \alpha \tag{3}$$

and the lower confidence limit is the value of L which satisfies

$$I_L(d,\, n\text{-}d+1) = \alpha \tag{4}$$

A Partial Orders Semantics for Constraint Based Systems

Steven A. Battle

Transputer Centre, Bristol Polytechnic
Frenchay, Bristol, England

Introduction

Expert systems have been traditionally cast in the mould of the decision tree and its implementational counterpart, the production system. The decision tree is an inappropriate semantics for many domains where flexibility is paramount. Decision trees often lead to massive structural repetition as a way of coping with decision paths that are highly sensitive to the data. Data interact in ways that make any sequential ordering both psychologically implausible and computationally inefficient. Humans are fundamentally sensitive to the input data rather than following any particular sequence of rules [3]. Constraint based reasoning is an improvement over production systems on these criteria and we can give it an appropriate semantics based on partial orders.

Two cases are introduced, each of which has been implemented as a system of concurrently executing processes running on a parallel computer based on the transputer. The semantics of each case are discussed.

Partial Solutions

Partial orderings provide a novel way of analysing the relationships within knowledge bases in general [2]. This paper addresses the problem of formulating a practical semantics for Constraint Based systems in particular. Central to this problem is the issue of partial solutions which naturally give rise to a partially ordered structure of representational states. The partial order and the operations that may be performed upon it provide a general way of talking about constraint based systems without needing to talk about the specifics of any particular representational scheme.

A semantics based on partial orders naturally favours representations which support partial solutions. A representation will start off in a general state and as more information is gathered its state becomes more specific in that the number of solutions picked out by the representation grows smaller. Partial solutions are essential in constraint based reasoning because where only incomplete information is available, this may yet be sufficient to trigger a constraint. Also, a triggered constraint will usually only restrict the range of solutions rather than specify a unique solution. Representations should support partial-solutions rather than the total-solution or no-solution dichotomy.

Case I

The first case is derived from a project to model the behaviour of a senior underwriter in a large Life Insurance company [1]. A major consideration when choosing a suitable insurance policy is the financial standing of the client, as ability to pay and other personal circumstances will affect underwriting decisions about the appropriateness of a policy. The constraint based paradigm was used to design a system that records simple data assertions, maintaining a representation of the states of various categories (age, job, salary, etc.) that remain possible given everything that it has been told so far. The system is purely data driven and each input constrains the range of possibilities until perhaps only one remains.

Each category is a set of mutually exclusive values, e.g., SEX = {male, female} . Our representation supports partial solutions by recording the set of values that remain possible labellings. If the system has no knowledge of any constraints on this category then the state of its knowledge about sex is represented by the full set. If it knows that the sex is female then the state is {female}. If the system is presented with the contradictory information that the sex is both male and female, then this inconsistency is represented by the empty set {}. As information is gathered the state of the representation will progress along certain well defined paths. The only transitions allowed in this example are to subsets of the current set. These state transitions define a partial ordering over the four possible representational states of the category, the powerset of the category: (SEX), the set of all subsets of SEX.

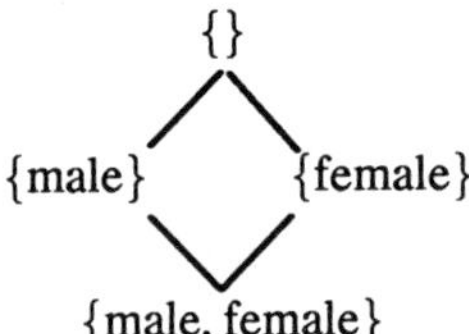

Figure 1: *Representational transitions occurring as information is gathered.*

What is it that drives the representation from state to state? Its knowledge can only increase if it receives external input (or it performs an action that has knowledge level consequences). Information from an external source will be equivalent to one of the above states; such an input might be {female}. The current state and the input must be combined in such a way as to preserve the information present in both. In this example the combined state is simply the set intersection; combining the initial state {male, female} with {female} gives {female}. Our semantics must, however, abstract from the particular representation used and express the meaning of this operation in terms of the partial ordering. Current state/input combination can be understood as finding the least upper bound of a pair of states. This is the lowest point in the partial ordering that can be reached from both states by moving only upwards (or not at all). The TOP element (here TOP is {}) is an upper bound on every pair of states. TOP is special in that it represents the state where no known solution exists; it is the over-constrained state. If the system receives contradictory information it is the only state it can sensibly adopt. Told that a person is both male and female it moves into the TOP state. Consider also a job category with two values: Anglican vicar and politician. This category is far from exhaustive; we do not claim that the knowledge base must be complete. If the system is informed that a person's job is neither vicar nor politician it is driven into the TOP state signifying an inconsistency; here between the knowledge base and reality.

A Knowledge Base System comprises knowledge about many objects and may classify a single object in many ways. We have so far considered only the unitary classification of a single object, now we can consider the multiple classification of an object. The two categories: sex and job may be used to classify a single person so that a single knowledge state specifies everything we know about them. These states are represented by the tuple (s, j) where each component is one of the partial solutions we have looked at previously, i.e., $s \; \varepsilon$ (SEX) and $j \; \varepsilon$ (JOB). The partial ordering over the tuples must be defined in terms of the ordering over its components such that $(s',j') \le (s,j)$ iff $s' \le s$ and $j' \le j$. The symbol '$\le$' is read as "is below (or identical to)" and corresponds to the diagrams in that $x \le y$ if we can reach y from x by moving up the lines (or by not moving at all).

This partial ordering over the tuples defines a hierarchy of specificity over the space of representational states. It does not yet define the admissible states and the valid transitions between them. Many tuples, though syntactically correct, will be semantically inadmissible. The system is prevented from entering inadmissible states by ensuring that there are no valid transitions from the initial state of no-knowledge, to such a state. These constraints are conveniently represented in matrix form. We place a '1' in the matrix where a particular combination of values is admissible and a '0' otherwise. At the present time a sex of female is inconsistent with the job of Anglican vicar. This fact is represented in the matrix by a '0' in the appropriate element.

$$M_{job,sex} = \quad \begin{matrix} & \text{male} \quad \text{female} \\ \begin{matrix} \text{vicar} \\ \text{politician} \end{matrix} & \begin{pmatrix} 1 & 0 \\ 1 & 1 \end{pmatrix} \end{matrix}$$

Figure 2: *A constraint between categories shown in matrix form.*

Consider the partial order in figure 3. START is the most general, initial state and TOP is the most specific, over-constrained state. We can see that A & B represent different and mutually exclusive solution sets. If the START state is combined with the input A the representation moves into state A, and similarly for B. But if we try to combine START with both A & B the inconsistency is acknowledged by moving into state TOP because their least upper bound satisfies $LUB(A,B) = TOP$. Now the solutions represented by state C are semantically inadmissible. It may for example represent all the states where vicar and female occur together, so we have removed all transitions leading into it. The combination of C with any other state will drive the representation into the TOP state.

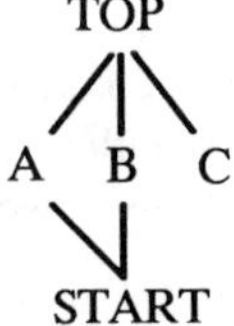

Figure 3: *State C is inadmissible so all transitions leading to it are removed.*

Movement up the transitional ordering corresponds to an increase in factual knowledge. We take the view here that knowledge must be explicit in the representation. This contrasts with information, which may remain implicit within a representation. Internal computation is at best information preserving, but even though it cannot create information it can still extract and make explicit, new knowledge. The intermediate representations of a computation will contain implicit information that is only made explicit in the final representation. The final representation will therefore be above its intermediaries. We wish to eliminate the details of computations from the semantics so we remove all transitions to intermediate states so that a combination with input can cause a transition only to their final state. Note that the intermediate states must still be included in the ordering because they themselves can form input states. Now we can see that the semantically inadmissible states are the intermediate states of a computation that lead to the final TOP state. In constraint based reasoning this internal computation corresponds to the application of a constraint. The information that is implicit in the state of one variable will be made explicit in the constraining effect it has on its neighbours. Figure 4 shows an intermediate state subordinated to its final state. Combining the START state with the intermediate state results in the final state.

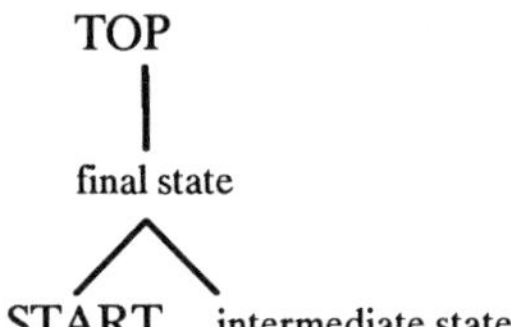

Figure 4: *An intermediate computational state subordinated to its final state.*

We will call all the states that are above the START state, valid states, since they are the only states that can be validly adopted as current states. Now we will formally specify the structure of the partial orders defining the specificity and transitional hierarchies.

The first thing we have to specify is the contents of the representation space. We consider only a small example of that space with the sex and job categories. In order to make the representation work with the constraint matrices, the range of values that each variable can adopt will be represented by a boolean vector; an element is 'true' when the corresponding value is a member of the set of possible values. The space of representational states REP is therefore:

$$\text{REP} = \{x \mid x = ((m,f), (v,p)) \} \text{ where } m, f, v, p \; \varepsilon \; \{\text{true, false}\}$$

The specificity ordering refers to the hierarchy of specificity over the space of representations, this is a purely syntactic relation since we compare only the form of the representations. The more specific representations must imply their generalisations, i.e., if a value is possible in the specialisation it must also be possible in its generalisation. The variables c and v index the categories and values within any particular state:

$$\forall x,y \; \varepsilon \; \text{REP} \; . \; x \leq_{\text{specificity}} y \text{ iff } \forall \; c \; \varepsilon \; C, \; v \; \varepsilon V(c) \; . \; y_{c,v} \Rightarrow x_{c,v}$$
$$\text{where } C = \{\text{sex, job}\}, \; V(\text{sex}) = \{\text{male, female}\}, \; V(\text{job}) = \{\text{vicar, politician}\}$$

A valid state is one in which no constraint can cause further specialisation; every constraint is satisfied. This can only be the case when the constrained variable is more specific (is above) the value derived from applying a constraint to one of its neighbours. The neighbourhood of a variable includes every variable to which it is connected by a constraint. The constraint between a pair of category variables x_i and x_j is expressed by a matrix M_{ij}. For convenience we order the variables in the tuple so that for any $i < j$, M_{ij} is defined rather than M_{ji}, so $M_{ji} = M_{ij}^T$. The effect on x_j is calculated from x_i by the vector-matrix conjunction (a disjunction of conjunctions), $x_i.M_{ij}$. The opposite effect on x_i is calculated from x_j using the transpose of M_{ij}, $x_j.M_{ij}^T$. Note that the relational symbols are subscripted by the name of the ordering to which they apply.

$$\text{valid}([x_1..x_n]) \text{ iff } \forall i,j : 1 \leq i < j \leq n \; .(\; x_j.M_{ij}^T \leq_{\text{specificity}} x_i \;) \text{ and } (\; x_i.M_{ij} \leq_{\text{specificity}} x_j \;)$$

The transitional ordering covers the same space of representations as the specificity ordering but includes only relationships that constitute transitions to valid states:

$$\forall x,y \; \varepsilon \; \text{REP} \; . \; x \leq_{\text{transition}} y \text{ iff } x \leq_{\text{specificity}} y \text{ and valid}(y)$$

This then defines the transitional structure over the representational states. When it comes to drawing inferences by combining an input with some current state then the resultant state must be a specialisation of them both, an upper bound on them. Inference is seen as specialisation only in the sense that it transforms implicit information into explicit information; no new information is gained. Inference stops when a valid state is reached, the inferential process is not open-ended as in first order logic. To ensure the validity of this inference it must choose a conservative upper bound, one that doesn't assume more than is given. The least upper bound provides the most conservative result that is a specialisation of the input and current state.

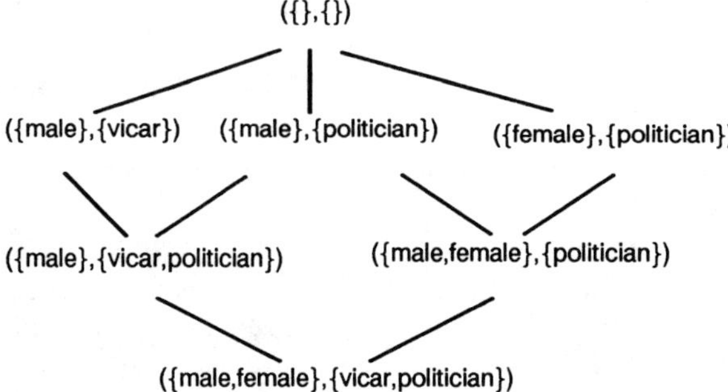

Figure 5: *A transitional ordering over (SEX)* x *(JOB). Only valid states are shown.*

The states shown in figure 5 include just the states the constraint system is able to adopt and at which it waits for more input. The states which are not shown represent input states and intermediate states in computational processes.

Case II

Another constraint system that has been constructed is based on Quinlan's Inferno, an inference network for probabilistic reasoning [4]. For comparison with the first system, we provide an exposition of Inferno using the semantics of partial orders. Inferno allows us to build a network of logical relationships between a set of truth variables.

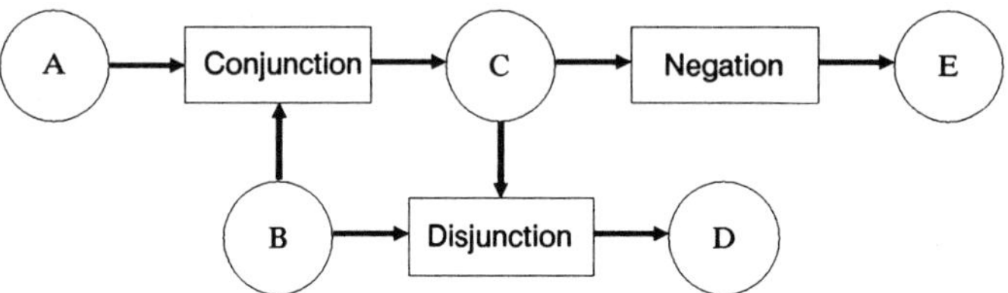

Figure 6: *A constraint network showing logical relationships.*

The logic is probabilistic rather than boolean and supports partial solutions, so each variable starts off in a state of zero information and is subsequently free to approach a unique solution in the form of a probability value. The representation of a truth variable consists of a pair of numbers from the interval [0,1], denoted by $t(x)$ and $f(x)$. They represent the degree of support for and against a proposition, or they can be used to derive the lower and upper bounds on the probability $P(x)$, i.e., $t(x) \leq P(x) \leq 1\text{-}f(x)$.

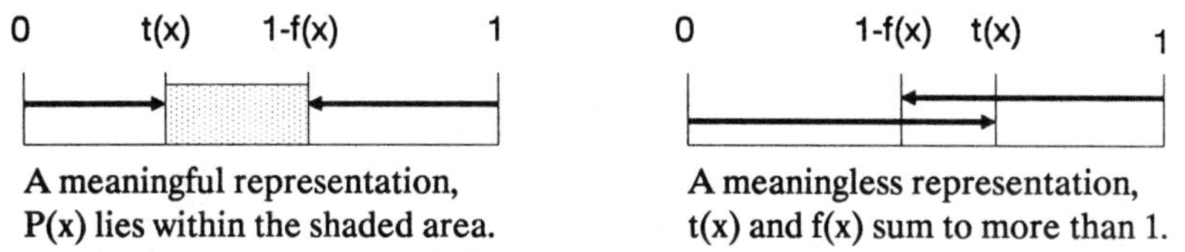

A meaningful representation,
P(x) lies within the shaded area.
A meaningless representation,
t(x) and f(x) sum to more than 1.

Figure 7: *The probabilistic representation of a single variable.*

The global state of the network is defined in terms of a tuple of variables, each of which has the two components described above (in practice we also work with numbers limited to a small number of decimal places to avoid infinite chains of states):

$$\text{REP} = \{x \mid x = [x_1..x_n] \text{ and } (\forall i: 1 \leq i \leq n . x_i = (t,f) \text{ where } t,f \epsilon [0,1])\}$$

Half of these states are meaningless. When t(x) and f(x) sum to more than 1 they have 'crossed over' and the interval within which the probability P(x) lies is empty. When this point is reached, no further constraints should be applied to that particular variable. In practice the user will be alerted to the contradictory nature of the variable.

Initially t(x) and f(x) are set to zero and as input is received they are only able to increase. The ordering over variable states is defined in terms of the numeric relationships between each of its components. A global specificity ordering is defined such that one global state is above another iff every variable within the former is above the corresponding variable in the latter.

$$\forall x,y \epsilon \text{REP} . x \leq_{\text{specificity}} y \text{ iff } \forall i: 1 \leq i \leq n . t(x_i) \leq t(y_i) \text{ and } f(x_i) \leq f(y_i)$$

The definitions of conjunction, disjunction and negation are shown in table 1 as a set of relationships, each of which must hold when a constraint is in place. In addition, each relationship is associated with a precondition of its use. This is to check that each variable involved in the relationship is meaningful, i.e., that its components sum to no more than one. For example the relationship $t(a) \geq f(x)$ will have the precondition:

$$t(a) + f(a) \leq 1 \text{ and } t(x) + f(x) \leq 1$$

Each relationship R is associated with its precondition P in a set of pairs C. A state is valid if every relationship holds or their precondition is otherwise false.

$$\text{valid}([x_1..x_n]) \text{ iff } \forall (P,R) \epsilon C . P \Rightarrow R$$

Finally, as before, the partial ordering of transitions is defined in terms of the specificity hierarchy and state validity:

$$\forall x,y \epsilon \text{REP} . x \leq_{\text{transition}} y \text{ iff } x \leq_{\text{specificity}} y \text{ and valid}(y)$$

Conjunction: a = x and y	**Disjunction:** a = x or y	**Negation:** a = not x
$t(a) \geq t(x) + t(y) - 1$	$t(a) \geq t(x)$	$t(a) \geq f(x)$
$f(a) \geq f(x)$	$t(a) \geq t(y)$	$f(a) \geq t(x)$
$f(a) \geq f(y)$	$f(a) \geq f(x) + f(y) - 1$	$t(x) \geq f(a)$
$t(x) \geq t(a)$	$t(x) \geq t(a) + f(y) - 1$	$f(x) \geq t(a)$
$t(y) \geq t(a)$	$t(y) \geq t(a) + f(x) - 1$	
$f(x) \geq f(a) + t(y) - 1$	$f(x) \geq f(a)$	
$f(y) \geq f(a) + t(x) - 1$	$f(y) \geq f(a)$	

Table 1: *The relationships defining the logical constraints. For full set, see* [4].

Conclusion

The examples have shown how the semantics is equally applicable to any subset of the system, from individual variables to the complete constraint network. The treatment of input is identical whether we are considering actual inputs at a terminal or the influence of a variable on its neighbour via a constraint. These properties make the semantics useful in the analysis of distributed systems and, indeed, both of the examples considered above have been implemented on the transputer, a microprocessor which provides internal concurrency and the connectivity required to support parallelism with other transputers.

References

[1]   Gammack, J.G. Battle, S.A. and Stephens, R.A. (1989) 'A knowledge Acquisition and Representation Scheme for Constraint-based and Parallel Systems', *Proc. 1989 IEEE International Conference on Systems Man and Cybernetics*, Cambridge, MA, Nov 89, vol.3, pp 1030-1035.

[2]   Morgan, S. and Gammack, J.G. (1989) 'Partial Orders as a Basis for KBS Semantics', *Advances in Artificial Intelligence, Natural Language and Knowledge-based Systems: Proc. Bar-Ilan Symposium on the Foundations of Artificial Intelligence*, June 89 .

[3]   Pitrat, J. (1984) 'An Intelligent System Can and Must Use Declarative Knowledge Efficiently'. in Elithorn, A. and Banerji, R. (eds.) *Artificial and Human Intelligence*, Elsevier, North-Holland, pp 271-280.

[4]   Quinlan, J.R. (1983) 'Inferno: A Cautious Approach to Uncertain Inference', *The Computer Journal*, Vol.26, No.3 pp 255-269.

Partial Orders as a Basis for KBS Semantics

Simon P. H. Morgan

Department of Computer Science
University of Exeter
Exeter, Devon, U.K.

John G. Gammack

Bristol Business School
Coldharbour Lane, Frenchay
Bristol, England

INTRODUCTION

Partial orders are a mathematical construct currently used in denotational semantics. This construct has several properties which make it more generally applicable to knowledge-based systems (KBS) design, and in this paper we consider the role of partial orders in describing the meanings of data states in knowledge based systems. Partial orders allow formal representation of the state of information and inferences made about the external world, as stored in dynamically generated data structures of the KBS. A partial order can be augmented with a single representation of the reasoning strategies of a KBS, which includes representation of how a KBS might adapt reasoning strategies depending on the information available to it. This gives a common theoretical framework for KBS methods.

Two case studies illustrate the practical use of partial orders in aiding the KBS design process. This gives the advantages of allowing greater flexibility of reasoning strategies and user interaction in the final system, while supporting modification in the design and maintenance processes.

To extend the case study findings that partial orders used in this way can be a generally useful tool for KBS design, we also show that:

> 1) use of partial orders overcomes restrictive knowledge engineering techniques, (e.g., commitment to a single representational formalism), while retaining scope to incorporate desirable features such as non-monotonicity and knowledge-level modularisation into a KBS.

> 2) describing partial orders of knowledge states provides many advantages in modelling human expertise.

Although not discussed in detail here, we also suggest that the potential of partial orders to accommodate other AI paradigms recommends their suitability as an underlying abstraction for a full description of KBS semantics.

First however, by way of example, we introduce our approach to partial orders with some formal details and definitions.

PARTIAL ORDERS OF MEANINGS OF DATA STATES

In our use of partial orders, a node is allocated to a state of dynamically generated data, and nodes are ordered according to the information those states of data represent, such that A ≤ B generally implies:

> 1) that the information represented by data state A is a subset of the information represented by data state B.

> 2) it is possible to arrive at state B after passing through state A in the execution of the program, or state A and state B are identical.

Nodes can be included which represent states of information, but without necessarily having corresponding data states in the knowledge based system.

Here we use a transitive, reflexive, non-symmetric partial order to relate the meanings of states of data structures. Any data structure in a given state may represent some information about the external world: this we can formalise as representing a set of possible world states. For example in figure 1a there is a state of data, marked by an asterisk that represents all the worlds where the red light is illuminated in a traffic signal.

The sets of states in the real world that are represented by each data state (e.g., 'red light on', 'red and green light on') designate the MEANINGS of data states, and can be placed into a partial ordering according to the subset relation. The set of states of the external world where the red and green light are on is a subset of the set of states where the red light is on.

Accordingly, a possible partial ordering could be:

DEFINITION 1:

> If B is a node above A in a partial ordering, then the set of possible worlds represented by the data state corresponding to B is a subset of the set of possible worlds represented by the data state corresponding to A. (e.g., A is red, B is red & green)

However if we look at the malfunction node, we see that it can derive from two nodes which are not compatible: 'red and green' and " not red and not green'. In order to conform to definition 1, we must draw out two distinct malfunction nodes, otherwise we must redefine the partial ordering only in terms of computational steps. This alternative definition could be:

DEFINITION 2:

> If B is a node above A in the partial ordering, then it is possible to arrive at the data state corresponding to B after passing through the data state corresponding to A.

Alternatively we could modify definition 1 as follows:

DEFINITION 3:

> If B is a node above A in a partial ordering, then the set of possible worlds represented by the data state corresponding to B contains a subset of the set of possible worlds represented by the data state corresponding to A. (e.g., A is red, B is red & green).

In general, the meanings we wish to represent are the meanings of any dynamically generated data structures, which may be all or just some of the data generated in a knowledge based system. This allows the possibility of using this partial ordering to separately represent the meanings of the data of separate modules within a system, whilst also being able to represent the meaning of data across more than one module. An example of this is given at the end of case study 1.

Partial orderings can be defined in other ways to give a broader notion of what data can represent. For example, rather than defining meaning only as representing possible states within the external world, meaning may be defined as possible states in the external world according to particular VIEWS of the world. In the traffic light example this is useful in the case where the system, detecting a traffic signal with no lights on, polls different distributed knowledge bases, one of which might infer that the lights are malfunctioning, whilst another might infer that they are switched off. The system could store these two conflicting views of the external world, before continuing. Our modified definition of meaning enables the holding of these two views to be represented within a partial ordering.

A further extension of the original definition would be to allow the ordering to represent the meaning of data which represent information about data generated by the knowledge based system. This might be the information represented in a program trace.

One point of interest to note here is that the partial orders may be used as a basis for constructing a knowledge level program trace, showing how information was built up, rather then an implementation level listing of what rules failed or fired.

So choice is given to the KBS designers, as to which kind, or kinds of definition of the partial ordering they wish to employ.

THE BUILDING UP OF INFORMATION

Rather than being concerned with the syntactic structure if the data, we are interested in modelling the progression of information built up within the knowledge base system. This is primarily traced by the stages of dynamically generated data, and can be supplemented by the position of the program pointer.

To see how the position of a program pointer can represent information, consider a set of rules listed in a program in a certain order, and each rule has preconditions and an inference. The preconditions of each rule are tested in turn and once met, the inference is made, represented in dynamically generated data, and the search stops. Information that a rule did not fire, and that an inference was not made is stored implicitly by the position of the program pointer as it goes through the rules. There does not have to be a program pointer explicitly implemented, there could be a stack, for example, from which rules are removed, as they fire or fail to fire. However there is still implicit representation of information that could be represented in the partial order.

Our work is inspired by the use of lattices in denotational semantics, [Scott 1976]. We deviate from that work in denotational semantics in that we do not always use a top node, or over-specified states. Also, as denotational semantics is concerned with what programming language expressions specify , it tends to emphasise syntactic aspects of data structures and processing, rather than what the programmer intends the data to represent in the real world external to the computer program. In contrast, our use of partial orders is aimed specifically at this latter aspect, i.e., what the programmer intends a state of data to represent about the world, rather than the syntactic aspects.

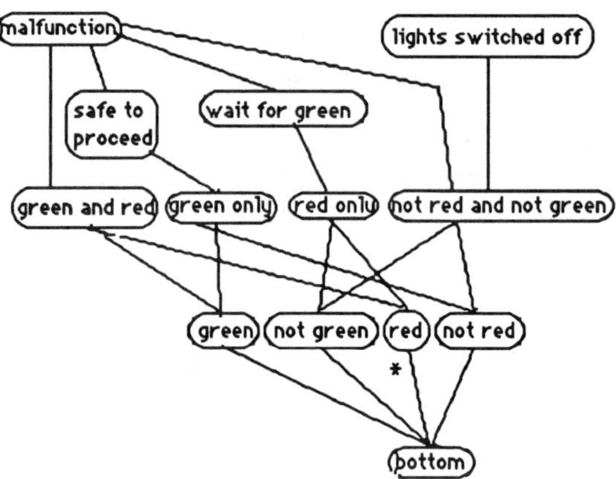

Figure 1a.

Figure 1a shows a partial ordering of the meanings of states of data in a knowledge based system which follows traffic   light signals. The bottom state is the state with no information. As information comes in, (e.g, from sensors which detect red and green), the partial order is ascended.

One of the features of our partial ordering is transitivity. In mathematical terms and in terms of our definitions of the partial order relation, this transitivity is given by the transitivity of the subset relation. However there are two practical implications of this:

> additivity of information as paths of the order are ascended, that is restriction of the remaining set of permissible world states,

> the possibility of making transitions that jump over several nodes in an order, going up a pathway, corresponding to the knowledge based system inferring a conclusion in one step, bypassing all the possible intermediate stages.

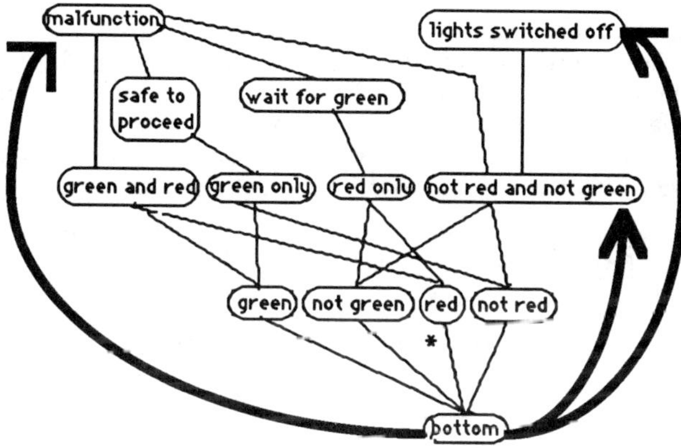

Figure 1b.

Jumping is illustrated in figure 1b, by the bold lines to represent the case where the system gets information immediately that the lights are either malfunctioning or switched off, (e.g., by detecting a road sign saying so).

We will now consider two case studies which demonstrate the utility of the partial order paradigm in practical KBS development.

CASE STUDY 1

The first case study concerns a diagnostic KBS in the domain of simulation modelling of computer performance: a domain described in Lazowska, Zahorjan, Scott-Graham and Sevcik (1984). This study reports co-operative design work that took place between the first author and a domain expert - a computer professional without formal training or experience in the areas of knowledge based systems, AI or cognitive psychology. As the project developed, emphasis turned away from conventional knowledge elicitation towards a series of co-operative design discussions, with no clear demarcation between the two.

The KBS was intended to diagnose errors made in building simulation models by comparing the predictions made by the simulation models, with actual measurements taken from the computer system being modelled. The diagnosis system would have access to ways of testing whether or not an error had been made in model building. These tests however would be time consuming as many of them would involve asking human users to go and check things which cannot be done automatically. As a brute force approach would waste user's time, the need to find the quickest way to the error, provided the main technical challenge for the project.

Expert model builders can diagnose what errors had been made in a simulation model merely by comparing the output from the model with statistics taken from the computer system being modelled. They would usually eliminate the errors and achieve an accurate simulation within a few attempts at finding the error. This was based on years of experience both of computer system performance and also of simulation model building.

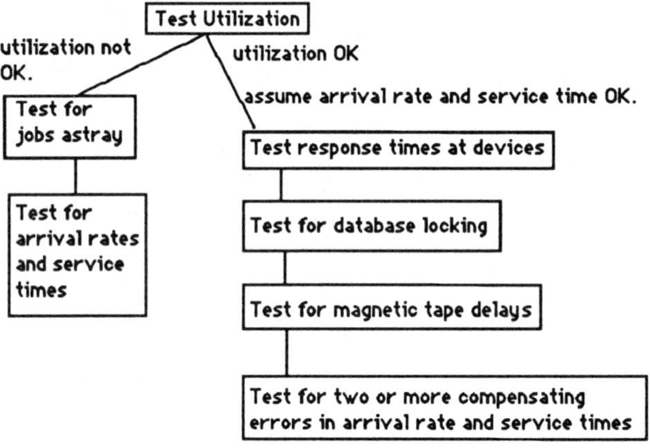

Figure 2a.

Figure 2a shows the initial result of a knowledge elicitation exercise. It shows a procedure of diagnostic tests to identify a single error that had been made in building a very simple model: a model of a computer system performing only one type of job. The procedure is a rigid sequence of tests for different types of error. The tests have been ordered according the likelihood of an error having been made, ease of testing for an error, and the order in which tests have to be carried out so that errors can be inferred by a process of elimination where necessary.

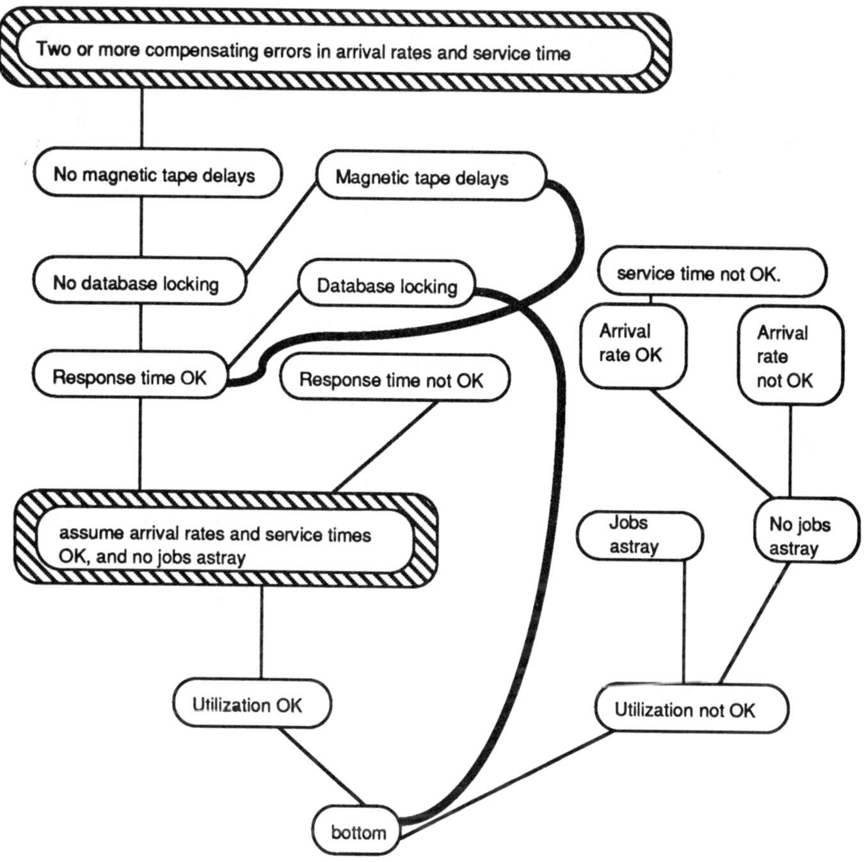

Figure 2b.

An important observation   from that elicitation session is that the domain expert had great difficulty in trying to consider how to extend the procedure for it to be able to cope with more complex cases. He said he was sure that this was the basis of how to deal with more complex cases, but he could not see how, and that it was too difficult to continue with the   exercise in   that session. This reflects the general fact that experts find difficulty in expressing procedural aspects of their knowledge. The   simulation models for which this system was being designed generally had between five and fifteen types of job, so the main task was to find a way of extending the procedure to cope with many jobs.

Persisting with the knowledge elicitation to identify domain methods for achieving a more powerful system, the expert commented   that experienced model builders will use their judgment to take short cuts if they feel that certain things are more likely to be wrong in a given situation.

In figure 2b, the procedure shown in figure 2a has been represented in a different way. Firstly it is displayed from bottom to top, and instead of the different tests, it shows the information gained from each test. In addition it shows short cuts that were mentioned by the domain expert. Figure 2b is not however a partial order according to the strict definition 1, given above.

Figure 2c, is a transformed version of figure 2b, made into a partial order according to definition 1 above. Non-monotonicity in figure 2b is shown by the items in hatched boundaries; an assumption shown in the lower item is invalidated in the upper item. This violates the definition of the partial ordering in definition 1, because the information is not additive. A separate path is created in figure 2c, so that the upper item can be reached without passing through the lower item, removing the violation.

Also, on the new path is a new item labelled 'other combinations of the original errors listed'. This begins to extend the original procedure as required, to cover more complex situations, and derives from the application of the strict semantics of definition 1. Thus the use of the partial ordering representation can help in the design process by prompting the generation of new items.

Figure 2d goes on to show how this can be continued to include more complex models with multiple job types. Note that the additional parts of the partial order are shown in bold lines, and that the original procedure is replicated.

Figure 2d does not represent KBS code, but represents the meaning of dynamically generated data structures. Figure 3 shows the syntactic structure of an example of dynamically generated data corresponding to figure 2d. Figure 3 also shows the syntactic data structure overlaid with boxes, showing parts A and B which correspond to figure 2d.

The operational semantics, (i.e., the order in which things are carried out) is not represented in the diagrams, and, although not described here, can be represented additionally. We suggest also that representations such as figure 2d, by explicitly showing the information states, make it easier for domain experts to think about the procedural steps. After being helped to map out the information by a KBS developer employing our proposed representations, a strict semantics for possible jumps and entry points according to context etc., can be introduced for these procedural aspects.

Two or more compensating errors in arrival rates and service time
No magnetic tape delays
Magnetic tape delays
No database locking
Database locking
service time not OK.
Arrival rate OK
Arrival rate not OK
Response time OK
Response time not OK
assume arrival rates and service times OK, and no jobs astray
Jobs astray
No jobs astray
Utilization OK
Utilization not OK
Other combinations of errors
one error only (assume)
more than one error
bottom

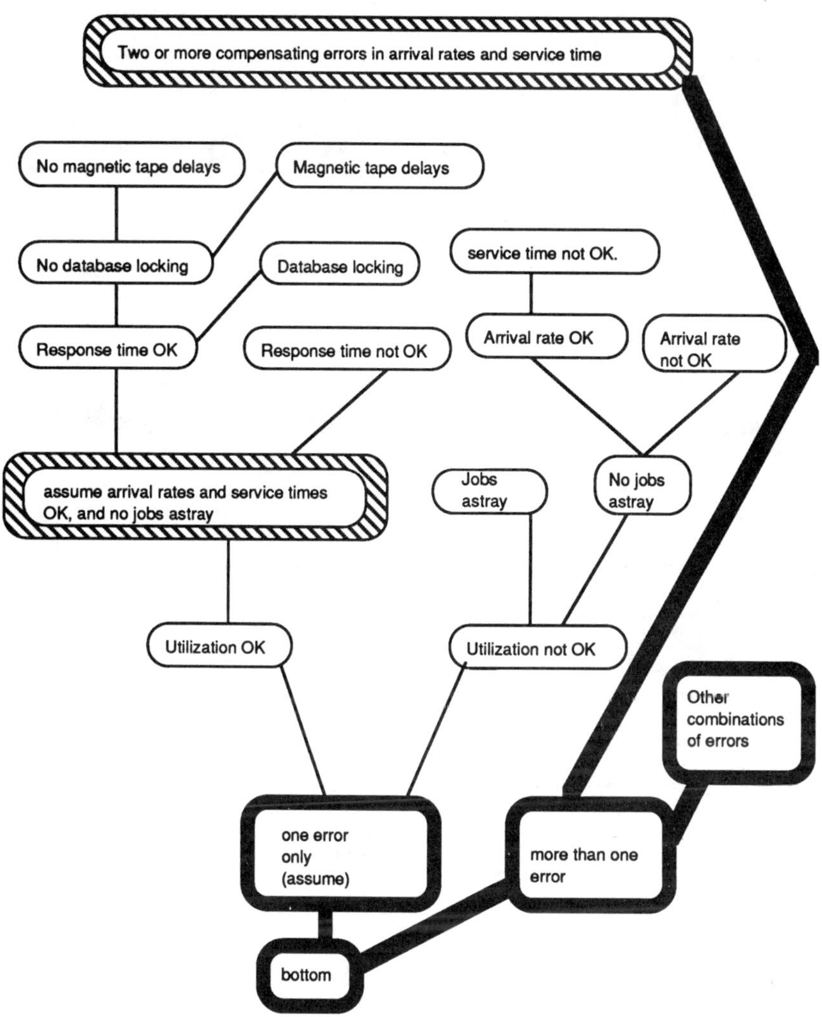

Figure 2c.

B
BASIC ORDERING CORRESPONDING TO THE INITIAL
SET OF TESTS AND CAUSES FOR THE SINGLE WORKLOAD
As below except information applies to the group
of workloads of equal priority, not just to one.
Other combinations of errors
one error only (assume)
more than one error
BASIC ORDERING CORRESPONDING TO THE INITIAL
SET OF TESTS AND CAUSES FOR THE SINGLE WORKLOAD
(See figures 2b and 2c)
Other combinations of errors
one error only (assume)
more than one error
All other workloads of same or higher priority as this workload, error free
Error on higher priority workload (in this case diagnose the workload)
Error on an equal priority workload
single workload model
multiple workload model
bottom
A

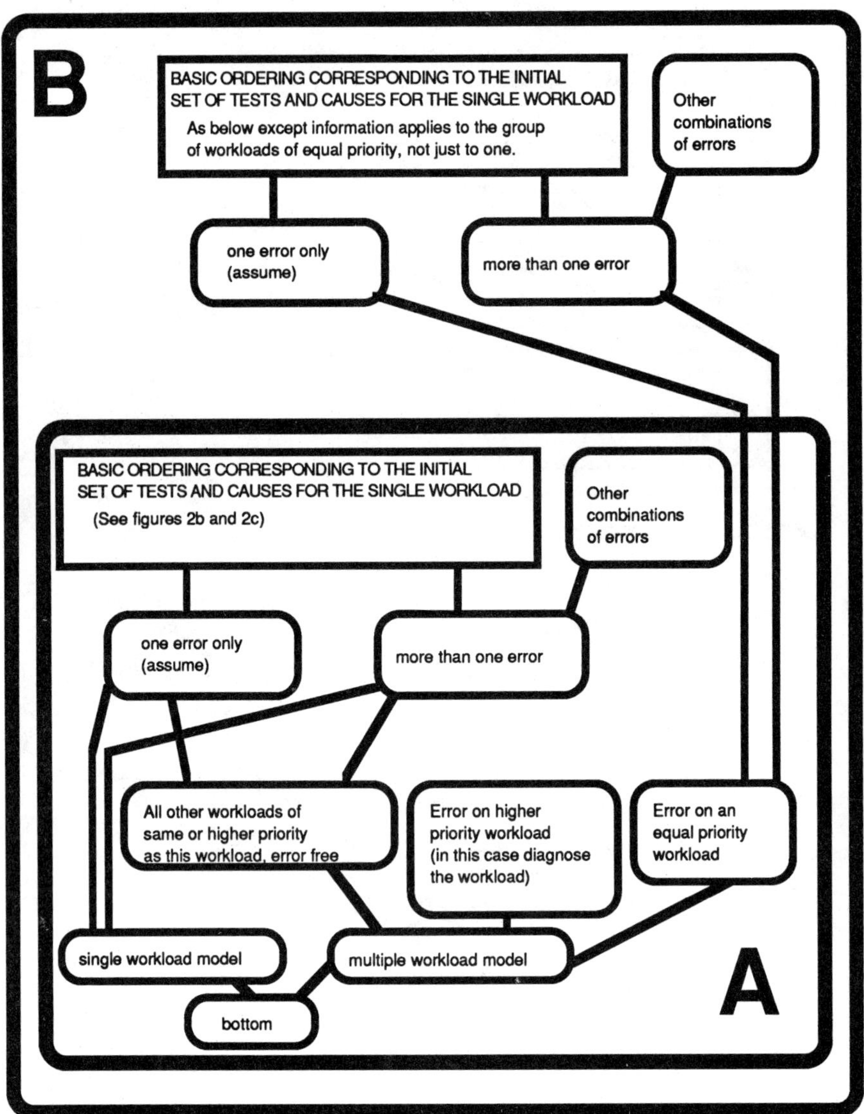

Figure 2d.

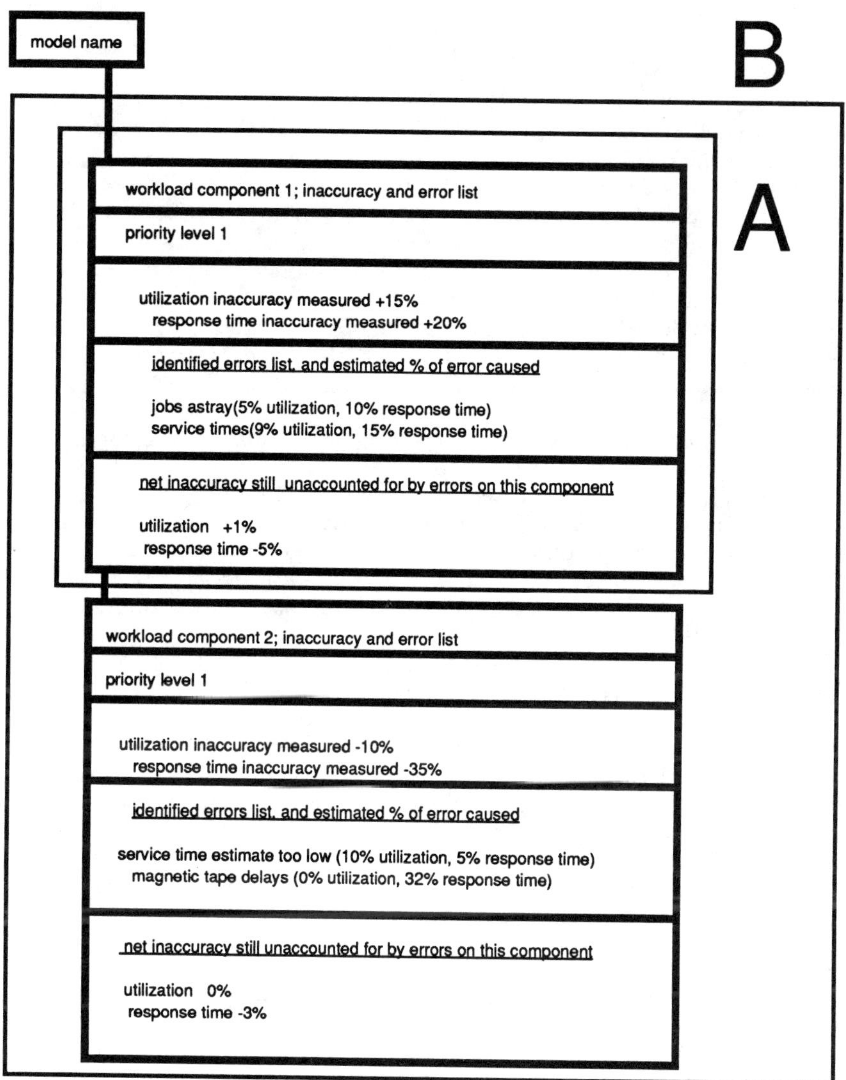

Figure 3.

The recursive data structure in figure 3 is one implementation of a general design concept, that of intercommunicating   modules, each of which has its own dynamically generated data representing information about the external world.

Figure 3 represents the model as a name and a string of structures, each corresponding to a type of software job on the system. These types of job are "workload components", and each with a priority level in competing for resources. This priority is represented in figure 3, and is important in diagnosis of inaccuracies   in simulation models.

Each workload data structure contains information about accuracy of the simulation model's predictions, compared with measures from the actual system being modelled. Also stored is a list of errors, that had been made in characterising those jobs when building the model, and which had subsequently been identified.

So in the example, the model has overestimated   the amount of processing used and the total response time of the computer system for jobs in workload component 1, but has underestimated them for jobs in workload component 2. The overestimations in workload component 1 have been caused by jobs astray and overestimating the amount of processing each job requires.   The amount of inaccuracy for utilization and response time caused by each error is given. The assumption of linearity is valid for cases where the diagnosis system is to be used.

Looking at workload component 1, the inaccuracy in utilization can be accounted for to 1% accuracy, but the effects of the errors were to increase response time by 25%, whereas the final estimate was only 20% over the correct value. So, having eliminated all the errors made in building workload component 1, the model's predictions, are underestimating response time by 5%. This underestimation is probably caused by errors made in building workload component 2. The   amount of resources used by workload component 2 have been underestimated. Now if for example, workload components 1 and 2 have to access the same disc many times, then there is probably more queuing at that disc than predicted in the model. So fully to diagnose why the inaccuracies occur in workload component 1, errors in workload component 2 must be identified, and their effects on the accuracy of predictions made by the model, evaluated.

The partial orders by themselves do not represent the actual numerical values of figure 3. We suggest that a simple augmentation of the partial order is used to achieve this, that is the numerical value (eg 15% inaccuracy of utilization in workload component 1, in our example) can be attached to the appropriate node ("utilization not OK").

CASE STUDY 2

A simple example of modularisation is illustrated by a second case study concerning the assessment   of financial risk   in life insurance underwriting

[Gammack, Battle and Stephens, 1989; Battle, this volume]. Risk is assessed by considering combinations of values for AGE, SALARY, SUM ASSURED, etc. available from a proposal form. Domain knowledge was expressed as constraints between category values (e.g., AGE < 16 and MARITAL STATUS = married would be inadmissible). The system propagated known values among a set of communicating modules connected in parallel. This modularity is at the knowledge level , i.e., in terms of real world semantics rather than in terms of purely computational considerations [see Pearl, 1985, p11].

Separate modules maintained representations of the admissible states of various categories consistent with all currently known information. The system was purely data driven so that entering a specific value for say SALARY, would constrain the remaining categories to have fewer admissible values. Within each module (category) is a data structure (here an array of labelled options) representing the remaining allowable values that each category can take. A piece of information may or may not affect the data structure labels within any one module, for example, a proposer's AGE may have eliminated the possibility of taking out a policy with a 40 year TERM: represented in the TERM module by labelling the 40 year option as no longer allowable.

Adding information progressively tightened the partial solutions from the most general (bottom) state. The system functioned as a decision aid by identifying appropriate members of the FINANCE PLAN category given a particular set of personal circumstances.

These partial solutions correspond to dynamically generated data states, which result from incoming information and subsequent computation according to the system of constraints (implemented as matrices of admissible relationships among specific category values). The communication among modules was thus closely related to the ordering of the partial solutions, and we found partial orders a useful design tool in helping define this intercommunication.

Because of the numerous ways in which information may be ordered or volunteered in this system, a single decision tree or production system is an inappropriate semantic basis for description, although partially ordered lattices can support specific realisations of this form.

PSYCHOLOGICAL AND KBS DESIGN CONSIDERATIONS

The above case studies illustrate several phenomena of intelligent processing exhibited by human experts and desirable in knowledge based systems. For instance humans are fundamentally sensitive to the input data and will jump from one line of reasoning to another according to the data's demands. Given one piece of decisive information, experts will not waste time asking irrelevant questions, and can conclude quickly. Since a critical piece of information may be volunteered at any time, a representation with flexible entry points is desirable, since humans can clearly respond to new information regardless of its order of arrival.

Flexible reasoning which is contingent on, or sensitive to circumstances is a hallmark of intelligence. For instance an intelligent diagnostician will look for specific information that is highly informative given the current state of knowledge. The information specifically sought will naturally depend on what is already known, and thus the ordering of states of data in an IKBS modelling expertise should vary dynamically across circumstances. This possibility is not available to a simple decision tree or (sequential) production system with their commitment to a fixed ordering of information, and rigid flow of control. As a descriptive abstraction of a knowledge base these can be inflexible and computationally inefficient, as well as lacking psychological plausibility as a model of intelligent processing. Instead, representing the underlying abstraction of data states using partial orders leads to a specification of possible state transitions, without a rigid commitment to evaluation order.

Other phenomena of human reasoning for which partial orders provide a basis for a semantics include an expert's propensity to reason forwards from the givens of a problem, switching to backward chaining as appropriate [Patel and Groen 1986]. Moreover, human reasoning tends not to be subject to pathological deadlocks, circularity, infinite recursion and the like: humans can make intelligent jumps out of pathological situations. Partial orders can be used in modelling these phenomena and non-monotonicity more generally.

Since experts may fabricate spurious explanations, which do not correspond to their actual reasoning, a cooperatively designed facility, directly linked to actual states of the knowledge base is clearly desirable. By emphasising the semantics of data states, partial orders provide a facility to incorporate explanation that is more promising than a mere evaluation trace. Despite superficially similar inputs and outputs, there may be no relation between a stack of program states and the reality of expert cognition, and accordingly explanation based on a program trace may have little or no validity. Because partial orders model both the semantics of data and the valid transitions between states of data, explanation can be allied to each transition. Such explanation can take into account the meaning of the data before and after transition, showing the rationale for the reasoning rather than merely its mechanistic implementation, as offered by the conventional program trace. This enhanced facility is more useful both to user and KBS designer.

Pearl [1985] notes three objectives for intelligent reasoning systems: 1) knowledge based modularity 2) intuitive transparency of elementary inference steps and 3) flexibility of control, and describes a belief maintenance system using Bayesian networks which meets these objectives. Partial orders also give a basic construct for achieving these desiderata, they can be given a strict semantics (leading to better modularity) and without being limited to

Bayesian calculation.

Finally, for knowledge acquisition purposes systems based on partial orders have several worthwhile properties. Experts find declarative knowledge easier to express than procedural, and a declarative specification of knowledge has many other advantages in knowledge engineering [Pitrat, 1984]. General declarative knowledge can support numerous specific programs, each corresponding to different dynamic contexts of use - the constraint-based insurance system described above contains this possibility, [see also Leler, 1988]. Expressing acquired knowledge in a partial order gives the designer the logical separation of function and structure, or reasoning strategy from factual constraints on reasoning. Because the states of data are specified independently of derivation path, the products of reasoning may be defined separately from the reasoning process. The graphical nature of partial orders, with nodes corresponding to information and links corresponding to reasoning steps, supports effective knowledge acquisition and can indicate omissions and possible short cuts.

MODELLING UNCERTAIN INFORMATION

We have seen how partial orders can used in modelling information based on discrete value logic paradigms including, chaining, non-monotonicity and constraint satisfaction. Finally we consider the accommodation of probabilistic information, and continuously variable confidence levels.

Figure 4a shows the partial order for two boolean variables, A and B, which can each be instantiated to true or false, and shows probabilistic expressions directly represented on the order as an augmentation, and also the implicit probabilities that can be determined from the expressions. One may or may not wish to include the implicit, meaning of the probabilities, until they are explicitly represented in the data, that is an option for the designer.

Since the whole augmentation pattern is used to represent the meaning of a data state the order requires redefinition. Each node directly represents a set of possible worlds instead of the meaning of a data state.

Definition 4:

> If B is a node above A in a partial ordering, then the set of possible worlds represented by node B is a subset of the set of possible worlds represented by node A.

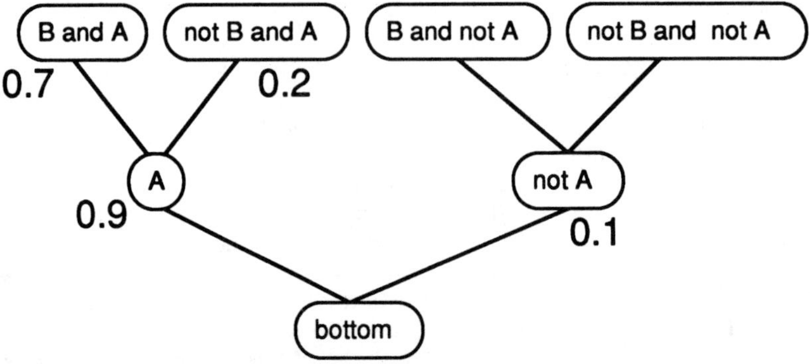

Representation of the meanings of data states corresponding to the probablistic expressions;

$$p(B \text{ and } A) = 0.7$$
$$p(A) = 0.9$$

Additional implicit probabilities are;

$$p(\text{not } A) = 0.1$$
$$p(\text{not } B \text{ and } A) = 0.2$$

Figure 4a.

The redefined use however is not incompatible with that of definition 1, if we consider the discrete case, where we only know that the probability of "B and A" is 1.0. In definition 1, the node "B and A", would be the current node, and in this use, it and nodes below it, are set to 1 and the rest to zero. This is shown in figure 4b. In general, if we wish to convert the ordering of definition 1 to this ordering, then we must set the current node and all nodes below it to "1"; set all nodes above it to "unknown"; and set the rest to "zero".

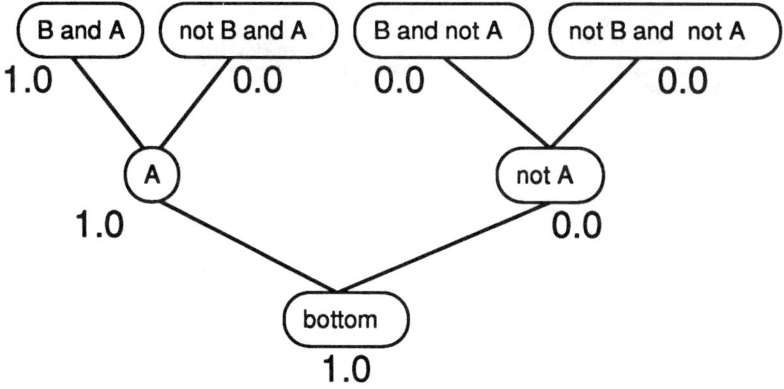

Representation of the meaning of data corresponding to the expression,

$p(A \text{ and } B) = 1.0$

Figure 4b.

REPRESENTATION OF OPERATIONAL SEMANTICS AND AN INFORMATION BASED APPROACH TO TRACE AND EXPLANATION FACILITIES

If we return to figure 2b, as an example, we see that there are 6 possible causes of error, figure 5 shows these, by blacking out intermediate nodes of information. Now the information nodes are laid out in a tree structure, with short cuts shown in bold. To show all such transitions between nodes becomes complex, figure 5, shows all the possible short cut routes to just three of the nodes.

Figure 5 shows the combinatorial explosion of possible search paths as combinatorial explosion of possible transitions. Therefore it is recommended that the partial order shows only the transitions corresponding to certain reasoning paths only.

This leads naturally to consideration of a trace facility based on partial orders that shows how information was built up as the knowledge based system ran, by showing the actual transitions that occurred in the knowledge based system. These will be transitions between nodes, or updating of augmentations of nodes corresponding to the numerical value associated with that node. With

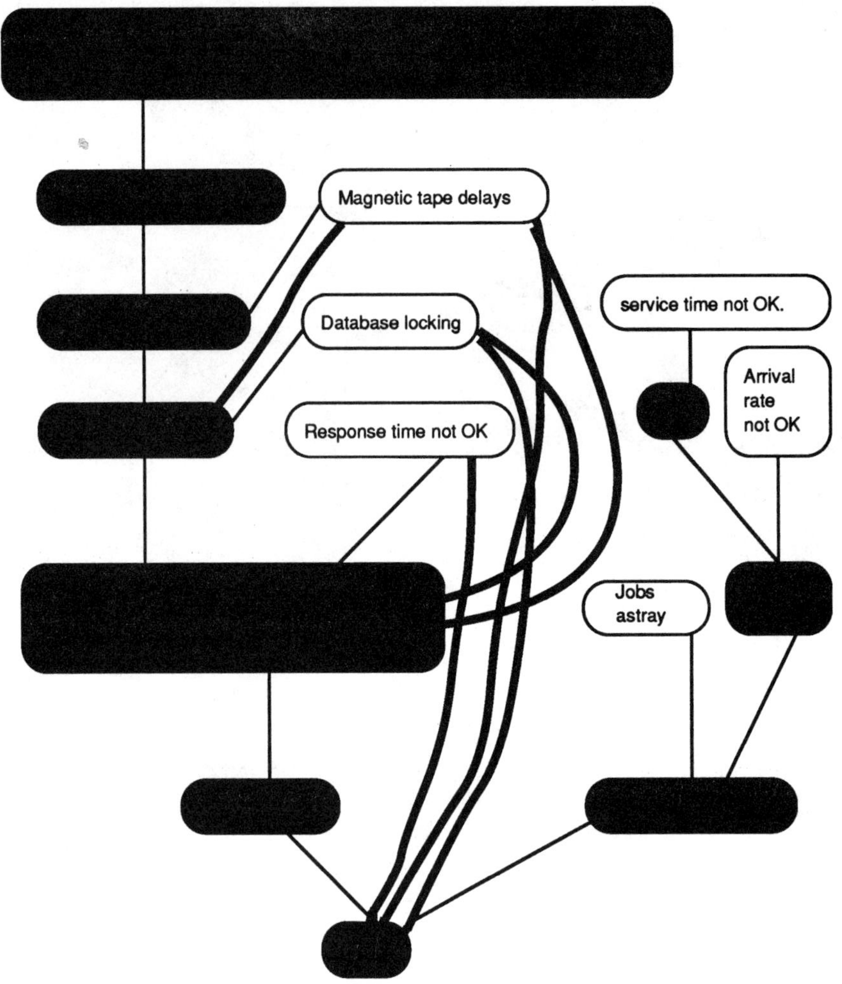

<u>Figure 5.</u>

each transition, there will be a corresponding link between nodes on the
diagram, and attached to each link can be an explanation, such as an inference
being made, or information being entered by the user. Similarly, for the
updating of augmented numerical values, a list can be kept of successive
values, and for each update of value, an explanation can be given. This
amounts to a knowledge level trace and an associated explanation facility.

CONCLUSIONS

With two practical applications, we have shown that partial orders can be used as a basis for the semantics of knowledge based systems, and also that it can accommodate various AI paradigms; chaining, non-monotonicity, constraint based reasoning and methods for representing uncertainty. We have also shown that the partial orders can be used to provide a "knowledge level" representation of how information is dynamically built up in knowledge based systems.

Augmentation to the partial ordering is necessary to represent continuously variable numerical values and also the operational semantics of the reasoning processes and user interaction. By separating information states from reasoning processes and user interaction we gain the advantage of orthogonality of information and processing.

KBS development can be strengthened by the use of partial orders in several ways. The orthogonality enables: 1) different AI paradigms to be combined; 2) greater flexibility in user interaction; and 3) easy modification of designs and prototypes. Graphical techniques enhance knowledge acquisition and co-operative design prior to implementation. Finally, knowledge level modularisation and knowledge level trace and explanation facilities are explicitly supported.

REFERENCES

Gammack, J.G. Battle, S.A. and Stephens, R.A. (1989) A knowledge acquisition and representation scheme for constraint-based and parallel systems. Proc. IEEE conference on Systems Man and Cybernetics. Cambridge, MA. vol. III, p1030-1035.

Lazowska, E.D., Zahorjan, J., Scott-Graham, G. and Sevcik, K.C. (1984) Quantitative System Performance., Prentice Hall, New Jersey.

Leler, W. (1988) Constraint Programming Languages, Addison-Wesley.

Patel, V.L. and Groen, G.J. (1986) Knowledge based solution strategies in medical reasoning. Cognitive Science, 10, 91-116.

Pearl, J. (1985) How to do with probabilities what people say you can't. C.R. Weisbin (Ed). Artificial Intelligence Applications: The engineering of Knowledge-Based Systems North-Holland 1985.

Pitrat, J. (1984) An intelligent program can and must use declarative knowledge efficiently. In Elithorn, A. and Banerji, R. (Eds.) Artificial and Human Intelligence, Elsevier, North-Holland.

Scott, D.S. (1976) Data types as lattices. Society of Industrial and Applied Mathematics(SIAM) Journal of Computing vol 5, no 3.

ACKNOWLEDGEMENTS

The work on case study 1 was carried out with, and entirely funded by Metron Technology Ltd, 50 North St., Taunton, TA1,1LX, U.K. Comments and help from Steve Battle, Dr Antony Galton, Carlos Martinez-Mascarua and Dr Ajit Narayanan are gratefully acknowledged.

A Heuristic Search Approach to Planning and Scheduling Software Manufacturing Projects

Ali Safavi and Stephen F. Smith

School of Computer Science
Carnegie Mellon University

1. Introduction

In today's highly competitive and constantly growing market for software products, planning and scheduling of software projects has become a bottleneck to increasing software production productivity [20]. There are several reasons why software manufacturing planning/scheduling is hard:

1. Even idealized formulations of the problem are NP-hard in the general case [8].

2. It involves face-to-face human negotiation between multiple agents to resolve the scheduling conflicts (i.e. unsatisfiable resource requests) that arise due to differences in goals, technical judgements, etc [6].

3. There is typically considerable uncertainty in budget (i.e. resource requirement) estimates and other project planning/scheduling constraints that must be accounted for [3, 11].

4. Software project planning and scheduling is not a static problem. Schedules must be continually revised over the course of the project as changes in planning/scheduling assumptions become known [7].

Given these characteristics, it can be argued that software project planning and scheduling is really much more of a schedule revision problem than a problem of schedule generation. This claim is supported by studies of actual software development organizations, which have indicated that the majority of scheduling time in a software project is spent on revising a pre-existing schedule [6, 18].

In this paper, we describe a heuristic approach to incremental revision of an existing software project schedule. We focus specifically on the design of a set of schedule revision operators and a control strategy for applying these operators during the scheduling process. This work extends previous work in the area of incremental schedule revision [5, 13]. Moreover, it represents the first major effort in building a *problem solving model* for software planning and scheduling. Other artificial intelligence approaches to software project management have focused primarily on the development of high-level specification languages for specifying planning/scheduling knowledge and frame-based knowledge representation schemes [1, 9, 16]. A program called NEGOPRO that uses our model to support the reactive refinement of software plans/schedules for large software projects has been implemented. NEGOPRO can be used both to improve a given (e.g. human generated) input schedule and to respond to unanticipated circumstances as the project proceeds. Extensions to support negotiation among multiple decision-makers during software project planning and scheduling are not discussed in this paper but can be found in [14].

A software project schedule is a specification of resources to be allocated to a software project plan and the intervals during which each is to be allocated. This specification must obey the temporal restrictions of production processes and the capacity restrictions of available resources. We also include the selection of a project plan (process plan) in the scheduling process because the selection of a process plan can not be separated from the scheduling of that plan. As opposed to the initial development of a set of process plans, the selection of a particular process plan from this set depends directly on how well it can be scheduled. This implies that selection of a process plan and the scheduling of that process plan should not be considered independently.

Our approach to software project scheduling is rooted in a formulation of the process as a heuristic search through the space of possible schedules. The search is initiated with respect to an input schedule that contains one or more unsatisfiable resource requests (conflicts), and the goal is to transform this schedule into one in which these conflicts are eliminated (or reduced). The heuristic search model is composed of three principle components: a set of *search operators*, each of which modifies a subset of the commitments comprising the current schedule to produce a new schedule, an *evaluation function*, which provides a basis for comparing the transformations produced by the application of alternative operators to a given schedule, and a *scheduling strategy*, which specifies knowledge relating to use of the search operators and the evaluation function within the search (e.g. conflict prioritization heuristics, operator selection heuristics, termination criteria, etc.).

We can contrast such a heuristic search model with traditional search-based planning models (e.g. [21]). In these models, the general objective is to find a feasible solution relative to a given set of non-negotiable constraints (i.e. a course of action that brings about a particular goal state in a manner consistent with the physics of the domain) and it is assumed that it is plausible to explore the entire search space (even if knowledge that enables more efficient search is seen as fundamental in practical applications). This assumption, even as a worst case scenario, is unworkable in the context of most scheduling problems, where the crux of the problem is balancing a conflicting set of preferences, each of which can be satisfied to varying degrees (i.e. optimizing within the space of feasible solutions). The search space is too large to ever exhaustively explore, and reliance on heuristic strategy knowledge and heuristic evaluation functions to restrict search is imperative.

Several previous efforts in manufacturing scheduling have considered the problem of incremental schedule revision[1]. The ISIS job shop scheduling system [4, 5] provides the capability to reschedule an order in response to the unexpected loss of required resources. This is accomplished by transforming the commitments pertaining to the problematic order into scheduling preferences, and generating a new schedule for the order. In situations where multiple orders are found to have schedule conflicts, the priorities of orders are used to determine the sequence of rescheduling them. Thus, in terms of the above heuristic search model, ISIS can be seen as utilizing a single search operator (i.e. the order rescheduling procedure). The overall revision strategy (highest priority order first) dictates a single trajectory through the space and thus there is no use for a global evaluation function[2]. The OPIS factory scheduling system [13, 19] implements a more sophisticated approach to reactive schedule revision. It emphasizes the use of several schedule revision operators, each with selective advantages in resolving certain types of scheduling conflicts, and operates according to an *opportunistic* scheduling strategy. More specifically, a heuristic theory relating the implications of current solution constraints (e.g. important reoptimization needs and opportunities) to the strengths and weaknesses of various revision operators is used as a basis for conflict prioritization and operator selection. This enables the scheduler to focus immediately on those decisions most critical to overall schedule revision objectives as opposed to encountering them only after other restricting commitments have been made. This heuristic theory (scheduling strategy) is used in lieu of a global heuristic search[3]. In the approach to schedule revision described in this paper, we also adopt an opportunistic scheduling strategy, but not to the exclusion of global heuristic search. A final approach to incremental schedule revision is implemented in the RESOURCE REALLOCATOR system [17],

---

[1]Both the ISIS and OPIS scheduling systems mentioned below also address the problem of schedule generation. We limit our attention here to issues relating to schedule revision.

[2]It should be noted that the "order rescheduling" procedure itself employed a heuristic beam search to locally explore alternative sets of commitments for the order being scheduled, and this search was focused by an evaluation function that reflected scheduling preferences relevant to the order (e.g. meeting the due date, utilizing preferred resources, etc).

[3]Although, as in ISIS, OPIS operators do exploit local heuristic search.

although in this case the problem addressed is quite different in that it is strictly a resource reallocation problem which is void of any temporal constraints. Nonetheless, the approach constitutes a heuristic search model that includes each of the principal components identified above.

The approach presented in this paper extends the previous work in schedule revision in several respects. First, it develops a problem solving model for a more general formulation of the scheduling problem than has previously been addressed. In particular, a search space is defined that includes selection among alternative process plans, and a problem solving model that integrates the search for a process plan with the search for a schedule that implements that process plan is provided. This enables preferential concerns relating to process plan selection to be appropriately balanced against those relating to resource allocation and time interval selection.

A second contribution of the present work relates to the development of alternative heuristic strategies for opportunistic scheduling. Specifically, the present work focuses on minimization of disruption (or change) to the schedule as the primary criterion for operator selection. Within any opportunistic scheduling scheme, the revisions prescribed by a selected operator to solve a particular conflict can lead to considerable disruption of the original schedule (i.e., create new conflicts and necessitate a large number of additional schedule revisions). Given the existence of a complete schedule, the search space is often highly constrained and thus provides little flexibility for revision. Disruption of the schedule over time (or alternatively lack of stability in the schedule over time) is a particularly important concern in software project management domain, as a project schedule serves to coordinate the interdependent activities of a large number of individuals. To minimize this phenomenon, we have studied the amount of disruption that is caused by each search operator, and have developed a set of heuristics to control the application of each operator on the basis of the disruption that it causes.

A third contribution of the present work is that it introduces and formally defines a criterion of *navigational minimality* for measuring the utility of design of a set of search operators. A set of operators is navigationally minimal if and only if it is the smallest set of operators that ensure that any given schedule is reachable from any other schedule. A navigationally minimal set of operators insures that it is feasible to start the heuristic search from any point in the search space while minimizing the overhead associated with operator selection at each cycle of the search. With respect to our formulation of the software planning and scheduling problem, we define such a set of search operators.

The remainder of the paper is organized as follows. First we formalize the problem of software project planning/scheduling to provide a basis for discussing the underlying problem solving model. We then describe, in turn, a set of operators for revising software project schedules, and the scheduling strategy employed to control their use. Finally, we present some experimental results obtained with the NEGOPRO program.

2. Formal Definition of the Problem

The notation used is described in two parts: symbols and constructs. The symbols will be formally defined as they appear in the formal definition of the problem. The symbols uniquely identify a planning/scheduling concept while constructs are used to manipulate them. Let r, p, and q be resources, G denote a software developing organization, Π denote a project, Φ denote a set of product feature requirements, Γ denote a process plan, and Λ be a schedule. Moreover, let Λ^* and Γ^* denote the set of all schedules and all process plans of a product respectively, $\{A_i\}$ denote a set of objects A_i, $[A_i]$ denote an ordered list of objects A_i (if A is declared as an ordered list, then A_i is used to refer to its i-th element), $Card(A)$ denote the cardinality of an ordered list or set A, 2^A denote the power set of A, membership test for ordered lists be defined and be referred to by the symbol $\in$, f, g, *and* h be functions, $[a\ b]$ *s.t.* $a,b \in N$ denote the inclusive set of rational numbers between a and b, and $(a_1\ a_2\ ...)$ denote a multi-dimensional domain.

We begin by considering the resources that must be allocated to support a given software project and the specification of the temporal constraints surrounding resource usage.

Definition 1: Resource

Let R be the set of all resources that can be used and produced in an organization G.
Then $R = R_{pro} \cup R_{pri}$ where $R_{pro} = \{r_j \mid r_j$ is the product of some project$\}$
and R_{pri} is the complement of R_{pro} in R.

R_{pri} denotes the set of *primitive resources* in G and includes those resources that are not produced inhouse. In contrast, R_{pro} denotes the set of *products* in G and includes those resources that are produced inhouse[4]. A file server, an office, any type of software, hardware, documentation, staff, or time are typical examples of primitive resources. Furthermore, all products in a software project are either software or documentation and are considered to be "infinite capacity" resources (therefore they need to be produced only once).

There are three types of temporal resource constraints: available capacity constraints, required capacity constraints (in the form of resource requests), and resource reservations (allocations). All temporal resource constraints share a common representation. We use the symbol ζ to refer to a prototypical temporal resource constraint. When multiple temporal resource constraints are needed, we use subscripts to distinguish between different temporal resource constraints. Furthermore, for a product p, we use r_ζ to refer to the resource requested by ζ, $\zeta(p)$ to refer to the set of all resource requests of the schedules of p, and $r_\zeta(p)$ to refer to the set of all resources requested by the schedule p[5].

R_{pri} itself includes two types of resources: unshared primitive resources which is denoted by R_{Upri}, and shared primitive resources which is denoted by R_{Spri}. A file server, an office, and any type of software or documentation are typical examples of shared resources while a system analyst, a coder or a workstation are typical examples of unshared resources. A system designer is an unshared resource despite the fact that it can be allocated to different projects at the same time. This is because if the size of time window is chosen small enough (e.g. manhour) a system designer can be working only on one project. *Time* is considered to be a shared resource since many activities (if their temporal ordering allows) can execute in parallel thus share the same unit of time. However, time has a special status that no other resource has, namely it is not treated as a separate resource and instead is implicit in the specification of ζ that involves other resources.

Definition 2: if ζ is a temporal resource constraint for a resource r by a product p, then ζ is of the form:

$$\text{if } r \in R_{Upri} \text{ then } \quad [(t_{2i}\ t_{2(i+1)}\ q_i)\ \ \forall i \in 0..n]$$
$$\text{else if } r \in R_{Spri} \text{ then } \quad [(t_{2i}\ t_{2(i+1)})\ \ \forall i \in 0..n]$$
$$\text{else if } r \in R_{pro} \text{ then } \quad t$$

such that t is a negative offset from the date that p is expected to be completed (initially mapped to zero) and denotes how early r has to become available in order to complete p on schedule, q_i is the quantity of r that is requested over $(t_{2i}\ t_{2(i+1)})$, and $(t_{2i}\ t_{2(i+1)})$ is the period during which r needs to be reserved where t_i and t_{i+1} are also offsets from the date that p is expected to be completed and $\forall i \in 0..n$ $t_{2i} < t_{2(i+1)}$.

Example 1: Consider the resource requirement specification *[(-5 -3 2) (-1 0 1)]* for a senior programmer. The specification requires 2 senior programmers for the first three months, no senior programmer for the fourth month (therefore the specification of this month is left out) and

---

[4]In software projects, these resources will remain available indefinitely once they are produced.

[5]Since our notation allows r_ζ to be used both as a function and as an object, we use the context of usage to determine whether it is a function or an object. More specifically, if it is followed by an argument which is enclosed in a parenthesis, then it is a function (the function value is a set). Otherwise, it is an object.

1 senior programmer for the last month of development.

Example 2: Consider that to develop a debugger (a product) we need a simulator (also a product). Furthermore, suppose that the simulator has to be available at least three months before the debugger can be completed. This resource requirement can be specified as -3. The specification of the upper bound of the interval is redundant because the required resources which are products will remain available once they are produced for the first time.

Definition 3: Resource Availability Constraints

$\rho = \{\zeta_j\}$ s.t. $\forall \zeta \in \rho$ r_ζ is unique, and in the specification of p, t is the date from which r_ζ becomes available, q_i is the quantity of r_ζ that will be available over $(t_{2i}\ t_{2(i+1)})$, $(t_{2i}\ t_{2(i+1)})$ is the period during which r_ζ will be available, and $\forall i \in 0..n$ $t_{2i} < t_{2(i+1)}$.

Given the above formulation of resources and temporal resource constraints, we are now in a position to formalize the overall software project planning and scheduling problem. A software development organization is an organization that can carry out orders from several clients concurrently:

Definition 4: Software Development Organization

$G = <\{\Pi_i\}, \rho>$

This definition implies that all projects within G compete for resources that are globally shared.

For every order, a project is created to undertake that order. However, our definition of a software project is recursive in that every inhouse order generated to meet a client order can be considered a project in its own rights.

Definition 5: Software Project

$\Pi = <p, \Phi, \alpha, \beta, \theta>$ s.t. p is the product of Π, Φ is the ordered list of feature requirements Φ_i that p has to meet, $\alpha = [\alpha_i]$ s.t. α_i is the ordered list of levels that feature requirement Φ_i of p can be met at[6], $\beta = [\beta_i]$ s.t. β_i is the ordered list of desired levels of meeting each feature requirement[7], and θ is a set of heuristic evaluation functions (definition 6).

The above definition implies that each feature requirement Φ_i of a product can be satisfied at multiple levels l $(1 \leq l \leq \alpha_i)$ from which one, β_i, constitutes the desired level. Of course a schedule can be constructed to satisfy a feature requirement above its desired level but this might be undesirable or incur additional cost without satisfying any new objectives. Modeling the satisfaction of feature requirements at multiple levels allows us to study the consequences of relaxing the desired level of meeting a feature requirement or alternatively the consequences of reserving additional resources to assure that a feature requirement will be met at a level which is closer to what is desired.

Definition 6: Heuristic Evaluation Functions

---

[6] y_j is a discrete variable that can assume only natural numbers. Furthermore, the elements of x_i are assumed to be organized in the increasing order.

[7] This can be formally stated as $\exists f$ 1-1 onto Φ $f: \alpha \to \beta$ s.t. $\forall \alpha_i$ $f(\alpha_i) \in \alpha_i$.

Let θ be the set of heuristic evaluation functions of Π. Then $\theta=\theta_{uh}\cup\theta_{mh}$ (where θ_{uh} denotes the project dependent heuristics and θ_{mh} denotes the project independent heuristics[8]) and $\forall\theta_i\in\theta$ $\theta_i:A\rightarrow n$ $n\in N$, s.t. A is a new commitment at the commitment point Λ[9] and n is the rating of A.

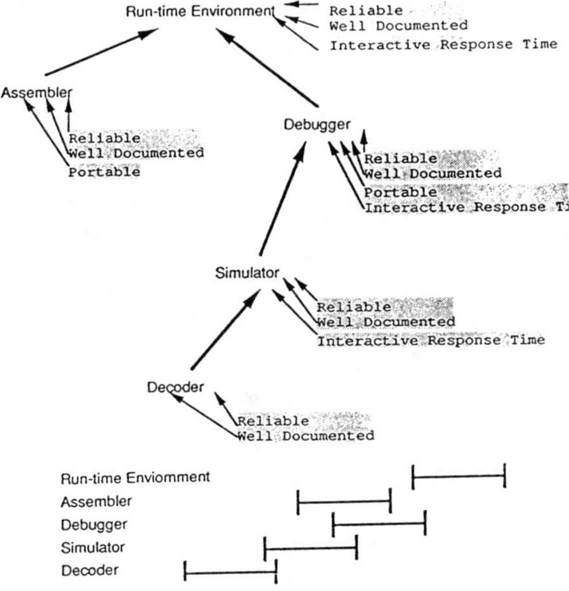

Figure 1: Production Dependency Graph of the
TMS3020 Runtime Environment

Consider a software project to develop a runtime environment for a TMS3020 chip. Furthermore, consider that the environment has to provide interactive response time and integrate the debugging and assembly functions. Once the project is awarded, the developing organization produces a *production dependency graph* of the final and intermediate products that need to be developed along with the feature requirements of each product (figure 1). In the production dependency graph of figure 1, products are represented by nodes while activities (productions) are represented by directed arcs. For instance the activity of producing the debugger is denoted by the directed arc that is incident from the simulator on the debugger.

According to definition 5, the project to develop a run-time environment in figure 1 only includes the activity to produce the run-time environment once the assembler and the debugger are completed. In general, the production of every single product (e.g. a simulator in figure 1) is formalized as a project. A *complete project* of producing a run-time environment is constructed by recursively replacing each intermediate product by its complete project.

---

[8]"Meeting the deadline is the most important feature requirement of a product under a rush mode" is a typical project independent heuristic that prefers the meeting of one feature requirement over the others if all can not be met together. In contrast, θ_{uh} includes the heuristics that are specific to the project being planned/scheduled and is specified with the problem.

[9]A *commitment point* refers to the plan/schedule that exists before it is revised by making a new commitment.

To illustrate the use of our representation language to specify the constraint knowledge of a problem, consider again the example of developing a runtime environment for a TMS3020 chip (figure 1). Figure 2 depicts the basic topology of the resource requests of each product that has been specified in our specification language under a fixed process plan. Hardware description *(HD)* is the only shared primitive resource that is included in the resource request graph while the unshared resources consist of junior programmer *(JP)*, senior programmer *(SP)*, graphic generator *(GC)*, and lexical analyzer *(LA)*. The labels of the arcs that connect two nodes reflect the resource requirements (temporal resource constraints) of a product end of the arc for the resource end of the arc. For instance, *HD* is required one month into the production of assembler while to

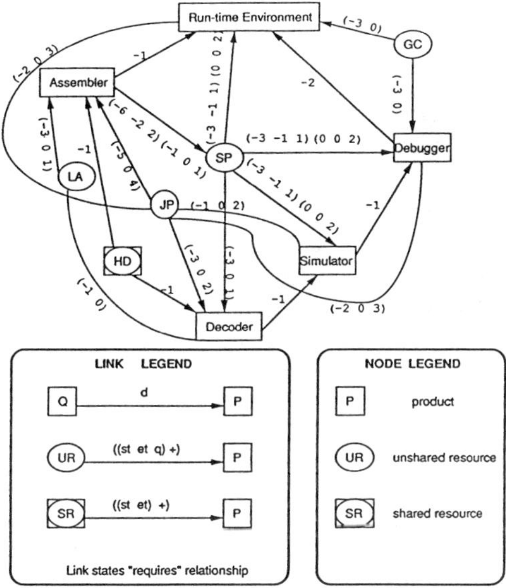

Figure 2: Resource Request Graph of the
TMS3020 Runtime Environment

develop the run-time environment 2 senior programmers will be required for the first two months and only one senior programmer for the third month.

Each project can typically be implemented through many process plans. A process plan specifies how a product can be produced from its required resources but stops short of allocating resources and temporally instantiating that plan. Furthermore, the process plan of a product does not specify how its required resources are acquired or produced. A *complete* process plan of a product p can be constructed by recursively merging p with the *complete process plans* of all products that are required by p.

Process plans of a product are different in the type of resources that they use to produce the product. For instance, a business data base application software can be developed by acquiring a business application generator and hiring an application generator expert to develop the application, or by designing and then developing the entire application inhouse using database designers and data base coders.

Among the set of resources required to produce a product under a process plan, some resources can be replaced by others. For instance, it might be possible to implement a process plan of a product by either 2 senior programmers and 3 junior programmers or 1 senior programmers and 6 junior programmers. The set of resources required under a process plan can be broken down to disjoint partitions υ such that each resource is in the same partition as all other resources that it is replacable with. For each partition, the user can specify multiple mixes of resource allocation requirements (e.g. two senior programmers and 3 junior programmers vs. one senior programmers and 6 junior programmers). We denote the set of these mixes for all partitions by τ.

Definition 7: Process Plan

Let Γ be a process plan of project Π which produces p. Then $\Gamma = <R_p,\upsilon,\tau>$ s.t. R_p is the set of names of resources required to implement Π, $p \notin R_p$, $\upsilon \subseteq 2^{R_p}$ is a set of disjoint partitions of R_p denoting substitutable resources, $\tau=[\tau_i]$ s.t. τ_i is the ordered list of resource mixes of each partition in υ[10].

Each process plan can be implemented through many schedules. A schedule is characterized by

1. determining which feature requirements (if any) have to be compromised (to avoid violating more important requirements such as missing a delivery deadline). For instance, the testing of a software module might require conducting formal reviews periodically, however, the development organization might decide to abandon this requirement if a major cost overrun would occur otherwise. We use ψ to denote the actual level at which each feature requirement of a product is met in a schedule.

2. committing to a set of resource requirements among all alternative sets of resource requirements for each set of substitutable resources. We let χ be the ordered list of indices of the selected resource requirement mixes.

3. committing to a set of resource allocations denoted by π to budget (allocate resources to) the process plan which the schedule implements.

Definition 8: Schedule

Let Λ be a schedule of Γ and p be the product of the project for which Γ is a process plan. Then $\Lambda = <\pi,\chi,\psi>$ s.t. π denotes the reservations of members of R_p[11], χ is an ordered list of integers denoting the selected resource requirement mixes[12], and ψ is an ordered list of natural numbers that denotes the actual level of meeting each feature requirement[13].

Definition 9: Resource Reservations of Λ

$\pi = [\zeta_j]$ s.t. $\forall \zeta \in \pi$ r_ζ is unique, and in the specification of
p, t is the date from which r_ζ becomes available,
q_i is the quantity of r_ζ that is allocated over $(t_{2i}\, t_{2(i+1)})$,
$(t_{2i}\, t_{2(i+1)})$ is the period during which r_ζ is allocated, $\forall i \in 0..n$ $t_{2i} < t_{2(i+1)}$.

The duration and start time of a schedule can be derived from the resource requirement specification of that schedule as follows:

Definition 10: Duration of a Schedule

Let $\forall \zeta \in \pi$ t_ζ = $if\ r_\zeta \in R_{pro}\ then\ t\ else\ t_0\ endif$
where t and t_0 are as defined in definition 2. Then d_Λ = $max(|t_\zeta|\ \forall \zeta \in \pi)$.

Definition 11: Start Time of a Schedule Λ

---

[10]This can be formally stated as $\exists$ 1-1 onto $f{:}\upsilon \to \tau$ where $\forall \tau_i$ $f(\tau_i)$ denotes the alternative resource requirement mixes of τ_i and $Card(\tau_i)=Card(\zeta)$ $\forall \zeta \in f(\tau_i)$).

[11]This can be formally stated as $\exists$ 1-1 onto $h{:}R_p \to \pi$.

[12]This can be formally stated as $\exists g$ 1-1 onto $g{:}\tau \to \chi$ s.t. $\forall \tau_i$ $1 \le g(\tau_i) \le Card(\tau_i)$ (a position within a).

[13]This can be formally stated as $\exists f$ 1-1 onto $f{:}\alpha \to \psi$ where $\forall \alpha_i$ $f(\alpha_i) \in \alpha_i$.

Let e_Λ be the value of the level at which the deadline feature requirement of p has to be met. Then $s_\Lambda = e_\Lambda - d_\Lambda$.

Therefore these parameters need not be specified as independent variables.

Normally we are interested not only in the schedule that describes how p is produced from its required resources but also the schedule of all intermediate products that need to be produced in order to develop the required resources of p. The complete schedule of p, Λ_{p*}, can be defined as the union of the schedule of p and the *complete schedules* of all required products of p. This can be formally written as follows:

Definition 12: Complete Schedule

Let Λ_p and Λ_{p*} denote the schedule and the complete schedule of producing p respectively. Then $\Lambda_{p*} = \Lambda_p \cup \Lambda_{q*}$ s.t.
$\forall q \quad p \in product\text{–}transitive\text{–}closure(q)$

Λ_{p*} can be constructed by starting from p working back recursively and including the schedules of all resource requirements of p that are of the type product.

Definition 13: product-transitive-closure

Let R and R_{pro} be as defined in definition 1 and ζ be a resource request. Then
$\forall x \in R_{pro} \quad \forall y \in R \quad x \in product\text{–}transitive\text{–}closure(y) \quad iff \quad y \in r_\zeta(x) \quad \vee$
$\quad \exists w \in R_{pro} \quad (y \in r_\zeta(w) \wedge x \in product\text{–}transitive\text{–}closure(w))$

The *scheduling problem* for a project consists of developing a schedule which is *consistent*. A project schedule Λ is consistent if and only if it meets the resource requirements that are necessary to satisfy the feature requirements of the product of that project (e.g. p). Since meeting the resource requirements of p is tied to meeting the resource requirements of the resources that p requires, then *consistency* needs to be measured across the *complete schedule* of p.

In our formalism, the consistency of a schedule Λ for a product p can be verified by comparing the aggregate demand[14] and the available capacity for r, for every resource $r \in R_p$. The aggregate demand for a resource by a schedule Λ reflects the capacity of r that is essential to satisfy all feature requirements of p. Λ is consistent if and only if the aggregate demand for every $r \in R_p$ never exceeds the available capacity of r. This can be formally stated as follows:

Definition 14: Schedule Consistency

Let Λ be a schedule to produce p. Then Λ is *consistent* iff
$\forall \tau_i \, \forall q \quad p \in product\text{–}transitive\text{–}closure(q) \quad n\text{–}th(\tau_i \, , \, g(\tau_i)) \subseteq h(q)$
s.t. τ is as in definition 7 and h,g are as in definition 8.

During the scheduling process, for every resource r, the aggregate reserved capacity of r (portion of the aggregate demand that has been met) should never exceed the available capacity of r. This is because a capacity can not be allocated unless it is available and can be formally stated as follows:

Definition 15: Scheduling Process Consistency

Let $Q = \{q \mid p \in product\text{–}transitive\text{–}closure(q)\} \cap R_{pro}$. Then $\forall r \in$

$\{r \mid p \in product\text{–}transitive\text{–}closure(r)\} \cap R_{pri} \quad \sum^{q \in Q} h_q(r) \subseteq \rho_r$
where h is as in definition 7.

Although the goal of scheduling is to develop a consistent schedule, incremental scheduling in our framework can be characterized as a process that continuously refines an intermediate schedule with the goal of achieving consistency. To guide this process, we need to measure the

---

[14]Aggregate demand for a resource can be constructed by aggregating the requests for that resource by all products produced under Λ.

distance between the present schedule and the goal schedule during each problem solving iteration. The value that the evaluation function returns for a schedule can be interpreted as the *consistency-distance (cd)* of that schedule.

We define the *cd* of a schedule as the ratio of the cost to the project of budgeting the schedule and the benefit (degree to which a schedule meets the requirements of the project) of the project. This suggests that *cd* calculates the balance between the satisfaction of a more important subset of feature requirements of the project product and the cost overrun that is incurred in order to meet those feature requirements in a project. A thorough description of *cd* and its measurement is provided in [14, 15].

In the project planning and scheduling literature, the end result of a scheduling process is often called a schedule only if it is consistent. However, we also refer to the output of a scheduling process as a schedule even if it is not consistent. If the schedule that is constructed is not consistent, it can still serve as a guide to the human user to help him decide which requirements can not be satisfied and therefore need to be compromised or alternatively which additional resources need to be made available if the requirements are to remain intact.

3. Operators

Given a formal characterization of the problem to be solved, we can now consider the specification of an appropriate problem solving model. In this section, we address the issue of search operators. We first define the concept of *navigational minimality* as an operator design objective, and then describe a set of operators for software project schedule revision that satisfy this property.

Let S be the search space of the problem (which includes the set of all possible schedules Λ that can be constructed) and Δ be the set of all possible revision operators that is defined on that space. Then

Definition 16: Composition of Operators

$C: (\delta_1,...,\delta_n,S) \to S$ s.t. $C(\delta_1,...,\delta_n,\Lambda_1)=\delta_1(\delta_2(...\delta_n(\Lambda_1)))=\Lambda_2$ where
$\delta_1,...,\delta_n \in \Delta \ \wedge \ \Lambda_1,\Lambda_2 \in S$

Definition 17: Orthogonal Set of Operators

Δ is orthogonal iff $\forall \delta_j \in \Delta \ \forall \Lambda_1,\Lambda_2 \in S \ \neg \exists \ \delta_1,...,\delta_n \in \Delta-\{\delta_j\}$ s.t.
$C(\delta_1,...,\delta_n,\Lambda_1)=C(\delta_j,\Lambda_2)$

Definition 18: Navigational Completeness

A set of operators Δ to navigate through a search space S is
navigationally complete iff $\forall \Lambda_1,\Lambda_2 \in S \ \exists w=\delta_1...\delta_n \ \delta_1,...,\delta_n \in \Delta \ $ s.t. $C(w,\Lambda_1)=\Lambda_2$.

According to this definition, Δ is navigationally complete if and only if a machine scheduler that uses it can navigate from any points within the space of possible schedules of a project to another point within that space. A navigationally minimal set of operators would assure that it is feasible to start the heuristic search from any point in the search space (i.e. any $\Lambda \in S$) in order to converge to a solution.

Definition 19: Navigational Minimality

Δ is navigationally minimal for S iff Δ is orthogonal and navigationally complete.

Our principal goal in designing Δ for software project scheduling is navigational minimality. We divide the design process into two steps: (1) formal declaration of the space to be searched, and (2) development of a set of operators that are orthogonal and navigationally complete with respect to this space. In the previous section, we formulated a search space S for software project scheduling that involves search along the following dimensions (which we refer to as D):

1. the amount of resources that are available for allocation to a project can vary over

time.

2. the same production (activity) can start at different dates.

3. the same production can be carried out with different mixes of resource capacities.

4. different productions might require the same resource. Then, if there is not enough of the resource to satisfy all requirements, a scheduler has to decide which production the resource should be allocated to or whether a product should be preempted from its resource so that the resource can be reallocated to another product.

5. product feature requirements can be compromised thus multiplying the number of ways that the requirements of a product can be satisfied.

6. The same production can be carried out with different process plans.

We now define a set of search operators that span this search space.

Definition 20: Operator Supply

$\delta_{supply}(\rho_x, \zeta) = \rho_y$ s.t. ρ_x and ρ_y denote
the available capacity of r_ζ before and after adding the capacity ζ.

Supply involves resolving a conflict by providing the disputed resource. A project is an *open-ended* system that communicates with the outside world by receiving budgets and delivering products. The commitments that a parent organization has made about the budget of a project could change if the major requirements of the project can not be met under the current budget. An operator, *supply*, is defined to increase the supply of that resource when major requirements of the project can not be met under the current level of supply. Similarly another operator, *take-away*, can be defined to decrease the supply of a resource dynamically.

Definition 21: Operator Move

$\delta_{move}(\Lambda_x, l) = \Lambda_y$ s.t. Λ_x and Λ_y denote the schedule of a product p
before and after the move, and $l \in [n\ m]$ denotes the amount of move (n represents
the maximum possible left shift and m denotes the maximum possible right shift of Λ_x).

Move is to move the start date of a schedule by delaying or expediting it: the start date is expedited if the schedule is moved left and delayed if the schedule is moved right. Let p be a product and χ_j and τ_j denote the j-th element of χ and τ. Then, to expedite the completion of p by l days, the following steps need to be executed in the order presented:

1. $\forall \zeta$ *s.t.* $r_\zeta \in (R_{pri} \cap R_p)$ first remove r_ζ from R_p and then return ζ to the list of available resources i.e. let $\rho_{r_\zeta} = \rho_{r_\zeta} \cup \zeta$. This would preempt p from the primitive resources that are allocated to it.

2. Let Φ_i denote the deadline feature requirement of p. Then let $\psi_i = \psi_i + l$ (this moves the completion deadline of p forward by l days).

3. $\forall \chi_j \in \chi$ and ζ the χ_j element of τ_j; if $r_\zeta \in R_{pro}$ then translate ζ by l on the time line.

4. Rebudget p. This would rebudget the primitive resource requests of p after they have been temporally moved.

5. $\forall q \in R_p$ move the schedule of q by $k \leq l$ such that q is completed before p requires it. If q already becomes available prior to the shifted completion time (i.e. q already enjoys a *left slack* which is larger than l) then the schedule of q need not be moved. However if q holds no left slack w.r.t. p or holds a left slack that is smaller than l, then a left shift in the schedule of q is essential. The left shift has to be *propagated* to any q that holds an insufficient left slack w.r.t. to their product.

If Λ_p is moved left, then not only the schedule of s s.t. $s \in product\text{--}transitive\text{--}closure+(p)$ remains unaffected, but also the slack of s w.r.t. p will grow.

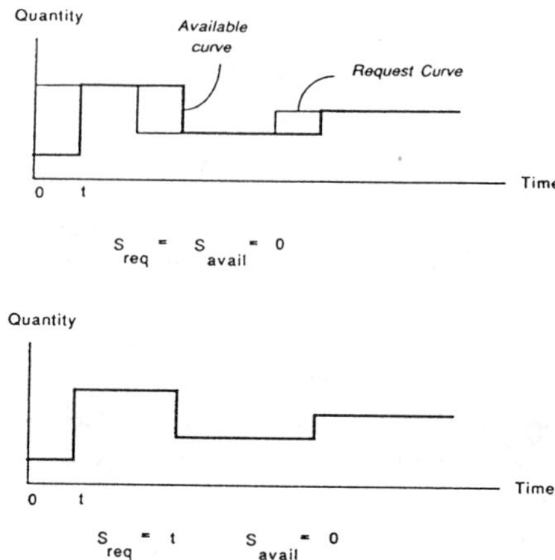

Figure 3: A Request Curve (a) prior to the Move (b) after the Move

If Λ_p is moved right by l, then the move needs to be propagated to q *s.t.* $q \in$ *product–transitive–closure*$+(p)$. If the *right slack* of p w.r.t. q is larger than l then q need not be moved. The right shift should be propagated recursively until the final products of the project are reached.

If the propagation reaches the final products of a project, then there is a chance that the duration of that project will increase. Duration of the project could increase even before the project has reached its final products. The recursive application of move-right along the path that starts with p should stop if the propagation causes the duration of the project to become the dominant cost factor.

Definition 22: Operator Substitute (Switch-Mix)

$\delta_{substitute}(\chi_x, y) = \chi_y$ where x and y are the indices of the set of
selected mixes of resources before and after one of the selected mixes is changed.

Substitute involves switching from one mix of levels of resources that produces a product to another mix of levels of the same group of resources producing that product. For instance, by allocating more manpower to a project that includes many parallel tasks, the duration of that project could be reduced; figure 4.

Definition 23: Operator Reallocate

$\delta_{reallocate}(\pi_w, \pi_x, r) = (\pi_y, \pi_z)$ s.t. w and x are the present indices of the schedules of p
and q, r is the resource to be reallocated from p to q, and y and z are
the new indices of the schedules of p and q.

Reallocate is to reallocate an unshared primitive resource from one product to another. The application of *reallocate* to a schedule does not affect the overall cost of resolving the conflicts in that schedule; figure 5.

Definition 24: Operator Compromise

$\delta_{compromise}(\Phi_x, y) = \Phi_y$ where x is the index of the set of levels of meeting each feature
requirement before the compromise and y is the index of the set of compromised levels
of meeting each feature requirement.

Compromise is to lower the desired level at which the feature requirements of p should be met.

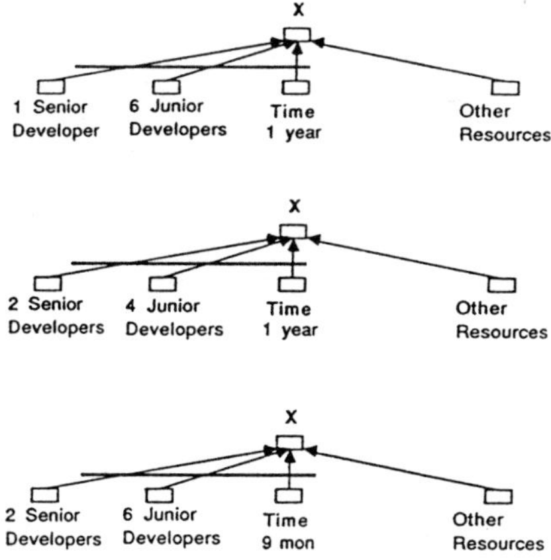

Figure 4: Different Mixes of Levels of Resources Produce the Same Product

	Module X	Module Y
Before Reallocation	10 Senior Prog 40 Junior Prog	2 Senior Prog 20 Junior Prog
After Reallocation	8 Senior Prog 40 Junior Prog	4 Senior Prog 20 Junior Prog

Figure 5: Reallocation of Senior Programmers From Module X to Module Y

Lowering the desired level at which the feature requirements of a product should be met in turn might affect the amount of resources that will be needed to meet the feature requirements of the product; this is illustrated in figure 6. Although it appears that a lower amount of resource requests will always lower the cost that is incurred for satisfying those requests, if the request that is lowered belongs to a shared resource r and the lowering refers to shortening the period l that a product p requires r, then the relaxation might save no new cost. This is because although the request of p for r is lowered, other products could continue to require r over l. The demand for r over a designated period l can be eliminated only if all requesting products drop or compromise their requests for r together.

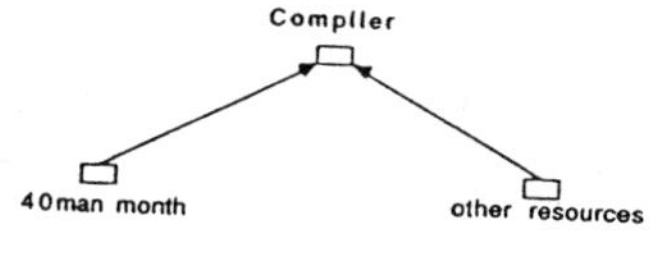

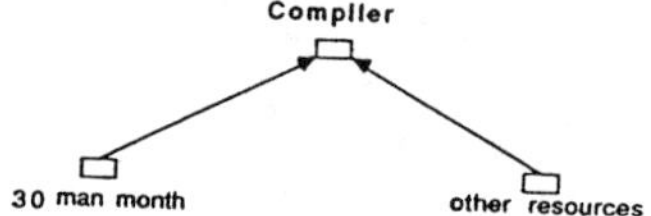

Figure 6: Compromise: Compiler (a) Has (b) Does not Have a 'High Reliability' Requirement

Definition 25: Operator Switch-Plan

$\delta_{switch-plan}(\Gamma_x, y) = \Gamma_y$ where x is the index of the present process plan among all process plans of the present schedule and y is the index of the new process plan to which the switch is to be made.

Switch-Plan is to switch from the present production plan to another. Suppose Z is an application software. Moreover, suppose that Z can be produced in three different ways:

1. Acquiring an application generator off the shelf to expedite the development.

2. Subcontracting the entire production to another firm.

3. Producing Z entirely inhouse.

In each case an entirely different process plan will emerge (see figure 7).

The procedures that implement each operator that we have described invoke two primitive operators: *release* and *allocate*. However, the procedures that implement each operator can not be expressed as a sequence of calls to *release* and *allocate* because they also include other decision constructs and heuristics [14].

Definition 26: Operator Release

$allocate(\Lambda_x, \zeta) = \Lambda_y$ where $\zeta = \pi_x - \pi_y$.

The capacity of r_ζ that is released from p will be added to ρ_{r_ζ}.

Definition 27: Operator Allocate

$allocate(\Lambda_x, \zeta) = \Lambda_y$ where $\zeta = \pi_y - \pi_x$.

The capacity of r_ζ that is allocated to p will be subtracted from ρ_{r_ζ}.

For instance, *reallocate* can be constructed from *release* and *allocate* as follows:

$$\delta_{reallocate}(\Lambda_w, \Lambda_x, r) = (\Lambda_y, \Lambda_z) \text{ s.t. } (release(\Lambda_w, \zeta) = \Lambda_y) \wedge (allocate(\Lambda_x, \zeta) = \Lambda_z)$$

Let $S^* = \{supply, take\text{-}away, reallocate, move, substitute, compromise, switch\text{-}plan\}$. Then

Claim1: S^* is Navigationally Minimal

Proof: We show that S^* is navigationally minimal by proving that it is navigationally complete and also it is orthogonal. Let $f{:}D \rightarrow S^*$ be a function that returns the name of the operator that spans the search space dimension denoted by the domain value such that $f(1)=supply$ $f(2)=take\text{-}away$ $f(3)=move$ $f(4)=substitute$ $f(5)=reallocate$ $f(6)=compromise$ $f(7)=switch\text{-}plan$. Clearly f is 1-1 onto. Therefore, S^* is navigationally complete. Furthermore, since the dimensions of the

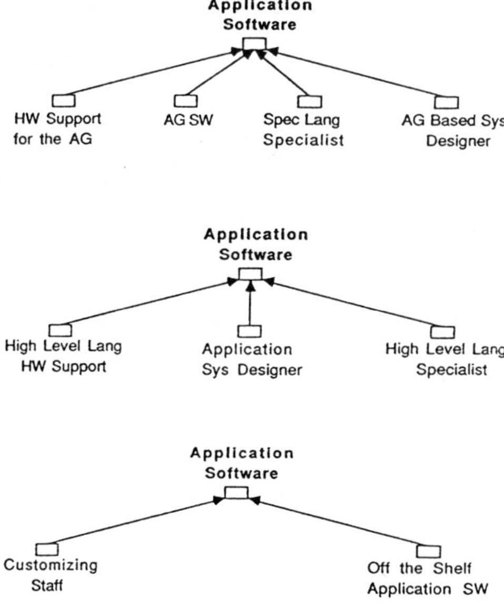

Figure 7: Three alternative production plans for developing an Application Generator

search space are orthogonal (by the definition of each dimension), the cardinality of S^* is minimal.

Given the generality of our formulation of the problem, we argue that S^* can be used to realize the same results as the "larger-grained" operators employed for incremental schedule revision in previous approaches[15]. In the following, we demonstrate how two operators employed by RESOURCE REALLOCATOR [17], a *transaction* and the more complex *cascade* of transactions, can be constructed by a sequence w of operators in S^*.

Suppose that G is a multiproject software developing organization. G begins a new project Π in an environment that several projects are already in progress each controlling a set of resources. Π usually has to deal with the problem that there are less resources available than it has requested. One way to resolve this problem is to reallocate the resources that are demanded by Π from other in-progress projects. This alternative is preferred if other projects can replace the reallocated resource with other resources that are available. RESOURCE REALLOCATOR refers to this sequence of *reallocation* and *replacement (substitution)* as a *transaction*. A chain of transactions is called a *cascade* [17]. For instance, group G_a might be in possession of $r1$ but have no skilled personnel, $r2$, to operate it. In contrast, G_b might be in possession of skilled personnel $r2$ but lack resource $r1$ to operate on. As a result of a transaction, both G_a and G_b could possess $r1$ and $r2$.

The semantics of a transaction in Sathi [17] is slightly different from the one we defined above because of the different rules that govern the organization that they assume. According to Sathi,

---

[15]Of course the advantage of doing so from the standpoint of scheduling efficiency is another issue.

the set of available resources consists of the resources that are under the discretionary control of some organizational unit. G_a can obtain a new resource (e.g. r) only from other units within G (e.g. G_b) that control r. The only method to obtain r in G is to trade a resource that G_b requires and G_a controls with r, a resource that G_b controls and G_a requires.

The main difference between the setting that Sathi define and the one used here is that here an organizational unit is not allowed to maintain its control over a resource unless that unit keeps the resource at work. This however does not prevent G_a from bidding for r and at the same time offering s which it currently uses.

Claim2: $\exists w=\delta_1...\delta_n\ \delta_1,...,\delta_n \in \Delta\ s.t.\ C(w,\Lambda)=\delta_{transaction}(\Lambda)$.

Proof: The main point in the proof is that a conditional release such as "G_a will give up s only if it can obtain r" can be broken down to "G_a will give up s" and "G_a will obtain r." Consider the sequence "*substitute reallocate substitute*" of operators in S^*. First *substitute* substitutes r for s in G_a, then *reallocate* reallocates r from G_b to G_a, and finally *substitute* substitutes s for r in G_b. Since the initial substitution has released s from G_a to ρ, s will be allocated to G_b from ρ.

Claim3: $\exists w=\delta_1...\delta_n\ \delta_1,...,\delta_n \in \Delta\ s.t.\ C(w,\Lambda)=\delta_{cascade}(\Lambda)$.

Proof: Recall that a cascade is a sequence of transactions and consider all sequences of operators in S^* that is represented by the regular expression e of the form "*substitute (reallocate substitute)+*." Then the same argument that we used to prove claim2 can be used to show a cascade of length n (a sequence of n transactions) is the sequence e such that the sequence *(reallocate substitute)* in it is repeated exactly n times.

4. Operator Selection

In this section, we describe an operator selection strategy which attempts to keep schedule disruption at a minimum while making the most progress toward resolving a given conflict. To reduce disruption during schedule revision, we have studied the amount of disruption that is caused by each search operator, and have developed a set of heuristics to control the application of each operator on this basis. To break ties among operators that are likely to cause the same degree of disruption, we consider the progress that each will make toward solving the target conflict. This implies that operators will first be sorted in the decreasing order of disruption and then in the decreasing order of progress made toward resolving the conflict. The advantage this heuristic strategy for opportunistic scheduling (which is a goal oriented process) is that it helps to maintain the solution structure that earlier opportunistic operators have shaped unless it is found not to be converging to a solution. For instance a disruptive revision might undo the commitments made during previous iterations of opportunistic scheduling by creating new conflicts at the points where previously resolved conflicts used to reside.

Although the minimization of disruption is not a major concern during the initial construction of a schedule, it becomes critical during the reactive refinement of an existing schedule (which characterizes the software project scheduling process). This is because decision making is much more constrained in the presence of a pre-existing set of commitments. Although the importance of non-disruptive (local) operators is noted in OPIS [13], it is considered as secondary to reoptimization concerns during operator selection.

An analysis of the operators in S^* illustrated that *reallocate, supply, take-away,* and *compromise* are the only operators that always have strictly local effects. For instance, *reallocate* only affects the allocation of resources in the product that the resource is reallocated from and the product that the resource is allocated to. Since *reallocate, supply, take-away,* and *compromise* can cause no disruption, then they are considered first during the operator selection. Discrimination between these operators is made by comparing the degree of progress that each makes toward resolving the intended conflict.

The remaining operators namely *substitute, move,* and *switch-plan,* can cause disruption. Substitution of a mix of required resources for another in the schedule of a product p will be disruptive only if

1. a resource r in that mix will be required earlier by p after the substitution is made. In this case disruption will occur if the new required date of r is earlier than the available date of r.

2. the duration of p increases after the substitution will be made. In this case disruption will occur if the new available date of p is later than when other product require p.

The disruptiveness of *move* and *switch-plan* can be studied in a similar way. Intuitively, we anticipate that *move* will be more disruptive than *substitute* since it requires that the entire schedule of p be shifted. We also anticipate that *switch-plan* be more disruptive than either *move* or *substitute* since not only the schedule but also the process plan of p (consequently the required resources of p) is altered. In our approach, we first determine which of the operators *move, substitute,* and *switch-plan* will actually be disruptive in the context of the current conflict. This is accomplished by simulating the effect of each on the schedule[16]. If none are found to be disruptive, then the operator that makes the most progress toward resolving the intended conflict is chosen. Otherwise, if all three operators are found to be disruptive then we choose them in the following order: *substitute, move, switch-plan.* This ordering lends itself to the least-anticipated-disruption-first heuristic which we briefly described above.

The policy of prioritizing the operators on the basis of how local their consequences will be could also be generalized to operator arguments by considering the arguments that cause a smaller disruption in the schedule first. Figure 8 shows the implementation of this policy in the action manager.

In the remaining of this section, we describe two alternative methods to approximate the degree of progress that an operator makes toward resolving a conflict. The first method involves explicit measurement of the cd (discussed in section 2) of both the current schedule and the schedule that results from applying the operator, and then calculating their difference. Although the cd of a schedule can be measured for the entire schedule, it is often preferred to restrict the measurement to a subset of the schedule in order to avoid the computational complexity of repeated measurements. [14] provides a detailed description of how the cd of a schedule (or part of a schedule) can be measured.

An alternative method to approximate the degree of progress that an operator makes toward resolving a conflict is to use a set of heuristics that has been developed to selectively choose as operator by assessing the parameters of the conflict or the schedule. These heuristics eliminate the need to measure the cd altogether when they are successful in selecting an operator. If they fail, however, we need to fall back to the first alternative. These heuristics have been developed by studying the effectiveness of each operator in resolving different conflict scenarios and also the degree of disruption that the operator might cause in each case, and are outlined as follows for the case that the conflict is over a resource r:

1. If the aggregate demand for r (combined demand of all products for r which is not satisfied) is constant throughout most of the project, then increase the *supply* of r uniformly across the entire project schedule.

2. If the available capacity of r increases in the neigbourhood of the disputed period, then *move* one of the products that requires r over the disputed period.

3. If the request for r can be substituted in one of the products that requires r over the disputed period and one of the resources that r can be substituted with is largely unutilized over the disputed period, then *substitute* is recommended.

---

[16]This type of simulation is not computationally expensive because it will stop as soon as it learns that other parts of the schedule need to be changed.

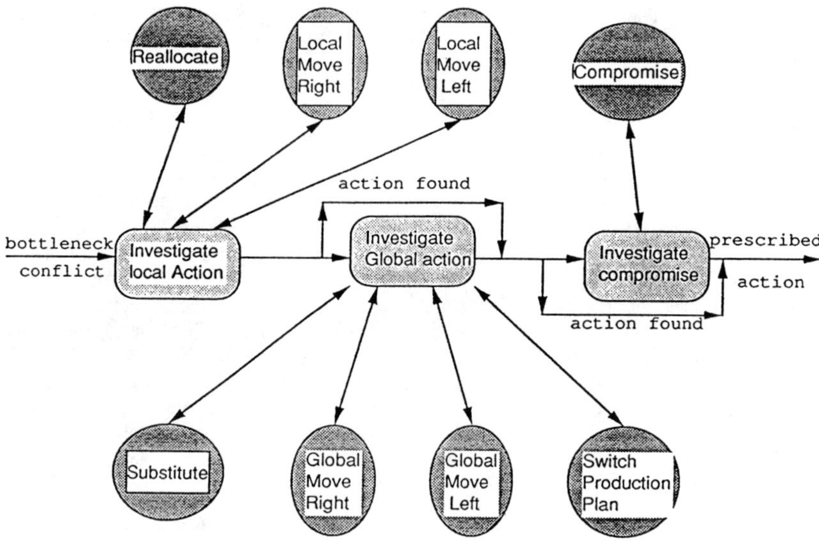

Figure 8: A Diagram of the Action Manager

4. If *r* can be reallocated from another product which has the choice to substitute or compromise *r*, then a *reallocate* is recommended.

5. If the conflict can be entirely resolved by agreeing to a marginal loss in the feature requirements of the project product, then a *compromise* is recommended.

A heuristic for selecting "switch-plan" is not recommended because the switch from a process plan to another might affect many schedule parameters which in turn significantly reduces the accuracy that can be achieved by providing a heuristic which relies on the value of only a small subset of those parameters.

5. Selection of Operator Sequences

In addition to improving the efficiency of search by developing a set of heuristics that approximate the effect of an operator on a schedule without measuring the *cd* of that schedule, we have also recognized the utility of heuristics which prescribe a *sequence* of operators once the schedule is known to satisfy a set of properties. The advantage of these heuristics is that they require only a single iteration of the algorithm to decide a *sequence* of operators that should be applied while normally each iteration is able to prescribe only one operator. Although the present prototype of NEGOPRO does not include these heuristics, we expect that they improve the efficiency of search significantly.

A typical situation where a whole *sequence* of operators can be prescribed is when we are certain that many conflicts in the schedule can be resolved by the repeated application of the same operator/argument pair to each conflict. For instance, when there is a manpower shortage across the board and formal review can be eliminated from the quality assurance requirements, the machine scheduler could enforce a *policy* to relax (compromise) the need for formal reviews altogether. This can be implemented by coding a heuristic that is triggered once a pattern of shortage of manpower across the board is detected during the reactive scheduling.

Some of the heuristics that we described in section 4 also provide a crude way of prescribing a *sequence* of operators. For instance the heuristic that approximates the applicability of "reallocate" examines if the resource to be reallocated can be later "substituted" or "compromised". In contrast, the direct measurement of *cd* can provide information on only one operator (*reallocate* in this case). It is important to be able to approximate the *cd* due to a sequence of operators since occasionally a sequence of operators should be applied to a schedule before the effect of them on the schedule can become apparent. For instance, a reallocation of *r* from *p* to *q* might have no affect on the consistency of the schedule. However, if *p* can substitute the resource *r* with another resource which is unallocated, then one could anticipate that the schedule become more consistent after a "*reallocate substitute*" sequence.

In the same way that a sequence of operators could provide a uniquely efficient way to converge to a solution, there exist sequences of operators that should be prohibited because they might cause redundancy or cause the formation of cycles. We use additional heuristics to prevent the formation of these sequences. For instance, consecutive *moves* can be simulated by a single move in order to prevent redundancy. In this case, we check that if the previous operator was "move", then "move" is prevented from being the next operator because any number of consecutive moves could have been achieved by a single move.

6. Experimental Results

Our goal from conducting experiments was to study the feasibility of our heuristic search approach. In order to fully assess our approach we need to use human subjects and compare global impact of the user provided utility value with that of the machine generated one under different scenarios. We however limited ourselves to compare the overall improvement in the schedule using our approach with the schedule that we started with in each case. We were unable to compare our results with those of other approaches [1, 9, 12] since they do not provide the type of problem solving capabilities that NEGOPRO offers.

Two groups of data were used to conduct these experiments. The data in each group sketched a multi-project organization that is engaged in the concurrent execution of three projects. The total number of products that were being scheduled in each group was 5 and 12 respectively. The experiments within each group varied in the number of resources being scheduled, substitutability of resources, number of process plans, complexity of compromises, and the schedule used as the seed. In contrast to the data within each group, the data between the two groups were not correlated. However, the second group of data contained a greater degree of assembly and had a considerably larger search space. The data within each group was not randomly generated because we had no strong reason to believe that there is no difference between a set of randomly generated data and a set of data that reflects a realistic micro multi-project case.

First, we conducted a total of 46 experiments and in each case we measured a number of parameters including the improvement in the quality of the final schedule in comparison to the quality of the seed schedule. This improvement was measured by comparing the *cd* of the seed schedule with that of the final schedule.

In designing a seed schedule, our initial goal was to minimize the duration of each project at the cost of other resources. This implies that initially we considered "time" to be the most expensive resource during the minimization of *cd*. Then we lowered the importance of time (i.e. meeting the deadline of the project) thus allowing the scheduler to rebalance the cost of other resources with time in order to lower the *cd* further for each experiment.

Once we conducted all 46 experiments, we analyzed the results by measuring the correlation between the input and output parameters. In each case one or two input parameters were allowed to vary while all others were fixed. Among the output parameters, those that we believed were interesting were recorded and then the results were tabulated into a number of tables [14] such that each cell of a table averaged all experiments that satisfied its rows and column attributes.

Below, we have included one of these tables. The budget overrun of individual resources were not accounted for since "cost" of the final schedule measured the combined effect of all of them. The use of an effective global measure in this case simplified the analysis.

Table 6-1 compares the effect of the two different groups of input on the output. The headings of the three middle columns *conflict analyzer, action manager,* and *progress analyzer* refer to the three components of NEGOPRO used for conducting incremental heuristic search. Progress analyzer has implemented a simplified version of an evaluation function to measure the *cd* of a revised schedule (intermediate solution) at the end of each incremental search step. Table 6-1 shows that by increasing the overall size and the assembly nature of the problem, the time that is spent in the conflict analyzer, action manager, and the progress analyzer all increase. However, the rate by which the computational complexity of action manager and progress analyzer increase is smaller than the rate by which the computational complexity of conflict analyzer increases. This suggests that operator selection is not a bottleneck and therefore may be coupled with other scheduling strategies as well. We also learned that the speed by which a schedule can be revised is mainly a function of the complexity of the assembly because the more assembly oriented nature of a project, the slower the propagation of a local revision to the rest of the schedule.

Group No	AVG # of Operators	Time in Conflict Analyzer	Time in Action Manager	Time in Progress Analyzer	Quality Improvement
Group1	6	1.2	0.7	0.1	490%
Group2	19	3.1	1.1	0.2	260%

Table 6-1: The effect of the size of the problem on the speed and quality of the final schedule (time in mins).

Table 6-1 also shows that with increasing the overall size and the assembly nature of the problem, the number of operators that are applied before the most qualified solution is constructed increases but that this increase is very much linear. Moreover, table 6-1 shows that NEGOPRO has improved the quality[17] of the seed schedule in the first group of experiments more than it has improved the quality of the seed schedule in the second group ,however, this result would be offset by the fact that the resource contention for the second group of experiments was chosen to be significantly higher than the in the first group of experiments.

7. Conclusion

In this paper, we have shown that software project planning and scheduling, an NP-hard problem under idealized formulation, can be characterized as a reactive scheduling problem. To solve the reactive scheduling problem, we described a heuristic approach to incrementally revise an existing software project schedule. This approach was rooted in a formulation of the reactive scheduling process as a heuristic search through the space of possible schedules.

In comparison to previous work in incremental schedule revision, the main contributions of our approach are,threefold. First, we have provided a framework that enables more general treatment

---

[17]The *quality improvement* is measured by taking the ratio of the *cd* of the seed schedule and the *cd* of the NEGOPRO generated schedule.

of process plan alternatives during scheduling, and thus allows preferential concerns relating to process plan selection to be more effectively balanced against those relating to resource allocation and time interval selection. Secondly, we have defined the concept of *navigational minimality* as a design objective in formulating a set of operators with respect to a given search space, and specified a set of navigationally minimal operators for the software project scheduling problem. Thirdly, we have focused on the minimization of disruption in the schedule as the principal criterion for opportunistic operator selection, and developed a heuristic strategy for operator selection based on this criterion.

With respect to the domain of software project planning and scheduling, our work represents the first major attempt to develop a computational model of the problem solving process. This can be contrasted with other approaches to software project management [1, 9, 16], which have emphasized issues relating to specification and representation of project management knowledge but have largely ignored issues of interpretation of this knowledge by an automated scheduler. We have implemented a program called NEGOPRO that uses our model to support the development and maintenance of software plans/schedules. Experimental results obtained with this program indicate the utility of our approach in reducing the level of conflict in a problematic software project schedule.

The current NEGOPRO model for software project scheduling takes several types of project scheduling knowledge and constraints into account. At the same time, there are several other types of project scheduling knowledge that are not currently handled and must be integrated into the model before it can be put into practical use. In particular, we need to extend our model to consider various organizational policies and regulations (e.g. "each junior programmer should be assigned to work with exactly one senior programmer and at most three junior programmers can be assigned to each senior programmers") as well as idiosyncratic preferences for individual resources or groups of resources over other resources of the same type. Such extensions are currently under investigation.

8. Acknowledgements
We are greatful to Mark Fox from the center for integrated manufacturing decision systems at CMU, Charles Marshal at Digital Equipment, and Hamid Nabavi at Xerox for their valuable comments. This research was supported in part by DARPA under contract #F30602-88-C-0001, and in part by the Robotics Institute at CMU.

References

1. Kent Bimson and Linda Burris. "Assisting Managers in Project Definitions". *IEEE Expert* , 2 (1989).

2. B.W. Beohm. *Software Engineering Economics.* Prentice Hall, Englewood Cliffs, N.J., 1981.

3. B.W. Boehm. *Software Risk Management Tutorial.* TRW, 1988.

4. Mark Fox. *Constraint-Directed Search: A case study of job-shop scheduling.* Ph.D. Th., Carnegie-Mellon University, Pittsburgh, 1983.

5. Mark Fox and Stephen F. Smith. "ISIS - A Knowledge Based System for Factory Scheduling". *Expert Systems 1,* 1 (July 1984).

6. Les Gasser. "The Integration of Computing and Routine Work". *ACM Transactions on Office Information Systems* (July 1986), 205-225.

7. Abdel-Hamid Tarek. *Project Management Modeling.* Ph.D. Th., MIT, School of Business Management, 1984.

8. M. Garey and D. Johnson. *Computers and Interactibility.* Freeman, New York, 1979.

9. Richard Jullig, Wolfgang Polak, Peter Ladkin and Li-Mei Gilham. KBSA Project Management Assistant. Tech. Rept. RADC-TR-87-78, Kestrel Institute, 1987.

10. H. Kerzner. *Project Managment: A systems Approach to Planning, Scheduling and Executing.* Van Nostrand Reinhold Company, 1984.

11. K. McKay, J. Buzacott, F. Safayeni. The Scheduler's Knowledge of Uncertainty: The Missing Link. Proceedings of IFIP Conference on Knowledge Based Production Management Systems, August, 1988.

12. J. Moder, C. Philips, and K. Davis. *Project Management with CPM, PERT & Precedence Diagramming.* Van Nostrand Reinhold Company, New York, 1983.

13. Peng Si Ow, Stephen F. Smith, and Alfred Thiriez. Reactive Plan Revision. Proceedings of American Association of Artificial Intelligence, Saint Paul, 1988, pp. 77-82.

14. A. Safavi. Scheduling and Planning of Large-Scale Software Manufacturing Projects. Robotics Institute, Carnegie Mellon University, in preparation, 1990.

15. A. Safavi and Stephen F. Smith. A Heuristic Model to Compare Alternative Commitments During Machine-Based Manufacturing Planning/Scheduling. International Conference on Expert Planning Systems, London, Jun, 1990.

16. A. Sathi, T. Morton, and S. Roth. "Callisto: An Intelligent Project Management System". *AI Magazine* , Winter (1986).

17. A. Sathi. *Cooperation Through Constraint Directed Negotiation: Study of Resource Reallocation Problems.* Ph.D. Th., Carnegie Mellon University, 1988.

18. Walt Scacchi. "Software Engineering: A Social Analysis Study". *IEEE Transacations on Software Engineering* (Jan. 1984), 45-60.

19. Stephen F. Smith. A Constraint-Based Framework for Reactive Management of Factory Schedules. In *Intelligent Manufacturing*, M. Oliff, Ed., Benjamin Cummings Publishers, 1987.

20. Nam P. Suh. "The Future of the Factory". *Robotics and Computer Integrated Manufacturing 1,* 1 (1984), 39-49.

21. David Wilkins. *Practical Planning: Extending the Classical AI Planning Paradigm.* Morgan Kaufmann, 1988.

From Data to Knowledge Bases

Martin Charles Golumbic

IBM Israel Scientific Center
Technion City
Haifa, Israel

Dennis Grinberg

Department of Mathematics
and Computer Science
Bar-Ilan University
Ramat Gan, Israel

1. Introduction

The study of databases is a well developed area of computer science and technology. Theoretical and practical aspects of databases have been subject to investigation for several decades, and have been the topic of thousands of research papers and hundreds of conferences. The reality is that today very large databases are an integral part of our everyday life. The spotlight is now being turned to combining methods from artificial intelligence and databases into a broader discipline known as knowledge bases.

Research into knowledge bases has not yet matured into a form where one can identify specialized fields and related methodologies. It is an area still under evolution. Ideas are born and die. Mutants are resurrected only to gain some strength of support before being discarded. Slowly, however, several basic principles are emerging which seem to have the resilience to stand up to scientific rigor. Although we may be many years from a technology of very large knowledge bases, we can and should nevertheless reflect upon and analyze the progress made so far and identify problems which we can reasonably attack in the near term. The big challenges for the long term will be met by slow and steady research.

Databases represent information as large, shared data structures residing usually on secondary storage. The data may possibly be distributed over several machines and locations with access to the data available concurrently to multiple users. Database applications typically *retrieve, manipulate* and *filter*. In contrast to this, knowledge bases currently are relatively small, residing in main storage. Knowledge applications generally are more ambitious and must *deduce* and *induce* new facts and exhibit "judgement" based operations on the stored information.

The following distinction can be made:

- Database operations are algorithmic and deterministic --
      You know what you want and know how to get it.

- Knowledge base operations are probabilistic, use rules-of-thumb,
  and deal with uncertainty --
      You guess what you want and you try your best to figure out
      how to get a close approximation to it most of the time.

A primary difficulty in defining the notion of a knowledge base is that there is much disagreement over what constitutes knowledge. There are certainly many fundamentally distinct types of knowledge, and the classification of such forms of knowledge has been the subject of debate by philosophers for centuries. There would appear to be much less controversy over what constitutes data, and hence databases. If database technology is like exploring a solar system, then knowledge base technology will be more like exploring a galaxy.

Different people define the terms *knowledge* and *knowledge base* in different ways. Some may seem "more correct" than others. An added difficulty is that there are many terms, such as *intelligent database, deductive database* and even *expert system*, that could mean the same or almost the same thing as *knowledge base*.

Consider the following six possible definitions or descriptions of the terms *knowledge* and *knowledge base*:

1. A knowledge base is a database augmented by evaluation mechanisms (based mainly on inference) that allows us to derive implicit information, i.e., information that is not explicitly stored in the database [16].
2. A knowledge base emulates human reasoning in order to eliminate the human from the cycle of design, of performance, and of active roles in the system [11].
3. Knowledge captures in some way the decision making process as opposed to data which doesn't [29].
4. A knowledge base is the front end of a database. It is the application that uses the data in the database.
5. The knowledge in a knowledge base is any information that allows us to interpret what we keep in the database [16].
6. A knowledge base is knowledge made explicit with a specific purpose in mind, and then made utilizable to solve a corresponding problem [16].

A look at these definitions suggests that they be placed into three broad categories. The first definition (1) defines knowledge bases as extensions of databases; the next three definitions (2-4) define knowledge bases as expert systems or applications; the last two definitions (5-6) define knowledge bases in a more general way.

For our purposes we will define a knowledge base as a *collection of facts (data) and knowledge (rules) about the facts*. The knowledge might be explicit, it might even be stored itself in a database, but it can also be implicit, like knowledge buried in an application program. The knowledge can be passive, (e.g., knowledge that is used by an expert system that accesses the knowledge base), or the knowledge can be active. If the knowledge is active, then a tool like an inference mechanism is needed, a tool that builds derivations from the facts and knowledge. Our definition of a knowledge base thus encompasses a number of the six definitions.

In order to provide some insight into where the road from data to knowledge bases is headed, we explore the major trends currently being investigated followed by a detailed presentation of the more promising ones. The edited transcript of a panel discussion on the topic, which was held at the Third International Conference on Data and Knowledge Bases (Jerusalem, Israel, June 1988), appears in Appendix A. For further source material in this area, the reader is referred to [18].

2. Classification of knowledge base systems

How can we classify knowledge base systems? Can we find a methodology that will enable us to decide whether one knowledge base is inherently superior to another? One possible classification is based on how the knowledge base's knowledge is represented. Using such a classification, we can divide knowledge base systems into three broad categories: *inherent knowledge systems, buried knowledge systems* and *explicit, auxiliary structure knowledge systems*.

Inherent knowledge is any intrinsic knowledge about our data. One important example of inherent knowledge is a database schema. A database schema describes data in the database and is therefore knowledge about the data. Although a schema might not provide very much knowledge in simple database architectures, as more and more complicated database architectures evolve (e.g., object oriented systems) more and more semantics are expressed via the schema [16].

The problem with inherent knowledge systems is that inherent knowledge does not provide us with all the information that we would like. We must "know" much more in order to do anything nontrivial with our data. If we were to create a scale of measuring knowledge base systems ranging from "inherently bad" to "inherently good," we would have to place inherent knowledge systems towards the bottom of the list.

Buried knowledge is knowledge that is not made explicit. For example, database application programs contain knowledge about data, but the knowledge is (usually) not exposed, it is buried in the application program. For a system to be classified as an "inherently good," we would like knowledge to be as explicit as possible. We would like to be able to store, examine and modify knowledge without difficulty. Non-explicit knowledge does not allow us to do these things. Buried knowledge systems would therefore also rank towards the bottom of a list of "inherently bad" to "inherently good" systems.

Auxiliary structure knowledge systems store their knowledge in an explicit manner. There are many examples in this category including some of the techniques used in AI like logic programming systems. In these systems both data and knowledge are explicit and can easily be examined and modified. These systems would be placed fairly high on our list, and we will focus much of our attention on systems in this category.

One of the biggest problems of systems with auxiliary knowledge structures is that their performance becomes sluggish when they contain large numbers of rules and/or facts. This is the reason why most existing AI systems deal onlywith knowledge bases of small sizes. Many even store their knowledge in a computer's main memory, whose capacity is usually quite limited.

There are additional problems with systems based on auxiliary knowledge structures like providing services for recovery and protection. Instead of dwelling only on problems in existing systems, we will take a look at the types of knowledge base systems that we can expect to see (or that we would like to see) in the next few years. We examine some of the difficulties in creating these systems and discuss a few possible models for the implementations of these future systems.

3. Six types of future systems

Real-time Expert Systems

In many advanced applications, such as the United States' Advanced Tactical Fighter (ATF) and Strategic Defense Initiative (SDI), expert systems that operate in real-time are a necessity [11]. The biggest problem with expert systems is that when they reach a certain size limit, they become non-operational in real-time. It doesn't matter what type of computer the expert system is running on, when an expert system contains too much knowledge, it's performance becomes sluggish.

Large Knowledge Bases

Large knowledge bases will be used in applications such as engineering processes, manufacturing and communications. Systems such as these incorporate vast numbers of rules. According to Hayes-Roth [10], such systems are expected to contain 100,000 rules by 1990 [25]. In addition to storing large numbers of rules, millions of database clauses might also be needed. Some knowledge base systems are geared for large numbers of rules and facts, but many (such as most Prolog systems) fail at around 60,000 clauses [30].

Multi-user Knowledge Bases

Knowledge bases must provide for concurrent access by many users. When using the standard physical locking scheme employed by most databases, (*two phase locking protocol* [3]), problems arise even if only facts (and not rules) are being accessed concurrently by multiple users. Solutions to the problems of concurrent access of facts have been suggested [4, 20, 23], but the problems of concurrent access of rules still must be solved.

Multi-media Knowledge Bases

In many advanced systems, data can come from many sources. For example, expert systems aboard an aircraft would receive data from multiple sensors determining speed, weather conditions and knowledge about other aircraft in the vicinity. The system would also receive input from the pilot's actions (changes in rudders, flaps, etc.). Since only data (and not knowledge) is acquired from multiple sources, there should not be more difficulty implementing multi-media knowledge bases than multi-media databases.

Distributed Knowledge Bases

In order to solve some of the problems with large knowledge bases, we can distribute a knowledge base's data and/or knowledge among a number of different agents. When only data is being distributed, the problems that arise are the same ones that exist with distributed databases. Even if passive knowledge (e.g., passive rules) is distributed, no new problems should arise if we employ conventions similar to those employed for distributed databases to insure data integrity. The problems arise when we want to distribute active knowledge among multiple agents (e.g., a distributed expert system), which brings us to the next type of system.

Intelligent Distributed Cooperative Work (IDCW)

IDCW involves a group of intelligent agents (such as expert systems) who must cooperate with each other in order to perform collaborative and/or individual tasks. Each of these agents has its own reasoning capabilities and its own knowledge about the world. There might or might not be some overlap of reasoning capabilities or knowledge among some of the agents. One possible use for IDCW could be to solve problems of large real-time expert systems mentioned previously. Before we can implement IDCW we must first decide on the means of communication among agents, how agents acquire knowledge from one another, how knowledge is distributed among agents and how the agents are going to be managed. These questions are currently being researched, but it may be years until we see enough useful results that will enable us to build a nontrivial system based on intelligent distributed cooperative work.

4. Hybrid data and logic models

Although there are many knowledge base models that could incorporate some of the advanced systems, such as coupling a database and OPS rules, coupling a database to a neural network or coupling a database to a forward or backward chaining system, there is one category of models that is being widely used and researched: models that merge *database management systems (DBMS)* with *logic programming systems (LPS)*.[1] There are four basic models in this category: logic programming system enhancements, database management system enhancements, systems built from scratch, and DBMS-LPS coupling [13].

Logic Programming System Enhancements

An existing logic programming system is enhanced so that it also contains the functionality of a database management system. Work has been done to enhance logic programming systems with database capabilities [19, 24] but a lot must still be done before the enhanced systems will prove very useful in large systems. Extending an LPS to provide database capabilities requires adding features to the LPS including a data definition language, security, data integrity, backup and recovery [21, 24].

A system based on this model should be able to solve the problems of large knowledge bases. Many knowledge base systems keep all of their clauses in main memory and can therefore only can work with a fairly limited number of clauses. A logic programming system extended with database capabilities will not have this problem. The implementation of such a model would not be expected to provide fast enough results to be used in real-time expert systems, because even if the underlying logic programming system could support real-time, once we add database capabilities, the system would be too slow. Because multi-user access to a knowledge base is much more complicated than

---

[1] It is inevitable that this duet will expand to a triumvirate as the *artificial intelligence (AI)* community embraces this cooperative outlook during the next decade.

multi-user access to a database, we will probably not see many implementations of this model with multi-user (concurrent) capabilities. Incorporating multi-media capabilities in this model shouldn't cause any more difficulties than including these capabilities in a database system. Using this model, we might be able to create a distributed passive knowledge base by adding the capabilities of a distributed database system to the LPS, but intelligent distributed cooperative work is probably out of the question.

Database Management System Enhancements

Instead of adding database capabilities to a logic programming system, we can add logic programming capabilities to an existing database management system. For example, we could augment a database with evaluation functions that would allow derivation of information not explicitly stored in the database [16]. Several research projects [8, 12, 22, 26, 27] have added some level of logic programming capabilities to database management systems, but not all features of logic programming systems (e.g., structures) have been included [13].

Many decisions must be made before an extended DBMS can be implemented. For example, we must decide how the extended DBMS would represent recursive views which are expressible in logic programming systems. Depending on the underlying DBMS, we will be able to build multi-media knowledge bases, large knowledge bases and passive distributed knowledge bases. Extending the multi-user capabilities of the database might allow us to create multi-user knowledge bases. Real-time expert systems and IDCW are excluded because of their inherent activeness. By nature, databases are usually not active.[2] We will not be able to create an active knowledge base by extending an existing database.

Systems Built From Scratch

It is fairly obvious that a system built from scratch holds the greatest potential because it is not subject to the limitations of any existing systems. From the outset, such systems could be designed to our specifications. Unfortunately, much work is needed in order to build a system from ground zero. An example of such a system is the *Logic Data Language* (LDL) being developed at MCC [28].

When building a system from scratch we could theoretically build a knowledge base for any of the future systems mentioned earlier, although it would certainly be an overkill for some of them (e.g., multi-media knowledge bases). We feel

---

[2]   The term *active database* in this paper differs from that discussed in [9].

that this is the only model that could truly implement IDCW to an extent that will prove useful in many future applications.

DBMS-LPS Coupling

In this model both an existing DBMS and an existing LPS are somehow coupled together. Compared to the previous three models, DBMS-LPS coupling requires very little effort to implement because most of the system already exists. Many implementations [1, 2, 5, 6, 7, 13, 14, 15, 17] and some commercial systems are being built by coupling relational database systems with Prolog systems. Because both logic programming systems and relational databases are based on first order logic, the task of coupling them together is greatly simplified.

It will probably prove impossible to build a real-time expert system using this coupled approach. A coupled system would be too slow for any real-time application. Even if the retrieval of clauses from the database is done in a way that minimizes database access, (such as retrieving multiple clauses from the database at once instead of accessing the database every time a clause is needed), today's database systems are still too slow. Coupled with a logic programming system, we must also take the DBMS-LPS interface and the logic programming system into consideration. The time spent in the interface might be negligible, but existing logic programming systems are not yet ready for real-time applications.

Of the four models presented here, the DBMS-LPS coupling approach comes closest to providing a perfect solution for very large knowledge bases. The first two approaches -- enhancing LPS with DBMS or DBMS with LPS -- may turn out to be useful only for prototype experimentation. The third may be best for designing, selecting and integrating desirable features and capabilities, but requires a major investment and may be geared to special purposes. The fourth is the only solution (for now) having the potential for high capability of both database and logic programming features, but it sacrifices speed of coordination. It may be possible to implement the DBMS-LPS interface so that it will not be plagued by the lack of main memory which restrict many large knowledge bases today. But there is a trade off between the speed of the system and the amount of main memory that it needs, and a suitable compromise must be reached.

5. Conclusion and other issues

In order to build multi-user coupled systems, the DBMS' locking scheme must be changed. The standard locking scheme can cause two sets of problems if it is employed for coupled systems. The first set includes problems that arise from the access of facts by multiple logic programs. The standard two phase locking protocol used to lock data [3] causes problems known as *phantoms* and *postponed reads* [23].

The second set of problems comes from multi-user access of rules. If a rule is being changed during a logic program's execution, the program's results might not be correct. One possible solution would be the locking of sets of rules as a logic program needs them. Another similar solution would be to provide logic programs with a static set of rules. For example, if a Prolog program needs to access a predicate with a given name, we might freeze that program's view of all predicates with the same name. These solutions are far from being complete; in order to build multi-user systems based on DBMS-LPS coupling, we must first devise a locking scheme that can be used efficiently.

If the database system used provides multi-media access of data, then there should not be any problem with multi-media knowledge bases built using the coupled approach.

Given an underlying distributed database, there should be no problem creating a coupled distributed (passive) system. A logic program would send queries (or low level database primitives) to the distributed databases via the database-logic programming system interface, and the problems associated with distributed data would be left to the (distributed) database. We can even store the knowledge itself in the distributed database, by representing it in some way as data.

In order to achieve IDCW in coupled systems, a multi-user database could be a possible means of communication between agents (a *blackboard system*). Each agent could have a private database where its own data and knowledge are stored, and a multi-user database could be used to pass information between the agents and to store data and knowledge that is common to all. What is lacking in order to achieve cooperative work is a means for two or more agents to work together to achieve a common goal, or a way for one agent to help a different agent perform a task. Systems for IDCW are currently being researched, and it is still unclear which of the problems that arise in IDCW will be solved. An educated guess would be that although we might be able to implement IDCW by using a coupled database - logic programming system, we will eventually get much better results using different approaches.

References

[1] Bocca, J., "On the Evaluation Strategy of EDUCE," *Proc. of the 1986 ACM-SIGMOD Conf. on the Management of Data*, Washington, DC, May 1986.

[2] Bocca, J., "EDUCE - A Marriage of Convenience: Prolog and a Relational DBMS," *Proc. of the 1986 Symposium on Logic Programming*, Salt Lake City, UT, Sept. 1986.

[3] Bernstein, P.A., Hadzilacos, V. and Goodman, N., *Concurrency Control and Recovery in Database Systems*, Addison-Wesley, Reading, 1987.

[4] Carey, M., DeWitt, D.J. and Graefe, G., "Mechanisms for Concurrency Control and Recovery in Prolog - A Proposal," *Proc. of the First Int'l. Workshop on Expert Database Systems*, Kiawah Island, SC, October 1984.

[5] Ceri, S., Gottlob, G. and Wiederhold, G., "Interfacing Relational Databases and Prolog Efficiently," *Proc. of the First Int'l. Conf. on Expert Database Systems*, Charleston, SC, April 1986.

[6] Chang, C.L., Walker, A., "PROSQL: A Prolog Programming Interface with SQL/DS," *Proc. of the First Int'l. Conf. on Expert Database Systems*, Charleston, SC, April 1986.

[7] Cuppens, F. and Demolombe, R., "A PROLOG - Relational DBMS Interface Using Delayed Evaluation," *Proc. of the Third Int'l. Conf. on Data and Knowledge Bases*, Jerusalem, Israel, June 1988.

[8] Dayal, U., "Knowledge-Oriented Database Management," *Technical Report, CCA-84-02*, Computer Corporation of America, Cambridge, MA, 1984.

[9] Dayal, U., "Active Database Management Systems," *Proc. of the Third Int'l. Conf. on Data and Knowledge Bases*, Jerusalem, Israel, June 1988.

[10] Hayes-Roth, F., Invited Talk, IEEE Compcon, San Fransisco, CA, February 1987.

[11] Kandel, A., Panel Session, "From Databases to Knowledge Bases - Expected Benefits and Problems," [Appendix, this chapter].

[12] Ioannidis, Y.E., Shinkle, L.D. and Wong, E., "Enhancing INGRES with Deductive Power," *Proc. of the First Int'l. Workshop on Expert Database Systems*, Kiawah Island, SC, October 1984.

[13] Ioannidis, Y.E., Chen, J., Friedman, M.A. and Tsangaris, M.M., "Bermuda - An Architectural Perspective on Interfacing Prolog to a Database Machine," *Proc. of the Second Int'l. Conf. on Expert Database Systems*, Tysons Corner, VA, April 1988.

[14] Jarke, M., Cifford, J. and Vassiliou, Y., "An Optimizing Prolog Front-End to a Relational Query System," *Proc. of the 1984 ACM-SIGMOD Conf. on the Management of Data*, Boston, MA, June 1984.

[15] Lei, L., Moll, G. and Kouloumdjian, J., "Prolog-DBMS Coupling: a Hybrid Approach, Half Interpreted, Half Compiled," *Proc. of the Third Int'l. Conf. on Data and Knowledge Bases*, Jerusalem, Israel, June 1988.

[16] Lockemann, P., Panel Session, "From Databases to Knowledge Bases - Expected Benefits and Problems," [Appendix, this chapter].

[17] Morris, K., Ullman, J.D. and VanGelder, A., "NAIL System Design Overview," *Proc. of the Third Int'l. Conf. on Logic Programming* London, England, July 1986.

[18]   Mylopolous, J. and Brodie, M., *Readings in Artificial Intelligence and Databases*, Morgan Kauffmann, San Mateo, Calif., 1989.

[19]   Naish, L. and Thom, J.A., "The MU-Prolog Deductive Database," *Technical Report 83/10*, Computer Science Dept., University of Melburne, November 1983.

[20]   Naish, L., Thom, J.A. and Ramamohanarao, K., "Concurrent Database Updates in PROLOG," *Proc. of the Fourth Int'l. Conf. on Logic Programming*, Melbourne, 1987.

[21]   Napheys, B. and Herkimer, D., "A look at Loosely-Coupled Prolog Database Systems," *Proc. of the Second Int'l. Conf. on Expert Database Systems*, Tysons Corner, VA, April 1988.

[22]   Nicolas, J.M. and Yazdanian, K., "An Outline of BDGEN: A Deductive DBMS," *Information Processing 83*, North Holland, 1983.

[23]   Schreier, U. and Wedekind, H., "Supporting Concurrent Access to Facts in Logic Programs," *Proc. of the Second Int'l. Conf. on Expert Database Systems*, Tysons Corner, VA, April 1988.

[24]   Sciore, E. and Warren, D., "Towards an Integrated Database-Prolog System," *Proc. of the First Int'l. Workshop on Expert Database Systems*, Kiawah Island, SC, October 1984.

[25]   Sellis, T.K. and Roussopoulos, N., "Deep Compilation of Large Rule Bases," *Proc. of the Second Int'l. Conf. on Expert Database Systems*, Tysons Corner, VA, April 1988.

[26]   Stonebraker, M., Johnson, R. and Rosenberg, S., "Extending INGRES with a Rules System," *Memorandum No. UCB/ERL M81/93*, University of California, Berkeley, CA, December 1981.

[27]   Stonebraker, M., "Triggers and Inference in Data Base Systems," *Proc. of the Islamorada Workshop on Large Scale Knowledge Base and Reasoning Systems*, Islamorada, FL, February 1985.

[28]   Tsur, S. and Zaniolo, C., "LDL: A Logic-Based Data-Language," *Proc. of the 12th Int'l. VLDB Conf.*, Kyoto, Japan, August 1986.

[29]   Williams, M.H., Panel Session, "From Databases to Knowledge Bases - Expected Benefits and Problems," [Appendix, this chapter].

[30]   Williams, M.H., Massey P.A. and Crammond, J.A., "Benchmarks for Prolog from a Database Viewpoint," *Proc. of Second ALVEY Workshop for SIGKME*, 1987.

Appendix A. Panel Discussion

What follows is the edited transcript of the panel discussion "From Databases to Knowledge Bases - Expected Benefits and Problems," from the *Third International Conference on Data and Knowledge Bases*, held in Jerusalem, Israel, June 28-30, 1988. The moderator was Martin Golumbic of the IBM Israel Scientific Center. The three panelist were Peter Lockemann of the University of Karlsruhe, Abraham Kandel of Florida State University and Shalom Tsur from MCC.

Martin Golumbic: I am pleased to welcome you to this panel session. In preparing for today's session, I have given each of the panelists several questions which they might address in their opening remarks. These include some submitted to me in advance by Michael Brodie, Larry Kerschberg and Jack Minker. The opening questions which I posed are as follows:

1. What really distinguishes data from knowledge?
    Do we have a continuum or an "artificially-created" division?

2. What functions and features would a KBMS have?
    What are the implications of updates to the description or "schema" when moving from a database to a knowledge base world?

In addition, I asked them background questions concerning the following:

- Deductive databases as an outgrowth of automated theorem proving

- The role and impact of intelligent databases on expert systems

- Coping with the semantic boundary of a complex AI object

After the panelists give their prepared comments on data and knowledge bases, we will open the floor to questions and comments.

Our first speaker will be Prof. Lockemann.

Peter Lockemann: To begin with, I am perhaps not even the right person on this panel. I do not know what a knowledge base is, and nobody I asked so far has really given me a sufficiently precise answer. So let me just start out with a few *possible* hypotheses.

First, a knowledge base is nothing but a glorified term for databases that just makes it easier to raise funds because AI buzzwords are in these days.

Second, and a bit more seriously, knowledge bases are something entirely separate, specific to just AI or to expert systems, and about the only connection they have to databases is that database technology is used to implement them.

Third, a knowledge base is a database augmented by evaluation mechanisms that allow to derive implicit information, i.e., information not explicitly stored in the database. Note, however, that this would also include SQL-like systems because the inclusion of aggregation functions, and that runs somewhat counter to our convictions.

Fourth, as before, but the evaluation mechanisms are mainly based on inference. This is probably the most common understanding.

Fifth, and this is a generalization, a database is a collection of symbolic representations of facts, and a knowledge base is the rules for interpreting these data; in this case I use the term rules in a very loose sense as any information that allows me to interpret whatever we keep in the database.

Now, for me as a person that deals with applications and implementations, I need a definition that somehow allows me to draw conclusions and translate these conclusions into some technical solution. And the fifth definition, perhaps not the best one, is one that indeed allows me to do just that. Let me just repeat that a "database" is a collection of symbolic representations, and a "knowledge base" is the rules for interpreting it. Notice that this definition of what a knowledge base is, is always relative to the definition of what a database is, in this case to what the collection of facts is. And that seems to shift as database technology evolves. For example, if we just use file management, then clearly, everything that goes beyond file management like describing the layout of a record or its content would have to be called a knowledge base.

Now, today's databases are described and interpreted by a database schema. Consequently, our databases are so much richer in semantics, but in order to get the information out of the database we still need the schema. So the schema represents our set of rules for interpreting the data in the database. Hence, relative to today's standards a schema would represent a knowledge base.

We could certainly augment the schema information by deductive rules and thus come closer to what many perceive as the characteristics of a knowledge base. But notice how in the area of object-oriented databases more and more complicated data models evolve, and consequently more and more semantics are expressed via the schema. And the literature demonstrates that there is a certain tradeoff between schema and deductive rules, that the constructs in the schema can be expressed by rules of a certain type, and vice versa. I think this again demonstrates that there is no fixed borderline between databases and knowledge bases, and in fact what we call knowledge bases would evolve to more and more complicated kinds of things.

There is also another issue that fuzzes the borderline. Consider now a knowledge base, that is, the rules used for interpreting the data. We will also have to store the rules, so I would have a second database one level up that stores the knowledge for the first level. Clearly I could go on like this up and up which gets us into notions that we also find in literature quite often, like meta-information, meta-meta-information, etc., etc. This underlines my hypothesis that a knowledge base is something utterly relative. We can imagine a hierarchy of databases where a given level always represents a knowledge base for the next lower level, and a database for the next higher level.

If I take this attitude, it will also explain some of the questions that I've run into in the case of image sequence analysis which I introduced on Monday in the tutorial. There we described the schematic information as a deep *isa*-hierarchy which we could somehow equate with our hierarchy of levels that I just had discussed. It is entirely unclear how the established notion of a schema fits into the *isa*-hierarchy. Introducing a hierarchy where each level assumes a dual role, one with respect to the next higher level and one with respect to the next lower level may make it much easier to deal with that issue.

Now, if we accept my model for the moment, let me look at a few consequences. For one, the dual role forces me to realize a knowledge base as a database, and hence, by means of database system, but in such a way that interpretation and inferences are indeed efficiently supported. And I think that many of the discussions that we've had in this conference and in other conferences actually deal with the question of how one can realize knowledge bases by means of databases. Just take the support of front-end solutions for deductive databases, or the attempts to integrate deduction into databases for the use of recursive queries, or all the questions of how one can support efficient retrieval of rules that govern deductions on the next lower level, or the attempts to reinterpret certain features of data models in order to support deductive systems like the reinterpretation of the relational algebra as certain forms of Horn clauses.

A second consequence, and actually one I'm currently working on, is to explore a fuller potential of database schemas by adding inference mechanisms to them, to utilize knowledge bases for databases, so to speak. Knowledge bases for consistency control seem an ideal application. For example, in technical applications there are very complicated consistency constraints. In order to help the user when a consistency check fails, one would like to include a mechanism that allows to diagnose failures, communicate these to the user, and even to suggest therapies. Or take database design as a second example. Database design essentially looks first at all the knowledge we have on a given subject area, and then we decide what to put into the database whereas the remainder clearly serves to interpret the contents of the database. In this case knowledge bases could be used also as a means for supporting the database design in deciding what to put in the database and what to put in the knowledge base for interpreting the data. Or another topic that fits into that role is end-user oriented query languages which is at the very end of all the means for interpreting the data that we find in the database.

To summarize, what I'm suggesting is that if one uses the fifth definition of those that I gave at the beginning, then what we end up with is a hierarchical definition of a knowledge base related to what we put in a database; we get something like a hierarchy of databases where each upper one defines the knowledge base for the next lower one. And finally we have two technical consequences, two different areas of involvement in research, one that I call *databases for knowledge bases,* or better, database support for knowledge bases, and a second *knowledge bases for databases*, or more precisely, knowledge base support for databases.

Martin Golumbic: Thank you very much. The next speaker will be Prof. Kandel.

Abraham Kandel: I don't have a model, I don't have slides either. What I have are some questions because I think that there is a difference between the extension that information and data lead to the structure of information and knowledge or data and knowledge.

Databases were not the structures over which knowledge engineering was built. It is not a natural extension. It's not going from 2-D to 3-D. Knowledge engineering, knowledge bases, are mixed in here because you use the word "base." OK, you have a database so you have a knowledge base, and therefore you also have an information base. Maybe you should be calling it knowledge "roofs," I don't know. Something to distinguish from the "bases." Knowledge bases resulted from expert systems. They came from a different spectrum of computer science altogether, from AI. Databases were never a part, an integral part of AI, (if I may say so as an AI person and not as a database person.)   Knowledge bases resulted from the need to emulate human reasoning, to eliminate the human from the cycle of design, of performance, of active roles in the system.

Databases were never used to eliminate certain manual operations.   You are always helpful to your operations.   I have not seen banks and insurance companies that fire thousands of people because they put in a database system.   In contrast, they hired more people.   Here the goal was very simple.   I would like to eliminate the pilot.   I would like to eliminate a doctor.   I would like to eliminate a lawyer.   Sure, I would like to eliminate all of us but Computer Scientists.   And for that I must have now a system that very, very narrowly emulates human expertise.   And I think that the use of knowledge, and the use of even more plastic words such as "smart systems" are very confusing to the issue.   What we are doing here is taking a slice of the pie of a certain expertise, replacing it, trying to capture that knowledge in a certain system.   That knowledge is composed of several things.   And if you take a look at the words that we are using with knowledge, and the words that we are using with data, immediately you see a difference.

Somebody may argue that this is just a semantic difference, a matter of cosmetics.   But it's not.   You use words like "data gathering," "data collection," how do you make a database?   We collect data.   We never collect knowledge, we elicit knowledge.   We milk, it's a milking process, that we have to go into the human brain and really extract the core of the knowledge and then refine it.   Other words we use, "meta," the word was used before, we never used the word "meta-data" before knowledge was in existence.   And yet we use the word "meta-knowledge" (and "meta-meta-knowledge" and all kinds of hierarchies of meta-meta).   Is it just a semantic difference?   Or is it something that really distinguishes knowledge from data?

I think that the applicability off knowledge is what distinguishes data from knowledge. I'm not sure how precisely it distinguishes it.   For years I used to think that data and databases are algorithmic, in other words you perform algorithmic operations on the database.   In knowledge, we use more of a combination of algorithmic and heuristics. Then, for a year, I thought that databases are precise, are deterministic, are accurate, and that knowledge, by its own existence, (and I must use this word), is fuzzy.   There is an integral part of the imprecise, ambiguous environment in which we all operate. Then, I changed my mind, because I found out first of all you can work very well with fuzzy data, to develop fuzzy relational databases that perform quite well in an imprecise environment.   And on the other end of the spectrum, there is a very nice environment in which precise expert systems and expert knowledge can survive, that you don't need the fuzziness anyway.   That you don't have to just insert fuzziness because you are a fuzzy logician, or an ex-fuzzy logician.

The source of the difference is, I think, the applicability.   Now, what do expert systems of the future look like?   In my opinion you are going to see a blend, a need for a merge, of very large databases, or very small databases, with very efficient knowledge bases that use expert systems, that are used in expert systems.   You see, for databases, regardless how large they are, we have mechanisms to deal with them.   With expert systems and knowledge based systems, once you reach a certain size limit, the system is not operational in real time.   And by my reading of the situation, most expert systems that require knowledge bases, that are going to be developed in the next two decades, will have to run in real time.

Until now, an expert system for medical care might run for hours, days, who cares? The patient may or may not die, that's not critical, OK? An expert system to design a building, so the building takes another two days. The urgency was not here. This is all changing. Changing partly, as Professor Lockemann said, because of funding. Funding, at least in the States, implies now that the systems must be in real time, because the funding for expert systems comes from ATF (advanced tactical fighter), it comes from SDI (strategic defense initiative), it comes from environments like the AWACS environment which do require action by the knowledge in a real time environment. Once you begin to load the knowledge base the same way that all of us are loading data bases, the system becomes very very slow. And it doesn't matter on what system you put it, you can put it on a IBM-PC under MSDOS, or you can put it on an ETA-10 under NOS5. (The difference between the two of them by the way is between $500 and $16,000,000.) It doesn't matter. You can vectorize it, you can use all kinds of techniques. Unless you reduce the knowledge base to a very small knowledge base, the system is not going to be operational. If you reduce knowledge bases, you reduce the knowledge, there is no question about it.

So we must concentrate now on building new centers of knowledge, in other words what we are talking about now is, I don't want to use the word "distributed" expert systems but I'll use the word "cooperating" expert systems. Expert systems that have very, very limited knowledge and maybe very, very large databases. They cooperate through varied means like wide band communication schemes and all kinds of relevance protocols and issues of this sort. And you insert them. You insert them in an aircraft, you insert them in the cockpit, you insert them in missiles, you just insert very small intelligent systems that in a way look very much like the RISC, and you build sort of butterfly expert systems. In databases there was never a need for that.

Now the problem is: How do you manage that system? How do you manage a large system composed of cooperative knowledge bases that report to a certain expert system or to a set of expert systems, nourish that system with very large databases that deal only with data, nourish it also with the source of the data sometimes or a kind of sensors, and do it all in real time when the entire system is controlled by a certainty management system. The certainty management again can be fuzzy, can be probabilistic, it can be all kinds of management systems. That's one of the issues. The State of Florida, Martin Morieta, Honeywell, and some other companies just gave over $2 million to a project of this sort. Ehud (Gudes), myself, and several others are going to work on it this summer and in the future. This is a system which will take expert systems, (in this case rule based), databases, (which in this case were written for an object oriented code), insert some CAD/CAM applications which represent essentials from which the data will be extracted and the knowledge will be extracted, and compose all that with a nice umbrella of security and fuzzy sets, and, if it is going to be useful, you will read about it. If it's going to fail, well you won't read about it.

To summarize, I think that we have to look at the two concepts differently. In databases there is no knowledge, and because there is no knowledge the applications are different and all the structures and methods are different. In knowledge bases, there should be at least an extensive amount of knowledge. Because if there won't be an extensive amount of knowledge they won't do what they have to do. And without that premise that they are going to do what they are going to do, knowledge will be reduced to data. If this is going to happen then I think that knowledge engineering will have failed. If it is going to be successful, then knowledge engineering will be a superset which will include data, knowledge, sensors, and so forth.

Martin Golumbic: Thank you very much. Our third speaker will be Dr. Tsur.

Shalom Tsur: Since I'm the third speaker I'll be brief. Let me start with a few issues that have been raised here. First of all the proliferation of terminology that we have today: expert systems and expert databases and logic databases and databases without logic, and G-d knows what. There have been attempts to try and classify these attempts, to put them in categories, boxes, and I maintain that this is an exercise in futility. Basically, all that it indicates is that this area, however you want to define it, is in a very healthy state of development. People try all kinds of things. I suspect that eventually you will see a sort of settling down and an understanding of this area once people start building these systems and enable those who are not yet involved in this effort to use these systems and gain their own experience. I think that this has happened in the past, it has happened to databases, it has happened in other areas like programming languages, operating systems, and I have no reason to believe that it will be different here. So, however you want to call these things, eventually you will see the emergence of a class of systems having a set of features which are going to be useful. Now, since I was asked to come up with some kind of classification or distinction between knowledge and data, let me first of all state that I don't see any useful distinction; I concur with Prof. Lockemann here. However, being in the logic programming business, let me offer one.

```
knowledge(X)  <-- data(Y),
                  X = (Y).

deep_knowledge(X)  <-- knowledge(Y),
                       X = (Y).
```

Let me also state that lesser artists borrow and greater artists steal; this one was borrowed from my friend Shamim Naqvi. Essentially what it says is that knowledge is data with a lot of parentheses around it. You have to read this bottom up and it doesn't close; as you see, it goes on and on. The knowledge becomes deeper and deeper depending on the number of parentheses you add around it. In a slightly more serious way, take one of the concluding remarks of Professor Lockemann, that if you want a hierarchy of systems, you have a data system and the knowledge which manipulates this data at the next level. Here you have a formalization of this idea if you like it. So this is as far as a useful distinction between knowledge and data.

Prof. Kandel has said something about small systems versus large systems, that data bases are typically large and knowledge bases are small. I think that I agree with that. Basically, database systems don't do much, at least they don't prefer to do much; but whatever they do, they do well. What I mean here is that performance is a major consideration when we talk about database systems. It's not that the database people don't know what should be done, they simply don't know how to do it well. And that's the reason why most of database systems are restricted to a set of features that can be efficiently performed. It is not the lack of the desire to do more.

Now, what can we do? We have today what we may call *logic systems*, and we have the chance to combine logic programming with database systems. Again the emphasis is very heavily on doing it well, having good performing systems. I will have to present this view from a fairly biased viewpoint because the project I work on has adopted this kind of approach. What we want to do is to enable people to specify their abstractions and map these abstractions against queries that can be executed efficiently. We maintain that logic programming is a device to do that, and I think that the virtues of such systems, as we have in other systems, is the testimony to that belief.

I've also been asked very often, suppose we have such a language and you have such a system, now what do we do with it? What is it good for? After all, we can adopt another approach that says - take a database, take a knowledge base, the knowledge base presumably is the front end of some general purpose programming language like LISP or Prolog, or Fortran, or whatever you like, and let this knowledge base manipulate the database, retrieve data, do whatever is required. All the decisions, all of the "smarts" are in this front end, and the dumb back end will sort of come up a little later. The problem is that if you adopt this approach, particularly with respect to very large depositories of data, you get terrible performance problems again. You try to deduce a fact and then you go to your database and invoke very heavy machinery to see if you can retrieve this fact. By analogy, this is like hauling bricks, a brick at a time, from a 16 ton truck. It's very inefficient. You really don't want to do it, and hence you want to integrate these systems; you don't want to maintain this distinction. Now once you have done that, you may support fairly efficiently a class of new applications which you really come up with today, and this class is what we have tentatively called "data dredging."

```
            DATA DREDGING

  1. Formulate hypothesis.

  2. Translate (1) into query.

  3. Execute query.

  4. If (3) fails then reformulate and goto (3).

  5. Exit.
```

On the first day this conference there was a vice president of IBM who gave a speech about all that IBM had done; but he didn't mention this. What is data dredging? Well it's an activity that goes on all the time in almost any enterprise that is involved in some kind of design or synthesis activity in the following sense: you formulate a hypothesis, and you take this hypotheses which may be fairly abstract and you translate it into a query. I'll elaborate on this in a moment.

I should add that the source of the data is very often some kind of empirical process, for instance, measurement data or data that has been collected from some kind of experiment in the natural sciences or harmonic data or any of another matter of sources. Then you take your data, very large amounts of data, and you formulate a query. If this query produces an answer which tends to support your hypothesis, fine, you're satisfied, you've done it. If not, which is often the case, you reformulate your query, you try something slightly different, you try again. You have this iterative process whereby you try out a series of very high level and abstract queries, and eventually either you succeed or you decide that the data simply doesn't support your hypothesis and then you might go back and try a different source of data.

Now, this iterative process is something that goes on all of the time in many, many different contexts. Let me give you a few examples:

DATA DREDGING APPLICATIONS

1. Economic data analysis

2. Performance data analysis - the convoy problem

3. Medical/Pharmaceutical data analysis for negative
   side effects of drugs

4. Trouble report classification

5. VLSI chip design analysis

.
.
.

Suppose I try economic data, time series. Essentially what we want to get out of this data are certain economic trends - an increase or decrease in employment or anything of that sort. The definition of the thing that you are looking for is certainly not in terms of the stored data of the database you have recorded, but is rather abstract. The transformation of the data into this abstract definition is a very painful and complex process which you can seldom do on your own.

There is another problem that we've been more actively involved with at MCC, so let me briefly elaborate on item number 2 here. Suppose that you have a multiprocessor system, and typically what you record there is performance data at the low level. For instance, you have a network of processors that are connected by some topology, and you have processes or rather entities that move from one processor to another through this network. More often then not, performance analysis simply assumes that these entities are statistically independent in the sense that they move from one node through any of their successors in a stochastically independent fashion. In practice, this doesn't always happen.

We have some other examples here, say the testing of medical and pharmaceutical data for side effects of certain drugs which pharmaceutical companies would like to release as early as possible. Another thing that happens in reality is that you have telephone companies and these people receive problem reports of their equipment. What they really would like to do is classify these problems in the sense that when somebody comes up with a new trouble, they want to know if this is an existing flavor that they have seen in the past or if this is a new kind of trouble. Right now they have lots of manual labor - people "letting their fingers walk" over piles of data to see if they can find something similar or not. Really you want to mechanize this.

To conclude, there are many, many applications of the data dredging type where you have low level data and we look for very high level phenomena which we want to extract from this data. In fact, most of research is like that. So, what I maintain is that these *knowledge databases* are a very efficient tool to do that. The fact that we can integrate a high level programming language with a database and do it efficiently, and optimize very abstract queries, and have them easily modified is an enormous advantage over the methods that are being tried today, which are typically the writing of a Fortran or a C program which is then modified and recompiled all of the time in order to achieve the same result. This is a class of applications that is very well suited to be integrated into one logic based system.

Martin Golumbic: Thank you. Now I would like to open the floor to questions, and I'm sure that there are quite a few brewing in the hall. I would just ask you to ask your questions loudly, so that we can pick them up on the tape recorders. First question?

Ehud Gudes (Ben Gurion University): I actually have two questions. One is related to the area of the definition - what really makes a database a knowledge base? The first question is to Prof. Lockemann - how do you describe a knowledge base in a CAD environment? Usually if you have a data base and then you have application programs that work on this database, and most of what we think of as knowledge is in this application program. What I would like to know is what do you think would make up databases and knowledge bases in the context of CAD systems. The second question is, suppose tomorrow somebody comes and says, "Here is the first knowledge base management system on the market," can you gives some rules like Codd's rules for relational databases that will tell you that this is a KBMS?

Peter Lockemann: Before I try to answer, let me just make one comment about the three contributions that we've just heard. I've found them really interesting because they demonstrate three completely different viewpoints. My own is entirely data-centered as everybody may have noticed. I think that Kandel's view was system-centered, and Tsur's was process-centered. And clearly, you can take these three completely different viewpoints and come up with three completely different conclusions, all of them equally valid.

Now to come back to your question. Indeed, if I distinguish for a moment between knowledge and a knowledge base, a knowledge base being something that knowledge gets stored away in, then it is true that in today's CAD applications knowledge is pretty much buried in the application programs. In fact, hardly any database systems are actually utilized by them at all.

How would one move then to a knowledge base? But first of all, what is the knowledge to be put into knowledge base? In other words, some of the rules that interpret the data would have to be made explicit. What does that mean? Well, as I said, most of the CAD systems at the moment utilize file systems, that is, they do not employ database systems, and their developers or users are not forced to write down schemas. But where they have tried to do just that they had to resort to complicated constructs that did not really reflect the knowledge in any application oriented way, as everybody in CAD knows who has had to work with relations or the network model. Now take a further step and use an object-oriented database. This clearly forces one to make more of the knowledge explicit, although in terms of structure and not as rules.

What we discover in this case is that a next step is needed, because in CAD applications there exist a large number of constraints that can not be captured by the new database systems. Those again have traditionally been hidden in CAD application programs. As we have found out, not all of them have actually to be captured in a schema or in rules in order to be caught and checked by the database management system, because much of what is being designed is observed by the designer on the screen, and he is often much quicker in discovering inconsistencies in the data. But where you want to have certain constraints to be automatically checked you have to be explicit. And once you are explicit you can formulate them, store them, and then argue that there is a database on top of the original one, that is being utilized for checking the constraints. And such a system could go even further to what I mentioned briefly before, namely to try to diagnose what has happened and suggest therapies and send the diagnoses back to the designer. So for me it's a kind of continuum in which decisions have to be taken as to how much of what you know should be made explicit. And I claim that a knowledge base is knowledge made explicit with a specific purpose in mind, and then made utilizable to solve a corresponding problem.

The second question I don't think was addressed to me.

Abraham Kandel: As far as knowledge systems, I think until recently when we thought about the CAD/CAM issue, we thought basically about VLSI design. And all the effort was concentrated in that direction by the needs of the VLSI design. In other words, when somebody envisioned a system of using knowledge bases in CAD/CAM it was triggered by the those needs of the VLSI designers. There are many other CAD/CAM issues which are totally, or substantially different from VLSI design. When you look into the constraints that a CAD/CAM system must have, and I would rather not call it CAD/CAM because the problem in CAD/CAM is basically the integration of CAD and CAM. We do CAD very well; the problem is really implementing it in the manufacturing scheme so I would like to call it CAM, computer assisted manufacturing, or computer systems engineering, or whatever words you want to do, to separate the design from the manufacturing. And in that process, I agree with Lockemann, you must have total, explicit knowledge. But you also must insert into the system a very high learning process. Because experience shows that in all kinds of CAD/CAM systems but VLSI show that the learning process is really the system.

I must also disagree with a different point; this is not an answer to your question but to Dr. Tsur. I understand and appreciate the enthusiasm and the passion in which logic programming is sort of sliding into the knowledge engineering area. That's great.

Shalom Tsur: Snaking, I think!

Abraham Kandel: Yeah, I would agree with snaking, I don't want to use that word, so blending. But there is no crystal clear evidence that what you want to do you can not do with other types of programming. You can do it very well with C; you can do it very well with Pascal; if you work for the Air Force you must do it very well in Ada. You can do it, as a matter if fact very efficiently in Modula-2, we have done some even in Prolog, I agree. But I think that in the issue of the language, there is too much effort which is concentrated on the language.

Most "pure" knowledge people, "pure" experts people, come from a different background. They come from the area of pattern recognition; pattern recognition for the last 30 years worked without theory. You want to recognize something, you develop your own theory, you write your algorithm, you burn it in the ROM, and you recognize. The next day you burn another ROM. There is no unified theory of pattern recognition. And therefore, I don't think that we will ever see, maybe I'm wrong, (I've been wrong many times before), at least in the next five years we won't see a unified theory of knowledge bases. You can take the concept of a schema, modify it a little bit, make it a "knowledge schema" which doesn't work. There is all talking of this sort. But the question is "Do you really need a unified, overall, mathematical, explicit theory of knowledge engineering?" And anything one engineer doesn't know is basic It is really essential. This is often true of many things. This is going to be not applicable if such a theory does not exist or will not be found in the next five years. I'm not sure it's necessary. But I'm sure that there's going to be many other people who disagree with that.

Martin Golumbic: Let's take Ehud's second question. What was the question again?

Ehud Gudes: I wanted an analogue of Codd's twelve rules for a KBMS.

Shalom Tsur: Let me answer in one sentence. Codd's twelve rules are a violation of affirmative action in the United States. I doubt whether you will see anybody trying to class a system according to those rules or any other rules for that matter.

Martin Golumbic: Any other comments?

Shalom Tsur: I would like to respond to Abraham's comment. I agree that you can implement things in all kinds of ways. In fact, I once coded things in absolute octal. But there's more to it. I think that the issue of a language is much deeper. Because essentially, the issue of a language to a large extent muddles your thoughts, effects the mental process that goes on in your own head when you think of the problem. I fully agree that the language is the means and not the end, but it is a very important means. I think that with certain languages, particularly the certain languages that are hired to be used in knowledge and databases, however you want to define them, are very important and the problems which you're dealing with are highly complex. If you have to map these into any of the existing languages, you really can not do it. In graduate school you can do it, but in practice it becomes too tedious, too complex. And I think that the class of applications that I outlined is an indication of that.

Amir Donenfeld (Rafael):   I think that a panel like ours will become anachronistic in the near future; the two concepts - databases and knowledge bases - are slowly merging into a single, unified concept. Essentially both concepts deal with information, but each one was originally conceived to fulfill different purposes. Databases models "the world" using crude data models, but can handle large amounts of data very efficiently. Knowledge bases deals with conceptually accurate "structural and behavioral models of the world," but disregards (partially) other mundane aspects of the task.

From these starting points the two paradigms are converging towards each other. Users of databases demand increasingly complex data schemes, in which their object systems could be more accurately described. On the other hand the users of knowledge bases are pressing towards Knowledge Based Systems that can access large amounts of data efficiently. I believe that these tendencies will cause the initial distinction between DB's and KB's to become blurred to the point that they may, at a certain point, turn almost indistinguishable.

A common ground that constitutes a reasonable paradigm for both Data and Knowledge Bases is already realized by the object orientation paradigm. In this paradigm, objects are self standing entities, that include both data and behavior, and why not rules? At one extreme we have classes of objects which are pure data structures, not very different from the data structures that characterize databases. At the other extreme we have very elaborated classes of objects mimicking frames, scripts and other behavioral patterns that we usually associate with knowledge.

I realize that I have ignored here many (theoretical and practical) subtleties, but I think that the general picture is correct and we will indeed witness a synthesis of these two concepts which are the subjects of our conference.

Martin Golumbic: Could we have a question?

M. Howard Williams (Heriot-Watt University): Just a comment on the definition of knowledge and data, etc. I think that what Prof. Kandel says is true, identifying knowledge as a field coming out of expert systems. The difference is that knowledge captures in some way the decision making process as opposed to data which doesn't.

But, as Abraham said, at present we have small expert system applications. This is similar to the state of affairs prior to the development of databases. At first we had small applications using small sets of data, and as the data grew, so also did the need to manage that data. Since data can easily be shared, we have an increasing need to produce systems which will look after the data. Hence, the development of database management systems.

In the same way, on the expert systems side, more and more expert systems are being developed which will need to share common knowledge. For example, in the case of medical applications, you've got a variety of different expert systems which need access to common knowledge about the human body as a whole in order to diagnose specific complaints. From the need to store common sets of rules, you need a management system to look after the shared rules. But that would be a passive knowledge base in the sense that the decision making elements that you put into it are passive rules which are going to be pulled out to be used by the respective expert systems as applications. In this case, the knowledge based management system doesn't do any inference, it simply stores the knowledge and preserves it for the expert systems when they need it. It is still a problem because the problems of authorization and of sharing of rules are a lot more difficult to solve than the sharing of facts in a database system.

In addition to passive rules, you may also have active rules in a database. This is where deductive databases come in; where you can use rules to represent sets of facts in the database. In this case you have an inference mechanism in the database system to deduce the appropriate facts. This is where the link comes in with logic programming. However, if you are storing passive rules in a knowledge base system and not performing any inference over them, the problems are very different from those of a system where you are storing active rules for which you are going to invoke inference mechanisms in the execution of queries. In the later situation, you want some protection from other users; you want to be able to guarantee that a query will terminate and that someone doesn't tie up the whole knowledge base system by giving a query which invokes deductive rules which do things which are unsociable to other users, etc. So, for that kind of knowledge, active knowledge, we have to be very careful about the model that we are using, and this may well be different from that of passive knowledge.

Another example, that we are working on is in the area of CAD, applied to mechanical engineering design, where you're carving up blocks of metal to get an object which you are going to connect together with other objects in an assembly. The data, if you like, is your 3-D model. At the other extreme you have the knowledge which the engineer uses in deciding how to make a particular object from a model, what tools to use and in what sequence to carve up the metal to achieve the final product. Now the latter knowledge is not used by the database but by an expert system to apply to the model data which would illustrate a model of the object that we want to construct. Once again such knowledge can be viewed as passive knowledge.

Martin Golumbic: I have a question sent to me by Larry Kerschberg who isn't here, which I'll throw out to you. His question is, "Does the closed world assumption make sense in the heterogeneous, distributed, knowledge/data base system of the future, and what tools and techniques do we need?"

Shalom Tsur: The only comment that I think can really be made is that the closed world assumption makes sense if you are going to define something, if you don't want open ended questions or fuzzy or undefined answers. I don't think that it's a real practical impediment that people can not do things because of this assumption.

Martin Golumbic: Has this affected the development of intelligent database systems, and what aspects do you judge to be most important?

Abraham Kandel: I think the answer is yes. Yes, it has in the past. And the impact is in systems that were developed in the last five years. I totally disagree that AI is dead or AI is alive just because there is funding. Obviously, because of funding, we can deal with things that we could not do without funding. Earlier, Shamim Naqvi (MCC) brought up the issue of the masters thesis. In AI you produce master's theses by the minute, which obviously just kills this half, just half dead if you look at the funding. But you can do a lot with non-monotonic reasoning and belief systems, and some systems if anybody is interested there are some systems such as MADX which uses exactly that - in this case a fuzzy belief system.

There is a very interesting med shell which is now going around the country here that people are trying to sell, it's a fuzzy, very intelligent expert system, very, very powerful. It has the power of about 100 times any M1, especially in the uncertain management and it runs under MS-DOS, and it's using exactly a model of such a belief system. So there is MADX

Martin Golumbic: But what about uncertainty in a database?

Abraham Kandel: Well, if you look at fuzzy relational databases, the first time they put doubt in databases was developed in fuzzy relational databases, which tried to really insert fuzziness into the database. The other great believer is you know, or maybe I know, that fuzziness is an integral part of any system, any real world system - whatever you want to do with that. Every time that we don't use fuzziness, in a sense we put in some threshold. So artificially, we eliminated fuzziness from the system. The question of whether fuzziness is the only way to deal with uncertainty is still debatable. And it's going to be debatable for some time. The issue is that some people don't accept fuzziness as a tool to deal with imprecision in expert (intelligent) systems and others just personally don't like it. It's a matter of how you look at it. You can do it probabilistically, you can do it fuzzily, you can do it with other, maybe new means of dealing with uncertainties, but there is no question that the uncertainties in data bases and in knowledge bases will not go away. If we could change the world into a deterministic world it would be great. If someone would just give up the blue prints.

Peter Lockemann: I think I'll go back to some of the comments that we had before. First, the one that said that there is actually something like a unifying concept among the two, namely the notion of "model." I would agree with that. Because on the one hand, database people have been modeling for a long time in order to arrive at their schemas, by sort of crude means admittedly, and in the AI field, the area of knowledge representation has tried to do the same, by more refined means. And in both cases, models are only good, or successful, if they do not try to deal with the whole world all at once but restrict themselves to small, reasonably homogeneous portions of it. One of the concepts that seems to unify the two is the notion of object. I am a disciple of object-oriented systems as everybody knows. Nonetheless, I do not believe that that's the entire answer to it. You add complexity to the model because now you have to settle explicitly on both structure and behavior. Also, by writing procedures that mirror the behavior, one again tends to bury some of the knowledge in programs.

Now to the question of fuzziness. Whether the data is fuzzy or not is again a matter of interpretation. Data in a database are neither fuzzy nor non-fuzzy. In other words, if you wish to interpret the data as being fuzzy, supply the corresponding interpretation mechanism. One way to do this would indeed be by including behavior, where behavior is described in terms of fuzziness. Otherwise, if you wish to express the fact that the data is fuzzy it must be buried somewhere in the application.

Finally, let me get back to the comment that claimed that databases is dead as a scientific arena, and has been dead for a long time. Indeed, the comment raises in my mind a number of disturbing questions. Above all, what is the future of database research? Indeed, one good measure is how many Ph.D. theses one can generate in the field. I am happy to say that so far I have had no trouble, and sometimes more topics than candidates. So you can't talk about databases as being dead yet. I agree that perhaps there is some tendency in the database area, as elsewhere, that you do those things where funding is easier, and you don't do those things where funding is harder. But I also believe that the potential of databases, or at least of the technology that has evolved around the database area, offers a much wider potential. I think it is still an unbelievably lively area. We observe new major areas of database research every two years or so, and we also observe a major impact on database research by the growing attempts to use databases in new application areas, raising all the while new interesting research issues. I believe that if an area is dead, then it revolves around the same issues again and again and again. And at some point, I agree, there's no material any more for Master's theses and Ph.D. theses. I believe that point is still far away and that quite a lot of research right now is pushing into new areas because there is a feeling that the potential is much larger than what we have explored so far.

Martin Golumbic: Further questions?

Arie Shoshani (Lawrence Berkeley Lab.): Whether the database area is dead or the knowledge base or the expert system areas are dead, the fact is that there is a tremendous amount of data and knowledge that is present in a tremendous number of applications. I was told this Saturday that there is a new kind of particular data that "came to earth" which people did not know how to process or use, simply because they didn't know how. It's as simple as that. They don't know how to do it fast enough; they don't know how to manage the information fast enough. There is certainly some knowledge that is involved in that because in their particular database they've collected information foolishly by time. We have people running experiments who don't use databases for them. They have bad experiences, building things like B-Trees over and over again. Why don't they just join the database age? Take the database technology that exists and make it work. Then we should go out into the real world and find a few tough problems and make them work.

Abraham Kandel: I agree and I think that you made this comment just for the sake of the comment! Otherwise you wouldn't spend three days here! But I absolutely agree with you and not just because of what has been said here. I think we are on the edge of new frontiers. So maybe in that respect, expert systems won't be buried, it's just sitting on the fence for a while. Sitting on the fence not dead, just waiting to see if we can really believe it. And it goes back to the late 60's where AI people made tremendous promises that we are going to solve everything within one general system and then we failed to deliver. And I think what happened at the moment is that there are many, many people just sitting on the side, waiting to see if knowledge engineering can deliver what it promised to deliver.

Martin Golumbic: (To Peter Lockemann) Since the question referred to something in your tutorial, perhaps you'd like to make a final comment and then I'll ask Dr. Tsur to make a final comment, and then I think we'll go to lunch.

Peter Lockemann: Well I think this was well-stated and I don't have to add very much. In fact one of our experiences, and I think of many others, is that by just looking at the so-called trivial problems users have we may open up entirely new frontiers in database technology. And the world is full of new applications. CAD was mentioned very often, CAM is another one, the example you gave is still another one. I think that if you just go out, and that's what we do very often in our projects, teaming up with the application, we discover new problems that we hadn't faced before, that often require new answers in the database field, or if there is already one we adapt it. Surely, I would suspect, at some point we will agree that database technology is so mature that as researchers we move on to other fields. Why not? I think that will be exciting, too. But I don't think that we have reached that status yet.

Shalom Tsur: I hate to agree with people but we should be grateful to Arie for his comment. I think that the real acid tests obviously are applications, and our ability to solve problems that until now could not have been solved. I listed earlier a set of problems that I think that we ought to solve in the near future. That's the ultimate test. The ability to be able to attack new problems that until now you could not attack.

Martin Golumbic: I think that we've had a very interesting 90 minutes with some very controversial points made. I would like to thank the panelists very much for their comments and their presentations.

Index